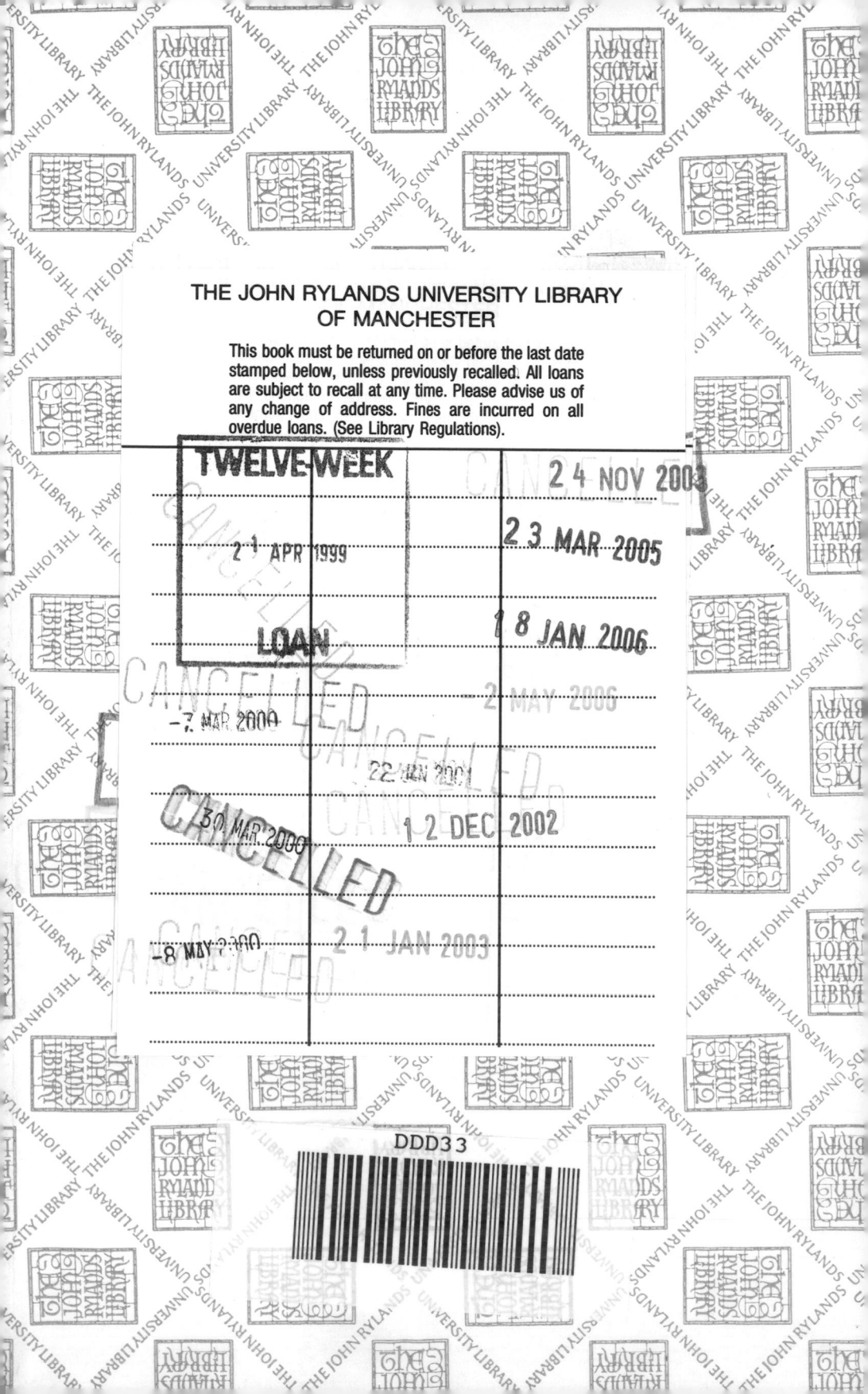

Essays on
WOMEN,
MEDICINE
& HEALTH

ANN OAKLEY

Essays on

*Women,
Medicine
and
Health*

EDINBURGH EDUCATION AND SOCIETY
General Editor: Colin Bell

Essays on

Women, Medicine and Health

ANN OAKLEY

EDINBURGH UNIVERSITY PRESS

© Ann Oakley, 1993

Chapters 1, 2, 3, 4, 7, 12, 14 and 17 first published
in 1986 by Basil Blackwell Ltd, Oxford.
Chapter 11 first published in 1992 by Carnforth,
Lancashire. Chapter 15 first published in 1991 in *New Scientist*.
Chapter 18 first published in 1990 by Routledge and Kegan Paul.

Edinburgh University Press Ltd
22 George Square, Edinburgh

Typeset in Lasercomp Palatino by
Vision Typesetting, Manchester, and
printed and bound in Great Britain
at the University Press, Cambridge

A CIP record for this book is
available from the British Library

ISBN 0 7486 0441 3 (cased)
ISBN 0 7486 0450 2 (paper)

Acknowledgements

Chapter 1 was originally given as the keynote address to the WHO/ Scottish Health Education Group Conference on Women and Health, Edinburgh, 25–27 May 1983; Chapter 2 was originally presented to the congress on *Women and Medical Science*, Helsinki, 25–26 January 1982; Chapter 3 was originally published under the title 'Doctors, Maternity and Social Scientists', in *Birth*, vol. 12, 3 (1985), pp. 161–6; Chapter 4 was originally given under the title 'On the Importance of Being a Nurse: nursing and the health-care division of labour, past, present and future', at a WHO Symposium on Post-basic and Graduate Education for Nurses, held in Helsinki, Finland, 4–8 June 1984; Chapter 5 was originally given as a lecture at Auckland Public Hospital, New Zealand, on 5 October 1989; Chapter 6 was originally given as the William Power Memorial Lecture of the Royal College of Midwives at the Royal Institute of British Architects, London, 21 November 1988; Chapter 7 was originally given as a keynote address to the symposium on 'The Impact of Children on Children': *Constructing Mothers*, Women's Studies Research Centre, University of Wisconsin, Madison, USA, 22 April 1982; Chapter 8 was originally given as a lecture to the Health Promotion Forum, Auckland, New Zealand, 4 October 1989; Chapter 9 was originally written as a background paper entitled 'Perinatal Mortality: problems of a social and health care policy' for a King's Fund meeting on the fortieth anniversary of the National Health Service in 1988; Chapter 10 was originally given as a seminar at the National Women's Hospital, Auckland, New Zealand, in October 1989; Chapter 11 was originally given at a symposium on 'Pregnancy Care in the 1990s' at the Royal Society of Medicine, April 1991, and published in G. Chamberlain and L. Zander (eds),

Pregnancy Care in the 1990s, Carnforth, Lancashire, 1992; Chapter 12 was originally given under the title 'Fertility Control – a woman's issue?' as the tenth Jennifer Hallam Memorial Lecture at the Royal College of Obstetricians and Gynaecologists, London, in October 1983, and published in *Journal of Obstetrics and Gynaecology*, 1984, 4 (Supplement 1), pp. 1–10, © John Wright and Sons; Chapter 13 was originally given as the Bernardijin ten Zeldam memorial lecture in the Nieuwe Kerk in Amsterdam, 12 October 1990; Chapter 14 was originally given at the Royal Society of Medicine Forum on Maternity and the Newborn, Ultrasonography in Obstetrics, 17 April 1985, under the title 'The History of Ultrasonography in Obstetrics'; Chapter 15 was originally published as Talking Point: 'Tamoxifen: in whose best interests?', in *New Scientist*, 22 June 1991; Chapter 16 was originally given at the Mellon Colloquium on 'The Invisible Majority', at the University of Tulane, New Orleans, USA, in 1990; Chapter 17 was originally published in H. Roberts (ed.), *Doing Feminist Research*, London, Routledge and Kegan Paul, 1981; Chapter 18 was originally published in H. Roberts (ed.), *Women's Health Counts*, London, Routledge and Kegan Paul, 1990.

Contents

Introduction

Essays on Women, Medicine and Health is a collection of essays, lectures and papers written between 1981 and 1992 in the interstices of a life variously committed to the pursuit of research, the promotion of a feminist social science, the writing of alternative versions of (her)story in the form of what is called 'fiction', and the usual labours that women perform in the maintenance of a home and the care and surveillance of children − what is called 'motherhood'.

There are a total of eighteen chapters in this collection. Eight were previously published by Basil Blackwell in 1986 in a volume called *Telling the Truth about Jerusalem*. Both that volume and this are stitching-together kinds of exercises; I suppose the appropriate domestic metaphor would be that of a patchwork quilt. Within the pattern of the quilt, there are favourite, well-worn and faded pieces, as well as the brighter colours of more recently-produced materials. But in the juxtaposition of the two, the aim is to create an overall impression in which the dissonances and similarities between the different pieces shade into one another to produce a vision that greets the eye as concretely whole.

Certain themes sew together both this and the previous collection. In *Essays on Women, Medicine and Health*, these are represented as the titles of the main sections: divisions of labour, motherhood, technology and methodology. Each of the chapters included speaks to the fabric and dialectic of women's particular construction in modern culture: the second sex, the other, an oppressed minority despite being a statistical majority; the mother, the carer, the one whose strength to society manifests itself psychically as weakness, as an overbred sensitivity to others, as an inability to take the self

seriously. There are many different ways to put it. The particular language used will depend upon the position from which the descriptions are offered. Most of the pieces in this book examine the situation of women from the standpoint of what is called 'health' and its cultural obverse, illness as medical work. The reasons for this standpoint are both pragmatic and profound. Pragmatically, much of my research over the last fifteen years has been occupied with women's experiences of health and illness and with the medical care system. Pushing back the frontiers of that conceptualization a little, it has also been concerned with women's own caring work – that is, their importance as producers of other people's health. Because my work has had this focus, I have been asked to talk about this topic at conferences and to write about it in invited papers – and most of the pieces in this book are the result of one or another of these activities.

The preoccupation with women and health has a deeper meaning, however. As some of the chapters point out, whenever we try to speak of women's experiences we are likely to find some difficulty with the conceptual and linguistic tools available to us. Language reflects culture and its socioeconomic structures. The forms of thought underlying it are dedicated to the position of the dominant group. Those who are socially subordinate may find that their ways of thinking do not fit the language – or, rather, that conventional linguistic forms cannot adequately express their experiences. So it is with concepts such as health and illness, mind and body, public and private, care and cure, nature and culture, self and other. Much of what research and scholarship has unearthed about women's experiences over the last twenty years convincingly displays the inability of these black-and-white distinctions to capture the creatively blurred ambiguities of the way in which women experience the world.

The distorting dichotomies of conventional forms of thought and language are responsible for a major difference between the format of the earlier collection and this one. *Telling the Truth about Jerusalem* mixed academic essays with poetry in a format organized around key themes concerning (some) lessons of history, motherhood's facts and fictions, health and gender, and the sexist methodology of social science. The poems and the essays were different ways of communicating the same issues. In *Essays on Women, Medicine and Health* there are no poems. This is not because I do not continue to see different ways of writing as reconcilable – parts of the patchwork quilt of the whole – but because it is apparently too early in the revision of our notions of writing for poetry to be accepted as a legitimate invader of the terrain of 'factual' writing. People are uncomfortable with the mixing of the two and with the implicit argument that fiction and fact may flow seamlessly into one another. In the same way, my use of fictional

episodes within an autobiographical text in *Taking it Like a Woman*[1] caused discomfort in some quarters. I wish this were not so, but, as a child of my times, I must respect their limitations, as well as chafing against them. Someone famous once remarked that a poet can survive everything except a misprint,[2] and, as there were one or two in the poems in *Telling the Truth about Jerusalem*, I am at least thankful to have been spared this disaster a second time.

The title of *Telling the Truth about Jerusalem* referred to the fact that Parry's often-played musical setting of William Blake's ecologically nationalist poem 'Jerusalem' was commissioned by the suffragette Millicent Fawcett and her friends to celebrate the gaining of votes for women in 1918. 'Jerusalem' was the suffrage hymn; it is still sung in British Women's Institutes today. Since few people are aware of this connection, it seemed to me a good demonstration of the need to ensure that when history is told it is not rewritten in the process. Women, in particular, need to make sure that they tell the truth about their experiences, and that other people, in recounting these, do not reshape the original truths as distorting fables and myths.

The title of the current volume, *Essays on Women, Medicine and Health*, is more straightforward. Part I, which is entitled 'Divisions of Labour', provides an overall context for the contributions in the rest of the book by examining the groundplan of gender differences in society generally and health care in particular. The last chapter in Part I, 'Who Cares for Women? Science and "Love" in Midwifery Today', was also the last in that section to be written; it discusses the conceptual divisions that parallel the social ones, and provide a powerful mechanism for distorting women's experiences. The problems which these pose for research methods, and for the codification of particular sets of experiences in the form of 'knowledge', are the subject of the last section of the book. In between these are two sections devoted to more specialist topics – motherhood and technology. As in *Telling the Truth about Jerusalem*, there is a certain amount of repetition between the different pieces. Although I have tried to reduce this to a minimum, internal coherence sometimes called for a point to stand, and I have respected that.

The general aim of the book is to make accessible to readers some of the more hidden fruits of my labours over the last fifteen years in the field of sociology and women's studies. Some of the fruits are hidden because unpublished, and some because, although published, they may be hard to find. In this context, I must acknowledge thanks for permission to reproduce material to: Basil Blackwell Ltd, Oxford; Carnforth, Lancashire; Holborn Publishing Group, London; and Routledge and Kegan Paul.

Finally, this book manifests certain tensions which are also the subject of

dissection in its pages. As I have said, this is not the book that I would have written had I had the freedom to alter received wisdom of what 'proper' books should look like. On the other hand, several of its chapters repeat the urgency of holding on to an alternative vision. In an essay written in 1924, the Danish writer Karen Blixen asked:

> Do some of you want to fly? Is it something you really want, and does the idea attract you more than anything else? Then hang on to your wish for a couple of thousand years and you will get wings.[3]

It is not uncommon to find in fiction that women want to fly, whereas men are attracted to the sea.[4] This may be because for men the sea represents women, whereas for women flying is something that men do. Equally, the resonance of the flying image may owe its strength to women's urge to get out of their confines.

Karen Blixen used a male name for her writing – Isak Dinesen. When the American writer Carolyn Heilbrun wanted to write feminist detective stories, she also used a pseudonym, for fear of having her alternative vision used against her in her academic life as an aspiring professor of English literature.[5] In her most famous alter ego work, *Death in a Tenured Position*, [6] one of America's most renowned and misogynist universities is given some money to fund its first female professorship. After a hard search, an appropriately non-feminist woman is found for this post. She is discovered dead after only a few months. Everyone suspects the male professors of having killed her. But the female sleuth, a considerably more uncompromising version of Miss Marple, works out that she killed herself. The whole environment was simply too inhospitable.

There are various messages in this. One is that women have their own ways of undermining masculine culture. Another is that things have got better, and there is no need to kill ourselves any more. A third is one to which the writer Carolyn Heilbrun herself draws attention: that no-one should be allowed to die seated comfortably in a 'tenured' position. If women achieve such positions, they must use them to go on being awkward.

With age comes a blessed relief from the strain of having to be a 'female impersonator'.[7] The chapters in this volume do, I suppose, speak of my own struggle to get away from impersonation. It is a fight for authenticity – both for tenure and for the right to say things that will ensure that this particular form of male-invented closure is unlikely ever to be available to women.

Part I

Divisions of Labour

1

Beyond the Yellow Wallpaper

The very idea of a conference on 'Women and Health' challenges two central myths of the industrialized world in the twentieth century. The first of these two myths is the one that says health is a medical product, that a state of health in individuals and societies is brought about principally through the efforts of members of the medical profession: illness is prevented or cured and death avoided through the beneficence of medical science. The second myth is that inequalities between men and women are surface blemishes only, and may be removed merely by cosmetic attention to the superstructure of social relations: all we need is a few good laws and minor social changes and women will be able to look men in the eyes as equals.

These myths are powerful organizing ideas in what is commonly, if misleadingly, referred to as 'the developed world'. The enormously important role in our cultural thinking and social policy of the myths challenged by the phrase 'women and health' makes this conference even more important. It is a radical departure for two national and international organizations concerned with health issues first of all to pay serious attention to women's role in health care; second, to confront directly the social, economic and political context of health – and, third, to do both at the same time.

In order to set the scene for this discussion, it is perhaps useful to run through some of the main issues to be tackled under the heading 'Women and Health'. From a global perspective, what burning questions need to be asked and answered about women as users and providers of health care? Next, what are the implications for women of the differences between these two conceptualizations: health as a medical product and health as a social

product? Finally, I will look at the implications for health-care systems of the differences between the two conceptualizations of women: the 'equal rights' view of women on the one hand, and on the other the rather more disturbing notion of women's oppression.

Before producing a shopping list of burning questions, we need to make a basic distinction among three terms: health, health care and medical care. The last is the easiest to define: medical care is that provided by a medical professional, with the aim of treating or preventing illness. Health care need not be provided by a medical professional, but can be an activity of non-medical, non-professional groups and even of individuals themselves. Health, as by far the most complex of the three terms, need not have anything to do either with health care or with medical care, and here I am, of course, referring to that substantial body of evidence demonstrating that changes in broad indicators of the health of communities are rarely brought about by changes in the provision of medical care. Although this type of evidence is limited by the indicators of health chosen (since the most oft-used indicator of health is death – which is more than strange, when you think about it), it does point in the direction of a certain definition of health which is relevant for us at this conference. The definition is that health requires, or is impossible without, a moral basis of good social relations.

The reason why we need a conference on women and health is because women are the major social providers of health and health care, and they are also the principal users of health- and medical-care services. In these two ways, the truth of the matter negates the dominant cultural message. The dominant cultural message is that doctors, not women, ensure health and that men, not women, are biologically the more vulnerable sex, with a mortality and physical morbidity record exceeding that of women from the cradle to the grave.[1] There is therefore something acutely paradoxical about women's relationship to health and health care which needs to be unravelled.

As providers of health and health care, women are important through their role in the division of labour. In their domestic lives, they provide health care by attending to the physical needs of those with whom they live. They obtain food, provide and dispose of the remains of meals, clean the home, buy or make and wash and repair clothing, and take personal care of those who are too young or too old, or too sick or too busy to take care of their own physical needs. These activities are known as housework, a somewhat

peculiar term, since most of the work done has nothing to do with houses, but a great deal to do with maintaining the health and vitality of individuals. Incidentally, or perhaps not so incidentally, it is a matter of great importance to policy-makers as to how this health-promoting work of women is described. Mostly it is described in terms of an ideology of women's natural commitment to family welfare, an ideology which attributes to women a feminine altruism that many would prefer to have recognized as unpaid labour.

To call women's household health work by the name of 'housework' is to ignore an extremely important aspect of the domestic division of labour, and that is women's role as the chief managers of personal relations both inside and outside the family. Emotional support promotes health: there is good evidence that a person's social relationships or lack of them are crucial influences on physical and mental functioning. As family welfare workers – as mothers, mothers-in-law, wives, housewives, sisters and daughters, and often neighbours as well – women take care of personal relations.

The impact of industrial economic development, although commonly seen in terms of the work–home division, also had this other effect: that personal relationships were equated with 'the family', and women were seen as responsible for them. 'The family' – increasingly the nuclear family of parents and children, with its incorporated division of labour – became the paradigm for all female–male relationships, for the division of all labour. Thus, also, before the modern industrial era, the domestic health care provided by women extended beyond the home and out into the community. Women were recognized as the main potential healers for the bulk of the population; hence such terms as 'wisewoman' and 'old wives' tale'; and hence the traditional role of midwives purveying a set of skills derived not from formal training but from personal practical experience. With the rise of professionalized medicine, many of women's traditional healing activities acquired a new definition as dangerous to health, if not actually illegal. This did not necessarily put an end to them, since, fortunately, women have almost always been strong enough to put up some resistance to the imposition of the state's power. It is because the subculture of women's healing and midwifery was never entirely eliminated by the combined misogyny of state and medical profession that, in a research project which we are doing in WHO, we are finding the existence of 'alternative' services for maternal and child health in most countries – a coming-out-into-the-open of an old tradition spurred on by the unresolvable dilemmas for women of the health-is-a-medical product idea.[2]

Even within official health-care systems, women remain extremely important as providers of care. To take Britain as an example, some

three-quarters of workers in the National Health Service are women. However, only about twenty per cent of British doctors are women: there is a division of labour by gender in professionalized health care, just as there is in every other sphere of social life. As doctors, as midwives and as nurses, women health-care providers in Britain and most other so-called developed countries are concentrated in the lower-status grades of health services. For example, while only some eleven per cent of British hospital nurses are male, a disproportionate twenty-three per cent of senior posts within the hospital nursing service are held by men.[3] When we look at the division by gender of specialities within medicine, we not surprisingly learn that women specialize in areas to do with children, mental illness, microbiology (perhaps a form of housework carried into the hospital setting?) and putting people to sleep, otherwise known as anaesthetics.[4] This pattern is not a reflection simply of choice, for research into medical careers has revealed much more dissatisfaction with existing career opportunities among female than among male doctors.[5] Individual women may struggle against the prescribed pattern, but a collective effort is needed to alter it.

There are many important questions here about the future role of women as health- and medical-care providers. The two which I would like to single out as the most deserving of our attention are, first, the family health and welfare work of women; and, second, female midwifery – women's work as managers of normal childbearing. Both family welfare and midwifery work are areas in which the rights of women are especially threatened today. In the family welfare domain, they are threatened because in most ways and in most countries the necessity to the economy and prevailing moral order of women's so-called labour of love has never been eroded by a recognition of their rights as individuals. With regard to the management of childbearing, and although most of the world's babies are still delivered by midwives, recent technological growth in obstetrics has eroded the independence of the midwife's role, and indeed promises to extinguish it altogether in the future. For women as a class, this, I believe, is more than a marginal retrogressive development, since, if allowed to proceed unimpeded, it will engulf motherhood in a masculine medical structure whose ideologies will, on the whole, project a different definition of health from that held by mothers themselves.

WOMEN AS USERS OF HEALTH AND MEDICAL CARE

The Yellow Wallpaper: Fact as Fiction

Before moving on to some of the important questions to be addressed in women's *use* of health services, I want to go back in time to a story written

nearly 100 years ago by the American feminist Charlotte Perkins Gilman. The story is called 'The Yellow Wallpaper',[6] and it illustrates the historical and cross-cultural continuity marking the unsolved problems of women and health. It also highlights three of the most central of these – those relating to production, reproduction and the medicalization, in the form of mental illness, of the psychological costs of women's situation.

'The Yellow Wallpaper' describes three months in the life of a New England woman diagnosed by her husband, a physician, as suffering from nervous depression following the birth of her first child. The physician rents a house for the summer and confines his wife to bed in a large room on the top floor, a room with yellow wallpaper. He prescribes total rest for her, and expressly forbids her to do any work in the form of writing, her chosen occupation. The story describes the progression of the invalid's feelings locked up in that room; it is an account at the same time (and depending on how you look at it) of an escape into madness and a discovery of sanity. The woman becomes increasingly obsessed with the yellow wallpaper since, deprived of companionship, exercise and any intellectual stimulation, she has nothing else to do but look at the walls. Finally, she becomes convinced that there is a woman in there behind the yellow wallpaper waiting to get out, a woman who creeps around the house and garden only by moonlight when no-one will see her. So, on their last day in the house, in an act of frenzy, she strips all the paper off the walls in order to let this other woman out, in order to free her once and for all from her prison. Her husband comes home, discovers what she has done, and faints with shock – a most undoctorly reaction – and thus apparently ends the story.

So, in 'The Yellow Wallpaper' we have the following moral lessons: don't put women with postnatal depression into solitary confinement; and avoid yellow wallpaper if possible. Actually, I think that the real moral is the one summed up in that dictum of the American writer Tillie Olsen: 'Every woman who writes is a survivor',[7] which, translated into everyday language, means that what is good for women's health is involvement in productive activity, involvement in, not withdrawal from, society. There is also a message in 'The Yellow Wallpaper' about reproduction. This is a complex message which runs as follows: childbearing, women's special biological and social contribution, may be either a source of weakness or a source of strength. Which it is depends less on the woman herself than on the social and medical context in which pregnancy, childbirth and childrearing take place. But I suppose the most profound message in 'The Yellow Wallpaper' (remember it was written nearly 100 years ago) is the one about how women's problems are constantly individualized: it is the individual woman who has the problem, and, even if many individual women have the same

problem, the explanation of a defective psychology rather than that of a defective social structure is usually preferred. Here we are up against not only individualization but also medicalization. The medicalization of unhappiness as depression is one of the great disasters of the twentieth century, and it is a disaster that has had, and still has, a very big impact on women.

Some twenty or so years after 'The Yellow Wallpaper' came out, Gilman published a note about it in which she admitted that the story came directly from her own experience.[8] She observed that at the age of twenty-seven, married and the mother of a two-year-old, and having felt unhappy for some time, she had visited in 1887 a noted specialist in nervous diseases who put her to bed and prescribed a fate much like that of the woman in the story. The eminent man told her never to touch pen, brush or pencil again as long as she lived. She followed his advice for three months and then, on the verge of what *she* felt to be total insanity, and with the help of a woman friend, she left her husband, moved to California and established a writing career for herself. She sent a copy of 'The Yellow Wallpaper' to the specialist in question, and, although he did not acknowledge receipt of it at the time, she learnt many years later that he had publicly said that not only had he read the story, but he had also altered his treatment of nervous depression in women after reading it. I think we may be justified in concluding that there is something intrinsically valid about personal experience and that, in coming clean about their own perspectives on health and illness, women may actually bring about the beginning of a change in those who hold powerful alternative views.

Women and Production

The first of the three burning issues which I mentioned under the heading of women and health services is women's economic role, their participation in production.

Whenever we discuss women's employment, we have the sense of being caught up in a circular, historical, but also timeless, debate: is women's employment a good thing or a bad thing; should women/wives/mothers work, or not? What is the effect of employment on health, both physical and mental; or, indeed, what is the effect of women's health and illness on employment? These questions cannot be given general answers. But we can easily note some important features about the employment of women. According to that oft-quoted United Nations Report, women perform two-thirds of the world's work-hours, receive one-tenth of the world's income and own less than one-hundredth of the world's property. Thus, whatever else work may be, it is a dead end in the business sense for women

– a bad deal. In undeveloped countries, the reality behind the myth of the male hunter–provider has always been the woman hunter–gatherer supporting her family through her own autonomous agricultural work. Once the process of urban industrial development sets in, what seems to happen is that women remain locked in the subsistence economy, while men become involved in the cash economy of the cities, and from then on the road is downwards, according to the rule that women's labour earns them less.[9] In industrialized countries today, women earn some thirty to forty per cent less than men, and it matters not a great deal from this point of view whether the country is capitalist or socialist in character – the same kind of earnings gap exists.[10] This is because most political structures ignore the politics of gender, or tend to pay lip-service to the idea of gender equality by passing a few weak laws referring to the illegality of certain forms of sex discrimination, or exhort women already overburdened with domestic work to enter the paid labour force for their own good, when they are not really talking about women's own good at all.

The paradox of working more and earning less than men derives from the double meaning of work for women: working inside the home for love and outside it for money; maintaining the health of families through housework and by earning a wage. In Britain and other industrialized nations, it now requires two incomes to maintain a family at the same standard of living provided by one income twenty years ago,[11] and many employed women are the sole breadwinners for their children or elderly parents. The notion that most of women's employment is accounted for by married women working for pin money or purely to escape the worst excesses of captivity in the home never had any real basis. It was a self-perpetuating myth rooted in the postwar sexism of social science, whose investigators found what the dominant mood of the culture told them to find, namely an apparently harmonious acceptance of the inequality model of family life. The idea of the family wage earned by a male breadwinner, with women's income as a luxury extra, is still the basis of many countries' tax, national insurance and social security systems – even though it has always been based on a fictionalized and therefore unreal middle-class view of the world. Further, the family wage presupposes an equal division of income inside the family. But the reality is income rarely divided so that women get their due share: women (and children) may well be in poverty when men are not.[12]

The relationship between the division of labour inside the family and the division of labour outside it has provided much fuel for theoretical debate. Which is the cause of which, and is it women's role in production within a capitalist economy that condemns them to relative disadvantage, or is it their role in reproduction within a patriarchal family that explains this

continuing discrimination? We see everywhere the interconnections between the two divisions of labour, and nowhere better than in the statistics of part-time employment, which the American sociologist Alice Rossi described many years ago as this century's panacea for the problems of women's disadvantaged social position. A part-time job individualized the problem by seeming to index a state of personal liberation while actually very often representing further exploitation. In Britain, some forty per cent of employed women work in part-time employment, an increase of twenty-eight per cent since 1956. Part-time employment is a large factor in the low status and low pay of women's work. Women are concentrated not only in a small number of occupations but also in those in which both male and female workers tend to be poorly paid and poorly unionized. There is also homeworking, working for pay at home, a 'solution' 'chosen' by increasing numbers of women and frequently carried out under appallingly unhealthy conditions.

A paid job may not signal liberation, but in the modern world it is an important basis for self-identity and self-esteem. The money which it brings in is important, and so is the kind of involvement in social relationships provided by it. That is the plus side, and supporting data come from various groups of studies on factors correlated with work satisfaction, on social factors in depression, and stress and employment. On the negative side, there is the interesting, but as yet unproven, suggestion that if women adopt male employment patterns they will lose the edge that they have over men in life expectancy and in cancer and heart-disease mortality – a kind of moral penalty for liberation, a reworking of the old Victorian idea that God will punish any woman who unsexes herself by doing anything except sitting or lying still with a blank mind and even blanker smile on her face.

We do not, of course, have any idea what would happen to men if they assumed women's typical double burden of unpaid domestic and poorly-paid non-domestic work. Perhaps they would die less often, or perhaps their health would suffer through their not having been socialized to the role. Since domestic accidents are a leading cause of death among young and middle-aged adults, if men tried their hands at women's juggling act there would certainly be some shift in causes of death. It is an interesting reflection of the cultural trivialization of housework that, when we think of fatal accidents, we think classically of the dramatic motorway collision, whereas the kitchen, seemingly a most innocuous place, is the place that ought to come to mind, the place that we must all try to avoid if we do not wish to die in an accident.

Of the less fatal and more chronically painful effects of housework we know very little for a similar reason – that the overlap of housework and

family life has underestimated the power of what happens in the home to shape life and death and public events. It is simply not the case that only the really momentous historical events and processes take place in the public arena; this alternative truth being, of course, implicitly, if dishonestly, recognized by patriarchy in the enormous preoccupation that has grown up over the last 100 years with the impact of mothers on children's health. Mothers have been held responsible for everything bad and everything good about children, a conflating of female power that, significantly, men have hardly created a protest about. As mothers create children's personalities, so they also create adult personalities in such a manner that all conformity to, and all deviance from, social norms has been laid at women's door, from homosexuality to schizophrenia, from the stuff of which the Yorkshire Ripper or American Presidents are made, to His Holiness the Pope – yes, even the Pope had a mother. This cultural fixation on mothers' ability to mould children's health and character has not been matched by any corresponding degree of concern with the impact of children on women's health. Indeed, the three questions of whether housework is good for women's health, whether motherhood is good for women's health and whether marriage is good for women's health are three very basic questions to which we can only give partial answers because the assumption that domesticity promotes health in women has been an obstacle to serious research for a long time.

Women and Reproduction

The place of childbearing in women's lives, like the competing claims of patriarchy and capitalism as controlling structures, has been a theme of debate for feminists. Whether childbearing is good or bad for women's health of course cannot be answered without paying attention to the exact historical context in which it occurs; it is one thing to talk about maternity in Europe or North America fifty years ago or the Third World today, where maternal deaths due to childbearing were/are one or more for every 250 babies born, and another to discuss it in a context where death is rare – so rare, fortunately, that epidemiologists have been heard to mutter under their breath that they will have to find some other way than counting deaths to measure health. However, to speak of the risks to physical health and survival of pregnancy and childbirth, one must remember the contribution of induced abortion, contraception and sterilization. These aspects of women's health care (or lack of it) have tended to make childbearing itself safer, but carry their own risks of death which need to be computed in order to obtain a complete picture of the impact of reproduction on the health of women.[13]

Having babies and trying not to have babies makes women sicker than

men in terms of use of hospital and other medical services. But here the question arises as to whether the management of childbearing itself has fallen under a medical rubric because there is something genuinely sickening about the process of having a baby, or for some other reason. In short, whose idea was it to treat having a baby as an illness, and was it a good idea? Taking the second part of the question first, there is no doubt that the rise of modern obstetric care has been accompanied by a fall in the mortalities of childbearing, but (as is usual with such issues) there is little evidence on which to hang the belief that medical maternity care was what did it. This point was made, some years ago, by a British epidemiologist who observed that, whereas perinatal mortality had declined as the proportion of hospital deliveries had risen, the figures could be alternatively presented to show that childbirth became safer the shorter the length of time mothers stayed in hospital after the birth.[14]

The extent of medical surveillance over pregnancy and birth is virtually 100 per cent in most industrialized countries today – that is, all women attend for prenatal care, and, in addition, the majority give birth in hospital. The extent of medical intervention in childbirth has risen exponentially over the last twenty years. In some European countries, operative deliveries are now in excess of twenty per cent. The evidence as to the benefits of individual obstetric technologies such as ultrasound scanning, other prenatal screening tests, instrumental or Caesarean delivery, induction of labour, etc., is equivocal, and an unexplained factor about obstetric technology policies is the enormous variation that exists between countries, between regions within countries, and even between hospitals and individual practitioners within the same region. This is a variation far greater than any 'biological' variation between different populations of women having babies.

Most of all, perhaps, we cannot answer from the available data three questions about reproduction and women's health. The first question is: what would have happened to the health of mothers and babies had the obstetric technology explosion not taken place? Might survival and health, for example, have been even better than it presently is? The second question is: what will be the long-term effect on women and children of this level of use of technology in childbearing? Some consequences of a high level of technology are already making themselves felt: for instance, Caesarean section rates rise geometrically as one Caesarean delivery becomes the reason for another in a woman's subsequent pregnancy. The third question, which cannot be answered so easily by an appeal to perinatal epidemiology (even an appeal to an appropriate perinatal epidemiology), is: what does it do to women to have their babies gestated and born so very much within such a closed structure of medical surveillance? It is hard to feel in control of one's

body and one's destiny during sixteen trips to the hospital antenatal clinic for the ritual laying-on of hands by a succession of different doctors, none of them especially trained in the art of talking to the faces beyond the abdomens, or in the science of knowing about the interaction between mind and body, the connection between peace of mind and a competent cervix, or between emotional confidence and a coordinated uterus.

What we see involved here are issues of control and responsibility that come up again and again in looking at women's health. Who is in control of the process — of having a baby, of being ill, of determining the relative balance between housework and employment work? Who is responsible for the outcome of any choice that is made, and is it really a choice? At the present time, it is not often women who are in control of matters affecting their own health, and this situation arises not only through the overall medicalization of life — a process which, after all, affects men too — but also through the infantilization of women as incapable of taking responsibility for themselves. Pregnant women are especially seen as being incapable of taking responsible decisions on behalf of themselves and their fetuses. What this conference is about is women's resistance to the patronizing professionalized health-care formula that women cannot take responsibility for their own health and illness. It is, indeed, a paradox that, although women's lives are all about providing health for others, as users of formal health-care services, custom decrees that they be no more than patient patients.

Turning to motherhood, we see this paradox written large. Infantilized in pregnancy, and delivered of their babies by others, women as mothers are liable to discover that the devotion of the state to the necessity of reproduction is too often a devotion in name only. Whenever the demand for out-of-home child care among mothers is surveyed, it is found to be many times greater than its supply. Time–budget studies of the division of labour in the home are not convincing on the topic of men's willingness to share child care, and insofar as men seem to be doing more for children than they were, they have chosen the more pleasurable aspects of child care — playing with the baby rather than changing its dirty nappy, or playing with the baby so that mother can get the dinner ready. If more active fathering along these lines is good for health, the question remains as to whose health it is good for.

So, there is a contradiction here at the heart of women's situation: women are both irresponsible and they have too much responsibility. They cannot make decisions and have to make all of them. In the privacy of the home, and as mothers, women are powerful, but in public they are not, for always there is a relationship between power and responsibility. You cannot have power without responsibility, and the taking of responsibility brings power; this is

why it is essential for women to resist the arbitration by anyone else on their behalf of their responsibilities in both health and health care.

Medicalization of Women's Distress

The last of the three issues which I extracted from the story of 'The Yellow Wallpaper' was the issue of the medical labelling of women's distress as mental illness.

Although women are physically healthier than men, it appears that they make up for this superiority by a certain mental instability. That is, when one looks at psychiatric admissions to hospital and at prescriptions for psychotropic drugs, women predominate over men. Hidden biases in the data are possible; thus it may be that unhappy or mentally ill men are more likely to be cared for by women at home than vice versa and/or that the more help-seeking behaviour of women as against that of men leads them more readily to take their unhappiness to doctors. However, it does seem that when men and women present essentially the same symptoms to GPs, the women are more likely to receive a psychiatric diagnosis.[15] A clue to this mystery is provided by a study of doctors' attitudes to patients carried out in this country in the 1970s. In this study, doctors were asked to say which types of patients caused them the most and least trouble. The least troublesome type of patient was defined as male, intelligent, employed and middle-class, with specific, easily treatable organic illness. The most troublesome patient was female, not employed, working-class, described vaguely as 'inadequate', and possessing diffuse symptoms of psychiatric illness that were difficult or impossible to diagnose and treat.[16]

What this suggests to me is that a psychiatric or pseudo-psychiatric diagnosis is most likely to be dragged in when men are unable to understand the problems that women have. It is not accidental that the two main biological events placing women beyond men's understanding, namely menstruation and childbirth, have both generated psychiatric diagnoses in the form, respectively, of premenstrual tension and postpartum depression. Since menstruation and childbirth are liable to make women ill, and all women menstruate and over ninety per cent of them give birth, the chances are that quite a lot of us will be out of action at any one time. The attribution to women as a class of mental instability is obviously highly consequential, since it affects one's claim to be a responsible person. Historically speaking, the evolution of these diagnoses of women's distress has gone hand-in-hand with a continuing cultural prejudice against the ability of women to hold responsible public positions.

The Catch 22 here is that, while the concepts of premenstrual tension and postpartum depression may have a particular meaning within medical

discourse and in terms of the structures affecting women's health, some women do have problems in the lead-up to menstruation, and some do feel especially distressed after childbirth.[17] How do we recognize the subjective validity of the problem without enclosing it in a terminology that inhibits political insight? How do we name it in such a way that we remain interested not only in what the problem is but also in how it might be caused and in what might be done to prevent it on a social and not purely individual level?

HEALTH AS A SOCIAL PRODUCT

In an essay on 'Professions for Women', written in 1931,[18] Virginia Woolf described two particular obstacles which she found had to be overcome in learning to be a writer. Although she was talking about writing, I think that what she said is important for all women. Woolf described first of all a phantom with whom she had to battle in her writing. She called the phantom after the heroine of a famous poem, 'The Angel in the House'. The Angel in the House was the ideal woman – intensely sympathetic, immensely charming, very domesticated, completely unselfish: 'if there was chicken she took the leg, if there was a draught she sat in it – in short she was so constituted that she never had a mind or a wish of her own'. This spectre of womanhood plucked the heart out of Woolf's writing, drained it of all strength, prevented her writing what she wanted to write. Many women recognize the same problem in themselves today. It is all too easy to hide behind the defence of feminity and to mask behind a facade of smiling and commendable altruism our own refusal to take ourselves seriously. The second obstacle which Woolf confronted concerned something of even more obvious relevance to this conference, and that is the problem of telling the truth about the experience of one's own body. As a novelist, Woolf felt that she had not beaten this problem, that no woman yet had, that the weight of convention, of male power and masculine history, was against such truth-telling.

Recognizing that health is a social product is a first task confronting women, as is to tell the truth about our own experiences. Our own experiences determine our health; they do so whether or not they are experiences which put us directly in contact with professional medical care, and whether or not professional medical care is able to provide any form of treatment which will make us feel better.

Not telling the truth about our experiences is equivalent to lying about them, and the social significance of lying is, as the American writer Adrienne Rich[19] reminds us, that it makes the world appear much simpler and also bleaker than it really is. Lying takes away the possibility of honour between

human beings, and the possibility of growth and change. It destroys trust and contorts history.

Another challenge following from an acceptance of health as socially determined is that women take a wider degree of responsibility for their own health and health-care decision-making in the future, even if this means in part taking such responsibility away from medical professionals. In a way, this is already happening with the growth of the self-help movement in health care. What comes under the heading of self-help is, however, a mixed bag. Some of it is fairly accepting of the conventional division of labour; for example, branches of the consumer movement in maternity care present themselves in terms of a defence of natural childbirth that sounds awfully like the Angel of the House; they may even worship charismatic male heroes along well-established angelic lines. But, on the other hand, other self-help groups could hardly be a more direct threat to the status quo, for example the early self-help gynaecology groups in the USA which led to women being placed under police surveillance because they had looked up their vaginas, an official response whose bizarre nature is perhaps only fully clear when one considers under what circumstances men might be subject to police surveillance for looking at their penises.[20]

HEALTH CARE AND OPPRESSION

Finally, I want to say something about what it means for the health-care system to recognize that women are not simply prone to suffer from the last vestiges of an unequal social relationship with men, but in fact constitute an oppressed social group.

Most modern medical-care systems, whether financed on a state- or private-insurance basis, have not succeeded in distributing medical care equitably throughout the population. Class, ethnic and gender oppression are all political facts affecting health and illness and medical care. However, the oppression of women is unique among the three forms of oppression, in that women's function as guardians of the nation's health forms the central core of their oppression. Women's role in reproduction, their role as unpaid family welfare workers, the personal emotional support that they provide for men and children – these activities, which are indistinguishable from the fact of being a woman in our culture, may also be said to encapsulate, to hold within them, the causes of women's ill-health. For example, a high proportion of physical problems in women (including maternity) are due to their habit of having sexual relations with men. I am thinking here not only of rape and marital violence, but also of diseases such as cancer of the cervix, which are apparently associated not only with women's own sexual history, but also with the sexual proclivities of the men with whom they live.[21] But

most of all I return once again to the ghost of the Angel in the House. The emotional, political and financial *dependency* of women's family welfare role is perhaps their — our — greatest disablement today. In being carriers of our society's unsolved problems of dependency in human relationships — how to love one another without giving up one's autonomy as an individual — in carrying this cultural dilemma, women are not helped even to articulate, let alone put forward for serious consideration, their own interests.

When I said that health depends upon a moral basis of good social relations, I meant that it is attempting the impossible to pursue health in a society in which one social group is systematically at a disadvantage in relation to another. It is attempting to erect a healthy community on the basis of unhealthy, that is exploitative, human relations. Whether the exploitation is rationalized, maintained and mystified in the name of love — the phantom Angel in the House of Woolf's essay — is, in a sense, neither here nor there. In contemporary industrialized cultures, female babies are not exactly thrown away, as they were in the past, but there is a painful metaphorical throwing-away of women still. While this continues to be condoned, there will be no radical change. And not condoning it means combatting the processes which I have been discussing: the medicalization of women's distress; the individualization of their problems; the infantilization of women. An isolated, unhappy child is not a political threat to anyone. But the political energy of a socially involved adult prepared to accept conflict and contradiction as a part of life is, on the other hand, enormous.

These issues possibly matter more now than they have ever done. Economic recession combined with the cash and confidence crisis of western medicine make 'women' and 'health' key words. Not all that women have gained in emancipation this century, but a good part of it, is threatened by new talk of bolstering the family, of a need to shore up the haven of community care for those who cannot care for themselves (what is community care but the work of women?) and of a need to take another look at the social costs of liberating women. All the traditional answers are the cheapest ones — of course. It is cheaper to edge women out of the paid labour force and traditional to say that nurturing others comes best to women. But we cannot say that these solutions are what women want, or what is good for the health of women. At the same time as the old answers are heard again, there is a growing and healthy recognition on the part of government of the need to curb the power of professionals to control people's lives. This offers a route even within conservative political dogmas to changing the traditional relationship between women and health care.

None of the tasks ahead of us are easy, and all of them demand confrontation of the conflict endemic in social relations between people and

professionals, women and men. In the end, everyone has a stake in moving towards a more humane society where health and illness are not split off from the rest of experience, in which bodies are seen as connected to the environment, and minds and emotions are understood to shape the way in which bodies function; everyone also has a stake in appreciating the limits of science, and in understanding the new technologies of our brave new world. What we want *is* a brave new world, not a defunct, dispirited and depressing old one. What we want is a world in which women who ask for change are taken seriously.

2

The Limits of the Professional Imagination

All human societies have to take into account the fact that only women can bear children. This is both important and unimportant as a biological constraint on the general division of labour between the sexes. It is unimportant because, in considering how different societies have responded to the biological fact of women's essential role in reproduction, it is not a question of nature determining culture but of different cultural interpretations of nature. Many examples of this are possible: in certain societies and historical periods, people have seen no contradiction between the female labour of growing and producing a child on the one hand, and whatever other labour it is customary for women to do on the other. In yet other times and places, it has been contended that women's function of reproduction is entirely threatened by work of any other kind: 'nature' forces on women a life of parasitic idleness in the interest of the preservation of the species.

Women's capacity to reproduce is subject to different interpretations. Biology is not destiny. But its very importance lies in the fact that it must enter in some form into the logic of every social system and every cultural ideology.

PROFESSIONAL PARADIGMS OF WOMEN AS CHILDBEARERS

Some of the most powerful images of women and motherhood are those held by the professional disciplines which lay claim to a special expertise in the field of reproduction – namely, medical science, clinical psychiatry and psychology. In order to review the images of women to be found in each of these professional perspectives, I am going to draw on a wide range of data,

from my own observations of work in a London maternity hospital in the mid-1970s and interviews with women having babies, to the assumptions made about women as patients in the medical literature. My basic argument can be simply stated: it is that, in the contemporary industrialized world, medical science and allied disciplines, in claiming specialist jurisdiction over all aspects of reproduction, have become the predominant source of social constructs of the culture of childbirth. The professional obstetrical view that childbirth is a pathological process and women are passive objects of clinical attention has become an integral part of the way in which the community as a whole sees childbirth. Science is in this sense itself ideology; it is certainly not a matter of objective 'fact'. However, we cannot let the matter rest there, for there is ample evidence that 'professional' images of motherhood conflict with the experiences of mothers themselves. Most women's experiences of becoming a mother are considerably and uncomfortably out of tune with the expectations which they have absorbed from professional advisers to mothers (among others) about what the process will be like.

IMAGES OF MOTHERHOOD AND WOMEN IN MEDICAL SCIENCE

The single most important aspect of medical attitudes towards women as mothers is their concealment behind a screen of what are presented as exclusively clinical concerns. The attitude is that there are *no* attitudes; it is purely a question of how medical knowledge determines the 'best' maternity care policy, one that will guarantee the lowest possible mortality rate for mother and child.

There is, in a sense, no answer to this – for what mother does not want to survive childbirth with a healthy child? But the issue is a great deal more complicated. In the first place, obstetricians and other makers of maternity-care policy have rarely possessed the evidence necessary to prove that any particular obstetric practice is really 'better' than another (or the alternative of no practice at all) as judged by the objective of the lowest possible mortality. In the second place, the assessment of the 'success' of childbirth in terms of mortality (and to a lesser extent physical morbidity) rates is itself an attitude of extreme, if benign, paternalism. It hides two assumptions: first, the usual but disputable medical-scientific claim, challenged convincingly by Ivan Illich,[22] Thomas McKeown[23] and others, that improvements in health care are due principally to medical treatment (rather than to changes in social and economic conditions); and, second, that all other indices of successful childbirth are irrelevant, or at least of very minor importance. The way in which obstetrics has developed has ensured a preoccupation with the *physical* model of reproduction. Social and emotional measures of reproductive success do not count, although the evidence is that such

measures are extremely important to mothers themselves. Such evidence is hardly ever collected by obstetric researchers investigating the efficacy of particular obstetric practices. Maternal attitudes to obstetric practice and maternal assessments of successful reproductive outcome as research topics have been considered by obstetricians to constitute the 'soft', and by implication inferior, material of social-scientific surveys – where, that is, they have been considered at all.

In modern obstetrics, the dominant image of women is a mechanical one: women are seen as reproductive machines. 'To put the matter rather crudely, obstetrics treats a body like a complex machine and uses a series of interventionist techniques to repair faults that may develop in the machine.'[24] The mechanical model is 'man-made' and needs regular servicing to function correctly. Thus, antenatal care is maintenance- and malfunction-spotting work. There is a most significant premise here, and that is that any machine can go wrong at any time; there is no distinction between those machines that are in good working order – in other words, the ninety-seven per cent[25] of pregnancies and childbirths that are unproblematic – and those machines with some apparent fault – in other words, the small minority of pregnancies and births in which medical intervention does literally save lives. Concretely, as well as ideologically, women appear to become machines. The language of obstetrics itself reflects this – consider such terms as 'uterine dysfunction', 'incompetent cervix' and 'bad reproducer'. Obstetric care in countries such as Britain and the USA is increasingly machine-oriented. In many hospitals, all pregnancies are monitored with ultrasound; in some, the mechanical assessment of gestation is so important that women are no longer asked for the date of their last menstrual period. Other technological assessments are a routine part of antenatal care. Machines are used to initiate and terminate labour. One machine controls the uterine contractions, while another records them; regional (epidural) analgesia removes the woman's awareness of her contractions so that these do, indeed, have to be read off the machine; and keeping all the machines going becomes what 'looking after' a patient in labour means.

This merging of the pregnant female body with the high-powered technology of modern obstetrics has many implications. But one implication that it does *not* have is that obstetricians are merely mechanics to be called in when faults develop, much as one takes a faulty car to the garage to have it repaired. It is usually obvious to a car-owner when her or his car goes wrong, but women cannot be trusted to be experts on their own pregnancies. Thus another prime feature of medical images of motherhood is that women lack the capacity to know what is happening to their own bodies. Doctors are the only experts in the entire symptomatology of childbearing.

This was very clearly demonstrated in the encounters between doctors and patients which I observed in a London maternity hospital in the mid-1970s. Perhaps the most striking encounter along these lines was the following:

> *Doctor*: [reading case-notes] Ah, I see you've got a boy and a girl.
> *Patient*: No, two girls.
> *Doctor*: Really, are you sure? I thought it said . . . [checks in case-notes] . . . Oh no, you're quite right, two girls.

Pregnancy and childbirth in the medical model are medical events. For it is only by an ideological transformation of the 'natural' or 'normal' to the 'cultural' and 'abnormal' that doctors can legitimate reproduction as a medical speciality. Any individual pregnancy or childbirth may be normal, but it is only so, according to medical dictate, in retrospect. The mechanical model of motherhood conspires with the model of reproduction as pathology to characterize women having babies as possessing only one role – that of pregnant patients, patients in the delivery room and postpartum ward. Being a patient is separated off from the rest of life. The impact of social, economic and psychological factors is admitted by obstetricians only insofar as it is liable to predict the physical symptomatology or outcome of pregnancy. Hence unmarried patients may receive special medical attention and be referred routinely to the medical social worker, while married patients who experience genuine medical and social problems are not routinely viewed as a 'high-risk' group. Low social class and being unmarried are frequently combined with obstetric factors in medical scoring systems for high-risk pregnancies.

The organization of much obstetric care is based on the assumption that a pregnant or parturient woman has no other responsibilities or interests which conflict with her function of producing a baby. Reproduction is a full-time role. In the antenatal consultations which I observed, as well as the medical literature, doctors rarely consider that pregnant women have homes to run, many have other children to look after, a significant proportion are involved in the care of elderly relatives, the majority are married and carry the domestic responsibilities attached to the role of a wife, while most are engaged in addition in some form of paid employment. One example illustrates this point:

> *Doctor*: Mrs Carter? How are you getting on?
> *Patient*: Horrible.
> *Doctor*: Why?
> *Patient*: I feel horrible . . . I feel so depressed.

Doctor: Why?

Patient: I don't know . . . I feel it's so difficult to walk.

Doctor: You shouldn't be walking much at this stage of pregnancy.

Patient: I don't. But I have my housework to do and I've got the in-laws staying.

Doctor: They should be doing your housework for you, shouldn't they? Isn't that what they're for?

Patient: They're not females . . . things aren't very good at home at the moment . . .

Doctor: You do seem to have put on a bit of weight.

Patient: What does that mean?

Doctor: It doesn't necessarily mean anything, but you must take things easy.

Patient: That's what my husband says. It's easy for men to say that.

Doctor: It's your set-up at home. You should have organized things better.

Patient: Well, I've got three children to look after.

Ninety-three per cent of the questions posed or statements made by patients about social matters and social role obligations in the doctor–patient encounters which I observed met with the response of irritation or simple avoidance from the doctor.

Because reproduction is a specialist medical subject, because parenthood is isolated from women's life circumstances, and because women are typified as essentially ignorant about the process of reproduction, the concept of choice as applied to users of the maternity services is nowhere in sight in the medical model of motherhood. Although many surveys of how women feel about their maternity care show that many wish to be consulted about what kind of medical treatment they receive, the obstetrical claim to unique expertise prevents the exercise of choice by those who have the babies. I am not talking here about those cases in which gross problems in pregnancy or labour clearly necessitate medical intervention, but about the majority of cases in which it is 'policy' in general that determines what proportion of women receive such procedures as ultrasonic monitoring in pregnancy, electronic fetal heart monitoring in labour, and elective induction of labour. Women themselves are often aware that the rules determining their treatment are arbitrary, in the sense that these rules vary from one hospital to another, or from one practitioner to another. Under such circumstances, it seems reasonable to mothers that they should have a say in what happens; but it is not reasonable to a medical profession whose claim to jurisdiction over the label of illness and any human life-event to which it may be attached

ensures the right (if not the responsibility) to disregard the wishes of the 'patient'.

Those who provide maternity care may see women as walking wombs, but they cannot discount completely the fact that women have heads as well. Thus we come to the second key model of womanhood in medical science – that of the biologically-determined 'feminine' female.

In the medical literature, including the advice literature available in Britain and other countries written by medical 'experts' for mothers, there is a clearly-set-out paradigm of 'normal' motherhood.[26] What is a normal mother? She is a person especially in need of medical care and protection; a person who is essentially childish; but at the same time fundamentally altruistic; she is married; and, lastly, she ought to be happy but is, instead, constantly beset with anxiety and depression.

These typifications of mothers are interrelated and also internally contradictory. Women's imputed need for medical care and control is demanded by the very premise of obstetric science – that women can only be 'delivered of' their babies: childbirth cannot be allowed to be an autonomous act. In turn, the need for medical care requires the imputation of ignorance, unreliability and plain silliness to mothers as immutably feminine characteristics. Women are people who suffer from an inability to remember important facts, like when they last menstruated or when to take iron and vitamin supplements prescribed by their doctors:

> Do remember to take the tablets your doctor has given you. No matter how well you feel, both you and your baby need them and the don't do either of you any good if you leave them sitting around on your dressing-table.[27]

Another instance of such advice is the counsel offered by much of the antenatal literature against moving house in pregnancy. This is described as a piece of idiocy guaranteed to jeopardize the baby's well-being. However, it is widely stated – I don't know whether this observation is to be found in Finnish literature too – that scrubbing the floor and cleaning out the kitchen cupboards constitute 'nest-building' of the type in which animals engage, and is a sure sign of the baby's imminent arrival.

In these ways, normal mothers in the medical paradigm are not really adults at all. They are like children; and, like children, have to be guided and disciplined into correct modes of behaviour. Yet, here we face a profound contradiction: for normal mothers, that is 'good' mothers, do not put their own needs first. They see the world in terms of their children's needs, which they gauge by a mixed and, again, contradictory process of listening to the experts, on the one hand, and intuition – the much-famed myth of the

'maternal instinct' – on the other. The stereotype of normal mothers as married refers to a central contradiction in obstetrical/gynaecological work (which reflects the illogicality of the association between the two disciplines) – and that is the conflict between the promotion and prevention of childbirth. The image of the nuclear family as the only valid context for childbirth is still immensely powerful in our society, and the medical profession is hardly renowned for its liberal moral attitudes. Husbands are important possessions for normal mothers because they constitute the sole orthodox channel for mothers' emotional and sexual satisfaction.

The final characteristic of normal mothers in the medical paradigm – their proneness to anxiety and depression – actually comes first in political importance in the social construction of motherhood and womanhood. It does so for three reasons. In the first place, the recognition that it is normal for mothers to be depressed before birth and afterwards proceeds from the recognition that the normal condition of women in general is depression. Second, the construction of women as depressed provides a rationale for them to be oppressed also. Third, the prevalence of depression in mothers and women raises the question as to why it occurs and what can be done about it. The standard medical explanation for female depression is a biological one – that mysterious term 'hormones'. The standard medical treatment is pharmacological, for it is by the widespread administration of psychotropic drugs that women are 'adjusted' to their situation. A Canadian study came to the interesting conclusion that women who use psychotropic drugs such as valium are consciously aware of taking them in order to cope with the social strains of their daily lives.[28]

PSYCHOLOGICAL CONSTRUCTS OF WOMEN

In an oft-quoted study carried out in the USA in 1970, a group of mental-health clinicians was asked to rate the applicability of a range of personal qualities to three different kinds of people: normal adult men, normal adult women, and 'healthy, mature, socially competent' individuals. The results of this study revealed that 'healthy, mature and socially competent' individuals were ascribed masculine characteristics. Normal women were seen as more submissive, less aggressive, less competitive, more excitable, more easily hurt, more emotional, more conceited about their appearance and less objective than the normal men.[29]

In this most significant manner, psychiatry and psychology have tended to reinforce the images of women extant in the medical model. They have underscored three particular aspects of the medical model: the failure to consider the *social* context in which childbearing occurs and women live; the assumption that psychological states (including depression as the normal

condition of women) are caused by physiological ones; and the refusal to treat women as human beings because women are a sex apart, 'nature herself'.

The term 'postnatal depression' is part of the language in which women discuss and experience childbirth. But it also exists as a technical concept, which is poorly defined in the literature. However, there is general agreement among the relevant 'experts' that postnatal depression is a form of reactive depression, that is, a response to particular environmental circumstances, in this case the prior circumstance of childbirth. The two main psychiatric theories describe its aetiology as, first, hormones; and, second, some disturbance of femininity. Now, while there are clearly considerable hormonal shifts during pregnancy and after delivery, to prove a causal association between these and the various forms of postnatal depression (from the 'blues' of the early postpartum days to a full-blown psychosis developing some time later) requires research of the kind that has simply not been done. Those few studies which have examined selected aspects of puerperal biochemistry have done so in relation to early postpartum mood only (because hospitalized women are captive subjects), and, for the most part, their findings have been inconclusive.[30] In other words, the hormonal aetiology of postpartum mental disorder is part of received medical wisdom about motherhood, and it is imported into the domain of commonsense understandings about motherhood, where its unscientific basis rests unquestioned. Most importantly, the biological explanation of postnatal depression is frequently taken to disprove the likelihood of this disorder being accounted for by any social influence. We are again back to the mechanical model of women as reproducers.

The second major theme in the psychological construction of maternity assumes that psychological problems result from intrapsychic conflict in the individual as she undergoes the stresses of reproduction. Postnatal depression is the outcome of this internal, individualized conflict. Of course, this interpretation also means that women are at the mercy of their bodies. It means, in addition, that a great deal of medical research has been based on the supposition that reproductive problems in general are caused by women's lack of success in achieving a mature femininity. For example, infertility, habitual abortion and premature delivery have all been analysed as psychosomatic defences, as a result of women's hostile identification with their own mothers, as symptomatic of a general rejection of the feminine role, or as evidence of disturbed sexual relationships with men. The same hypotheses have also been applied to other common complications of pregnancy, such as nausea and vomiting and toxaemia; and the literature is studded with attempts to relate the neonatal condition of the baby to its mother's personality.[31]

In one attempt to relate neonatal condition to maternal mental state, a group of research workers at the London Hospital involved in a longitudinal study of child development decided to begin with pregnancy and to collect a certain amount of 'social' data which they could then relate to pregnancy outcome. There appeared to be a significant difference in mean infant birthweight according to whether or not the mothers suffered from psychiatric illness in pregnancy. However, when factors associated with 'psychiatric illness' and 'non-psychiatric illness' groups were considered, it became apparent that the association of lower birthweight with maternal psychiatric disorder was probably a spurious one: women who were considered psychiatrically ill and had low-birthweight babies were also more likely to be smokers, aged under twenty and infrequent antenatal clinic attenders.[32]

Whether or not the 'feminine woman' makes the best reproducer cannot, like so many other professional suppositions about motherhood, in fact be established from existing research. One problem is: what is femininity? Clearly, it is something quite different from mere biological femaleness, or there would be no grounds at all for this debate that has raged for many decades in the psychiatric literature.

The first factor that stands out in this literature is that femininity is an ever-changing concept. Pregnancy nausea is taken as evidence of lack of femininity in some studies[33] and of its presence in others.[34] Pain in labour is a denial of femininity,[35] or the absence of pain is.[36] Are real women sick and prone to labour pain or are they not? One investigator, using a masculinity–femininity scale, found that the more 'masculine' women reported fewer pregnancy problems. He was forced to engage in the contortion of concluding that such women, because they wish to appear healthy, simply *deny* their symptoms.[37] For the most part, however, and not surprisingly, a feminine woman is defined in the psychiatric literature on reproduction as one who is married, devoted to motherhood and domestic life, unambitious, not highly educated; in short, rather a dull, second-class citizen. Factors such as playing boys' games in childhood, experiencing any kind of sexual problem, and worrying about how to care for the child are predictive of improper femininity[38] – which immediately disqualifies most of us from achieving this label.

The meanings of 'femininity' cannot be derived from the psychiatric literature but rather from the social world. As a final comment on psychological images of maternity, there is the paradox to which I have obliquely referred in mentioning the work of the researcher who was displeased to find 'masculine' women healthier than 'feminine' ones. The paradox is that femininity as conventionally defined is not conducive to

problem-free reproduction (nor is the 'normal motherhood' of the medical advice literature). In her study of *The Birth of the First Child*, Dana Breen found that the most feminine women in her sample of fifty were those who encountered a whole range of problems most often. She summed up the situation thus:

> those women who are most adjusted to childbearing are those who are less enslaved by the experience, have more differentiated, more open appraisals of themselves and other people, do not aspire to be the perfect selfless mother . . . and do not experience themselves as passive, the cultural stereotype of femininity.[39]

It seems to me that the question that should have been asked has not been asked. This question is: why should it have been considered so important in psychological research on reproduction to demonstrate the link between having a baby and having acquired that particular psychodynamic structure which expresses the socially secondary meaning of womanhood in a patriarchal society? One answer is that there exists a special and mistaken 'psychology of women' which 'implies the need for a special set of laws and theories to account for the behaviour and experience of females'.[40] Another answer is the dominance of the psychoanalytic perspective, according to which much of the sophistication of what Freud actually said has been lost in dogmatic connections between reproductive physiology and female psychology.

SOCIOLOGICAL SURVEYS

Because their subject matter is the social, surely sociological studies of women and reproduction have been able successfully to remove motherhood from its deterministic biological underpinnings? To some extent, this is true. But just as there has not been, until recently, even the beginnings of a 'sociology of women', so there has traditionally been no 'sociology of reproduction'. Why is this?

Like most professions, sociology has been male-dominated, although perhaps it has been so in less obvious ways than some. The truth is that the 'agenda' of sociology – its defined subject areas, issues and models of enquiry – has been grounded in the working worlds and social relations of men. The accepted fields of sociology – political sociology, the sociology of occupations, the sociology of deviance, and so forth – have been defined from the vantage point of the professional, managerial and administrative structures of our society. Women have been assigned a special place. Both as subject matter and as practitioners of sociology, women have been overwhelmingly relegated to the domain of marriage and family relations.

The consequence of this for sociological conceptions of maternity is that the psychodynamic structure of the marital relationship replaces the psychodynamic structure of the individual (in the psychological paradigm) as the locus in which the meaning of reproduction is to be found. This 'marital' bias is evidenced in four main ways:

1. research on reproductive intentions and practices has been focused on *married* women (much as gynaecologists are concerned to promote childbirth among the married and prevent it among the unmarried):
2. the reproductive behaviour of single women has been studied almost exclusively from a 'social problem' perspective, although in many countries 'illegitimate' conceptions are relatively common;
3. maternity has been viewed as of primary importance to the development of the marriage relationship, rather than to the development (or otherwise) of mothers themselves;
4. the examination of motherhood has been child- and not woman-centred, reflecting a concern with children's needs rather than with those of mothers.

Largely because of the influence of the functionalist school of thought in sociology, its practitioners were for a long time obsessed with the question 'What purpose does the institution of the family (and the category women–wives) serve for society as a whole?' The answer was couched in terms of families being the sole appropriate factories for the production of human personalities – which are, of course, to the sociologist not born but made. Ultimately, biology seeps in within the functionalist model as the fundamental explanation of gender-differentiation within the family. In particular, recourse is had to 'the division of organisms into lactating and nonlactating classes'.[41]

The functionalist paradigm of motherhood has exerted a tremendous influence on marriage and family sociology, and has got in the way of important alternative questions. These include 'what does the family do to women (and men)?' and 'how does the ethic of marriage and the nuclear family constrain the practice of maternity?' In other words, the sociological paradigm of reproduction as the cornerstone of the family has served to distance women from their reproductive experiences, just as medical appeals to biology or psychological constructions of womanhood have done.

The discipline of medical sociology, which has grown enormously in the last five years or so in Britain and the USA, has given more prominence to maternity than sociology in general. The British medical sociologist Sally Macintyre described four types of sociological approach to the management of childbirth, in a paper published in 1977.[42] These four approaches are:

1. *historical/professional*: an exercise in which the evolution of the professional (and lay) management of childbirth is examined;
2. the *anthropological* approach, focussing on the relation between the management of childbirth and prevailing belief-systems in different cultures;
3. *patient-oriented* studies, where the perspectives of those who use the maternity services are articulated; and
4. studies of *patient—services* interaction, where patterns of communication between users and providers of services are examined.

We now possess a sizeable literature of studies in each of these areas. Most important of all is the fact that the medical paradigm of motherhood has been reconceptualized as a potential influence on the meaning of motherhood to women themselves.

Once the medical paradigm is extracted from its scientific guise, it is possible to see it as a cultural project, and, as I have already said, it is a cultural product of enormous significance in shaping common sense understandings of women and motherhood. But we are still left with the problem of the fissure between the actuality of female experience and its dominant ideological expression. Why do professional paradigms of motherhood contain an image of women as, first and foremost, natural maternal creatures devoted to wifehood and housekeeping? Why does the attribution to mothers of the unselfish motive of reproducing the race hide their characterization as childish and incapable of control? Why are mothers seen at the same time as strong and central to the social structure and as weak and essentially marginal to all mainstream public issues? Why are motherhood and childbirth not themselves public political issues akin to, for example, education and the structure of electoral systems?

To answer these questions, we have to set the medical care of women within its broader political context. We must consider both medicine as an agency of social control, and the typical forms of social control to which women have historically been subject.

3

The Doctor's Problem

It has been said that history proceeds by changing the subject, rather than by a rational progression from one state to the next, or by the dialectical process of 'doing, undoing, and reassembling things'.[43] In the early nineteenth century, and even the early part of the twentieth century, doctors and midwives who provided care for childbearing women made no hard-and-fast separation between clinical success and the patient's satisfaction.[44] But, as time has advanced, so the profession of obstetrics has turned in on itself and focused more and more exclusively on biological and clinical influences and effects. By the 1980s, we even have babies described as 'the obstetrical product'. Over the horizon of this newly technological phase of perinatal medicine then came the consumer organizations, in uneasy and sometimes unspoken alliance with social scientists who wanted to change the subject and talk about the rights of women to make choices in childbirth, and other such liberal-romantic distractions. Now I think we are at a stage where it is at least possible to unravel and integrate these different points of view, rather than merely change the subject again. Let us concentrate on two closely linked themes. The first is the meaning of the current debate about hard versus soft outcomes.[45] The second is why so much is heard (on one level) about patient satisfaction and why so little is done about it, and why so little, correspondingly, is heard about the satisfaction of doctors when this is so clearly a powerful, albeit invisible, influence on patterns of obstetric care.

THE HEALTH-CARE DIVISION OF LABOUR

The most obvious division of labour in perinatal care is between people who are paid to provide obstetric care – doctors, midwives, nurses, paramedics

and so forth – and those who are not paid – so-called 'patients' and their families. This division of labour is one example of a general rule observable in all health care. This rule is that a great deal of health care is done by people who are neither paid nor acknowledged for their performance of this task. Indeed, it is a predominant myth of the modern age, an aspect of the 'theology' of medicine, to use Thomas Szasz's term,[46] that the only people who can care for health are those who have been formally trained and licensed to do so. (And our belief about the impropriety of lay people caring for health is, of course, why we are in such a technological fix about such matters as health education and health promotion; having said health is something that people get from the medical and allied professions, we are now trying to get people to supply it for themselves while at the same time keeping the professions in business.)

One of the consequences of this paid/unpaid division of labour in health care is unequal status between these two groups, both in general and in relation to specific issues such as the evaluation of care. In maternity-care policy, as in medical-care policy overall, a clear division holds between clinicians' autonomy to determine treatment and patients' attitudes to treatment. It is within this frame of reference that the attitudes of patients have traditionally been accommodated. To cite an accurate, although sexist, analogy used by Freidson:

> It is as if the housewife could choose the store she wished to patronize but not which of the articles in the store she could buy. The choice is made for her by those who run the store on the basis of their conception of what she 'really' needs which may be no articles at all, articles she does not want, or, if she is lucky, just what she wants.[47]

In the literature on doctor–patient interaction, there are some stark illustrations of constraints on patients' freedom to influence their medical care. In a study of 2,500 general practitioner–patient consultations in England, for example, the theme of doctors resisting any challenge to their expertise is manifested thus in one interaction where a patient is dissatisfied with the diagnosis given by the doctor. The doctor reacts by saying: 'I will tell you what is wrong with you, I will tell you what your symptoms are, and I will tell you what to do. I am the doctor and you will kindly not forget that fact.'[48] Most interesting of all, when the tape-recording of the consultation was played back to the doctor in question, he said that he could remember clearly what the patient had said but that he had no recollection at all of his own reaction.

ARE DOCTORS SATISFIED?

Naturally, it is unfair to quote an isolated instance of one doctor–patient consultation that obviously got out of hand. However, such examples serve to make an important point. This point was framed by Cassell, writing on the philosophy of healing some years ago in the following terms: 'we, as a society, have come to associate the doctor and his technology so closely and to attribute such power to the association that we have difficulty in seeing them separately when such a separate view is necessary.'[49] Generalizing from this, it could be said that a comprehensive evaluation of medical care or of obstetric care must include both the technical efficiency and effectiveness of medicine on the one hand, and its social relations on the other. Most importantly, it must not mistake one for the other. We need to know, for instance, not only whether particular therapies work, but also how important the social relations of doctor and patient are in making them work or in explaining why they do not work – an issue that is, of course, particularly well addressed in the literature on placebo effects.[50] In attempting this degree of understanding, I would argue that we must be as concerned with doctors' satisfaction as we are with patients' satisfaction. In fact, I would go further than this and observe that obstetric practice as an entity cannot be understood without appreciating that doctors are motivated by personal and professional feelings, and, among these feelings, perhaps the most influential is the need to maximize her or his own job satisfaction within a framework in which the major 'quality control' over obstetrical work is exercised by the somewhat fragile brake of 'peer review'.[51]

In her national survey of induction in England and Wales in the mid-1970s, Ann Cartwright[52] collected some interesting data on obstetricians' attitudes to induction, which are buried in the last chapters of her report on the study and are not often referred to by those who use it. A sample of consultant obstetricians were asked open-ended questions about the advantages and disadvantages of induction. Nearly half said that in their view it had increased the job satisfaction of obstetricians because it had enabled more planning of deliveries, tidier departments, and *happier* mothers. At the same time, some of the consultants contradicted themselves and three out of five said that induction had not improved the experience of childbearing for women, or had actually made it worse. When Cartwright looked at obstetricians' views on induction according to gender, age and type of appointment (university versus National Health Service), she found women doctors and those in university appointments somewhat less in favour of induction (there was no clear trend with age). The doctors in her sample were also in favour of epidurals as increasing their own job

satisfaction and were surprisingly certain about the effects on the patients of these interventions. For example, two-thirds stated that induction for non-medical reasons would have no effect on mothers' health or on the relationship between mothers and babies. Cartwright found that fewer than one in five midwives (compared to half the obstetricians) said that induction had increased their own job satisfaction.

These data belong with a wide range of others showing the importance of what could broadly be termed 'social' factors in determining the clinical behaviour of medical professionals and others engaged in providing care for sick or pregnant people. Perhaps my favourite among these studies is the one that analysed the educational background of British doctors in different medical specialities and found that those who in their youth had been to public (i.e. private) schools were more likely than others to work on living bodies rather than dead bodies, on the head rather than on the lower trunk, on male bodies rather than female bodies, and on the body surface rather than inside.[53] This raises the pertinent question of whether, and how, doctors are satisfied. What do doctors really want?

'PATIENT SATISFACTION'

What *is* satisfaction? How can it be measured? One way *not* to measure it is illustrated in a somewhat more exciting area of study, that of human sexuality. The pioneering work of Alfred Kinsey and his colleagues in the 1950s told us much that we did not know about the sexual behaviour of human beings, mostly because Kinsey and his team went into the community and replaced 'soft' speculation with 'hard' data. However, the team also committed some errors. In one special research project, the object was to find out which areas of the female genitals were most sensitive to sexual stimulation. To achieve this end, three male and two female gynaecologists touched more than 800 women at sixteen different points, including the clitoris, labia, vaginal lining and cervix. In order to be appropriately impersonal and scientific, the gynaecologists did not use their hands; they used cotton swabs. These produced a response in the clitoral area but not in the vagina, which, as we now know (and presumably some women knew then), is sensitive not to soft touch but rather to deep pressure. The researchers thus concluded, on the basis of an inappropriate methodology, that vaginas are insensitive, a myth propagated until Masters and Johnson came along with the more appropriately sensitive measuring instrument of the laboratory observation of human sexual behaviour.[54]

A broad but appropriate generalization from the 'patient satisfaction' literature would certainly be that most obstetric patients – ranging from sixty to over ninety per cent in different studies – say that they are satisfied

when asked somewhat unspecific questions about their satisfaction with care.[55] In this respect, it is reassuring to know that obstetric patients resemble other patients of the same sex and age.[56] This is partly because most patients do not readily admit to basic dissatisfaction with their care. In an exactly parallel fashion, most people, when asked by a researcher, will say they are happy.[57] The reason is presumably the same in both cases: there is little point in admitting to dissatisfaction unless there is some hope of changing the status quo. Readiness to declare dissatisfaction rises proportionately with the personal opportunity to bring about change. And most people are not in a position, at least in the short term, to change very much in their lives.

Patients may often feel an incentive to make the relationship work; they like the doctor; they cannot easily change doctors; they do not want to get involved in unpleasant hassles in pregnancy, and so forth. Not surprisingly, then, the highest rates of 'satisfaction' are reported in studies where patients are asked about their satisfaction in a medical setting by medical personnel or in a context which is unambiguously that of medical sponsorship.[58] At one extreme is the patient 'satisfaction' rate of ninety-five per cent reported by a doctor in a 'short internal study' of an antenatal clinic. In answer to the question, asked in the antenatal clinic by a staff member, 'Do you understand what your doctor has told you?' ninety-five per cent of women said yes.[59]

In another study, eighty-seven working-class women were asked (at home, by a social scientist) the meaning of thirteen common obstetric terms such as breech, membranes, rhesus, and so forth. A group of physicians was also asked (in hospital, by a social scientist) which of these terms they would expect such patients to understand. Results of the study indicated an 'overwhelming underestimation' by the physicians of working-class patients' ability to understand what they, the doctors, were talking about. I cannot avoid mentioning that the male physicians thought the pregnant women considerably more ignorant than did their female colleagues.

Rates of patient 'satisfaction' are considerably lower in non-medical studies.[60] In Cartwright's study of hospital care, sixty-one per cent of patients interviewed by a social scientist in their own homes after discharge from hospital complained that they had not been able to get adequate information about their treatment.[61] Direct rather than open-ended questions apparently produce more dissatisfied patients.[62]

An excellent rundown on the different data-collecting methods and their variable yields is provided by Cartwright in her recent book, *Health Surveys*,[63] which addresses the role of small-scale, more qualitative research studies as useful for providing insights and hypotheses to be tested in larger-scale work. Smaller-scale studies are especially likely to be

illuminating on the difficult question of alternatives to existing forms of care. Large-scale and questionnaire surveys have an inbuilt conservatism. They do not allow people to range freely in the realm of their more utopian visions of prenatal clinics, delivery rooms and obstetrical or midwifery bedside manners.

It is unlikely that the statistically common and personally disabling 'soft' outcome of postpartum depression, for example, will be tapped satisfactorily in a large questionnaire survey, and certainly its antecedent social and medical-care factors are unlikely to be found using this approach.[64] Another criticism of large-scale quantitative work is that the global rates of patient satisfaction found in these studies may conceal a large range of different rates in different subgroups of patients. Furthermore, they are able to give us absolutely no information about what patients expect or want from their medical encounters. What patients expect has been shown significantly to affect satisfaction levels.[65] Although continuity of care is a feature of patient expectations that is predictive of high satisfaction among obstetric patients,[66] other studies demonstrate that what patients are after is good clinical care together with intelligible and unpatronizing information about what doctors are doing. This may be one explanation of an aspect of patient behaviour infrequently set alongside the patient satisfaction data, but which very much deserves to be. While most patients may *appear* satisfied, between nineteen and seventy-two per cent — an average of thirty per cent — do not take the medications prescribed by their doctors. They are 'drug defaulters'[67] (though who actually is defaulting here would seem very much an open question).

DOCTORS, PATIENTS AND SOCIAL SCIENTISTS

In the debate about the management of childbirth over the last twenty years, the spectre of 'the happy mother' has emerged to haunt hospital corridors, medical journal editors and the hidden recesses of the obstetrical mind. The opposition between 'hard' and 'soft' outcomes is personified in the idealized objective of 'healthier babies and happier mothers'. The problem of how to achieve both at the same time or even, in some quarters, *whether* to, suggests that we are victims of a 'two-culture' dilemma. Childbearing women and their families on the one hand, and those who manage childbearing on their behalf on the other, bring different sets of cultural baggage to their mutual encounters, and these encounters are often experienced in confrontational terms for this very reason.

To what extent might social scientists offer a bridge between doctors and childbearing families? Studies of how pregnant women felt about their care have been a main strand in medical sociological work.[68] Some social

scientists have observed doctors,[69] or analysed the structure and power relations of medical professions, the state and society.[70] But these professional exercises have proved quite challenging, because doctors have a certain reluctance to be studied, or to give information to 'outsiders' about their practice.[71]

Moreover, communication is not an art taught in medical school; it is, rather, one that appears to be actually bred out of medical students in the course of their training programmes. As an illustration, there is the well-known tendency of doctors to present different faces to patients from different social class groups.[72] Social scientists are therefore best known for their research on obstetric patients, and most of these researchers have been women. As a result of this division of labour, social scientists have tended to play an awkward kind of marital counselling role in the difficult interplay between doctors and patients. Some of us are better marital counsellors than others. But it is an essential element in the counselling process that attention be paid to the perspectives of both partners in the communication difficulties that have developed between them.

CONCLUSION

I do not believe that a satisfactory mode of assessing and integrating soft outcomes will be found merely by co-opting into randomized controlled trials or such methodologies a few questions about what mothers think about this or that procedure. The relations between the profession of medicine and the profession of social science fortunately have a good deal more potential than that.

In the words of one social scientist, Richard Titmuss, written thirty years ago in an attempt to bridge the growing gap between medical power and social needs:

> Scientific medicine has let into clinical medicine a new spirit of criticism and questioning. . . . The danger is, however, that in the stage through which we are now passing a new authoritarianism will replace . . . the old one . . . for the greater the expectations we place on the doctor the more may we strengthen his [sic] need to maintain his role and, while attempting to satisfy others, satisfy himself. . . . There is a danger of medicine becoming a technology. . . . There is the problem of medical power in society; a problem which concerns much more of our national life than simply the organization of medical care. . . . The task of the future is to make medicine more 'social' in its application without losing in the process the benefits of science and specialized knowledge.[73]

4

On the Importance of
Being a Nurse

Illness and suffering are part of the human condition. They create dependency, for to be sick and in pain is to be dependent on, and vulnerable to, others. The very persistence of this dependency throughout history provides a motive for the rise of all forms of health care. All health care has a common aim, namely the relief of human suffering.

Nursing fits into this picture somewhere, though just where it fits depends on the time and the place and is, to some extent, in the eye of the beholder. Nursing needs to be looked at within two forms of the division of labour: the division of labour in health care, and the division of labour between the sexes. In what ways are nurses different kinds of people from doctors, or patients, or other health-care workers? What is, or should be, their particular contribution to the relief of suffering in any community? The second question is contained in the first, for no-one can really pursue a definition of nursing without examining the relations between the role of nurse and the general position of women.

The reason for asking these questions is not merely academic. In many countries of the world, health services are now in a state of crisis. There are two edges to the crisis. One is economic; a growing failure to match the demand for medical services with available economic resources. The other factor is a crisis of confidence in the ability of medicine to deliver the goods: adequately to prevent illness, to prevent disability and death when illness does occur, and to do so with treatments and technologies that are not more damaging than beneficial to the lives of patients.

THE INVISIBLE NURSE: A PERSONAL AND PROFESSIONAL APOLOGY

In a lengthy career as a medical sociologist studying medical services, I have to admit to a certain blindness with respect to the contribution that nurses make to health care. Indeed, over a period of some months spent observing health-care work in a large London hospital, I hardly noticed nurses at all. When I sat there with my notebook and tape recorder, watching doctors and patients interacting, nurses were around somewhere in these scenarios; I took their presence for granted (much as, I imagine, the doctors and patients did) – but the character of the nurse's role in no way impressed itself on me. If this sounds a bit like Florence Nightingale's definition of a good nurse – an invisible, good woman – then perhaps we should not be too surprised. In many ways, history *has* defined a good nurse as a good woman, and this can be counted as both the weakness and the strength of nursing as a profession.

Having apologized for not noticing nurses in my professional role, I shall now attempt to salvage my reputation by telling you when I did seriously begin to notice them. About seven years ago, I was in hospital, in a cancer ward, as a patient. As a cancer patient – I believe that is what we are called – I suffered from the usual, well-documented inability to obtain information about my condition. Doctors tended to lapse into mystifying technical-medical language in front of me, and my 'illness' was treated as a mechanical malfunction of my body without implications for my mind, my feelings, or my life. Of course I can describe my experiences accurately now, but at the time I was in a profound state of shock. I remember silently crying in front of the consultant the day the tumour was diagnosed. All he said was: 'What are you crying about? The treatment won't affect your appearance.' My appearance was not what I was worried about.

After that, I didn't cry again until the moment when I discovered the importance of nurses. I was lying in bed with a radioactive implant stitched into my tongue, and suddenly my resolve to face with a calm equanimity the experience of having cancer deserted me as I realized that I might, simply, not survive that experience. A young nurse came into the room to fetch the remains of my lunch, and she saw that I was distressed. Instead of taking my lunch tray away, or offering me drugs for the pain I was in, she sat down on my bed and held my hand and talked to me. I told her how I felt, and after a while she went away and read my notes, then came back and told me everything that was in them, and that, in her, of course unmedical, view, I would probably be all right. She stayed with me for nearly an hour, which she should not have done. I was radioactive and no-one was meant to spend any longer than ten minutes at a time with me. She was also, presumably, not

supposed to tell me what was in my case-notes, so she was breaking at least two sets of rules. I never saw this nurse again after I left hospital, but I would like her to know that she was important to my survival.

Since then, I have read some of the literature on communication with cancer patients. I have learnt, for example, that less than one per cent of cancer patients' discussions with doctors concern emotional or psychological well-being.[74] Many patients see their doctors as being too busy and interested only in their physical condition.[75] Both doctors and patients tend to define a 'good' patient as one who is compliant, and superficially cheerful. A patient who is openly distressed is as much a problem patient as one who is refusing to take her pills.

The moral of this story is that medical care is only a part of health care. Caring for someone's health means more than removing bits of disordered tissue, or bombarding the body with drugs and other 'therapeutic' influences. Above all, it means relating to the ill person as a whole person whose psyche is equally involved with her or his soma in the illness in question. This is the substance of many modern critiques of medicine. Ivan Illich, in his much-quoted *Medical Nemesis*,[76] observes that among the human experiences now 'medicalized' as the subject matter of medical work is pain. Under the medical regime, pain becomes merely a technical problem of the body, rather than an experience with an inherent personal meaning. This is not to say that people should suffer pain, but it is to say that pain is something felt by the individual and not simply within the diseased organ or body. Thus the relief of pain involves communication with the individual who feels it. A chemical intervention at the level of the body is not enough.

NURSING IN THE HEALTH-CARE DIVISION OF LABOUR

It has, at times, been enormously difficult for medical practitioners to ignore the potent relationships between bodies on the one hand, and minds and environments on the other. In order to do so, they have had to put on one side a great deal of evidence pointing to the social causation and prevention of disease – from studies showing the connections between life-events such as family arguments and the onset of infections such as streptococcal sore throats,[77] to the presence of 'stress' chemicals in the blood and urine of unemployed men whose wives are not being especially kind to them.[78] The 'placebo' effect in medical treatments themselves has been known for a long time to be often equal to the direct therapeutic effect of medical interventions, whether the focus of the treatment is pain,[79] preterm labour,[80] or apparently technical disorders such as urinary incontinence.[81] 'Placebo' means literally 'I shall please'. As evidence emerges about the mechanisms whereby the placebo effect may cure illness, it is becoming clear that the

patient's belief in the efficacy of the 'treatment' causes that 'treatment' physically to alter the body's condition. An especially vivid demonstration of the placebo effect is Norman Cousins'[82] description of how he cured his own crippling illness – ankylosing spondylitis – in 1964. He did this with two underrated therapeutic tools: vitamin C and laughter. With large intravenous doses of vitamin C, and a few Marx Brothers films, Cousins' blood sedimentation rate dropped, he no longer needed pain-killing drugs, and he was eventually restored to health (although he rapidly had to move out of hospital because his laughter disturbed the other patients, who were receiving more orthodox forms of medical care).

Despite this evidence as to the impact on health and happiness of what has been called 'therapeutic trust', the prevailing model of health and illness today is the one that says that medical care cures illness and preserves health. This model is closely tied to the evolution of the medical profession itself: the medical profession derives its legitimacy, its claim to fame, if you like, from its promise to cure illness with those resources that it, as a profession, exclusively controls – potent drugs, surgical operations, and complex, sometimes alienating technologies. But when we come to consider the history of nursing, we do not see at all the same relationship between what nurses do, or claim to do, on the one hand, and the curative model of medicine on the other. The origins of nursing lie in a totally different model of health and illness, namely the environmental one.

Nursing began to emerge as a separate occupation in the mid-nineteenth century. At that time, it was no more and no less than a specialized form of domestic work. Middle-class people did not use hospitals when members of their households were ill, but employed private nurses at home. Hospitals were for the sick poor, and in them nurses did everything that doctors didn't do, and also quite a lot of what we, in the twentieth century, are accustomed to think of as medical work (while very junior doctors also did some nursing work). Most hospital nurses were married women doing for patients what they did at home for their families. In addition, the dividing line between nurses and patients was blurred, and able-bodied convalescent patients were expected to help nurses with the domestic work of the ward. In one nineteenth-century London hospital, patients who failed to do this lost a whole day's meals for a first such offence and were abruptly discharged from hospital for a second.[83]

Having been a domestic servant was the only qualification required at this time for ordinary nursing, except that, once taken on, these women were also taught how to make poultices, an absolute necessity in the pre-antibiotic era. Hospital administrators of the period wondered what on earth nurses would do if they were deprived of heavy domestic work and if they only had to

administer to the sick. Even in the early professional training schools, competence at pudding-making, the making of bandages and the understanding of ward-ventilation were regarded as necessary skills for nurses to have. Conditions of work for the early nurses were poor, and nurses were expected to sleep on the ward, and were not provided with meals when on duty. It was hardly surprising, therefore, that some nurses were accused from time to time of stealing the patients' meals, and that Florence Nightingale, with her apt turn of phrase, remarked that nursing was done by those 'who were too old, too weak, too drunken, too dirty, too stolid, or too bad to do anything else'.[84] While food was not provided, alcohol *was* often given as part of the nurse's wages, or in return for particularly disagreeable work. A nineteenth-century British nurse would get a glass of gin for laying out the dead, or two glasses of gin for one spell of night duty, though it is not clear whether these were to be drunk at the time or afterwards.

As with all histories, there is an official history of nursing which selects certain kinds of developments and not others as important.[85] Hospital nursing training in Britain, for example, was begun before Florence Nightingale arrived on the scene, although, in the orthodox history, the profession of nursing was created by Nightingale virtually single-handed. Florence Nightingale's achievements on behalf of nursing were, in reality, quite mixed. An idle daughter of the upper classes, she was drawn to her work by visions of God, perhaps the only means available to her for making nursing seem respectable – God said it was, and Florence in due course proved it, with her labours in the Crimea which gave the impression of saving the entire British army.[86] What Florence Nightingale actually did was to wean nursing away from the cruder aspects of domestic work and attempt to establish it as a profession alongside the emerging profession of medicine. She saw nurses as a kind of hospital housekeeper whose job it was to supervise the health of the patient's environment as well as the patient's personal hygiene, and who, in order to do this, had to be members of a highly disciplined occupation with its own code of conduct and behavioural and ethical standards. While medicine sought to 'cure', nursing sought to care for the patient in both a sanitary and a moral sense.

Nightingale's efforts on behalf of nurses were aided by the growth of the demand for nurses in many countries at the end of the nineteenth century (in Britain the number of hospital beds tripled between 1861–91 and 1891–1911[87]), and by medicine's own insecurity about its professional credibility, and its consequent need to expand and control hospitals as places where captive patients could be used to teach future doctors. The new, trained nurses were a particular problem for doctors, since they often came

from a higher social class than the doctors themselves. This was one reason why the nurse's place in health care had to be very tightly controlled. What one could call the 'feminine' environmental model of nursing in fact changed little until the 1930s and 1940s, when nursing became clearly subordinate to medicine within a newly hierarchical technical division of labour. In the last twenty years, state intervention in health care has, in many countries, rigidified this pattern, and nurses have become one among many groups of ancillary health workers harnessed to the promotion of the technical-curative model of medicine. In the course of these developments, some elements in the trained nurse's work have been removed from it and relabelled the work of nursing auxiliaries or domestic staff. To fill the gap, and because doctors have become increasingly occupied with specialist technologies of one kind or another, doctors have passed on to nurses some routine parts of their own work. In this manner, the boundaries between different health-care occupations constantly shift, though an important question to ask is which occupation's definition of its role is the prime cause of changing occupational boundaries throughout the system. And, as with many social changes, the impetus to movement in health-care occupations comes from the top, from the highest-status, highest-paid and most powerful profession, and the one with the closest link to the machinery of state power. Indeed, doctors, politicians and top civil servants are liable to share the same social background and sets of values.[88]

'A GOOD NURSE IS A GOOD WOMAN': THE HEALTH-CARE FAMILY

This historical division of labour between doctors and nurses presents today's nurse with a definite set of constraints as to what nurses are able to do for patients and for themselves. But almost an equal constraint is the gender division of labour in health care. The details of this vary between countries, but we may make two generalizations about it. First, the vast majority of the world's health-care workers are women; many of these are nurses. Nurses thus provide more health care than doctors. The second generalization is that the medical profession is male-dominated. In most countries, it is male-dominated in a statistical sense, but, even where it is not, the stereotype of a doctor which is conveyed in medical training and practice owes a great deal more to cultural notions of masculinity than femininity. Doctors are rational, scientific, unemotional and uninvolved; indeed, their very value is sometimes said to reside in their detachment from the personal needs of their patients. In talking about this gender division between medicine and nursing, we have to add that, although women may become doctors and men may become nurses, there is a tendency within both professions for men to monopolize the top jobs. While it is possible to

understand why this happens in medicine – a science (or an art?) from which women were excluded so that they must now fight to be allowed back in – it is much harder to understand why nurses should allow their male colleagues to take an undue share of the top jobs. Don't women know more about nursing than men do? Of course I am being a little provocative here. But I have thought for a long time that what nurses, midwives and women in general need is assertiveness training. If Florence Nightingale had trained her lady pupils in assertiveness rather than obedience, perhaps nurses would be in a different place today. For nurses, like all women, have to contend with one important obstacle to change: real women are not supposed to be revolutionaries. If we complain about our situation, or the system, we are liable to be called ill, neurotic, menopausal, premenstrual, or in need of some curative relationship with a man. It is not good enough to say that there is something wrong out there, and we want to change it.

This was the iron link that Florence Nightingale did not challenge when she tried to professionalize nurses: the link between nursing and womanhood. The relationship between doctor and nurse in early nursing paralleled the husband–wife relationship in the family: *she* looked after the physical and emotional environment, while *he* decided what the really important work was, and how it should be done. 'Nursing is mothering.'[89] Or, 'To be a good nurse one must be a good woman', that is, 'attendants on the wants of the Sick – helpers in carrying out Doctors' orders.'[90] Nightingale, I want to add, was not quite as feeble as this much-quoted phrase makes her sound. She also ranted against the idea that nurses had to be nothing but devoted and subservient. 'This definition', she once said, 'would do just as well for a porter. It might even do for a horse.'[91]

But it is not just that doctor plays father and nurse plays mother: who is the child? The child is, of course, the patient. Mother and father (doctor and nurse) take care of, and make judgments about, the welfare of children (patients). Crucial to this triadic relationship is the fact that children are not asked to participate in making decisions about their own welfare; the role of children (patients) is to be passive recipients of parental (medical and nursing) treatment decisions.

THE 'CONSUMER' CRITIQUE AND THE NURSE'S ROLE

This analogy between the health-care division of labour and the family division of labour brings into focus a new social movement of our time – the movement formed by users of health care to protest about their infantilized position within the health-care system. In many countries now, there are organizations of health-care users whose agendas are very specifically asserting the rights of patients not to be treated like children. The emphasis

in these organizations is that health-care users be allowed choice in the matter of who gives them health care and how; furthermore, there is increasingly a demand that people be exposed only to treatments (whether of drugs, counselling, surgical operations or other procedures) which have been scientifically evaluated and been shown to be both effective and not unduly hazardous in either the short or the long run.[92]

This attack on the entrenched values and practices of the health-care system comes especially, of course, from those, including oppressed social minorities, women, and childbearing women in particular, who do not feel that they have totally benefited from medicine's curative claims. Indeed, the so-called 'consumer' critique is at its height in the area of maternity care, where people are able to add to all the other arguments the rejoinder that childbearing is not an illness, and therefore should not automatically be equated with a need to seek medical surveillance.

The word 'consumer' is, of course, really a misnomer in this context. People who use health care do not 'consume' it — they are also capable of producing their own health for themselves. Self-help health care is a mainstream development in the 'consumer' movement. Furthermore, 'consumers' of health care do not, in most places, really have the opportunity to choose the care they want. Choice requires alternatives, information and imagination. You cannot choose something if you do not know it exists and cannot imagine it existing. Similarly, we cannot really talk about 'patients' either, since that prejudges the issue in another way. The word 'patient' comes from the Latin 'patire', 'to suffer', and many people who use health services are not suffering, just as many who are suffering do not ever present themselves to health-care providers.

The inappropriateness of the terms 'consumer' and 'patient' points us in the direction of one extremely important generalization. This is that the new assertiveness on the part of users and would-be users of health care is but one aspect of a widespread challenge to professional authority today. It is not only the profession of medicine that is being challenged, but also others, including education, social welfare and the law. We in the industrialized world live in a society dominated more and more not by industrial production, but by the production of services. Control over service-production rests with professionals, whose power expands in importance as that of the older economic system declines.

What has all this to do with nurses? I think that there are two main ways in which the consumer health-care movement is signalling a future for nurses of which many may be unaware. In the first place, nurses do not form a profession along the same lines as doctors or lawyers make up a profession. Nurses are not members of the professional power elite whose authority is

currently being challenged. The fact that this is so provides nurses with a unique opportunity, namely to reshape their own place in health care so that they are more closely allied with the self-stated needs of patients, rather than with the self-stated needs of the medical profession. Second, much of what the consumer movement in health care is saying already has echoes in the history and ideology of nursing. Nurses need not, therefore, cover their tracks in order to map out an appropriate and successful response to the present health-care crisis. All they need to do is recover their past.

CARING VERSUS CURING

As I suggested earlier, nursing is associated not with a curative model of health and illness, but with a caring and an environmental one. The content of the first occupational training schemes for nurses emphasized not that 'patients' would be cured if their environments were clean and their personal needs were cared for, but, rather, that they would not be cured *without* this. Caring and attention to the environment were necessary, but not sufficient, conditions for restoring people's health. This ideology emerged as an accompaniment and as a support to the miracle achievements of modern medicine: the antibiotics and other chemotherapies; safe, organized blood-transfusion services; new surgical and complex new diagnostic technologies. But the irony is that, after some decades of experiencing the benefits of modern medicine, it is now clear that Florence Nightingale and other like-minded women the world over had got it right. Caring about someone and their environment is normally a necessary condition for maintaining their health.

When we look at surveys of how patients feel about nurses, the importance of caring emerges very clearly. People prefer nurses to be warm, kind, sympathetic personalities.[93] Rates of 'patient satisfaction' with nursing care are generally higher than those with medical care for two reasons. First, nurses offer an emotional support service. Second, patients frequently have problems acquiring sufficient information about their condition and treatment from doctors, and turn to nurses to fill this gap. Most of us who have had the experience of being hospital in-patients know the usual train of events. The doctors sweep through the ward on their ward 'round', and, once they have left, the patients ask the nurses what the doctors said (or meant). Surveys demonstrate that working-class patients, in particular, feel that nurses are not only good, but also appropriate, givers of information, and this fits into the general picture in which nurses have higher status among lower-class patients.[94]

On the theme of emotional support, one study by Rose Coser in the USA found that patients see the nurse's essential task as giving personal

reassurance and emotional support.[95] A more recent study in Britain by Evelyn Anderson had some interesting findings about how patients, nurses and doctors respectively see the role of the nurse. While both nurses and patients placed emotional support highest on the list of what a good nurse should provide, the doctors rated nurses' technical competence as most important, and were relatively uninterested in their capacity to provide emotional support.[96] Another survey with a bearing on this is that of Hughes and his colleagues in the USA. These researchers found that women in general see nurses more favourably than men do but that doctors see nurses less favourably than do men in general.[97] (In Anderson's study, thirty per cent of nurses had negative feelings towards doctors.)

Caring about, and for, the patient, is therefore an important part of the nurse's role in practice – whatever the theory. Yet, while nurses may pick up and respond to patients' needs for support and information, we have to add an important rider – that this sensitivity should not overrule nurses' perceptions of patients' physical needs. Marie Johnston's[98] study of patients and nurses in three gynaecological wards is not alone in suggesting that this sometimes happens: Johnston found that nurses perceived patients to have more worries than patients said they had, at the same time as significantly underestimating patients' pain and other physical symptoms.

NURSING AND THE POSITION OF WOMEN

Alertness to the needs of others is consistently picked out as the mark of a good nurse in surveys of people's attitudes to nurses. This is also the mark of a good woman. Altruism is a social strength. But, so far as the altruistic individual is concerned, it may well be a weakness: altruism serves the community but often gets the individual nowhere. Women, in living altruistic lives, nevertheless often feel quite bad about themselves and what they are doing, and somehow end up in a position where they are not at all equal shareholders with men in the world's economic and political wealth. As Jean Baker Miller has pointed out in her *Toward a New Psychology of Women*, ' "Serving others" is for losers, it is low-level stuff'.[99] But women's psychology and social roles are organized around the presumption that they *will* serve others; indeed, that from this serving of others will come the only self-enhancement that is culturally accepted as appropriate for women.

Taking care of others is a service required by every human community. Its value – good or bad, high or low – like the value of everything else that human beings do, is not intrinsic to the activity itself but is given it by the culture. And the problem with caring in modern Euro-American culture is that it is one-sided. While women do it and know it to be important work, men do not do it, therefore they do not know it to be important and are likely

to deny and deride its importance. But more than that, because these values are the dominant values, the dominant value is that caring is unimportant work. Women therefore are trapped. Their experience tells them that caring is important, but their culture tells them it isn't.

One of the most impressive mechanisms for denying the importance of caring work is to disenfranchise and disadvantage the people who do such work. The mechanism is effective, if not exactly subtle. The most outstanding example of it is childrearing, followed as a close second by housework. Both are unpaid occupations when located in the family and in conjunction with marriage, though of course in other circumstances both can be paid. But these occupations are not only normally financially unrewarded, they also disenfranchise their holders in important ways: a woman who gives up employment to rear children will generally lose out on her pension rights for those years, and, if she is in professional work, the missing years will set her permanently behind on the career ladder. Added to this is the deception of the cultural ideology about motherhood. Feminists from the eighteenth century onwards have remarked how mothers are idolized, how the sanctity and devotion of mothers is an absolutely core social value. Yet at the same time, as a real mother, one is liable to find oneself unable to go anywhere or do anything or be anyone: the shop doors which don't easily admit a pram, and the factory without a creche, are concrete illustrations of a symbolic order in which mothers and children are good only if they are controlled, confined to a limited place, prevented from infusing the rest of society with the values of nurture, sensitivity and creativity, and thereby turning the dominant ideology on its head. For, if relating rather than alienating, altruism rather than competitiveness, emotional expressiveness rather than intellectual rigidity, become the order of the day, what on earth will the world be coming to?

The dilemmas of doing good and feeling bad apply to nurses, just as they do to women in general. Insofar as caring is the signal quality and main work of nurses, they are likely to come up against two barriers: first, they will not achieve a social and financial status which underlines their inner feeling that nursing is good work – instead, the external rewards of nursing are likely to undermine nurses' confidence in the performance of caring work. Second, it will be difficult to feel, day in day out, and in the face of so many counterchallenges, that communication with patients and acting as a midwife to patients' own articulation of their own needs is truly as valuable work as microsurgery, diagnoses with body-scanners, and intricate immunological tests. I use the word 'midwife' carefully, since that word conveys exactly the part of health-care work which nurses have historically excelled in, but which has been their downfall; for they have, I believe, facilitated patients' own

abilities to cure themselves, just as midwives properly enable mothers to be their own deliverers.

NURSING – A PROFESSION?

A simple message could be extracted from all this – that nursing needs to lose its association with femaleness in order to achieve full professional status. The logic is undeniable, and it certainly appears to be the case that male nurses are more likely to emphasize the professional status of nurses than are female nurses.[100] On the other hand, and to complicate the issue, only a minority of doctors are prepared to accept male nurses at all, and two-thirds express a jocular or uncomfortable ambivalence to the whole idea. If male nurses are to be tolerated anywhere, it is apparently on violent psychiatric or urological wards.[101]

I am not in favour of simple answers, and so want to consider a few implications of this one – that the problem of nursing is that it needs more men to make it into a profession. First of all, what is a profession? Perhaps most obviously, a profession is a superior type of occupation, a non-manual occupation requiring advanced education and training. A profession thus has a specific and exclusively-owned body of knowledge and expertise. A profession organizes and to some extent controls itself by establishing standards of ethics, knowledge and skill for its licensed practitioners. Lacking these, people will not be admitted into its ranks. A profession is also recognized as such by its members, and by society at large. This definition of a profession is extracted from the sociological literature on professions and professionalization,[102] but is arguably not very helpful. According to it, some time ago, nursing was dubbed a 'semi-profession', along with others dominated by women (schoolteaching and social work). In fact, the predominance of women in these occupations was counted as a reason for their lack of full professional status, women being said to be less committed to employment than men and more interested in on-the-job personal relations than in such 'masculine' attributes as long training programmes.[103]

If a profession is by definition male-dominated, then nurses might as well give up. Alternatively, nurses might ask the truly radical question as to what's so wonderful about being a profession anyway? This question is a bit like asking what's so wonderful about the family, motherhood, Father Christmas and the space programme. It is self-evident that being a professional is superior to not being one, just as living in a family or going to the moon are better than being a single parent (which would, in any case, disqualify one for training as an astronaut). The point in each case is that the world which we know takes the goodness of some people, activities and objects, and the badness of others, for granted. Yet, so far as nursing and its

professional or non-professional status is concerned, the current crisis of confidence in medical care should tell us that professionalization is not only not the answer, but that it may indeed be positively damaging to health. It has been said that professions in the twentieth century have in general created a 'dependent, cajoled and harassed, economically deprived and physically and mentally damaged' clientele. They are more entrenched and 'international than a world church, more stable than any labour union, endowed with wider competence than any shaman, and equipped with a tighter hold over those they claim as victims than any mafia.'[104] This situation is disabling for everyone except the professionals – though Jean Baker Miller, and any decent analyst worth her salt, would say that it is disabling for professionals too, since to achieve success the 'true' professional must deny at least half of humanity's needs and potential – the need and capacity for caring about oneself and others as whole people, not merely as sets of specialized and segmented skills.

Interestingly, those radical critics who attack the evils of professionalism do not mention nurses. Just as I failed to notice nurses when researching doctors and patients some years ago, so in the orchestration of the 'doctor-bashing' theme, the motif of who nurses are and how they could help to make things better is not even heard as a single tune played lightly on the woodwind above the crashing of the brass and percussion and the persistent grinding of the wind section – the motif just isn't there.

THE WORLD WE KNOW, AND THE WORLD WE DON'T KNOW

To conclude, I will give a brief historical reflection, together with a pointer for the future. But first, I shall summarize my main points so far:

1. Nurses and nursing deserve more serious attention and research from all of us than they have hitherto received. A good nurse is not invisible, nor is she a ghost from the past.
2. Communication between those who provide, and those who use, the health services is of paramount importance in both curing and caring work.
3. Doctors try to cure and nurses try to care. Curing isn't possible as often as doctors claim it is, and it usually isn't possible without caring. This is because emotional support is good for people's bodies as well as their minds.
4. The doctor–nurse–patient relationship mirrors that of the traditional nuclear family. Neither structure is especially good for people's health, and it is damaging in particular ways for the health of nurses-wives and patients-children.

5. Users of health care and intellectuals who write about what is wrong with it tend to criticize the medical profession more than nurses. This suggests that nurses have got something right, even if, or even because, they are not professionals in the same way that doctors are. It also suggests that an alliance between nurses and health-care users is a strategy that could drastically improve the health-care scene.

6. Serving others, as nurses do, and as women have traditionally done, is an enormously good capacity to have, so long as it is developed at the same time as a sense of one's own self-worth and self-identity. Thus, specifically, dedication to the occupation of nursing is never an argument for taking bad working conditions and poor financial rewards without protest. In fact, it is extremely important to bring about improvements in the value attached to nursing work.[105]

The historical reflection comes from Florence Nightingale's *Notes on Nursing*, first published in 1859. She wrote:

> Keep clear of both the jargons now current everywhere . . . of the jargon, namely about the 'rights' of women, which urges women to do all that men do including the medical and other professions, merely because men do it, and without regard to whether this *is* the best that women can do; and of the jargon which urges women to do nothing men do, merely because they are women . . . you want to do the thing that is good whether it is suitable for a woman or not.[106]

And the pointer for the future is from Jean Baker Miller, who said that 'one of the major issues before us as a human community is the question of how to create a way of life that includes serving others without being subservient'.[107] That is the task ahead for all of us, and especially for nurses, who owe it to themselves to lift off the veil that has made them invisible, and make everyone see and understand how important they really are.

5

'Consumerism' and the Future of the Perinatal Health Services

Certain assumptions are embedded in the title of this chapter. These are:

1. that medical professionals and policy-makers are engaged in providing services for perinatal *health*;
2. that these services do have a *future*:
3. that there is this phenomenon which we can call *'consumerism'* that does have something to do with the services that are, or ought to be, provided.

These issues are clearly interrelated. Whether or not the perinatal services have a future depends both on the past history of these services and on whether they are seen as appropriate by their major constituents, who are neither the doctors, nor the policy-makers, but childbearing women and their families.

The first national survey of births to be carried out in Britain sampled 13,687 births in 1946. The main report of this survey, *Maternity in Great Britain*, concerned all aspects of pregnancy and childbirth, and the introduction to the book identified the key questions addressed in it, which were:

> What services are available to women bearing children? How far are they used and what are the factors affecting their use? Do they help women to regard childbirth as a normal process? How far do they prevent premature birth and infant death and promote the health of mothers and infants? Finally, what do parents spend on pregnancy and childbirth?[108]

These are very different questions from those asked by medical and governmental maternity-care policy-makers today. Most strikingly, of

course, there is the emphasis on helping women 'to regard childbirth as a natural process'. There is also the distinction between the prevention of death and the promotion of health, which are two different objectives. Last but not least, *Maternity in Great Britain* is concerned with the meaning of parenthood to parents: how much does it cost to have a baby, and are the services available the right ones? This emphasis is even more evident in the text of the report: for example, not only is the subject of maternal employment discussed, but there is also a whole chapter called 'Help in the House'. The emphasis on women's unpaid domestic work is there because the authors of the survey recognized that any epidemiological interest in the impact of work on pregnancy must include this less visible, but nevertheless important, domain. This insight is missing from the post-1960 reports.

Going back to the emphasis on normality in the 1946 survey, it is interesting to note that the report condemned the practice of having doctors at every antenatal visit on the grounds that this stresses 'the abnormal part of pregnancy and deprives midwives of an interesting and useful side of their work'.[109] Continuity of care was regarded as essential to a definition of pregnancy as a normal process, and for this reason 'concentration of supervision at a central clinic' was deemed undesirable – as it also was on the grounds that it could mean long journeys and long waiting times for expectant mothers. On home confinement, the report said that this was in general a low-risk event and it was also what many mothers wanted, so long as domestic help was available and housing conditions were good. The tone of the report reminds us of the arguments put by the medical profession in the 1920s and 1930s to the effect that the safety and other advantages of home confinement deserved a mass publicity campaign because too many women were choosing the unsavoury alternative of hospital delivery.[110] It is worth remembering that as late as the 1940s the main question was not one about the safety of *home* delivery, but one about the safety of having a baby in hospital.

WHO IS THE CONSUMER?

The 1946 survey did not mention 'the consumer' at all. So who is she and what is 'consumerism'?

Women began to complain publicly about medical services for motherhood in countries such as the UK and the USA some forty or so years ago. One of Britain's best-known and largest user-organizations, the Association for Improvements in the Maternity Services, was founded in 1960; the origins of AIMS lay in the experiences of its founder, a woman called Sally Willmington, who spent six weeks of pregnancy in an antenatal ward, did not enjoy the experience, and decided with the help of other similarly-

motivated women to form a pressure group to bring about improvements in maternity care. AIMS was originally called the Society for the Prevention of Cruelty to Pregnant Women, using the analogy of society's need to protect animals from the malevolent intentions of others. The primary aim of AIMS in 1960 was for more national resources to be given to the NHS and within this to the maternity services. A particular concern of consumers at the time was the shortage of hospital beds. More women wanted to have babies in hospital than could do so, and one of the intentions of AIMS was to ensure a rise in hospital maternity-bed provision. Second, AIMS wanted more midwives. Third, the association perceived a need for domestic support around the time of childbirth. Fourth, they were concerned at the many reports which they were receiving of women being left alone in labour. Finally, another topical concern was appropriate analgesia and appropriate training of health professionals, particularly in the psychosocial aspects of pregnancy, childbirth and parenthood.[111]

Another source of 'consumerism' in obstetrics was the movement for natural childbirth, which predated the use in many countries of specific organizations with specific complaints about maternity care. The origins of *this* movement do not really lie in the resistance of childbearing women to professional control, but rather in a particularly ideology of what childbirth *is* which has been promoted by another set of male experts. From Grantly Dick-Read to Frederick Leboyer and Michel Odent, the line is an unbroken succession to the title of knowing better than women how nature defines women's reproductive role. This alternative, though at the same time very traditional, vision of how to give birth has been responsible for fuelling consumer dissatisfaction, as well as for producing some very satisfied mothers. The American journalist Suzanne Arms' widely-publicized book *Immaculate Deception*, which was published in 1975, was written because its author, having anticipated a 'natural' birth, found herself the recipient of caudal anaesthesia, hormonally-accelerated labour and an instrumental delivery resulting in a torn cervix:

> I came out of delivery numb from the waist to the knees, dry and sour in the mouth, flat on my back, and strapped to a metal table four feet off the ground.[112]

Arms' objection was to the deception, foisted on women by doctors, of the 'no-risk' birth: the rule that natural childbirth is unnatural, that it is dangerous, and that the best protection for mother and child from reproductive risk is achieved by entering hospital and by relinquishing the female body and the process of childbirth to the control of obstetricians. She found herself trapped between two models: one of natural, and one of

medicalized, childbirth, neither of which was what she wanted. The obligation of service-providers to attend to the wishes of childbearing women, even if they do not fit existing models of what women want, is thus one central plank in the consumer challenge.

The word 'consumer' is hardly appropriate as a description of people using medical services, for two reasons. First, it implies that professionals produce health services and people consume them, whereas this counters the evidence which we have, that the most important producer of health is the person himself or herself. Indeed, this observation lies behind the whole contemporary health-promotion movement, the focus of which is on the improvement in living conditions and the need to boost self-help health care as the *only* effectice means of raising the standard of the public health.[113] The notion of patients as consumers is inappropriate for the further reason that it embodies the capitalist assumption of a free-market society. But, in practice, capitalism is a means of ensuring that people's right to choose is unevenly distributed in the population. Like health, choice is given to those who already have it, and it is consequently those who are most able to exercise choice who are the most vociferous defendants of the principle that we all can do so.

Health-care 'consumerism' is nonetheless so called in part because of a wider phenomenon – the recognition that has obtained in many spheres of life over the last twenty to thirty years that people who 'buy' products and services in industrial economies must be respected by those who sell such things, as the livelihood of the seller depends on there being a few willing purchasers around. This model does have a certain relevance to the maternity services, and it does so irrespective of the way in which the financing of the health-care system is organized. Where people buy medical services through private insurance, their power over the sellers of medical services is obvious – voting is via the feet, which take the purchaser elsewhere when the product is not satisfactory. In a country, such as the UK, with a national health service, people may, of course, turn to private medicine.

THE REVOLTING CONSUMER

The main recent criticisms articulated by consumer organizations in the maternity-care field are:

1. that pregnancy and childbirth are not illnesses;
2. that women are human beings;
3. that obstetrics should be scientific; and
4. that happiness is an important outcome of good obstetric care.

These criticisms directly challenge the notion that the perinatal health services are about health. Research on women's experiences of pregnancy shows that unpleasant symptoms are not uncommon: pregnancy does make a lot of women tired, many experience nausea or vomiting, and many have other physical problems as well.[114] When women make the point that pregnancy and childbirth are not illnesses, they are clearly *not* saying that these are experiences totally devoid of troublesome physical manifestations. The crucial point is how these symptoms are interpreted by the people who have them. One recent study of how lay people perceive and experience health and illness came up with an interesting conclusion here. From the accounts given to her, the author of this study[115] was able to say that people divided illness into three different categories. First, there were 'health problems' such as tiredness, indigestion, headaches etc., which everyone had to cope with and which were therefore a part of normal life. Second, there were 'normal illnesses' – for example, influenza and the common infectious diseases such as chickenpox and measles. The third category was of 'real' illnesses – conditions such as heart disease, cancer and tuberculosis – which were serious, not only in their daily symptoms, but also in their threat to life itself.

Pregnancy imposes certain health problems on women, but this does *not* mean that they see it as an illness in any serious sense. However, we immediately confront a paradox here – for, having become pregnant, what is the first thing that a woman does? She goes to a doctor and has a physical examination which is designed to see if she has anything wrong with her aside from pregnancy. Then, next, she probably goes to a hospital, and if she lives in the right (or perhaps the wrong) country, she goes on to give birth to the baby in a hospital too. Hospitals are for sick people, and doctors are in business to cure the sick. The whole basis of the obstetrician's craft is the devising of complex schedules for managing a condition which in most cases manages itself.

One way to look at it, then, is to see the obstetrician's challenge as precisely the task of converting pregnancy and childbirth into illness. This is the essence of the 'risk' philosophy – that no pregnancy and birth can be normal except in retrospect. Actually, when one looks at the history of the 'risk' idea, what happened is that a lot of people put a lot of energy into devising schemes for predicting risks to which pregnant women might be prone, but then they found that there are an unacceptably large number of false positives and false negatives in any such scheme. So, they came to the conclusion that the only thing to do was to say that all women are equally at risk of developing serious complications. The opposite conclusion, that all women are not at risk, could also have been drawn, but would have had a rather different set of implications for the maternity services.

[Childbirth *has* become exponentially safer for both mother and baby over the last 100 years.]The reasons for this are numerous, but most providers and users of the perinatal health services would regard medical care as having had an important input to this improvement in safety.]Careful research attempts to quantify the role of medicine compared to that of other biological and social factors – for example, the decrease in family size, leading to more childbirths at 'biologically safer' ages, and environmental improvements in the public health – cleaner, healthier homes, and so forth.[116] In examining which medical strategies may have been important in promoting perinatal health, it is important to consider the trade-off between benefits and costs, and particularly the implications of two critical components of medical work in this field – what has been called the 'as if' rule – the rule that all pregnant women should be treated 'as if' they are about to succumb to all known complications at any time – and the further dictum, widely accepted in medical circles, that an obstetrician or paediatrician who does everything that s/he can is let off the hook if something goes wrong, whereas the doctor who does not intervene as much as possible is considered morally culpable if mother or baby emerge damaged in any way. These rules protect the obstetrician who, on the evidence of ultrasound, wrongly diagnoses a growth-retarded baby and operates to produce by Caesarean section a child who is brain-damaged through having been born too early. So long as the doctor can show that everything reasonable was done in the light of currently accepted standards of medical practice, then a judgment of incompetence is unlikely to be made. However, the opposite case, in which a midwife attending a home birth sits by and waits for a mother to deliver on her own, and she does, but the baby is stillborn for no apparent reason, is likely to result in legal action being taken against her.[117] To trust nature – or the consumer – is an offence: it is being unprofessional. To use medicine is to dominate nature, to be scientific, to be a professional.] The term 'unprofessional' is interesting here, as it has come to mean the same thing as someone who behaves badly. This is a somewhat wider meaning than the original one, which was 'contravening the rules or etiquette of the profession concerned'.[118]

The second consumer criticism – that women are human beings as well as obstetric patients – also may seem a matter of common sense. In 1980, the British report on Perinatal and Neonatal Mortality summarized the many surveys of antenatal care that have been done by referring to

> the 'cattle truck' atmosphere of antenatal clinics where there is little privacy, little dignity . . . long waiting times, difficult access to clinics, lack of continuity of care, lack of opportunity to discuss things that

women themselves are worried about, and the feeling that they are going through a rather mechanical process and not getting as much out of it as they feel they should.[119]

The results of a Scottish survey[120] attach figures to these observations. In this study, no mothers found the thirty-four-week antenatal visit useful, although some could see a value to the booking visit. It is interesting too, how important the reassurance value of maternity care is: in this study, thirty-nine per cent of women found the booking visit reassuring and seventy-one per cent mentioned reassurance as an important factor later in pregnancy.

Patterns of satisfaction with perinatal services are not merely random, but are related to certain key aspects of the care provided. For example, there are differences in women's satisfaction according to whether care is provided by the same one or two people or by different people each time. Both for hospital and for GP care, seeing the same one or two people is the preferred option;[121] one important reason why care in the community may be preferred is that it takes less of mothers' time.

Some general assumptions about the respective roles of doctor and patient underlie these routines. One assumption is that the doctor's time is more valuable than the patient's. This became particularly clear to me during an observational study which I carried out in the 1970s in a London maternity hospital. Watching what happened to the new young housemen/women when they arrived to take up their jobs revealed the following pattern: at first, they would turn up to the antenatal clinic on time, looking rather eager and conscientious; then gradually they would arrive later and later, so that eventually they turned up only shortly before the consultant (who was always late). In other words, the young doctors had learnt the lesson that 'real' doctors keep patients waiting. Or, to put it differently, that women have nothing better to do than wait. This is, of course, not true. Women make up forty per cent or more of the employed workforce in many countries. In those countries – such as the UK – experiencing an economic recession, the only flourishing sector of employment is part-time, unskilled or semi-skilled work, and women are moving into these jobs in increasing numbers in order to support their families. In the home, the bulk of household work is still done by women, much of whose housework can be seen as a form of health care – for looking after children and men and homes are basic activities needed for survival.

OBSTETRICS SHOULD BE SCIENTIFIC

In a recent book called *Who's Having Your Baby?*, the British health rights activist Beverly Beech discusses women's participation in controlled and

uncontrolled research. She contrasts the invitation to participate in randomized controlled trials of health care with what she calls 'uncontrolled trials', which she describes in the following terms:

> Uncontrolled trials are trials where the staff feel they ought to try out a procedure on a number of women and babies to see how it goes; no attempt is made to compare the outcome with a comparable group; and very little information is given to those who are asked to take part in the trial.[122]

Beech goes on to suggest that, just as women who are asked to take part in RCTs should be given the fullest possible information about these, so those undergoing routine everyday obstetric practice should receive information leaflets concerning this practice. She suggests the following format for such a leaflet:

> Doctors at this and every hospital will come to a decision about what type(s) of care to offer you in a variety of ways. Sometimes there will be good evidence of the effectiveness and relative safety of the treatment recommended; more often, doctors will be influenced by tradition, prejudice, fashion or bad evidence in making their recommendations; occasionally doctors who want to ensure that they maximize the chances of you having whichever turns out to be the best of alternative treatments will select your treatment at random from the likely best alternatives. If you want to know anything about the basis upon which your treatment has been selected; or about the alternatives and their relative merits and disadvantages; or what doctors here are doing to try to minimize their unintended mistakes and protect their patients from them, then do not hesitate to ask for this information.[123]

According to a review by Tyson and colleagues published in 1983,[124] most recommendations for clinical practice are not justified by the evidence. The majority of routinely-used perinatal procedures have never been properly evaluated. In Britain, the procedure which caused a great deal of consumer reaction in the mid-1970s was induction of labour, which had become very fashionable in many hospitals in the early 1970s: in the UK, the rate tripled between 1965 and 1974. For many women, induction is painful. In one study,[125] only a minority of women were indifferent to either of the two main methods of inducing labour – rupturing the membranes and setting up an intravenous hormone drip.

Other complications of induction were also given some prominence in women's reports and the media at the time, for example, the increase in neonatal jaundice that appeared to be associated with it. Despite

obstetricians' objections that induction was not done for professional convenience but in the best interests of mother and child, research showed a curious pattern of a concentration of births on Tuesdays, Wednesdays, Thursdays and Fridays. Few births occurred on Sundays, or on public holidays, with Christmas Day – despite it being the best-known birthday of all – being the day on which the fewest number of births occurred.[126] There is a significant relationship between induction and doctors' job satisfaction.[127] By the time the results of this survey were published in 1979, induction rates had fallen. There is no doubt that the consumer critique had something to do with this, though – or and – research was also carried out and published showing that a high-induction policy did not demonstrate the kind of benefits claimed when compared with a low-induction policy.[128] One of the most interesting features of this research was that it was easy to mount because widely different induction rates coexisted in the *same* hospital – different consultants were differently persuaded of the value of this technique, and the care of women coming under them was subject to these arbitrarily differing policies.

HAPPINESS AS AN 'OUTCOME' MEASURE

As to the fourth 'consumer' criticism, that happiness is, or should be, a significant measure of successful obstetric care, by far the most basic assumption to be challenged here is that the perinatal health services are not concerned with the maintenance of *positive health* but rather are oriented towards the prevention of *death*, and towards a concern with *physical morbidity*. There are good historical reasons for this. The maternal and infant welfare movement started out around the turn of the century to remedy the enormously high rates of death among mothers and children – for every 3,000 or so births at that time, one mother and some 500 babies were dying. The situation today is somewhat different. Perinatal mortality rates of eight or nine per 1,000 may not represent the minimum achievable, but at least they give us the opportunity seriously to consider other indices of good care, including the impact of current obstetric practices on women's social and psychological health. For example, rates of postnatal depression go from fifteen to eighty per cent in different studies. Most agree that a majority of women these days experience something that they call depression after they have a baby.[129] Of course, obstetricians may not know about this. In the UK, some women will go back to the hospital consultant under whom they delivered at six weeks postpartum, but not all do so. In any case, most obstetricians are interested in the mother's physical condition and are not willing to listen to 'psychiatric' symptoms. Women who become depressed after childbirth often find it difficult to get their experiences taken seriously.

This is particularly strange when you consider how frequently the diagnosis of depression is made when women have any (other) kind of problem.

The observation that happiness is an important way of measuring the effectiveness of obstetric care means, of course, that the right questions must be asked in research studies. A study of women's experiences with a well-known antenatal test – amniocentesis – showed the importance of considering the impact of the test on women's emotional well-being. Reactions differed between women having this test because of an abnormal result on a previous routine blood test and those having the test because of some other indication – for example, the previous birth of an abnormal child. Women who had a *specific* indication for the test reacted considerably less badly than those without such an indication. Of particular interest is the fact that this particular medical intervention appears to increase forms of behaviour not medically recommended in pregnancy – the women in the first group reported starting to smoke and drink more alcohol during the period of waiting for the test and its result.[130]

WHAT DO WOMEN WANT, THEN?

One way to approach the question usually asked in the debate about the 'consumer's' role in perinatal care – what do women really want? – is to consider what it is that the perinatal health services *think* women want. The 1980 UK Short Report on Perinatal and Neonatal Mortality has a whole chapter – consisting of four-and-a-half pages – devoted to something called 'Humanizing the System':

> 'We are aware' say that Committee, 'that it is not enough, in our survey of perinatal and neonatal mortality, to concentrate solely on the physical well-being of the mother and her baby. The emotional support provided by the maternity services . . . is also of major importance . . . We would regard a mother who has produced a healthy baby but looks back on her pregnancy as an experience she does not wish to repeat, as evidence of a failure on the part of the maternity services.'[131]

The implication is clear: what women want is emotional support. And how should the services provide this? The Report goes on to make some concrete recommendations. The main ones are that health professionals should:

1. Communicate with women better.
2. Reduce overcrowding in antenatal clinics, provide continuity of care, and appoint more social workers to ensure that women attend.
3. Tell women what to expect (e.g. epidural anaesthesia and electronic fetal monitoring).

4. Make hospital rooms more attractive.
5. Not separate mothers and babies, and encourage women to breastfeed.
6. Appoint special midwives 'with warmth' to act as public relations officiers.
7. Rename Neonatal Intensive Care Units 'Intensive Care Nurseries'.

Twelve years later, the only areas where progress appears to have been made are the fourth and fifth recommendations. In some quarters, redecoration of hospital wards and labour rooms with flowery wallpaper and curtains is hailed as a major advance. 'Birth rooms' rather than 'labour wards' have also flowered: these are made to look like somebody's idea of an ordinary room, with pictures on the wall and a bed that looks like an ordinary one but which converts, at the touch of a button, into something unnervingly like the delivery bed in the room next door. While it is possible that these are important advances, there is no evidence to suggest that this is what women want. There are no studies in which representative samples of women are invited to give their accounts of desirable changes in the system.

One of the observations which women might have made, had they been asked, is that by and large what they do not want is to be separated from their babies. Instead, however, what happened was that medical professionals 'discovered' 'bonding'. In his book *Power and the Profession of Obstetrics*,[132] William Arney observes that one of the most important aspects of this discovery was that it enabled professionals to give in to some of the demands of the consumer movement; science discovered something that women have always known. For childbirth is not only about the physical production of another human being, it is about the relationship between two beings, about falling in love. Arney suggests that obstetrics knew that it needed to change because of the pressure that women were exerting on the profession to change, but merely to allow women's experiences and opinions as valid data would have been too threatening. So, instead, a new scientific theory was developed which enabled medical practice to 'Help Mothers to Love their Babies', as an editorial in the *British Medical Journal* put it.[133] 'Bonding' of mother and baby together for a few minutes or hours soon after birth became the answer to all sorts of social problems – from child-abuse to juvenile crime. In 1979, the President of the American College of Obstetricians and Gynecologists called home delivery 'the earliest form of child abuse'.[134] In America, some couples having home births have indeed been reported by paediatricians to State authorities under statutes covering child-abuse and neglect.[135] This kind of response to parents' wishes to determine where, and thus how, their children are born tells us that the argument is not on the level of rationality but is on a very deep level – one of

control. The perinatal health services are a battleground in which two opposed factions are fighting for control. On the one hand, the health professionals need to justify their own professional position by having work to do. A widespread return to home birth, for example, would leave many obstetricians with nothing to do. Many years ago, the psychologist Martin Richards made a relevant observation when he showed that the strongest predictor of admission rates to special care nurseries was not the condition of the babies born but the number of cots available.[136] Costs, beds and the bank balances of obstetricians have to be filled. These economic and professional considerations are culturally more highly prioritized than the wishes of childbearing women.

CONCLUSION

The message of 'consumerism' for the future of the perinatal health services would therefore include the following points. First, these services should be oriented to *promoting health* as distinct from *preventing death*. Second, some of the 'faddism' about natural childbirth which has never been about the desires of women at all needs to be discarded. The best scientific evidence concerning what childbearing women want comes from the study of induction of labour carried out in the UK in the mid-1970s.[137] Table 5.1 shows preferences for place of birth, analgesia and induction according to what happened in the previous delivery. Seventeen per cent of the women who were induced last time wanted the same kind of delivery next time, compared with seventy-eight per cent of those who were not induced last time. Sixty-three per cent of women who had an epidural wanted the same

Table 5.1: Women's preferences for care if they had another baby.

| | For survey birth | | | | | |
| | Induction | | Epidural | | Place of birth | |
	Induced	Not induced	Had epidural	Did not have epidural	Home birth	Hospital birth
	%	%	%	%	%	%
Prefer same as last time	17	93	63	82	91	83
Prefer not same as last time	78	5	34	13	9	15
Other comment	5	2	3	5	—	2
Number of mothers (= 100 per cent)	522	1,593	110	2,053	97	2,083

Source: A. Cartwright, *The Dignity of Labour?* London, Tavistock, 1979, p. 107.

again, but eighty-two per cent of those who did not have an epidural would not have one the next time either. Eighty-three per cent of women who had their last baby in hospital wanted hospital again, and ninety-one per cent who had a baby at home wanted home again.

Third, it is important to understand that the nature of the consumer revolt cannot be subsumed under the heading of 'patient satisfaction'. One implication of the focus on patient satisfaction is that professionals and policy-makers are not interested in what women *think* about maternity care — they are only interested in how women *feel* about it. But the real problem with women is that they have minds as well as hearts, and both their minds and their hearts are connected to their reproductive systems. As a matter of fact, as any well-brought-up medical sociologist will tell you, maternity patients are actually *not* more dissatisfied with their medical care than other patients of the same sex and age.[138] The recurrent question, 'Are women satisfied?', or rather 'Why aren't women satisfied?', hides a powerful set of assumptions about women and their role in society, and these assumptions themselves constitute an important part of the problem. Just as different doctors want and indeed do different things, so do women. Women do not constitute a homogeneous, unitary group among whom, if we search hard and long enough, we will uncover a single set of answers about what the future of the perinatal health services should look like. The needs and wishes of women with different backgrounds and living in different social conditions will vary. It has, for example, been shown that socially disadvantaged women may have a less negative attitude to analgesia in labour than their better-off sisters, and may regard childbirth as more in the way of something to be 'got over' rather than as a peak emotional event.[139]

But whatever different women want, there is the important question of resistance to change, as in one version of the famous light-bulb joke:

> *Question:*   'How many psychotherapists does it take to change a light bulb?'
>
> *Answer:*   'One, but the light bulb really has to want to change.'

Women need to work hard on the light bulb so that it is able fully to understand the advantages of its own illumination.

6

Who Cares for Women?
Science and 'Love' in Midwifery Today

To use a fashionable phrase, midwifery today is 'in crisis'.[140] In part, this is because the maternity services in many countries are themselves suffering from the cumulative effects of economic starvation, political neglect and enduring, health-damaging social inequality. The case for the protection of motherhood is not helped by the erosion of the gains of the 1970s in women's employment, financial and legal positions. In the UK, one adverse sign is the removal of the right to maternity-leave provision, so that pregnant women in Britain now have no universal, legally enforceable right to maternity leave; the qualifying conditions and level of payment imposed on British women are more stringent than in any other European country.[141]

While mothers' rights are being eroded and undermined in this and other ways, midwives themselves are having a difficult time. There are not enough of them, and the importance of their work in both hospital and community does not seem likely to be recognized by the new clinical grading structure which is being imposed on them in the UK. The dissatisfaction that many midwives feel with this situation matches the lack of continuity of care about which many mothers complain. Perhaps most sinister of all these developments, a series of legal challenges to the autonomy of particular midwives in the UK and elsewhere is effectively questioning the extent to which midwives are today able to protect the interests of mothers and babies without being seen as meddlesome witches intent on emasculating the medical profession and damaging the moral fabric of society. Some of the same issues are arising in these cases as were aired in the inquiry into obstetrician Wendy Savage's suspension.[142] It is clear that the confrontation

between the different groups of care-providers is also across gender lines (much as it was historically with the persecution of witches).

THE ART OF OBSTETRICS: GENDER (AND OTHER) DIVISIONS

In a book entitled *A Textbook of the Science and Art of Obstetrics* published in the USA in 1902, a doctor called Henry Garrigues referred to American midwives in somewhat unenthusiastic terms. Having admitted that more than half of childbearing women in New York City were attended by midwives, he deemed these 'half-taught' and 'totally ignorant' persons, maintaining that the 'science and art' of obstetrics belonged to physicians. He went on to argue that

> Midwives do harm not only through their lack of obstetric knowledge, their neglect of antiseptic precautions, and their tendency to conceal undesirable features, but most of them are the most inveterate quacks. First of all they treat disturbances occurring during the puerpery, late gynecological diseases, then diseases of children, and finally they are consulted in regard to almost everything. They never acknowledge their ignorance, and are always ready to give advice. They administer potent drugs, such as ergot and opium. Their thinly veiled advertisements in the newspapers show them to be willing abortionists; and since they have the right to give certificates of stillbirth, who knows whether or not an infant's death is due to natural causes or to criminal manipulations? . . .
>
> The institution of midwives is a remnant of barbaric times, a blot on our civilization which ought to be wiped out as soon as possible.[143]

The uncompromising allegations made by Dr Garrigues and his peers against midwives had serious implications, marking their decline in that country as legitimate providers of maternity care. Over the same period, the fate of midwives improved in other countries, including the UK, where, in the year that Garrigues' book was published, the Midwives Act came into force, obtaining for midwives the role and position which has for long been the envy of their transatlantic colleagues.

There are certain critical assumptions in Garrigues' text. These are that:

1. Midwives are ignorant and dirty, therefore their practice is dangerous.
2. Even trained midwives are incompetent.
3. Midwives are especially unscientific because they care for women and children's health generally.
4. Men know more about obstetrics than women.
5. Doctors know more about obstetrics than anyone else.
6. Obstetrics is a science.

Many medical men at the time had written, or were writing, similar kinds of anti-midwifery tracts. We have in such texts a certain polarization of concepts which sums up the terms of a continuing debate about the occupational identity and unique contribution of midwives to the care of childbearing women. On the one hand, there are concepts such as health, normality, social, subjective, experience, practice, intuition, nature, femininity, family, community and care, and, on the other, terms such as disease, abnormality, medical, objective, knowledge, theory, intellect, culture, masculinity, work, institution and control.

These oppositions represent something that goes beyond the domain of obstetrics and midwifery. But it can be argued that the dilemma of all the various parties involved in the maternity services today (the midwife, the obstetrician, the paediatrician, the mother, the baby, the father, the policy-makers) is that of being trapped within this language of opposition. It is an intensely misleading language, and as a consequence we are unable to make any real progress in our understanding either of the processes involved in reproduction or of how best to help the key actors in the drama of childbirth – the mother and the baby.

Childbearing does not fit the language of the mind–body divide. The theory dominant in western medicine that the body is an organism, and that the functioning of particular bits of it can be explained by looking at functioning elsewhere in the body, simply does not fit the facts so far as childbearing is concerned. The best evidence of the lack of fit is the well-documented relationship between social stress and childbearing difficulty,[144] and the counterpart of this, which is the benefits in terms of healthy childbearing conferred by the provision of social and other non-technical supports.[145] The body as a machine model produces certain well-known analogies, for example the garage analogy, according to which the doctor is a mechanic and the pregnant woman is a broken-down Ford (or Mercedes, depending on her social class). Here is the supposedly ideologically advanced Grantly Dick-Read in 1942, talking about women's increased efficiency at motherhood:

> Since when have repair shops been more important than the production plant? In the early days of motoring, garages were full of broken-down machines, but production has been improved; the weaknesses that predisposed to unreliability were discovered and in due course rectified. Today it is only the inferior makes that require the attention of mechanics. Such models have been evolved that we almost forget the relative reliability of the modern machine if it is properly cared for . . . The mother is the factory, and by education and care she can be made

more efficient in the art of motherhood. Her mind is of even greater importance than her physical state, for motherhood is of the mind. . .[146]

The language of metaphors embodies the interests of the user. In another medical field, Susan Sontag[147] has written about the military metaphors used by oncologists. Male infertility specialists apparently refer to the genetic material in human sperm as 'nuclear war-heads'.[148]

In reality, pregnant women are not machines, or cars, or even ambulant pelvises, but individuals with minds, emotions and complex personal and social lives. So where did the male-dominated mechanical model of childbearing come from? Why is it still around today? And how does its effectiveness compare with what 'ignorant' midwives are able to do?

The basic outline of the story is familiar. First of all, Dr Garrigues was right in associating the role of midwives with the more general role of women as carers for the community's health. Throughout history, and in all human cultures, it has been predominantly women who have cared for dependent and vulnerable individuals, including children, the old, the sick and the disabled. Female midwifery fitted easily and logically within this overall caring function – as an early version of what we now dignify with the technical label of 'continuity of care'. Onto this traditional fabric was then grafted the new imprint of the emergent medical profession. This laid its claim to fame not on caring – with or without continuity – but on technical expertise: science as opposed to love; forceps and the lying-in hospital as opposed to the purely domestic art of 'catching' babies at home. It is characteristic of such developments that the new professionals also write their own history – which means effectively *rewriting* history – so that what actually happened is recast to fit the contours of what the new professional group believes it has to offer. To be more specific, Dr Garrigues and others like him had to argue that the practice of female midwives was dangerous and unscientific, and that the status of midwives in society was low. They had to do this in order to get people to accept obstetricians. Naturally, they equated obstetrics with science, but what is striking when you read the history of the obstetrical takeover of midwifery is that the discreditation of midwifery as unscientific sufficed *instead* of proving the scientific credentials of the new medical discipline. The obstetricians' attack on midwives was a substitute for any sustained defence of their own case. They did, however, mention the fact that they could work technical wonders that midwives were unable to. This was a claim unsupported by scientific evidence. In the early 1900s, for example, obstetricians argued that they possessed the technical knowledge to prevent miscarriage, preterm delivery and toxaemia.[149] These goals have yet to be achieved today.

The contemporary evidence suggests that the practice of obstetrics did not represent an advance over that of midwifery. For example, in 1913 in New York City, midwives attended forty per cent of all births but had only twenty-two per cent of maternal deaths from sepsis. Physicians, with sixty per cent of births, had sixty-nine per cent of the deaths. Although midwives may have attended some less complicated cases, they were also the only attendants for poorer women, who are likely to have been in the worst general health.[150] Illiterate midwives are likely to have spread a good deal less infection than doctors. In Europe as well as North America, introduction of the forceps – the major technical advance claimed by obstetricians – is likely to have increased, rather than decreased, mortality.[151]

Some of the reasons for this are clear from the arguments of the early obstetricians. Joseph DeLee, the American doctor who recommended the routine prophylactic use of forceps, described obstetrics in 1915 as 'a major science of the same rank as surgery' and went on to assert that 'even natural deliveries damage both mothers and babies, often and much. If childbearing is destructive, it is pathogenic, and if it is pathogenic it is pathologic.' In short, DeLee concluded that childbearing could no longer be considered a normal function; thus, in relation to it, 'the midwife would be impossible even of mention'.[152] Such allegations were, naturally, self-fulfilling. Between 1918 and 1925 in the USA, when midwifery declined nationwide, infant deaths from birth rose forty-four per cent.[153] Perhaps fortunately and not coincidentally, when the first male midwives established instruction courses in England in the eighteenth century, the art or science of instrumental delivery was not taught to women (who paid lower fees for the course), only to men.[154] This may be regarded as recognition of the fact that doctors specialized in treating childbearing as abnormal, whereas midwives were the guardians of the normal.

A common medical therapy in pregnancy and childbirth for many centuries was bloodletting. Iatrogenic haemorrhage was the treatment of choice for many complaints. Some doctors even bled women into unconsciousness as a remedy for delivery pain. Bloodletting, emetics and mustard plasters (for the feet) were recommended for toxaemia of pregnancy. Routine maternity care as practised by William Goodell, Professor of the Diseases of Women at the University of Pennsylvania in 1874, took the following form:

> When the patient came to the hospital, some days or weeks before delivery, she was put on a regular dosage of quinine, then a kind of all-purpose preventative. Each woman received drugs for constipation, headaches, and sleeplessness. When labor began, each received a

cathartic and a bath. The staff then ruptured the amniotic sac, used forceps to expedite delivery, gave ergot when the head appeared, and hurried the expulsion of the placenta by pressing on the stomach. After cutting the cord and bathing the woman again, they gave her morphine each hour until she felt no more afterpains, and gave her quinine 'until the ears rang'.[155]

In the early twentieth century, obstetricians' desire to expand the influence and increase the status of their profession seems to have been the basis of their opposition to midwives. At the height of the anti-midwife phase, there *were* some medics who acknowledged the lack of scientific evidence against the midwife; some were prepared to say that women were safer in the hands of ignorant midwives than in those of 'poorly educated medical men'. However, according to one prominent and outspoken obstetrician in the early part of the century, 'such a conclusion is . . . contrary to reason', and what reason dictated was that 'the obstetrician should not be merely a male midwife but a scientifically trained man'.[156] Money was an important part of the picture, too. As a group, nineteenth-century doctors were not particularly affluent; although midwifery itself was not a particularly lucrative speciality, it *was* guaranteed income and, more important, it opened the door to family practice.[157]

But the vehemence of much medical opposition to midwifery cannot be understood on rational or economic grounds. There is a well-established historical connection between midwifery and witchcraft. Midwives were associated with witchcraft because not all witchcraft was bad; from medieval European times, there were recognized to be good witches and bad witches. Another name for the good witch was 'wisewoman'.[158] It is for this reason that the modern name for midwives in French is 'sage-femme'. The midwife was the practitioner of health care for a community that had no access to any other kind of health care, maintaining family health by the use of traditional medicines such as herbs and other empirically-tested strategies. Also, the claim that midwives were bad witches was an important part of the Church and the State's attempt from the fifteenth century onwards to control both the role and the power of women, and to restrict the practice of medicine to the new, university-trained, male medical practitioners. This is evident in one of the earliest preserved oaths made by an English midwife applying for a Church licence in 1567. After being questioned by the Archbishop of Canterbury – no less – and eight women (presumably experienced midwives themselves), the midwife had to swear that she would 'not use any kind of sorcery or incantation in the time of travail of any woman' and would baptize every infant with pure, clean water, notifying the parish curate of each

baptizing. It is of interest that same oath obliges the midwife to promise 'to help and aid as well, poor and rich women' and not 'permit or suffer that women . . . shall name any other to be the father of her child'.[159] Witnessing the biological connections in kinship systems was an important social function of the midwife.

SCIENCE AND THE 'MASTERY' OF CHILDBIRTH

The rise of obstetrics and its eventual dominance over midwifery was achieved in part by the argument that those who care for childbearing women can only do so properly by viewing the female body as a machine to be supervised, controlled and interfered with by technical means. Science, or reason, were given (are given) in support of this approach; but were, on closer inspection, figments of the medical imagination. Childbearing had many mysterious and untreatable aspects, and towards these the obstetrical attitude prescribed the 'mastery of birth'. In the absence of understanding, control and management were important – childbirth and women had to be 'mastered'. The masculine gender of this word is highly significant. The male role in obstetrics paralleled the male cultural role; socialized to be masters of their own fates, families and environments, the same kind of impulse possessed the men who first took over childbirth from the traditional carers of women, midwives.

Some common themes here with the management of childbearing today must be obvious. In the first place, what we might call the 'technological imperative' in obstetrics remains dominant and continues to be problematic. Over the last twenty years, the use of such technologies as induction of labour, electronic fetal heart-rate monitoring, ultrasound, episiotomy and Caesarean section has risen; although the accumulated evidence of randomized controlled trials has suggested that frequent and/or routine use of these technologies cannot be justified, nonetheless such strategies continue to be used. In general it can be said, as Richard Taylor in his book *Medicine out of Control* has done, that

> The infusion of science and technology into medicine, which began on a large scale during the Second World War, promised a more rational and effective version of an ancient caring craft. This promise has been largely unfulfilled. Most of the supposed 'rationality' and 'effectiveness' is illusory. What we now have is a malignant proliferation of technological intervention with important adverse effects and little result in terms of improved health for the community.[160]

Some very crucial perinatal problems have been little affected by obstetric intervention – one outstanding example is the incidence of low-birthweight

births; despite many imaginative attempts to prevent preterm labour and/or improve intrauterine growth by means of drugs or other strategies, obstetricians have had virtually no impact on this common cause of death.[161] Indeed, some of their most cherished remedies – for example, bedrest in twin pregnancy – have been shown in controlled trials to make the problem more, and not less, likely.[162]

As the late Ian Donald, who pioneered ultrasound in Britain, once wisely said:

> A tool exploited for its own sake is no better than a saw given a small boy for cutting wood who must presently look around the home for suitable objects of furniture wanting amputation.[163]

In part, this is a problem that extends to the whole of medicine. According to a World Health Organization report, the three most common criticisms of health care expressed today are: that its benefits are distributed in a socially unequal way; that it has harmful effects; and that it is characterized by excessive technological intervention.[164] But the place of technology in maternity care is also a peculiar one. Control and intervention versus the different attitude of watching and waiting – the prescription of normality as against the belief that childbearing is an inherently pathological process – is a division which has a unique professional representation in the form of two distinct groups of care-providers: the obstetricians and the midwives.

If technology is the obstetricians' weapon, what is the midwives'? What is a midwife anyway? According to the Oxford English Dictionary, the word 'midwife' comes from Middle English, 'mid' and 'wife' meaning 'a woman who is *with* the mother at birth'. The rather more technical definition, which lays emphasis on formal training and registration procedures put forward by WHO and the professional midwifery organizations, stresses that a midwife must be able to 'give the necessary supervision, care and advice to women during pregnancy, labour and postpartum period, to conduct deliveries *on her own responsibility* and to care for the newborn and the infant'.[165] This definition critically emphasizes the continuity of care provided by the midwife, and her proper independence in delivering the baby – that all-important phrase – 'on her own responsibility'.

So, midwives care for women and obstetricians control and master childbirth. If obstetric technology has been shown often to rest on weak scientific foundations, its *routine* use being neither effective *nor* safe, then what evidence is there for the effectiveness and safety of caring? What is the scientific value of love?

THE VALUE OF CARING

One approach to answering this question is a formal review of studies that have been done of midwifery care, social interventions or 'social care' during pregnancy. An important underlying assumption is that these three categories of care can be equated. Their common denominator is the absence of technological intervention – for historical reasons, and for reasons to do with professional imperialism, most forms of this, as we have seen, are reserved for doctors. So, the key question here is: what is the potential of *non*-technological care to promote the health of women and babies?

The rest of this chapter presents the evidence for the effectiveness, appropriateness and safety of non-technological midwifery care. The strategy adopted is a review of studies which have used the approach of randomized controlled trials. Use of this design is the only reliable way of establishing whether differences observed in obstetric outcomes between women who have received such care and women who have not done so are likely to be due to the form of care offered rather than to extraneous factors. It enables one to examine the effects of different forms of care in groups of women who are as similar as possible.[166]

There have been few properly-controlled studies of midwife care. In the us, Lilian Runnerstrom[167] conducted one of them some years ago, comparing nurse-midwifery care with care provided by obstetric residents for 4,500 women with uncomplicated pregnancies. Some of Runnerstrom's findings were that nurse-midwives, compared with doctors, more often used no or only inhalational analgesia, and had mothers with shorter labours, a much lower operative delivery rate, a somewhat lower low-birthweight rate and fewer women with complications in the puerperium. A second study, also American, was carried out in the mid-1970s in North Carolina.[168] In this, nurse-midwives achieved a higher spontaneous delivery rate and less use of low forceps. The third study is French and is interesting because its findings are somewhat more complex than the others.[169] The results of this study appear to show that home midwifery care adds to the risks of childbirth. However, on closer inspection, the data yield the finding that socially disadvantaged women did benefit from home care; but those with medical risks did not. As the epidemiologist Judith Lumley has pointed out, the high rate of obstetric complications and cervical cerclage among the 'home' group in this study raises the possibility that the randomization did not work as intended, so that these women were, in fact, a higher-risk group anyway.[170]

A study by Olds and colleagues[171] looked at the effect on pregnancy outcome of home-visiting nurses. During their visits, the nurses provided parent education and set out to enhance 'the woman's informal support

systems'. A central aspect of their approach was to 'emphasise the strengths of the women and their families'. Significant differences in favour of the home-visited group were found for a mixed bag of outcomes, including 'awareness of community services' (a direct effect of the parent education, presumably), attendance at childbirth classes, discussions with family and friends of stress-related issues, paternal interaction with babies, smoking in pregnancy and the incidence of low birthweight – though this applied to the younger (adolescent) mothers only. Similar findings were obtained in a smaller, more recent study by Judy Dance[172] in Birmingham, where a social support intervention was provided by linkworkers to pregnant Pakistani women. The linkworker group experienced fewer medical problems in pregnancy, more happiness (and less unhappiness), shorter labours, less use of analgesia in labour, higher mean birthweight and fewer feeding problems.

The effectiveness of childbirth preparation in improving pregnancy outcome has never been scientifically proved, though it may of course have increased women's satisfaction. The very expectation of a pleasant delivery can affect the length of labour, as Nelson and colleagues found in their Canadian study of 'Leboyer' deliveries.[173] In one study, which compared the effects on labour outcomes of prenatal education versus knitting classes versus nothing at all, birthweight in the prenatal-class group was lower than in the no-class group, which in turn was lower than among the knitters. Use of medication was, however, lowest among the prenatal-class attenders and highest among the knitters.[174] Such findings are, of course, likely to be mediated by women's attitudes to knitting. There is a study of the effect of music on fetal activity which demonstrates precisely this: that it is not music per se that affects the infant's prenatal activity, but whether or not the mother liked the music being played.[175]

Some social interventions consist of reorganizing the pattern or the location of care so that it is more satisfying to the mother. A Scottish study[176] compared care provided in a peripheral community as distinct from a centralized hospital clinic. It is clear that community-based care is of material and practical benefit to the mother – it costs less, and half the mothers – as opposed to none in the hospital group – were able to walk there. It is also of interest that a community clinic facilitates conversation between midwives and mothers. A somewhat different study[177] looked at pregnancy 'outcomes' in women cared for in birthrooms as against more conventional hospital settings. Use of oxytocin, forceps and episiotomy was significantly lower, though the two groups of women receiving the different patterns of care had a similar level of risk.

One of the interesting messages that comes out of reviewing these social intervention studies is the relatively powerful effect that even an apparently

insignificant intervention can have. One study[178] examining the impact of one pregnancy interview with medical students found significant effects on pregnancy anxiety and use of pre-delivery medication. If one interview with a medical student can work such wonders, what miracles attend many prenatal conversations between mothers and midwives? The answer to this question is provided by the world-famous study carried out by Caroline Flint[179] in London. Flint wanted to examine the scientific effectiveness of the value to women and their babies of continuous personal relationships between mothers and midwives in pregnancy. Women in what Flint called the 'Know-Your-Midwife' Scheme, as distinct from those receiving standard antenatal care, felt encouraged to be more questioning antenatally, more often experienced spontaneous onset of labour, felt in control during labour, had no analgesia or entonox only, had few episiotomies, slightly bigger babies that needed less resuscitation, were more likely to be breastfeeding at six weeks and found it easier to be a mother.

In other words, communication increases women's 'mastery' of their childbirth experiences (and all these studies show that mastery is as important for women as it is for obstetricians). This effect can be achieved by putting mothers, rather than hospital bureaucracies, in charge of personal medical information. Two randomized controlled trials[180] looked at the effects of mothers holding their own case-notes rather than the somewhat less informative, so-called maternity 'co-operation' cards. The increase in feelings of control among women holding their own notes was a marked beneficial health effect. Similar beneficial effects of information, though with more directly measurable health effects, were found in a trial[181] of different ways of carrying out ultrasound examinations of pregnancy: when talked to about the image on the screen, women were more likely to adopt healthier lifestyles.

Counselling and/or non-specific social support also have the potential to influence a range of pregnancy outcomes. For example, discussing with pregnant women the likely realities of motherhood in advance will significantly reduce problems after delivery, as the Gordons[182] showed in a now classic 1960 study of postpartum emotional problems. The results of the study by Margaret Gutelius and colleagues[183] of child health supervision (which included pregnancy counselling) were quite dramatic, not only in making children whose mothers were receiving counselling sleep through the night and give up nappies earlier, but also in affecting the likelihood with which husbands kept their jobs in the first three years of the child's life!

Finally, there is the study of the effectiveness of social care in pregnancy which I have been responsible for undertaking with colleagues in England since 1984.[184] This was a randomized controlled trial of midwife-provided

social support in women at risk of delivering low-birthweight infants. There were about 500 women in the study, and half of them were offered a package of home visits and social support from research midwives in addition to their normal antenatal care, while the other half had normal antenatal care only. At the end of the study, we compared pregnancy 'outcomes' in the two groups of women – those who were offered this extra support and those who were not. Some of our results were that women offered social support more often had babies above normal birthweight; were more likely to have experienced spontaneous onset of labour and spontaneous delivery; were more likely to have babies which were healthy at delivery and afterwards; and experienced better postpartum physical and psychological health themselves. These differences between the two groups of women are accounted for by the simple provision of a listening ear during pregnancy. Our 'social support' midwives gave no clinical care. When asked what they had appreciated most about this type of help, the mothers put the fact that 'she listened' first; eighty per cent of them said that this was important.

WHO CARES FOR WOMEN? THE LOGIC OF INTRAPROFESSIONAL DISPUTES

Love is a scientific concept, and its effects on the health of childbearing women can be quantified. Conversely, there is much in obstetrics that claims to be science but does not have this status. Behind these differences, the motives of midwives and obstetricians are also different. The whole ideology and professional training of midwives qualifies them to care for normal women, while that of obstetricians orients them towards controlling the abnormal. Though these different qualifications would seem at first sight to provide an excellent 'package' when taken together, the problem is the psychology of what has been called the 'as if' rule. By treating all pregnant women as if they are about to become abnormal, obstetricians are inclined to make them so. On the other hand, the disposition to regard pregnant women as a normal class of beings will help to facilitate this. This is one of the processes lying behind the findings described above. Midwifery care encourages the normal, both directly and by enabling women, through information and greater self-confidence, to take control of their own reproductive fates. Such control is difficult, but not impossible, when childbirth is characterized by technology.

None of this is really surprising when you consider that obstetricians are doctors and thus trained in the diagnosis and management of disease. A review by Carol Sakala[185] in the USA of midwives' and obstetricians' attitudes to pain in childbirth highlights this particularly clearly. Looking at published information on approaches to pain as well as empirical practice, Sakala found

that, in the medical domain, pharmacological approaches to pain-relief were discussed almost exclusively, while midwifery practice emphasized other ways of dealing with pain, including relaxation, massage and social support. In medical practice, relief of pain was regarded as almost obligatory, while midwives recommended relying on the mothers' individual preferences. In line with this, it is significant that, in Jean Walker's[186] study of how midwives and obstetricians perceive the role of the midwife, most midwives thought that midwifery was different from obstetrics, while most doctors thought that they were the same.

Intraprofessional conflicts between the perceptions and practices of midwives and obstetricians are not uncommon today. In Jean Walker's study, for instance, midwives were less likely to see the responsibility for a normal delivery as lying in the medical domain. Within the same setting, midwives and doctors may be operating with different views of the same situation. Another study[187] showed quite a lot of disagreement, with, for example, four times as many doctors as midwives claiming that doctors manage normal labour. However, when it came to the question of who *ought* to do what, the obstetrical claim to exclusive expertise reared its head again: the doctors did not mind midwives sewing and sticking clips on (natural feminine functions anyway), but they were unhappy with the idea of midwives carrying out breech or forceps deliveries or intubating infants. Accordingly, the number of midwives actually performing these tasks was much lower than many midwives would have liked.

Love – caring – is as important as science – technical knowledge, monitoring and intervention – in the maternity services today. Rather than being a soft option, it is a fundamental necessity. For those who wish to concern themselves with scientific proof, this can be demonstrated from published studies examining the effects of social support as distinct from clinical care. Consequently, the goals of satisfying mothers and producing healthy babies, which are so often deemed by obstetricians to be at odds with one another, are in reality the same goal. The definitions of caring given by midwives on the one hand, and obstetricians on the other, have been different and opposite from the very beginnings of the uneasy collaboration in this complex, but wonderful, business of helping babies into the world. Midwives must do everything to reclaim this concept of care (and the rest of us must do everything we can to help them), both for the sake of women and babies and for the sake of themselves. As one mother, who gave birth in Cambridge in 1987, said, 'I think that, in a perfect world, every mother should have what I had – a midwife's face that said "look, we have performed a miracle together". (And there was nothing to it!)'[188]

Part II

Motherhood

7

The Cries and Smiles of Babies

In her autobiography *Blackberry Winter*, the anthropologist Margaret Mead describes her own struggle to achieve both personhood and motherhood. In 1931, at the age of thirty, she set out for New Guinea with her second husband, Reo Fortune, to work on the question of the extent to which differences in temperament between the genders might be conditioned by culture – work which led eventually to the publication of her famous *Sex and Temperament in Three Primitive Societies*. One of the three cultures which she encountered in New Guinea and later wrote about was the Mundugumor. The Mundugumor lived on the banks of the Yuat river in New Guinea and appeared to have set up a particularly unpleasant form of social organization based on head-hunting. The culture was aggressive, rivalrous and exploitative in the extreme. Even so-called 'love-making' was performed deliberately in other people's gardens so as to spoil their yams, and was accompanied by scratching and biting. People committed suicide by getting into a temper tantrum and drifting down the river in a canoe towards the unenviable fate of being captured and eaten by a neighbouring tribe. Such a culture is hardly likely to cherish children, or women as the bearers of children. Indeed, this proved to be the aspect of Mundugumor culture that Margaret Mead found most hard to take. 'Women wanted sons and men wanted daughters,' she wrote, 'and babies of the wrong sex were tossed into the river, still alive, wrapped in a bark sheath. Someone might pull the bark container out of the water, inspect the sex of the baby, and cast it away again. I reacted so strongly against the set of the culture', Mead goes on to say, 'that it was here that I decided I would have a child no matter how many miscarriages it meant.' (She had already, at this point in her life, experienced

several miscarriages.) 'Further, it seemed clear to me', she observed, 'that a culture that so repudiated children could not be a good culture, and the relationship between the harsh culturally prescribed style and the acts of individuals was only too obvious.'[1] Well, of course, there does have to be some relationship between the broad values of a culture and the acts of individuals. But what is a 'good culture', and should it be a child-orientated one? What happens to women in a child-orientated culture? Can a culture both be child-orientated and permit, or foster, the liberation of women as individuals with non-motherhood identities?

Let us think for a moment about the Mundugumor, about the values and practices they espoused which led to Mead's own resolution to become a mother. Were Mundugumor women free from the motherhood-versus-personhood dilemma experienced by Mead and her sisters in Euro-American culture? One striking feature about Mundugumor culture was that the prevailing negative attitude to children meant the application of a similar attitude to women. Everything specifically female about women – their sexuality and capacity to conceive, gestate and lactate – was decried. Any echo of maternity was a vulnerability and a liability. Women as women were hated and hated themselves. Motherhood was quite simply an entirely negative identity.

Leaping unjustifiably from one culture to another, let us now consider one of the laws pertaining to motherhood that operated in New York State when Mead herself achieved motherhood in 1939; newborn babies had by law at that time to be kept in a separate hospital room from their mothers. What does such a law tell us about the values of American culture and the position of women as mothers in it? I suggest that it transmits a message about women which is in many ways not terribly different from the head-hunting Mundugumor.

In both the Mundugumor case and the case of the New York mothers in the 1930s, the essential point is that women are alienated from certain aspects of their potential identities as mothers. How they are able to perceive themselves in relation to motherhood is not an open-ended question. One fixed notion *is* given to them by their cultures, and that is the notion that being a mother is a problem. In the New Guinea case, biological motherhood itself is bad, while in the New York case, motherhood itself is good, but women are not good enough to do it properly without the expert guidance of the state via its institutional, ideological apparatuses – education, the law and the medical profession. In both cases, there is a split between women's concept of themselves and the manner in which they see themselves as mothers.

BIOLOGICAL VERSUS SOCIAL REPRODUCTION

In discussing the relationship between women's identities and motherhood, it is, of course, necessary to specify what the term 'mother' means. And it is here that we meet the first difficulty – or the first enlightenment – for what 'mother' means is both the capacity for *biological* reproduction and the exigency of *social* reproduction – childbearing as opposed to childrearing.

Biological Motherhood

Dramatic historical changes in definitions of both biological and social motherhood have occurred quite recently within our own society. Women have been bearing fewer children, have been dying less, and have been subjected to more medical control. While we may presume that unwanted childbearing and unwanted deaths are *not* benefits for women, the increase in medical control which has accompanied (and may even at times have accounted for part of) the improvement is another matter altogether.

The most profound impact of modern methods of childbirth management on the situation of women is the unfortunate connection between the attitudes and practices of medicalized childbirth, and the psychological constitution of women within patriarchal culture. The relationship between women's psychology and that of men is most easily described as that between a subordinate and dominant social group. The psychological characteristics of subordinate groups form a certain cluster: submissiveness, passivity, docility, dependence, lack of initiative, inability to take decisions, and so forth. Subordinates embody weakness while dominants embody strength. A degree of weakness and dependence is part of the feminine stereotype. 'Real' women obtain their reality by being the very opposite of the assertive, aggressive, empire-building masculine stereotype. And yet these features of femininity (which have been found to characterize actual women in numerous psychological and social studies) are precisely those features which identify the patient in what most doctors consider to be a good doctor–patient relationship and most patients experience to be the *normal* doctor–patient relationship. The doctor tells the patient what is the matter with her or him and the patient believes the doctor. The patient also complies with the doctor's orders in terms of any treatment or change in lifestyle that is thought by the doctor to be required in order to dispel the patient's symptoms. After all, it is said, there wouldn't be any of this nonsense about natural childbirth and delivering babies standing up in the dark and/or underwater, if women understood what is good for them – or, rather, what is good for their *babies*. The naivety of the medical profession in relation to such questions often leads its practitioners to pose an artificial conflict of interest between women and

their fetuses, to remark on an apparent absence of that effortless altruism which is itself a hallmark of femininity. (This is not to say that the interests of women and of their children always coincide. Clearly, this is not the case. But the point is that it should be women themselves who determine both the circumstances under which their and their children's interests coincide and those in which they do not.)

Social Motherhood

This is the century of the child. It became the century of the child for a number of related reasons: the decline in infant deaths and births, the emergence of child labour into the public limelight of the industrial workplace, and the requirements of an industrial economy for specialized and educated labourers. These factors forced the state to take an interest in the protection and preservation of childlife. The population losses brought about by war reinforced this eugenic rationale, for, as one British commentator put it in the early 1900s, 'out of the mouths of babes and sucklings . . . the strength is ordained which shall still the Enemy and the Avenger'.[2] Not only the British variety of imperialism, but all brands of nationalism, came to be seen as rooted in the home. It is interesting, and most important for our purposes, to note that in the USA, Britain and many other European countries, two strategies were developed absolutely simultaneously for the preservation and improvement of childlife. These strategies were, first, the control of biological reproduction by the medical and midwifery professions; and, second, the control of social reproduction by the rise of paediatric 'experts' and the education of mothers for hygienic housewifery and motherhood. The major initial impetus for the medicalization of biological reproduction was not the aim of decreasing infant mortality but the aim of keeping mothers alive, because, of course, a dead mother could not be educated to be a better mother.

From the start, women were seen as the key to the whole problem. The economic climate and the reaction against feminism combined in the first decades of this century to produce an atmosphere most unfavourable to a vocation for women outside the home. Women had, therefore, to be the child*rearers* – a conclusion supported by the new enlightenment about breastfeeding as the answer to one of the great infant killers – gastrointestinal infection. As Ellen Key wrote in her 1909 bestseller *The Century of the Child*: 'the transformation of society begins with the unborn child. . . . This transformation requires an entirely new conception of the vocation of mother.'[3] Or, as President Roosevelt put it:

> The good mother, the wise mother – you cannot really be a good mother if you are not a wise mother – is more important to the community than

even the ablest man.. . . The woman who, whether from cowardice, from selfishness, from having a false and vacuous ideal, shirks her duty as wife and mother, earns the right to our contempt just as does the man who . . . fears to do his duty in battle when the country calls him.[4]

The battle in the home and the battle outside it: an appropriate gender division. Of course, the focus of the experts' advice to mothers has shifted over the years between the early decades of this century and now. *Then* it was on physical aspects of child care: on the simple mechanistic elimination of 'dirt' from the environment, for example. Now attention is focused on the development of the child's psychology and personality. Rather than a sound body producing a sound mind, the formula is reversed, and our modern emphasis on the possibility, if not prevalence, of psychosomatic disturbance enables us to know absolutely that the basis for a sound body is laid in the mother's creation in her child of a sound mind. It is worth noting that the earlier concentration on the physical side of child care meant, for women, a total continuity with their function as homemakers. The production of a sanitary environment was the prime goal of both good housewifery and good motherhood. But later on in the century, a discontinuity becomes increasingly evident. What is good for the home is not always good for the child. Charlotte Perkins Gilman was in advance of her time when she called family life neither marriage nor child-culture but 'the running of the commissary and dormitory departments of life, with elaborate lavatory processes', and curtly observed that although 'the mother loves the child, always and always . . . the principal work of her day is the care of her house. . . . Follow the hours in the day of the housewife,' Gilman admonished, 'count the minutes spent in the care and service of the child, as compared with those given to the planning of meals, the purchase of supplies, the labour of . . . cleaning things. . . . In what way', Gilman asked, 'do the meals we so elaborately order and prepare, the daintily furnished home, the much trimmed clothing, contribute to the body-growth, mind-growth and soul-growth of the child?'[5]

To bring Gilman's observations up to date, let us note that, if a market value is assigned to the housewife-mother's domestic services, more than a third of the gross national product in both the USA and Britain is accounted for by housework. The major part of the unpaid work which women do at home is not concerned with what the paediatric experts declare to be the most significant function of motherhood.

WHAT DO YOU EXPECT WHEN YOU BECOME A MOTHER?
It is hard to avoid the fact that there is something really depressing about motherhood. In my own study of the transition to motherhood,[6] four out

of five mothers experienced a short-term 'blues' reaction to the births of their babies, three-quarters an anxiety state on first assuming responsibility for the baby, a third depressed moods, and a quarter had a more serious symptomatic depression in the early months of motherhood. I looked separately at the women's feelings about the social role of mother and at the relationship which women described with their babies. A third of the women were not satisfied with the social role of mother, and two-thirds expressed negative feelings/ambivalence in their relationship with their babies.

I do not believe that these findings are unrepresentative either of the general situation in Britain or of that elsewhere. The fact that depression is most characteristically a female disorder is well known. The amount of depression in mothers that is postnatal only in a tautological sense – you have to acquire a child to be called a mother, but mothers can be, and are, depressed at any stage in their motherhood – is enormous. A very carefully-done community survey in London found a prevalence rate of fifteen per cent in what psychiatrists would call depression.[7] The highest rate was for working-class women with children under six – forty-two per cent of these were clinically depressed. But when 'borderline' cases were included, the rate in the community as a whole rose from fifteen to thirty-three per cent. Such statistics provide the background for the very high rates of psychotropic drug-prescribing that now characterize the relations between the medical profession and mothers – in some general practices in Britain more than a fifth of all women patients are in receipt of such drugs.[8]

Studies that have examined the factors associated with depression in mothers have shown the importance both of the conditions under which women mother and of past factors in women's lives that appear to make them especially vulnerable to 'depression'. The factors which I found to be significantly associated with the outcomes of depression in my own study are a somewhat mixed bag. The medical factors seemingly predictive of depression are those relating to an unsatisfying birth experience in which the mother felt that she was not the person delivering the baby, while the social factors relate to the absence of supportive conditions for childrearing and to the lack of previous job experience – that is, little contact with babies before the acquisition of one's own. The community survey mentioned earlier suggested that four factors in particular predicted women's vulnerability to depression: lack of an intimate relationship, having three or more children under fourteen, loss of one's mother before the age of eleven and not having a job outside the home. In my own study, the occurrence of depression was associated most strongly with four 'vulnerability factors': lack of a job outside the home, housing problems, a segregated role-relationship with the

baby's father and little previous experience of babies. In the presence of four vulnerability factors, the depression rate was 100 per cent, falling to twenty per cent for those with one factor. It may well be that a relatively simple index of housing conditions, such as tenure, is more predictive of maternal depression than any number of enquiries into mothers' psychological constitutions. Thus, another British survey of motherhood showed a highly significant difference in rates of depression according to housing tenure – from seventeen per cent in women who were owner-occupiers to sixty per cent of those living in council accommodation.[9] Clearly, the application of this index to the situation in the USA is not simple – but the basic point is that poverty causes unhappiness, and that motherhood, despite being a morally idealized state, does not guarantee (economic) wealth.

As to possible theoretical pathways between such vulnerability factors and the onset of clinically-recognized depression, the theory is that vulnerability factors produce an ongoing state of low self-esteem. When a provoking agent – a life-event or a chronic difficulty – occurs, the feeling of hopelessness that is evoked becomes a generalized state of hopelessness which in turn produces the features of clinical depression. Both the factors that make women vulnerable to developing a depressive disorder and the life-events and long-term difficulties that are liable to provoke depression are more prevalent in the lower socioeconomic groups. This is but one manifestation of a general phenomenon – the process whereby economic class and gender class are interlocking axes of inequality for women.

According to theorists such as Jean Baker Miller[10] and Nancy Chodorow,[11] everything hinges on the question of self-identity and self-esteem. The fact that women do the mothering in our society accounts for a certain unbroken relationship between mothers and daughters. A consequence of the lack of a daughter's need to repudiate an identification with her mother (which is what a son must do to achieve masculinity) is the difficulty that women may have in developing an autonomous sense of self, a certainty about the stable core of qualities which one attributes to oneself *through and beyond the circumstances of any particular relationship*. The problem of motherhood for women is that the tendency to seek one's identity in relationships with others is liable to continue, even when the original tie with the mother seems to have been outgrown. Also, an attitude of unreality about the *gratifications*, about the *satisfaction*, of motherhood is bred in women by their earliest experience of the mothering relation.

I think that this interpretation helps to explain a number of otherwise puzzling features of motherhood. Perhaps the first question is: why do women continue to want children? Between eighty and ninety per cent of adult women in the industrialized world have at least one child, and,

although fertility has fallen in the sense that there are more small families these days, the experience of mothering *at least one child* is now spread more widely across the female population than it was fifty or a hundred years ago. Like many questions in this field, this question, why women want chidlren, is impossible to answer on the basis of existing research, since the dominant paradigm has equated biological femaleness and the impulse to maternity: non-achievement of motherhood rather than its achievement has been the problematic of most inquiries. When it *is* asked, the question 'Why did you want a baby?' is usually greeted with some response along the line of 'I never really thought about it', or 'I always have done'. And this is what would indeed seem to be the case; for, as long as women mother, women will always want to *become* mothers in order to recreate the same apparent satisfaction of their relational needs as they experienced as children with *their* mothers.

Another way to put this is to say that what the gender-differentiated nuclear family produces is two classes of people – men and women – who cannot satisfy one another's relational needs. Men want their relational needs to be satisfied in a heterosexual connection with women, while women look, throughout their lives, and in one way or another, back to the original symbiosis of the mother–child relationship. When one compares contemporary industrial society with non-industrialized cultures, the absence of patterned cooperation and friendship between adult women is one of the most striking differences. Women in many other cultures look to each other for daily help and support and emotional gratification. They did so in our own society before industrialization and before the rise of the nuclear family ethic, according to which the love between man and woman is every woman's salvation. In fact, of course, the promise of this love is every woman's downfall; for, as long as women believe in *men* as their saviours, they will not be able to find themselves. The nuclear family provides women with only one culturally accepted solution to their own gendered, family-produced needs for intense primary relationships: and that is to invest their emotional futures in their children.

The second puzzling feature of motherhood that is illuminated by this particular interpretation concerns what is *difficult* about mothering. According to Chodorow, those very capacities and needs which create women as mothers lead to potential contradictions in mothering. Mothering involves a dual identification for women, both as mother and as child. Women make good parents because they can take the place of the child, understand the child's needs from the child's point of view. But the mother–child relationship is also marked with inherent conflict, and women run the risk of projecting their own childish needs onto their children, of

finding the temperaments, capacities and interests of their children less than satisfying, and of living out problems in their relationships to their own mothers with their own children.

Third, we can see how, in turning to the idealized fulfilment of the mother–child relationship, women do not begin to solve their basic problem, and that is of an insufficiently individuated sense of self. Nor do they begin to solve this problem for their daughters. This conclusion, which is not intended to be 'victim-blaming' in any sense, helps to identify what may be good for women and their children about women having a job outside the home. There is no doubt that, as we have seen, having another work role that is economically rewarding and publicly valued improves the mental health of mothers, probably because it increases their perception of themselves as individuals and adds to (or provides them with a basis for) self-esteem. At the same time, children of employed mothers, especially daughters, appear to be more independent, more self-reliant, less 'feminine' and less rigid in their conceptions of gender roles.[12] Such findings are slightly curious when one considers that most employed mothers work in low-status, relatively ill-paid jobs which do not themselves appear to be intrinsically rewarding. It would appear to be principally the opportunity for non-domestic identification that is important – for mothers and their daughters. And yet the full exploitation of such an identification may involve short-term hardship, for, as most mothers know, it is still going against the set of the culture to insist that one is oneself first, and somebody's mother second, and extremely difficult for a five-, ten- or even fifteen-year-old to realize that such self-assertion is in her own best long-term interests.

Fourth, and most fundamental of all, the mother–child relationship is pre-social and in a significant sense 'unreal'. It is the infant's first love experience and it is one in which the infant has little sense of her/his separateness from the mother. The infant attributes to the mother an idealized and sacrificial love, and these attributes of motherhood are never entirely lost for either male or female children. The males grow up with a double image of women – as pure and selfless mothers and, on the other hand, as sexy bitches or aggressive careerists. The females grow up possessed of a profoundly unreal fantasy of what it is like to be a mother.

So, one of the problems of motherhood in a patriarchal, family-oriented culture, which assigns childrearing to the female parent, is that women come to motherhood with quite unrealistic expectations of what they will achieve *for themselves* through biological reproduction. *A certain idealization of the state of maternity is itself built into the mothering relation as presently defined.* So long as childrearing continues to be assigned to women, this idealization can be counted as a form of 'transmitted deprivation'. Women are deprived of

the chance to understand not only the benefits but also the hazards that motherhood will pose to their own identities and lifestyles.

WHAT KIND OF CHILDREN DO WE NEED?

It was the American sociologist Alice Rossi who, in 1968, drew attention to the fact that the bias in almost all existing research on parenthood within the behavioural sciences is towards finding out the right kind of mothers for children to have.[13] It was assumed that if enough were known about styles of mothering and attitudes of mothers to children, then much of the evident variation among children could be accounted for. As David Levy put it in his much-quoted book *Maternal Overprotection* in 1943, 'It is generally accepted that the most potent of all influences on social behaviour is derived from the primary social experience with the mother . . . the most important study of man [sic] as a human being is a study of his mother's influence on his early life'.[14] The contrary assumption – that if enough were known about the attitudes of children to mothers and children's impact on maternal identities and lifestyles, then much of the variation among mothers might be explained – was, however, never made. If we shift the emphasis – as research over the past few years has increasingly done, though not by any means sufficiently thoroughly yet – then we can see that the important questions for women include: 'What is the effect of motherhood on women's lives?' What does maternity deprive women of?' and 'What is the best kind of child for a woman to have if she is to obtain the most gratification and the least deprivation from the status, role and identity of mother?'

I do not know that we can really answer this question, given the present state of the art. Margaret Mead, those initiation into motherhood I referred to earlier, once recalled a letter written by Harriet Beecher Stowe, in which Stowe said that she had in mind to write a novel about slavery, 'but the baby cried too much'. Mead's comment on this was that 'it would have been much more plausible if she had said 'but the baby smiles so much'.[15] The pleasures of motherhood may well be an obstacle to writing books about slavery or being involved more generally in publicly productive activity – but a crying baby is more likely to cause maternal dissatisfaction than a smiling one. An interesting study in Cambridge, England, which followed a group of first-born children from birth to school age, found that children who persisted in waking at night after the first year were those who cried and showed the highest levels of irritability in the early days of life. The only differences in maternal behaviour between the night-wakers and the non-night-wakers were attributable to, rather than causes of, this early difference on the part of the babies.[16]

Given that the sex-differences literature demonstrates that it is more

usually boys than girls who provide their mothers with such problems, it is not very heartening to discover that, according to a number of studies, women more often find mothering a daughter more depressing than mothering a son.[17] One researcher has suggested that female babies are more often depressing to women because they re-enact the initial, unworked-out ambivalence of the mother–daughter relationship, and because to have a son is to achieve what our culture continues to hold out as the highest achievement for women. If you can't become a member of the dominant group yourself, I guess the next best thing is to give birth to one.

MOTHERS AND CHILDREN AND THE 'GOOD' SOCIETY

Female parenting is the first and most lasting determinant of women's subordinate group psychology. Daughters are never rid of their mothers — either of their mothers' weaknesses or of their mothers' extraordinarily valuable emotional capacities and sensitivities. Biological motherhood is not the primary problem. Without resorting to a test-tube and artificial-womb technology (which, anyway, would not solve the problem because in the present social order this technology would be male-controlled), it *is* possible to see how biological reproduction could be managed so that it did *not* alienate women from their own bodies and identities in the way in which it does at the moment. What is needed is a condition that is at the same time both most simple and most complex, and that is to ensure that women experience themselves as the central actors in the drama of childbirth and motherhood. All the evidence points to this essential requirement, because mother–child relations are severely jeopardized if they begin with the medical infantilization of women, with an insistence that women have to be instructed in the business of childbirth and childrearing by a male-dominated profession of experts and must have their bodies attended to and manipulated like, and indeed, by, machines in order for the child to be safely extracted and set out on the even more hazardous journey to autonomous adulthood. The terms 'control' and 'mastery' — a most telling word in this context — occur often in the literature dealing with what constitutes successful biological reproduction from the mother's point of view. Where a woman does not feel that she in some sense directed the course of her own childbirth and is able to direct the course of her own motherhood, she is more liable to come out of it with damaged self-esteem, and with a perception of her baby and herself as strangers produced by strangers. Motherhood as a form of colonial imperialism is something that women can do without.

So, it is not too difficult to specify the conditions for biological reproduction that are needed to provide a *positive* self-identity in women and that heightened self-esteem which is the reality behind the cultural myth of

maternity's automatic enhancement of all women to a state of grace. But childbearing constitutes but a tiny fragment of time in our total experience of motherhood. Motherhood is not only an experience, it is an institution, and it is with this institution that our greatest problems lie. The strong association between the social and economic circumstances in which women mother and their mental health, which is clear from some of the evidence that I have quoted, points very firmly to this conclusion. In fact, it is *because* of the determination of mother–child relations and the psychology of women by the gender-differentiated family that the element of so-called 'mastery' in childbearing and childrearing is so profoundly important. Can you imagine *men* putting up with the kind of indignities and assaults imposed on mothers by the medical profession over the last twenty years? I can't. The victimization of women is facilitated by their own victimization of themselves. We need to embark on motherhood with strength, assertiveness and a clear sense of ourselves as individuals. But most of us become mothers too early in our own development to have begun to understand that a secure sense of self-esteem is a prerequisite for, and not a consequence of, motherhood.

In order to understand *why* the institution of motherhood takes the form that it does in modern industrialized society, it helps to grasp one other consequence of women's mothering within the family. That consequence I have already obliquely referred to, and it is men's contradictory need both to put mothers on a pedestal and to keep them down – in their place as domesticated, resented, unliberated dependants. It has been observed for a long time, by both feminist and non-feminist defenders of motherhood, that motherhood is high in our scale of values – it is a prized and necessary occupation – yet at the same time it is the most socially undervalued occupation of all. Simone de Beauvoir put it well in her classic *The Second Sex* when she said: 'There is an extravagant fraudulence in the easy reconciliation made between the common attitude of contempt for women and the respect shown for mothers'. Women who are denied the opportunities and responsibilities of men have babies put into their arms 'without scruple, as in earlier life dolls were given to them to compensate for their inferiority to little boys. They are permitted to play with toys of flesh and blood.'[18] Motherhood is a labour of love. Motherhood is non-work. But more than that, society need not provide for mothers. The pre-social or antisocial character of mother–child relations is reflected in the unflagging determination of our policy-makers to divide the world into two: mothers and others. Mothers do not belong to the public world, but to the private domain of the family in which the state must not intrude to advance mothers' own self-determined needs. One sign of the enormity of the state's failure to

take account of the real situation of mothers is the fact that, in Britain, only some thirteen per cent of the under-fives whose mothers have a paid job are in receipt of some sort of state-provided day care, and only about one per cent of the total public money devoted to health, education and social services in Britain is used for helping employed mothers (parents) with their child-care responsibilities.[19]

Adrienne Rich has said that 'There has been a basic contradiction throughout patriarchy: between the laws and sanctions designed to keep women essentially powerless, and the attribution to mothers of almost superhuman powers'.[20] The other side of the contradiction is the negation of women who are not mothers, who are woman-identified, or who identify with the woman (person) in themselves. And it is, as Rich points out, immensely ironic that the first and last verbal attack slung at the woman who demonstrates a primary loyalty to herself and other women is 'man-hater'.

Is the experience of motherhood under patriarchy ultimately a radicalizing or a conservative force for women? That is a question which Rich asks herself. Does motherhood extract from us an obedience to convention and a social order which we know to be morally bankrupt, or does it really put us in touch with the way things are, with the callousness of patriarchy towards women's interests? Either way, women tend to be the losers. I think this is one of the things that Margaret Mead meant when her excursions into New Guinea forged the conclusion in her own mind that a culture engaged in the repudiation of children and of the creativity of motherhood is not a good culture. A good culture is one in which human relationships come first — a good culture is a *humane* culture. Note here that both the words 'human' and 'humane' come from the same root, but that their usage diverged in the eighteenth century so that 'human' meant 'characteristic of man [sic]' and 'humane' came to mean 'kind, benevolent, civil, courteous, obliging'. As men became, linguistically and socially, the standard for human civilization, so kindness and benevolence ceased to be attributes of the human community as a whole. Kindness and benevolence are hardly defining characteristics of men in our society today. But to flourish as mothers and as people, women *require* a kind society. There is nothing intrinsically unfeminist about a culture that is oriented to the needs of children, so long as it is so in more than a superficial, eugenic, woman-hating sense, and so long as it is understood that the needs of women are not the same thing as the needs of children, and that the needs of women are not the same as the needs of mothers. We do not, in fact, know what it would be like to be mothers in a society that affirmed and respected women as individuals; nor can we imagine how the situation of women who are not mothers might be transformed by a different social valuation of motherhood. We do not know

what it would mean for all of us if children were to be valued sufficiently for men to be truly involved in their care. We have no idea how motherhood might be transformed in a world rid of the extremes of class and race inequality, as well as sex inequality. We can only guess at the effect on motherhood of a culture that affirmed peace and life instead of war and death. But we do most desperately need such a vision if we are to pass on to our daughters more than our own impoverished heritage.

8

Promoting the Health of Childbearing Women

According to the World Health Organization, health is something that we all must have by the year 2000, and health is a positive concept, implying a definite sense of complete physical and mental well-being, rather than merely an absence of disease.[21] This often-quoted definition must be misleading, because taking it literally means that few of us can really be considered healthy. However, the WHO definition has been useful because it draws our attention to two points: first, the best measure of health is not death rates, despite the traditions of epidemiology and official statistics which say that the only way to compare the health of populations is to count the numbers of people who die; and, second, when we talk about health, we are talking not only about a functioning body but about a mind and a psyche as well. People cannot be separated into bits that either function or do not function. What we should be concerned with is the whole individual, and not only the individual but also the way in which he or she fits into the particular bit of the social world in which they live.

WHAT IS HEALTH?

In her diary, writer Katherine Mansfield showed that she also knew about health. At the end of a life which had been increasingly dominated by illness, she wrote that health was something that she wanted and needed in order to write, for 'Nothing of any worth can come out of a disunited being'. But what was this elusive condition? 'By health,' she wrote, 'I mean the power to lead a full, adult, living breathing life in close contact with what I love – the heart and the wonders thereof – the sea – the sun . . . Then I want to *work*. At what? I want so to live that I work with my hands and my feelings and my brain . . .'[22]

These three words – health, power and work – are the themes of this chapter, which considers the promotion of women's health in relation to them. But first we need to get rid of some misconceptions. The most important of these is the word 'medicine', which always springs to mind when people talk about health. Health care is not the same thing as medical care. Caring for health – the health of a person, a family, a population – may imply the use of medical services or it may not. The second most important misconception concerns the meaning of the word 'work'. When Katherine Mansfield used it, she did not mean first and foremost something that gained her financial reward. She meant the use of herself, her skills, in an activity that would create something other than itself.

The need to get rid of these misconceptions is particularly important in relation to *women*. The progress that is needed to promote the health of childbearing women is contingent on new understandings of the terms 'health' and 'work'. The old understandings have failed us because of their inherent limitations. And we need the word 'power' as well, because redefining health and work draws our attention to the dimension of power that is hidden in all this: on the most simple level, the partial understandings that we have about health being the same as medicine and work being the same as waged labour result from the fact that these old definitions are those of the powerful, i.e. men and the medical profession. Payment for work in the labour market outside the home is what men mean by work; clinical monitoring and intervention is what most doctors mean by health care. The alternative understanding is the world as seen from underneath, the view of those who do not have power and therefore by definition do not have the power to impose their views on anyone else.

The argument proceeds on two different levels. The first, general, level requires the description of the condition that childbearing women are in, and what is healthy or unhealthy about it. Second, there is the micro-level of behaviours relevant to health. Here, I take one particular example of a health-related behaviour – cigarette-smoking – and ask what we can learn about appropriate ways of promoting women's health from looking at research on smoking.

WOMEN'S CONDITION

To outline aspects of women's condition, I begin in a very obedient place with Florence Nightingale, the woman generally hailed as the founder of one of women's main occupations today – nursing. In 1852, at the age of thirty-two, Florence Nightingale wrote an essay called 'Cassandra'.[23] She was still, at this advanced age, living at home with her parents, and from the outside it must have seemed as though she were doing exactly what

everyone wanted her to: as a middle-class daughter, she had no professional occupation, indeed no occupation at all, save that of being a respectable, domesticated, and therefore essentially idle, woman. It took Florence Nightingale a very long time – around nine years of concerted argument – to persuade her parents, and especially her father, to release her into the outside world. If this battle had raged a century later, no doubt social workers, family therapists and a whole army of professional health workers would have been called in to solve the problem of Florence's position in the family, including her father's intense need for psychological domination. In fact, the writing of this essay, 'Cassandra', was an important moment in Nightingale's own liberation from the narrow world of the home and the family – and from those Victorian sentiments which said that any woman who wanted to do something for herself must be absolutely crazy, and certainly not a real woman, which was, of course, the most important thing to be. These were the days in which higher education for women and employment outside the home were generally considered not only morally bad but also dangerous to women's health. Doctors at the time warned that, if a woman used her mind, her ovaries would shrivel up and other absolutely diabolical things would happen, so that there was really no point in even thinking about doing anything else apart from having periods and babies, and, of course, a husband or two.[24]

This essay of Florence Nightingale's is essentially a diatribe against the view, held by doctors and most other people at the time, that activity in the world outside the home is incompatible with the possession of two X chromosomes. Nightingale begins by asking: 'Why have women passion, intellect, moral activity – these three – and a place in society where no one of the three can be exercised? . . . Look at the poor lives which we lead', she goes on. 'It is a wonder that we are so good as we are, not that we are so bad.'[25] By 'poor', Nightingale meant restricted in terms of activities and choices. A great deal of 'Cassandra' is given over to complaining that the reasons why women have failed to become great painters, great writers, etc., is because they have never been given the chance. To quote her again,

> Women never have half an hour in all their lives . . . that they can call their own, without fear of offending or of hurting someone. Why do people sit up so late, or, more rarely, get up so early? Not because the day is not long enough, but because they have 'no time in the day to themselves'.[26]

Nightingale sums up her description of the position of women in 'Cassandra' using the following words: 'We go somewhere where we are not wanted and where we don't want to go . . . Women dream of a great sphere of steady,

(not sketchy) benevolence, of moral activity, for which they would (fain) be trained and fitted, instead of working in the dark . . .'[27]

To update Nightingale's picture, it can be said that most women in industrialized countries today get married, most women do housework, most women have children. Childbearing, in other words, happens in the context of women's other labours to do with wifehood and domesticity. Domesticity — looking after other people — is a theme running right through women's lives, now, as well as when Florence Nightingale wrote 'Cassandra'. Most of the world's health care is of the environmental and personal kind, and it is carried out by women, free — as a 'labour of love' at home. As one sociologist has put it,

> The most fundamental responsibility carried by mothers is that of providing for health. It is the most life-sustaining and labour-intensive aspect of women's health work; the activity through which the basic material resources of housing, fuel, food and transport are used to make healthy children and healthy parents. Providing for health keeps the family going. Moreover, it provides the setting in which the other health responsibilities are pursued: nursing the sick, teaching for health and mediating with professionals . . . Providing for health involves all the basic domestic activities we associate with the maintenance of a home. It involves the provision of a materially-secure environment: warm, clean accommodation where both young and old can be protected against danger and disease . . . the purchase of food and the provision of a diet sufficient in quantity and quality to meet their nutritional needs . . . the provision of a social environment conducive to normal health and development . . . orchestrating social relations within the home, to minimise . . . health-damaging insecurities . . .[28]

This meaning of health-promotion — as the labours which childbearing women perform for other people — exhibits stability and consistency over time. However, there have been important social changes affecting both marriage and biological reproduction which have altered the context within which this work and childbearing itself is done. At the turn of the century, the average woman (in the UK) would have spent a third of her life — about fifteen years — either pregnant or lactating. By 1950, the fifteen years had reduced to about four — or seven per cent of an average female lifetime.[29] Today the figure is about three years, or four per cent of average life expectancy. As to marriage, it remains popular, but the nuclear family is nuclear in two senses: it is the core, the kernel, the nucleus of the extended family; and it also, like nuclear reactors, has a tendency to blow up. Divorce rates have risen sixfold in a quarter of a century. This means that many

women who begin childrearing within marriage find themselves eventually childrearing on their own. Increasingly, too, some women are choosing to have babies without being married, or find themselves in this position: in 1982, a third of all conceptions in this country took place outside marriage. In some countries, for example Sweden, conception inside marriage has now become the exception and non-marital motherhood the rule.[30]

Despite these demographic changes, the idea of the family as a haven in a heartless world, as a place where secrets are kept and intimacies shared, and where everyone is happy, is an image that haunts both those of us who live in families and those of us who do not do so. So far as the role of men is concerned, the evidence about fathers' participation in childrearing has always been at odds with the twentieth-century notion of the liberated male. Studies have consistently shown that playing with the children while the mother gets on with the housework or cooks the dinner is the main contribution that men in dual-couple households make – aside, that is, from financial support.[31] Here, again, the image of the family as a harmoniously functioning unit breaks down in the light of research showing that, within dual-couple households, the idea that financial and other material resources will be shared equally between men and women is very often a fiction. Women do not receive their fair share, and are in any case dependent on the man's goodwill *to* receive it.[32] Adequate material support for mothers and children rests on the fragile basis of the emotional relationship between 'man and wife', to use the old phrase: where this flourishes, so do women and children; but, where it is divided and marked by conflict, the health of women and children is in jeopardy. Accordingly, one of the single most important consequences of the increase in single-parent households is that, both in Britain and the USA since the 1950s, women and children on their own have emerged as the single most important social group living in poverty. In Britain, more than one in four of the population now lives in poverty; this includes a third of all children and a large number of mothers rearing children on their own. It has been calculated that, in the USA, the poverty population will consist entirely of women and children in the year 2000.[33]

For a complex of reasons, then, reproduction exposes the social fragility of women, not as the weaker but as the *second* sex, to use Simone de Beauvoir's[34] term. Women's existence as childbearers is subject to a central paradox: although the *most* socially important activity, it is also rendered the *least* important, as cultural ideologies and practices enforce women's marginalization. This fact must be central to any attempt to conceptualize women's health and its promotion. It is also, literally, a depressing fact; women are depressed by it. Material disadvantage is related to women's depression or unhappiness;[35] so are those medical interventions justified in

the name of perinatal health in the specific sense that the use of technology in childbirth is associated with women's reports of being depressed in hospital after the birth.[36]

This, of course, illustrates another critical characteristic of the condition of childbearing women today: their status as recipients of professional advice, exhortations, instructions, education, monitoring, surveillance and intervention. The single most difficult aspect of motherhood today is that *other people are always telling mothers what they ought to do.*[37] The advice literature is enormous, and the range of professionals who have all got something to say is quite considerable – from the health visitors to the health educators, from the social workers to the sociologists, from the psychiatrists to the psychologists and the paediatricians and the agony aunts, and not forgetting the teachers, general practitioners, politicians and policy-makers. It has been said that being told the meaning of your life by other people is one of the most depressing things of all. It is certainly difficult to come to terms with when it is at odds with your own experience of who you are and what your life is all about. One powerful example of this is mothers' smoking.

THE PREGNANT SMOKER

Smoking among women today is regarded by health professionals and policy-makers as a major public health concern, in part because the reduction in smoking rates which is the aim of health education campaigns has affected men far more than women. In 1982, thirty-eight per cent of men and thirty-three per cent of women in Britain smoked.[38] Among young people, smoking is now a predominantly female habit, with eighteen per cent of eleven- to fourteen-year-old girls and fifteen per cent of eleven- to fourteen-year-old boys reporting smoking.[39] In the USA in the seventeen to nineteen age group, there are five female for every four male smokers.[40] Within this professional and policy debate about women's smoking, the impact of smoking in pregnancy on the unborn child is given special prominence. Indeed, it is *the* major health effect of women's smoking that is considered,[41] being mentioned in policy documents and professional texts far more often than the health hazards to women themselves of smoking at any time in their lives, including in pregnancy.

In turn, this professional/policy concern with smoking during pregnancy identifies a series of adverse health consequences for the children of smoking mothers, ranging from reduced birthweight to more health problems in later life. The terms of the debate are not only gender- but also class- and race-specific. Both smoking among women and low birthweight are more common among socially disadvantaged women. Precise statistics for the

proportion of women smoking when pregnant are hard to come by; in the USA, the figure is estimated to lie between twenty and thirty per cent.[42] In Britain, the 1970 British births cohort found that forty-five per cent of mothers were smoking immediately after the birth of their baby. Smoking in the 1970 cohort was higher than in the 1958 one, when thirty-four per cent of mothers were smokers after the fourth month of pregnancy.[43] The first report to identify the health-damaging aspects of pregnancy smoking was published in 1957.[44] It showed a higher incidence of both low birthweight and preterm delivery in mothers who smoked, and the report subsequently sparked off a tidal wave of medical interest in the hazards to the infant of maternal smoking in pregnancy. The finding that smoking affects birthweight has since been consistently reported in the perinatal literature. The size of the effect appears to be relatively constant and dose-dependent and to characterize diverse ethnic, geographical and social settings.[45] Work on the long-term effects of pregnancy smoking claims to have identified an excess of hospital admissions in infancy, more bronchitis and pneumonia, more delayed motor development, increased risk of sudden infant death syndrome, and increased risk of childhood and teenage cancer (the latter via a mechanism named 'transplacental carcinogenesis').[46] Smoking has also been claimed to result in poorer social adjustment and general intellectual achievement, and in retarded development in maths and reading at ages seven and eleven.[47] The latest claim in this literature is that children whose mothers smoked become adults who at age twenty-three are less likely to have attained high educational qualifications than those whose mothers did not smoke.[48]

The health education message derived from all this 'evidence' is uncompromisingly simple: smoking in pregnancy is dangerous to babies and women ought to stop doing it. Moreover, following the oversimplistic health education model, according to which knowledge about health results directly in changed health behaviour, large amounts of time and money have been expended on telling women that smoking is dangerous and they ought *therefore* to stop doing it. But what effect does anti-smoking publicity and/or persuasion have? Smoking-cessation programmes have varied in their effectiveness. About twenty to twenty-five per cent of pregnant women who smoke will stop on their own during pregnancy; on the other hand, some eighty per cent of those who stop in pregnancy will start again afterwards.[49] Anti-smoking interventions in which women receive individual, non-judgmental counselling and/or self-help programmes are the most successful in terms of affecting pregnancy smoking rates.[50] 'Shock' tactics such as demonstrations of the level of carbon monoxide in alveolar air[51] or admonitions not to smoke 'for the sake of the baby' appear to be ineffective.[52]

CARING AND SMOKING

Why do pregnant women smoke? The assumption of the health education literature that they smoke through ignorance about the damaging effects of cigarette-smoking on the fetus are not borne out by the evidence. Most studies show that most women say they know smoking is supposed to be bad for babies.[53] In the face of this evidence, it has been suggested that pregnant women continue to smoke because they disagree with health professionals about the status and relevance of the evidence on smoking and reproduction; and, more importantly, because smoking is a means of coping with the stress of caring work.[54] Some of the findings of our social support study[55] illustrate this. Forty per cent of the women in this study smoked at the beginning of pregnancy; the numbers of cigarettes which the women reported smoking dropped a little during pregnancy and then increased after childbirth. Smoking was associated with low income, with 'marital' status as single, with unemployment and with a higher number of children to care for: all these factors made it more likely that a woman would smoke. Smoking was also associated with stress: with life-events, and with crises such as family illness, relationship problems, financial difficulties and violence. It was linked with depression in pregnancy and afterwards, and with perceived control over one's life.

These findings reflect those of other work, which demonstrate that smoking among mothers is most likely to occur among working-class lone parents who are involved full-time in domestic work.[56] According to one such in our study,

> I tried to give up, but I get so as I want to kill everybody. I don't think it's worth it at the moment. I'd have to get right away. From everyone . . . at the hospital, they have asked me [again] if I smoke . . . The doctor at the clinic, he said I really should give it up. He was the same doctor I had last time. I felt so sorry for him. I couldn't give up. I told him I would cut down.
> *Interviewer*: You had or would cut down?
> I would . . . I felt like giving it up just for him. Not for me. If I'd gone back and he'd said 'Have you?', I would have said 'Yes' . . . you don't want to hurt their feelings.

Such stories do amuse, but of course they also drive home the two important points that women are not likely to tell the truth to doctors when they know the doctors will then 'get at' them for their 'bad' behaviour; and that doctors' attitudes to women's smoking are part of the very problem that women confront. Here is another example:

I was under 5 lbs, my brother was 4 lbs 2 ozs, so it's hereditary . . . [But] the doctor asked me to take a deep breath and I went . . . and he said, how many cigarettes has it got here, ten? It's more like twenty or thirty. How long do you expect to live after you have given birth to this child? Horrible. The nurse was going like that [gestures] behind his back, so that made me feel better.

In this and other ways, women reported that medical encounters could actually lead to increased smoking by causing worry:

Interviewer: Did the doctors say anything about smoking?
They don't say anything, they just say how much do you smoke and that's it . . . I know it goes into the bloodstream and makes the baby's weight less and it's possible that the baby will be less bright, able to read later than normal . . .

Later in pregnancy, this mother described how problematic her life had been over the past weeks, with her relationship with the baby's father breaking up, resulting in her taking an overdose of paracetamol and being admitted to hospital. She reported the same level of smoking at the end of the pregnancy as at the beginning.

Some doctors go to extreme lengths to stop women from smoking:

When I had the scan, he said to me, do I smoke. I said yes. He said, it's bad for the baby, it makes them small. He tried putting me on bedrest when I was in hospital to stop me from smoking, but I still went down for a fag . . .

Or:

Interviewer: How about smoking now?
Well, I was doing very well with that. I mean, since finishing work I haven't had any, until last week, when I went to the hospital, and they said something about something not being quite right with the placenta, which made me want to smoke more . . . It's just that everybody knows cigarette-smoking interferes with the placenta, and it just makes you feel more guilty when you know that . . . that placenta can do without interference!

All the women in this study said they were aware of the medical message about the health effects of cigarette-smoking. This is an extremely important point, because it means that health promotion strategies in relation to women's smoking are unlikely to succeed if all they do is simply reinforce the

moral message – the individual culpability of women who smoke and the exhortation to stop for the sake of someone else – the baby. This emphasis on women's altruism is really the heart of the matter; for, as we have seen, women are involved here in the paradox that health-promoting work may be health-damaging for those who do it. There may well be parallels between cigarette-smoking and other variables associated with caring work, such as the poorer mental health of married women compared with single women and married men.[57] The health consequences for women of caring work are highlighted with particular poignancy in a population of women who have already experienced what is said to be an adverse consequence of smoking – the production of a low-birthweight baby. If the conventional health education model is to be believed by such women, then what they are being asked to confront is the paradox that it is in the very activity of caring that they damage those for whom they care. In the social support study, smoking rates rose with poor obstetric history and with the worry about having another small baby.[58] After the baby is born, worry about its development then ensures that smoking continues.

THE POLITICS OF HEALTH

There are a number of conclusions to be drawn from this sort of evidence about ways in which *not* to promote women's health. In view of the connection between social deprivation and stress on the one hand, and women's smoking on the other, the argument that health is a matter of individual choice ignores the *social determinants* of choice – it ignores the fact that health is itself a social product. So far as the reproductive effects of smoking are concerned, a particular paradox with which the individualistic model cannot deal is that of passive smoking. Most women who smoke in pregnancy and who live with men are, along with their fetuses, exposed to the reproductive effects of *his* cigarette smoke. It has been shown that sidestream cigarette smoke often contains higher concentrations of toxins than the mainstream smoke directly breathed by the smoker.[59] One study of ten- to eleven-year-old children found a blood co 6.1 per cent higher in children with one smoking parent, but 15.1 per cent higher in children whose parents both smoked.[60] In pregnancy, a Danish study suggests that fathers' smoking may be almost as closely (and independently) associated with a depression in birthweight as mothers' smoking.[61]

But the limits of the conventional health education approach also come in a rather perverse way from the limits of medicine itself in promoting health. For example, the causes of low birthweight are not known, and the condition itself cannot be prevented by medical care. It is because of this ignorance that cigarette-smoking by mothers is identified as important. Thus, when the

Secretary of State for Social Services was asked in 1988 a parliamentary question about 'the main known factors in prematurity and low birthweight in babies', he replied in accordance with this view, that:

> The cause of prematurity or low birthweight in babies is in most cases not known. Apart from clinical factors of various kinds relating to the pregnancy, it is becoming increasingly clear that smoking by pregnant women and significant consumption of alcohol may be important in some cases.[62]

Much the same arguments apply to other health-related habits, such as drinking and the use of tranquilizing and anti-depressant drugs, which form important alternative coping strategies. If these habits are proving resistant to the efforts of health educators, then it is in large part because they are a manifestation rather than a cause of the problem. So far as smoking is concerned, it remains for socially disadvantaged women almost the only way they have of asserting the independence with which cigarette-smoking among women was associated when it first gained popularity; the emancipation of women remains, in other words, problematic.

To say this is to draw attention to the health hazards of being a woman, or at least of belonging to a social group whose health concerns are often rendered invisible to public attention. An example of this comes from another study carried out in London. This study is of work conditions and women's health; its findings show that women are more likely to be exposed to dangerous working conditions at home than in the formal labour market.[63] The considerable amount of public attention focused these days on the health hazards of particular occupations ignores those obtaining in the home, which, from this point of view, cannot be considered a safe place.

CONCLUSION

Based on the research evidence, a number of principles should inform policies for promoting the health of childbearing women in the future. First, and most important, is recognition of the *material*, or *social*, basis of health – the social factors and conditions that make health possible, or militate against it. Second, promotion by governments and by health professionals of health-promoting, rather than health-damaging, social conditions is essential. Reducing social inequalities – between genders, classes and different ethnic groups – is part of what this means. Third, the centrality of the *informal* health-care work of women should be accepted, both as regards the claims made about the contribution of formal medical care to health, and as regards the burden on women of performing such work. Fourth, it needs to be recognized that powerless individuals are not in a good position to

promote their own health. Within both the domestic and labour market economies, and as patients in formal health-care systems, women are in a position of relative powerlessness. Thus, measures to improve women's position in society generally, resulting in their feeling less alienated and more powerful, would be as good a means of promoting their health as any, and better than most. This argument has been put in relation to *children's* health, particularly in the Third World, and in the specific sense of mothers' education level emerging as the most important single factor associated with reduced infant mortality worldwide.[64] But the same argument has not been applied to the promotion of women's own health. This is, of course, yet another example of 'the unimportance of important people' – the cultural imperative which renders women as individual beings invisible, while inflating their social roles in relation to others.

And last, but by no means least, we have medicine itself. When Florence Nightingale established nursing, she saw it as an *environmental* model of health care – caring rather than curing. Not coincidentally, this is the model that applies to women's health-care work more generally. But it is not the model appropriated by the modern medical-care system. A WHO expert report summed up the three common criticisms of health care today as: unequal distribution of benefits, alleged harmful effects, and excessive technological intervention.[65] These criticisms form part of a wider picture of a crisis of confidence in modern medicine to deliver the goods. Accordingly, a major requirement for promoting reproductive health in the future is a very stringent attitude to the claims of professionalized medicine that it holds all the answers. Women must therefore ask of doctors and other health professionals who wish them to undergo particular therapies: 'What is the evidence on which you base this recommendation?' 'Is it good evidence?' And, 'If I agree to have it, what will be the likely consequences for me and my children not only today or tomorrow, but five or ten or twenty years hence?'

These questions invoke another particular problem of medical practice – the preoccupation with measurable, short-term outcomes as proof of effectiveness. A glance through almost any medical literature results in the clear impression that most doctors are in fact not interested in health at all. Their interest in death is much greater than their interest in health. Because western medicine does not have a definition of health apart from health as the absence of disease, health promotion defined as 'the process of enabling people to increase control over, and to improve, their health' can scarcely be conceived within the medical framework.

As the word 'power' is very closely allied to the word 'political', the promotion of the health of childbearing women is above all a *political* exercise. It is about how people live and why they die, and it is about the

responsibility of both the governors and the governed to ensure a healthy social environment in which health is no longer something to be striven for, the prerequisite of a few, but everyone's birthright.

9

Perinatal Mortality – Whose Problem?

'The laws of life', wrote William Farr, first statistician to the British Registrar-General's office in 1885,

> are of the highest possible interest, even if the knowledge of these laws gave man no more power over the course of human existence than the meteorologist wields over the storms of the atmosphere, or the astronomer over the revolutions of the heavens. But all human laws proceed on the belief that the lives of individuals and of communities can, within certain limits, be regulated for good or for evil . . . it becomes necessary to discuss the problem – can lifetime be prolonged by a knowledge of the causes that cut it short, or by any means within a nation's power?[66]

The causes of mortality are, as Farr observed, of both academic interest and practical concern. On the one hand, there is the urge to accumulate knowledge about a topic of crucial significance to the human condition. On the other hand, the interest of policy-makers is in applying this knowledge so as to prevent disease, disability and premature death. Farr compiled his pioneering work, *Vital Statistics*, at a time when the prevention of deaths among mothers and children was beginning to be recognized as a concern of central government. His own work in this area exemplified many of the themes to be found in the debate about the causes and prevention of perinatal mortality today. These themes can be grouped under various headings:

1. *Biological versus social causes*. How much of the observable mortality at

any one time is attributable to biological facts and how much to the influence of the social environment?

2. *Preventability*. What proportion of deaths can reasonably be regarded as preventable? On what basis can this calculation best be made?
3. *Strategies for prevention*. In the attempt to reduce deaths, how much investment should there be in medical services as such, and how much in wider policy changes aimed at improving the social basis of environmental and personal health?
4. *Mortality versus other 'outcome' measures*. To what extent does it make sense to isolate the aetiology and preventability of particular categories of deaths from the patterns of morbidity associated with them? Is preventing death necessarily the same thing as preventing illness? Should quantity as well as quality of life be regarded as measurable, and included in analyses of health-care policy?

This chapter focuses on these four themes within the context of the long and continuing debate about perinatal mortality. As well as aiming to isolate key arguments in these areas, it aims to step back and look at the debate about perinatal mortality within its own sociohistorical context. Enumerating the exact causes of fetal and infant deaths is clearly critical to the exercise of reducing these, but so is an understanding as to why the reduction of perinatal mortality emerges in certain historical periods as a major health-policy concern.

INTERNATIONAL AND OTHER COMPARISONS

In the section of *Vital Statistics* dealing with childhood mortality, Farr noted that the number of children in every 100 who survived the first five years of life varied in different European states. The figures which he cited are shown in Table 9.1. Death rates among young children were more than double in some countries what they were in others, with the Scandinavian countries ranking top, followed by England in fourth place. Factors such as midwifery (or obstetric care, as it would now be called), nutrition, clean water and other 'sanitary conditions' are mentioned by Farr as underlying this picture. However, as instructive as the *inter*national comparisons are the *intra*national ones: in England's 'healthy' districts, child mortality was very nearly as low as in Norway, whereas in the least healthy English districts the rate was as high as in Austria and Spain. If the analysis was restricted to children of the English peerage or clergy, the rate became a mere ten per 1,000. The right-hand column of Table 9.1 shows the somewhat different measure of perinatal mortality for the same countries almost a century later, in 1980–1. Comparing the two sets of figures, we can see that the extent of

Table 9.1: Childhood and perinatal mortality in selected European countries, 1885 and 1980–1.

Country	Deaths 0–5 years 1885		Perinatal mortality 1980–1	
	Rate	Ranking	Rate	Ranking
Austria	360	7 =	12.6	9
Belgium	270	4	9.0	5
Denmark	200	2 =	8.8	4
England*	260	3	11.8	8
France	290	5	9.8	6
The Netherlands	330	6	8.6	3
Italy	390	9	14.3	10
Norway	170	1	8.1	2
Russia	380	8	27.7	11
Spain	360	7 =	11.1	7
Sweden	200	2 =	6.7	1

Source: 1885 data from W. Farr *Vital Statistics*, 1885, p. 205. 1980–1 data from US Department of Health and Human Services, *Proceedings of the International Collaborative Effort on Perinatal and Infant Mortality* vol. 1, 1985, pp. 11–16.

*Great Britain 1980–1 data.

the variation appears to have increased: the highest rate, 27.7, is more than four times the lowest rate of 6.7. There is a fair degree of consistency in ranking positions, with only two countries – England and the Netherlands – changing their position between the top half and the bottom half of the league table over this period.

Such comparisons of how different countries 'perform' in the field of perinatal and infant mortality become increasingly commonplace in both the technical and lay literature from the late nineteenth century on.[67] At first, the foci of these comparisons are the infant and maternal mortality rates. By the 1920s, the latter has become of more concern: rates of infant death show consistent decline, but the deaths of women due to childbearing continue at about the same level as when statistics on this first began to be systematically collected in the 1830s. Writing about *The Protection of Motherhood*, in a Ministry of Health Report for 1927, Dame Janet Campbell included a table showing puerperal mortality in eighteen countries. Her statistics supported the general idea of a paradise in Scandinavian countries.[68] This had become so alluring by the time the Departmental Committee on Maternal Mortality and Morbidity came to produce its Final Report in 1932 that a special delegation of experts was sent to Denmark and Sweden (and the Netherlands) to find out whether or not it was true (and, if so, why). The investigators came to the conclusion that 'there is a wide difference between the social conditions and habits of life in these countries

and in many parts of England and Wales'.[69] Other factors such as different methods of death-classification were important in explaining the differential; midwifery services played a part — the Committee was particularly impressed by the Dutch avoidance of anaesthesia in normal midwifery — but, overall, the superior social conditions and general health of the population were considered the single most important factor.

In the late 1930s, maternal mortality in Britain finally began to fall, thus clearing the stage for the new central character of perinatal mortality to emerge as the focus for essentially the same debate about social versus medical determinants of health. The term 'perinatal' was introduced in 1936 by a German paediatrician, who argued that deaths towards the end of pregnancy and in the early days of life are united by similar causes, and so should be grouped together.[70] Various commentators noted that the fall in infant mortality was almost wholly accounted for by reduced deaths among babies surviving beyond the first few days of life, largely because the infectious diseases of infancy were killing less than they had. By comparison, fetal mortality and deaths shortly after birth had changed little.

Once 'perinatal' mortality had been accepted as the appropriate term, it, too, was subjected to the league-table treatment. In 1959, for example, the Report of the Maternity Services Committee (the Cranbrook Committee) occupied itself with observing that perinatal mortality was higher in Britain than in Australia, the Netherlands, New Zealand and Sweden. The Committee went on to emphasize that 'we are of the opinion that the present perinatal mortality rate could be lowered by a better maternity service, in particular by more careful ante-natal care'.[71] The wording is significant — especially the term 'opinion' and the singling-out of antenatal care as the key preventive strategy. More recently, during the 1970s, perinatal mortality again acquired the status of a major public-health problem. Britain's 'poor record on perinatal mortality' was widely referred to; a Select Committee of the House of Commons investigated and reported on it, and a team of experts was sent abroad — this time to France — to find out why other countries managed what Britain apparently could not. Publicity was given to the apparently large fall in the French perinatal mortality rate for 1976, and to the parallel investment in specialist neonatal training and care that was said to have taken place there.[72] Shortly after this, the Spastics Society ran a national press campaign drawing attention to regional differences within Britain in perinatal mortality rates. Under captions such as 'The urgent need to reduce baby deaths'[73] or 'Why do babies die?',[74] the media called for investigation as to why some Area Health Authorities seemed to do well and others less so.

Evidence given to the Short Committee on Perinatal and Neonatal Mortality, which published its Report in 1980, reiterated the international

motif. A major theme of the text is international trends in perinatal and neonatal mortality, with the fall observable in developed countries taken as evidence of preventability. 'It did not escape our notice', commented the Committee, 'that the highest rates are in regions that have long been, and still are, at a socio-economic disadvantage.'[75] Substantial media coverage was given to the Committee's estimate that about 10,000 British babies annually died or were handicapped for reasons that could be avoided by greater efforts in the domain of medical care.

The main drift of all comparisons of perinatal mortality rates between and within countries has been to arrive at some estimate of preventability, and to argue the case for particular kinds of policy changes – for example, increased expenditure on neonatal intensive care, 'humanization' of the antenatal services, so as to increase take-up, or health education and income support targeted at the diet of pregnant women. But the problem with such arguments is that they interpolate causal relationships from crude statistics which are often not collected in uniform ways, and which say nothing about some of the most important factors underlying international and other differences in death rates.

A large proportion of the world's infant deaths are reported incompletely and/or inaccurately – ninety-eight per cent, according to a United Nations Population Commission estimate in 1969.[76] Even in developed countries, different definitions of what constitutes a 'perinatal' death and how the rate should be calculated (on the basis of live births and stillbirths, or live births alone?) complicate the attempt to draw meaningful conclusions from international comparisons. Moreover, the choice of countries to be included in the league table affects the impression created – Papua New Guinea had a lower infant mortality rate than France in 1972, for example, but its statistics and health-care system were not quoted in the British media in the 1970s as a model to be emulated in British health-care policy.[77]

WHICH BABIES DIE?

A more serious charge levelled at the league-table approach to perinatal mortality from a policy point of view is that it ignores two particular reproductive differences between populations that substantially affect death rates.[78] Most perinatal deaths are associated with low birthweight and/or congenital malformations. A country with a high proportion of low-birthweight babies and a high congenital malformation rate has a population of babies at higher risk of death than a country where congenital malformation and low-weight births occur less frequently. The same is true of populations in different regions within a country. This 'weighting' is of critical importance to policy, for no amount of expenditure on neonatal

Table 9.2: Perinatal mortality and low birthweight in seven countries, participating in the WHO collaborative study, 1973.

	Per cent total births <2500g	Perinatal mortality rate	
		Crude	Standardized
Hungary	10.8	29.1	16.6
Cuba	10.8	26.9	20.1
USA (part)	6.0	14.9	11.7
Austria	5.7	21.4	18.2
Japan	5.3	17.0	18.9
New Zealand	5.2	17.3	17.3
Sweden	3.9	12.6	14.5

Source: A. Macfarlane and I. Chalmers 'Problems in the interpretation of perinatal mortality statistics' in D. Hull (ed.) *Recent Advances in Paediatrics* Edinburgh, Churchill Livingstone, 1981, p. 4.

intensive care is likely to salvage babies with congenital handicap, and the distribution of investment in social versus health-policy changes required to improve birthweight distributions must take account of the complex and poorly-understood aetiology of low birthweight.[79] Countries with high infant mortality rates also tend to have high congenital malformation rates.[80] However, the single most important factor contributing to the risk of perinatal death is low birthweight, which accounts for between fifty and eighty-five per cent of all perinatal deaths.[81] Like congenital malformations, low-birthweight births vary in incidence both inter- and intranationally. The first column of Table 9.2 shows the percentage of low-birthweight births among total births in seven countries in 1973. These kinds of differences have led to the suggestion that, whenever comparative statistics are used for evaluating perinatal health care, birthweight-specific mortality rates are a more appropriate yardstick than crude mortality rates.[82] Adopting this suggestion shifts the ranking of different countries; the USA, for example, moves up the table, as, although it has a relatively high proportion of low-birthweight births, the mortality of these babies is relatively low. The second and third columns of Table 9.2 demonstrate the effect of 'standardizing' rates so that each country's birthweight-specific mortality is held constant but the birthweight distributions are assumed to be the same. (In Table 9.2, birthweight distributions have been standardized to the pattern then obtaining in New Zealand.) This standardization exercise results in five of the seven countries changing their rank position.

WHY DO BABIES DIE?

To say that a small or malformed baby is more likely to die than an average-sized or normally-formed one is to say nothing about the causes of

Table 9.3: Perinatal mortality by social class, England and Wales, 1985.

Social class	Perinatal mortality rate
All	9.8
I	7.7
II	7.5
IIIN	8.8
IIIM	9.2
IV	11.1
V	12.4
Illegitimate	12.1

Source: OPCS Monitor DH3 87/1.

Table 9.4: Low birthweight by social class, England and Wales, 1985.

Social class	Percentage of live and stillbirths weighing <2500g
All	6.8
I	5.5
II	5.9
IIIN	6.0
IIIM	7.2
IV	7.7
V	8.2
Others	6.9

Source: OPCS Monitor DH3 86/2.

these conditions, nor to give any indication of how their incidence in any community can best be reduced. Cause and prevention are of course intimately connected. Effective prevention requires some notion of aetiology, though – as in the famous case of Snow and the water-borne cholera epidemic – it may be sufficient to identify the general category of cause rather than to possess a detailed understanding of the mechanism of its effect.

Perinatal mortality, congenital malformations and low birthweight are all greater in lower social classes, virtually whatever dataset is examined.[83] Tables 9.3 and 9.4 give figures for perinatal mortality and low birthweight by social class for England and Wales in 1985. These suggest that social factors underlie population differences in perinatal risk. In turn, it seems logical to conclude that prevention of these conditions should include action at the social or environmental level, or at the level of enabling individuals to adopt healthier lifestyles. To concentrate on health-service factors may be equivalent to hauling drowning persons out of a river instead of moving

upsteam to find out what is causing them to fall in in the first place. While the evidence supports such a view, it is necessary to look more closely at the associations that exist between perinatal risk and social factors, and at the possible meanings of these associations.

In 1978, a WHO Report on *Social and Biological Effects on Perinatal Mortality* documented an association for all countries covered in the Report between socioeconomic status and perinatal mortality.[84] The Report showed gradients in perinatal mortality rates by father's occupation, more or less continuously from the professional, technical and administrative groups through to the agricultural, productive and service groups. This pattern, though startlingly consistent, does not in itself constitute an explanation; rather, it constitutes the problem to be explained. Is the association of social class with perinatal mortality causal or artefactual? It is clear that social-class differences in perinatal risk have persisted throughout periods which have seen considerable changes in the definition and status of occupations and in the occupational distribution of the employed population. (Semi-skilled and unskilled work in particular has declined in importance, with the result that social class V represents an increasingly extreme group.) Changes in fertility patterns have altered the contribution made by each social class to overall births. (In 1978, for example, in England and Wales, social classes I and II and the 'illegitimate' category contributed more, and social classes III and IV and V less, than each class had done in 1951.) These considerations are consistent with the 'biological drift' hypothesis, according to which some of the excess reproductive risk of lower-social-class mothers is due to a tendency of those who are less 'good' reproducers, biologically speaking, to move downwards in the social-class scale. Scottish data analysed by Illsley confirmed the existence of such a pattern. What Illsley's analysis showed was that women brought up in social classes I and II who marry into social classes IV and V are shorter, have poorer physiques and diets lower in calcium, protein and vitamins A, B and C, leave school earlier, achieve lower scores in IQ tests, enter less prestigious occupations and run a higher risk of perinatal loss than their counterparts who marry within their social-class group.[85] The effect of such movement must be to maintain the social-class gradient, but it is not sufficient to explain it. As Chalmers concluded in a leading article in the *British Medical Journal* on this subject in 1985, selective social drift may reflect genetic influences, but 'There is little direct evidence with which this possibility may be assessed'.[86]

Insofar as social-class membership influences perinatal risk (rather than vice versa), it is necessary to separate out those specific social factors that appear to be related to increased risk. These factors include type of occupation, education, housing, income, ethnicity, marital status, sexual

activity, interpregnancy interval, smoking, alcohol and stress.[87] Many of these factors are interactive: thus, for example, while smoking increases perinatal risk overall, the deleterious effect of smoking appears to be greatest among working-class mothers.[88] Occupation is a good example of a social factor whose connections with perinatal outcome are more complex than they might at first appear. French research suggests that, while women who are economically active during pregnancy have a generally more favourable perinatal outcome than economically inactive women, there are certain features of employment that are associated with poor outcome. These include a long working week, standing during work, having few work breaks, a long and difficult journey to and from work, and performing especially tiring work.[89] There is very little research which attempts to unravel the relationship between 'women's two roles' and perinatal outcome – the second role – in the home – also including a substantial work component. Housework disappeared from perinatal epidemiology sometime in the late 1940s, when Douglas, analysing data from the 1946 birth cohort, described a beneficial effort on birthweight of household help during the last trimester of pregnancy for women having their first child and for those giving birth to a subsequent one after an interval of two years or less.[90]

Social-class differences in perinatal mortality parallel those for many other categories of death and illness,[91] where questions of aetiology and preventability must confront the issue of the relative weight of short- and long-term factors. Health is affected by childhood environment, but to what extent is it determined by it? Can policy changes overcome historical effects, or does the past always limit possibilities of change in the present?

These questions are perhaps even more relevant to the issue of perinatal mortality, because it is possible to make some assessment of the extent to which the health of women as children influences the health of their own children. Many years ago, Dugald Baird in Aberdeen demonstrated cohort changes in reproductive risk as improved childhood health was manifested in greater reproductive 'efficiency' in adulthood.[92] Similarly, improvements in perinatal mortality in the early 1970s have been linked to the redistribution of health resources, including food, which occurred during the Second World War in Britain. So far as diet is concerned, and despite current enthusiasms among maternity pressure groups for attention to diet in pregnancy, there is very little evidence showing any beneficial effect on perinatal mortality of dietary supplementation during pregnancy itself.[93] Contrary to received wisdom in the 1960s and 1970s, a high-protein diet appears to be bad, rather than good, for birthweight.[94] Such conclusions should not, however, be taken to mean that diet in pregnancy is *not* important; rather, they mean that we do not yet know in which ways diet *is* important, and in particular we do

not have the necessary information to evaluate the short-term versus long-term effects of dietary manipulation.

SERVICES FOR PERINATAL HEALTH?

It is impossible to answer the question as to whether social factors, biological influences or factors related to the provision of health care are more important in reducing the risk of perinatal death. Some of the most convincing evidence of the importance of social factors comes from the period before the introduction of the National Health Service in Britain. During the First World War, a dramatic improvement in infant mortality and narrowing of the social-class gap in life-chances was associated with concerted government action to protect vulnerable groups in the population from the adverse health effects of the war. There was a reduction in medical services at the time – sixty per cent of doctors were in uniform.[95] The Second World War saw the largest absolute fall in perinatal mortality ever, with dramatic improvements in stillbirths and early neonatal mortality rates, and even greater reductions in maternal mortality.[96] These falls were not preceded or accompanied by improvements in medical care. Between 1939 and 1943, the number of doctors in public-health work fell by twenty per cent and general practitioners by twenty-five per cent; the remaining medical staff were 'generally either very young or elderly, or unfit for military service'.[97] At the same time, the national food policy achieved a more equal distribution of resources; but, as we have seen, the effects of diet on perinatal outcome are unlikely to manifest themselves in the short term. More convincingly, it has been argued that improved health and survival among mothers and children during the war reflected long-term improvements in national health. Women having children in the 1940s had experienced healthier childhoods than those who became mothers a decade or two earlier. Furthermore, larger families were becoming less popular, so that the extra perinatal risk contributed by high-parity births was reduced. At the same time, the national health benefited from full employment, which is probably one of the factors contributing to the collective picture of wars in general having a paradoxical health-promoting effect on civilian populations.[98]

Despite such evidence, it is widely believed that perinatal mortality rates serve as proxy measures of the quality of perinatal health services. Thus, over the years, antenatal, intranatal and postnatal medical care have all been suggested as areas where resources need to be invested in order for further reductions in perinatal mortality to take place. During the 1920s and 1930s, it was antenatal care that received the most attention, as maternal education and clinical surveillance were identified as likely to preserve the life of the unborn child.[99] After the war, and increasingly in the 1950s and 1960s, the

argument refocused on care during labour and delivery, with place of birth becoming a major concern of maternity-care policy. More recently, the spotlight has shifted to the efforts of paediatricians in caring for small, sick babies. It is the 'need' for technological and staff investment in neonatal intensive care that now occupies the central place in the medical script. As with other areas of medicine and health, the contention of medical care's effectiveness is difficult to support from the evidence available. The growth of antenatal medical care, the centralization of intrapartum care in the hospital and the invention of the specialist technical nursery have all taken place over the same period as perinatal and other reproductive mortalities have fallen, but contemporality is no proof of causality.

The appeal of antenatal care as a means of saving babies was summed up in the Short Report's much-quoted dictum: 'Antenatal care is a perfect example of preventive medicine'.[100] However, in its previous paragraph, the Committee had revealingly noted that what antenatal care consists of and how it works was considerably more puzzling than its intuitive appeal. Some aspects of pregnancy are more clearly appropriately dealt with by antenatal medical care than others. These include diabetic pregnancy, women with essential hypertension, and the diagnosis of fetal abnormalities, where medical care has had, and continues to have, an undoubted impact on perinatal mortality.[101] But the consequent treatment of all pregnant women as potentially high-risk, the religious faith that more visits are a passport to better outcome, and the inhumane organization and impaired communication that characterize many antenatal clinics, can hardly be said to make a contribution to perinatal health. So far as medical care during labour and delivery is concerned, there is no firm evidence that the increased use of interventions such as Caesarean section and induction of labour, which have been a feature of perinatal health care in many countries over the last twenty to thirty years, have been responsible for lowered mortality.[102] Perinatal mortality rates have fallen considerably in countries with quite different patterns of medical perinatal care.[103] After birth, improvements in neonatal intensive care since the 1970s have led to increased survival for low-birthweight infants in Britain and other countries (though the rate of low birthweight has not itself changed).[104] Some caution needs to be exercised, however, as it is theoretically possible that the effect of such care is merely to transfer mortality from the perinatal to the neonatal period. There is some evidence that a shift of this kind has taken place.[105] The benefit of enhanced survival must also be measured against quality of life. Aggressive medical care of small infants may result in more handicapped children in the community.[106] There is evidence that the increased use of neonatal intensive care has led to rising cerebral palsy rates.[107]

One attempt to answer the question as to how much of a medical-care input lies behind declining perinatal mortality is Alberman's[108] analysis of different categories of deaths. For low birthweight, Alberman shows that the rate increased slightly over the period from 1979 to 1983 (rising from 6.42 to 6.74 per 1,000 live births), while at the same time perinatal mortality decreased for these babies, masking the increased rate of low birthweight itself. The same pattern of secondary prevention concealing a failure of primary prevention was evident for congenital malformations, the other main contributor to perinatal deaths. Stillbirths due to congenital abnormalities fell faster than those due to other causes, associated with increased diagnosis and termination of affected pregnancies rather than with improvements in maternal health resulting in a lower conception rate of such babies.

A CAUSE FOR CONCERN?

Whatever the input of social and health-care factors, perinatal mortality rates are falling persistently in most countries. From the mid-1970s in England and Wales, perinatal mortality has been decreasing at the rate of about one per 1,000 births per year. As a leading article in the *British Medical Journal* in 1980 commented, the reason for this fall

> is not clear. It has occurred before there has been any chance to introduce measures such as monetary incentives for mothers to attend antenatal clinics . . . the setting up of more intensive care neonatal units, and the provision of better nutrition for mothers – all campaigned for by well-intentioned reformers, including the BMJ. Nor can the improvement be due to increased monitoring of the fetus; controlled trials have shown little difference between perinatal mortality in those who are and those who are not monitored.[109]

The BMJ noted that availability of abortion must be a factor, as perinatal mortality is considerably higher in illegitimate births. And, as with earlier periods of improvement in perinatal health, changes in the age and parity of the childbearing population continue to be a significant factor. Mothers are younger and have fewer children, thus the children that are born are at lower risk. Analyses of the statistics of different countries suggest that these factors account for between a quarter and a half of the overall decline in perinatal mortality in countries such as Britain and the USA.[110] For further decline or sustained low levels of perinatal mortality, it may therefore be as important to focus on factors affecting the overall health status of women, including fertility-control services, as on the provision of medical care after conception has occurred.

Figure 9.1: Perinatal mortality per 1,000 live births, by year.

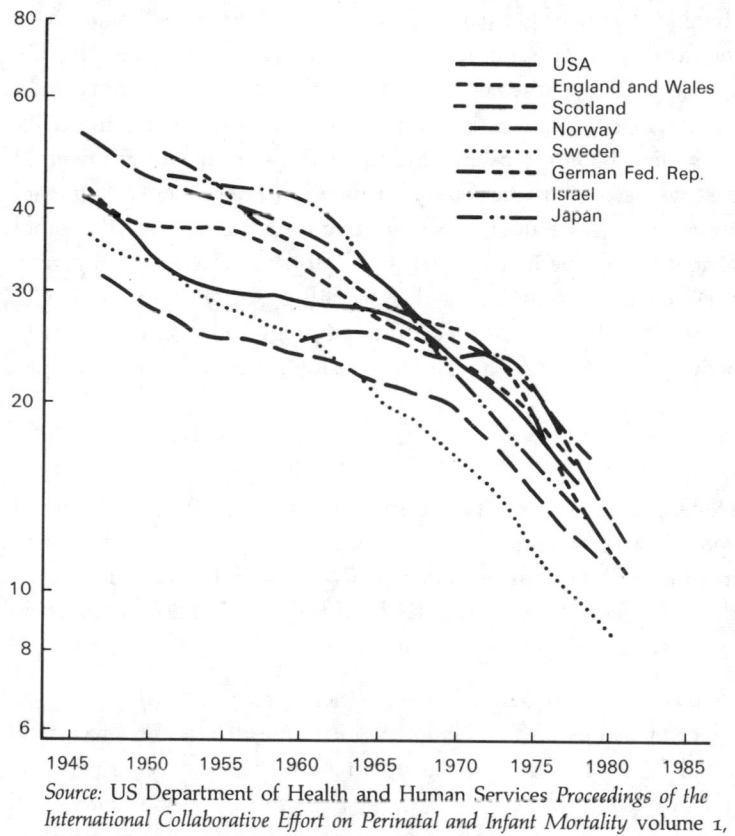

Source: US Department of Health and Human Services *Proceedings of the International Collaborative Effort on Perinatal and Infant Mortality* volume 1, Hyattsville, Maryland, Center for Health Statistics, 1985, II–98.

During the present period of declining perinatal mortality, international differences remain, because the reproductive risks characterizing different populations, including their vulnerabilities to low birthweight and congenital malformations, continue to be an important determinant of overall perinatal mortality. Figure 9.1 shows perinatal mortality for eight countries from 1945 to 1985, and Figure 9.2 the trend in postneonatal mortality. It has long been recognized that infant, and especially postneonatal, mortality is more responsive to social conditions than perinatal mortality; this may account for the widening gap between countries as one moves from Figure 9.1 through to Figure 9.2. To take a concrete example of this, research on housing status and childhood mortality in England and Wales has shown a significant association between poor housing and mortality up to the age of four, after controlling for the effects of unemployment and low social class.[111] In a study in Scotland, Martin[112] and colleagues established that children's health was more affected than the

Figure 9.2: Postneonatal mortality per 1,000 live births, by year.

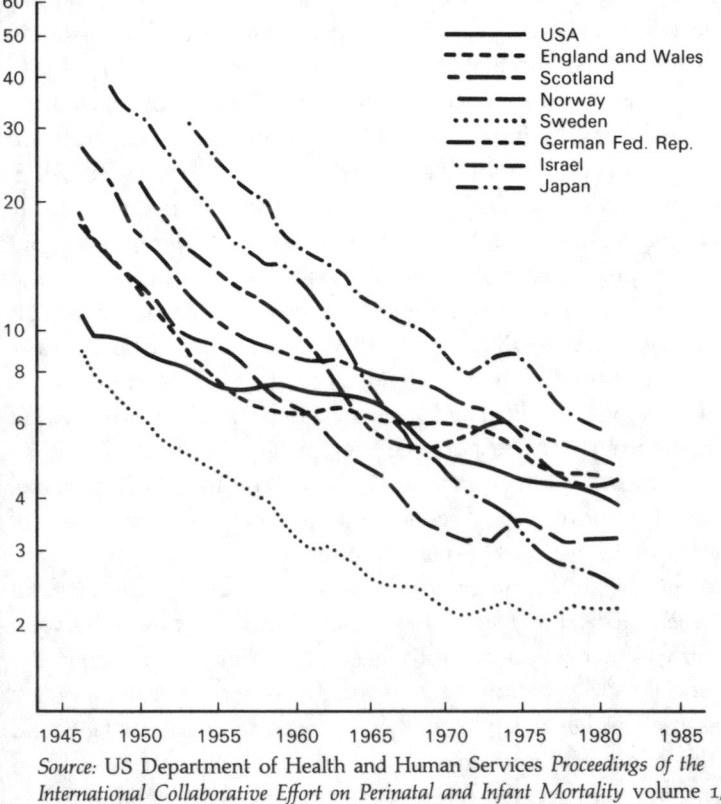

Source: US Department of Health and Human Services *Proceedings of the International Collaborative Effort on Perinatal and Infant Mortality* volume 1, Hyattsville, Maryland, Center for Health Statistics, 1985, II–98.

health of adults by living in poor, and especially damp, housing conditions.

There is a strong association between adverse socioeconomic conditions and postneonatal mortality, as there is also between such conditions and the two main factors – low birthweight and congenital malformations – underlying perinatal mortality. In the light of this, the capacity of medical care to prevent perinatal death is clearly limited by conditions determining the public health in the widest sense. For this reason, the ratio of doctors in the population or per capita expenditure on health care show no consistent relationship to perinatal or infant mortality;[113] conversely, such factors as the size and distribution of the GNP of a country[114] and the proportion of this devoted to military expenditure[115] do show some association with mortality rates.

Concern about perinatal mortality is hardly mysterious; every community is understandably occupied with the prevention of premature death among its citizens. Yet what is puzzling is why this concern surfaces at particular

times and not at others. As Chalmers has observed, the 1970s debate about perinatal mortality erupted at a time when not even crude international perinatal mortality data supported the idea that Britain was doing particularly badly.[116] At the height of this debate, the rate was actually falling faster than at any time since the 1930s, when stillbirth registration began. To argue the case for increased health-care resources to be devoted to the care of mothers and babies in this climate is therefore not, as Russell[117] suggests, simply a rational deduction from the statistics of perinatal death. Rather, it is to make a case based on a set of values and assumptions about *who* are the appropriate people to promote health in any community, and about the allocation of moral responsibility for health to particular groups within it. In every period in which reproductive mortality has been cast as a public-health concern, health has tended to be constructed as an individualized, personal product, and women have been identified as failing to behave in appropriately responsible and maternal ways.[118] Such an ideological framework naturally conceals the extent to which perinatal mortality is a matter of social and economic well-being and so an aspect of the national life on which *social* policies are required.

Critical to the debate about perinatal mortality is an arid and artificial division between medical and social models of health.[119] Those who view perinatal health as a medical-care product find it difficult to admit the influence of social factors, and the same is true the other way round. Policy interventions that bridge the two models by making social changes and evaluating the effect of these on clinical and other outcomes point an important way forward for the future of health and social policy in the perinatal field.[120] Such interventions demonstrate that social care for pregnant women can improve their health and that of their babies. This and other evidence suggest that improving health may be a more appropriate goal for perinatal services in the developed world than reducing mortality.

It is not accidental that the issue of perinatal mortality can be made to fit in different ways into the ideological framework of party politics. A Conservative government may use the evidence of social determinants to disclaim any commitment to the problem at all: the social factors causing babies to die are either beyond the scope of government or too expensive to manipulate, or both. Investment in medical technology is a simpler (but not necessarily cheaper) answer. On the other hand, would it be wise to increase the monopolistic power of professionals over people's lives? From a Socialist point of view, people have an equal right to be healthy, and this includes an equal right to access to health — and medical — care. Perinatal health care owes its origins at least in part to the arguments of women's organizations in the early decades of the twentieth century, that women and children were

disadvantaged through lack of medical attention, but that this was not an argument for ignoring the importance of social conditions. Similar debates are in progress today concerning maternal mortality. In some parts of the world, for example Bangladesh and rural India, mothers are still dying at the same rate – about nine per 1,000 live births – as babies do in the developed world.[121]

In England and Wales, the decline in perinatal and other mortalities now appears to have levelled off – postneonatal mortality rose in 1985/6 after falling in 1983/4. This is more likely to be associated with a deterioration in public health than with pressure on the maternity services.[122] 'Descent is easy,' wrote William Farr a century ago, 'and onward motion over a level road is not difficult; but every step upwards to a higher state encounters obstacles, and so it is in the improvements of the human race.'[123]

10

Birth as a 'Normal' Process

The aims of this chapter are limited, but I hope not limiting. In it, I discuss what is essential (and by implication) valuable about sociologists' contribution to the understanding of birth. I also explore the ideas of *risk* and of *responsibility*, and, in particular, how sociologists, doctors and women see these, and how their different perceptions fit in with different attitudes to the normality, or otherwise, of birth.

PROFESSIONAL IMPERIALISM AND ITS CONSEQUENCES

In many places in the world today, birth is considered an abnormal event. It is an episode in women's lives and in the lives of families which is not part of everyday life, but an occasion for medical surveillance and treatment. Thus, to think about the possible normality of birth requires a deliberate refocusing of one's attention. But what is significant is that such a refocusing was not necessary before birth became the province of experts. Obstetricians and paediatricians are not the only experts on birth who have helped to make it special in this way. Other professional groups have also participated, and benefited, including childbirth educators, social workers, health visitors, psychiatrists, psychologists, sociologists, anthropologists, epidemiologists, technicians and other members of the commercial world surrounding birth. While these different professional groups have had different perspectives on birth, we have all, in effect, collaborated in transforming birth into a professional subject. In making it something which is endlessly debated and dissected in the pages of the academic and scientific press, we have conspired to take it out of the taken-for-granted world and turn it instead into an expert mystery.

One of the characteristics of birth that has got lost in the process of professionalization is that most people in the world, including the so-called professionals, are themselves personally involved in birth. Many of us have given birth or have experienced fatherhood. Yet, because modern industrialized societies are organized around the work–home divide, personal experience has become separated off from professional expertise. We talk about birth as professionals, or as individuals, but these two perspectives are not integrated with one another.

A third difficulty with discussing what sociologists have to say about birth as a normal process is that sociologists, on the whole, have not actually seen birth as a normal process. They have viewed it as a *social* process, which is not quite the same. Indeed, sociological research and commentary in this field really adds up to a statement that there is nothing intrinsically 'normal' or 'natural' about birth. It depends on who you are, where you are and when you are talking about.

RITES OF PASSAGE (AMONG OTHERS)

Thus, one of the most valuable aspects of the sociological perspective is not so much the statement that birth is a normal process, but that it is normal for societies to take different views of birth. It is also the case that these views are not regarded as *separate* from other cultural values and ideologies but as contingent on them. A frequently-quoted analysis here is Arnold van Gennep's classic work *Les Rites de Passage*,[124] which focuses on the tendency for all societies to treat birth and new motherhood in a ritualistic way, but always one that 'fits' with the local culture. The rites surrounding birth are akin to those concerning puberty or death and burial – they serve to mask an individual's transition from one status to another, and are particularly likely to be expressed in relation to changes seen by society as difficult or dangerous in any way. Van Gennep drew attention to the fact that, characteristically, rites of passage have three stages: separation, transition and incorporation. Individuals undergoing them are first removed from ordinary society; second, they are taken through a period of change; and, third, they are returned to the everyday world – albeit in a state different from the original one.

Such observations as these about the cultural management of childbirth put a somewhat different gloss on one's view of normal obstetric practices. Taking up van Gennep's challenge directly, the psychoanalyst Peter Lomas provided a reinterpretation in 1978[125] of modern obstetric practice in which he drew out its ritualistic and irrational aspects. Lomas listed aspects of the contemporary obstetric regime as including:

1. nutritional advice;
2. confinement away from home and family;
3. shaving of the birth area;
4. the medical control of the timing of the birth process, and the use of drugs to relieve labour and pain;
5. the use of a passive position for birth and the treatment of the mother as ignorant and childlike;
6. surgical extraction of the child and/or enlargement of the vaginal orifice;
7. postbirth separation of mother and child.

Described in this way, certain interrelated elements of the prevailing management of birth reveal themselves. First, mother and child are passive patients; the mother's contribution to the birth is minimal. Second, the occasion is one of suffering rather than joy. Third, the predominant mode is impersonal, emphasizing control rather than spontaneity. Fourth, there is a break in the continuity of the mother's life. Fifth, cleanliness, order and formality are emphasized.

Lomas's reinterpretation tends to make normal birth in the industrialized world sound as though it has come out of an anthropological account of life in exotic places. This, of course, is precisely the point. Lomas says:

> Even after as much credence as possible has been given to medical justification for this practice, and even when allowance has been made for the effects of rationalistic-technological philosophy, the phenomenon is sufficiently striking to make us wonder about the meanings that may lie behind it. At a period of history when the importance of individual rights and freedom of expression is not in doubt how can an obstetric regime so antipathetic to these rights gain wide acceptance? . . . Why do professional helpers so usurp the mother's function and why does she let this happen?[126]

Lomas's main answer to this cites male envy of women's reproductive power – not, probably, an explanation that most obstetricians would accept. Yet, the existence of strong professional feelings about the need to control women, and indeed about women themselves, have been amply documented. Two out of many possible examples follow. The first is a 1977 paper by John Beazley entitled 'Controlled Parturition'.[127] Beazley was writing at a time when high induction rates were common, and when the philosophy of 'active management' was gaining support within obstetrics. His paper is a good illustration of this point of view. It begins: 'Many mothers consider that the usual course of spontaneous labour is normal parturition. Nature, however, is not always a reliable ally . . . The logical

extension of good antenatal care is control of parturition.' The extent and timing of such control, according to Beazley, is determined by the extent to which either mother or baby or both may be considered 'at risk', this being established by 'clinical acumen but confirmed by data such as the daily recording of fetal movements, the ultrasonic measurement of fetal growth and development, fetal cardiotocography, and studies on maternal urinary oestriol excretion, liquor amnii and enzymes'. Controlled parturition means that a decision is always made by the obstetrician either to deliver electively or not. He [sic] is advised to consult the paediatrician but not the mother, who is referred to in the following terms: 'Usually the onset of labour is diagnosed by the patient herself and not surprisingly, therefore, the diagnosis is often incorrect'. The final paragraph of Beazley's paper comments that this type of active management of labour has not been properly evaluated. However, 'while statistical support must be of interest to obstetricians . . . a statistical approach to obstetrics does not always reflect the satefy margins involved and should not be the sole determinant of patient management'. This latter statement is rather odd, suggesting as it does that obstetrics is not about science so much as it is about what obstetricians want to do to women.

The second example concerns one of the things that obstetricians have been responsible for doing to women – shaving their pubic hair in labour. When midwife Mona Romney challenged this in a randomized controlled trial and subsequent paper dubbing it an 'unjustified assault',[128] the question arose as to how to infiltrate the trial's findings – that shaving was not only not beneficial but positively harmful – into routine practice. The difficulty was that many midwives were easily persuaded that peak moments in a woman's life are better experienced without being attacked by a razor first, but the doctors were harder to persuade. In one hospital, one consultant became particularly angry and informed the midwives that *his* women would continue to be routinely shaved. One very brave midwife came back with the reply to this consultant: 'well, in that case you'll have to do it yourself'. Since he did not fancy such close encounters, routine shaving was allowed to lapse as a policy.[129]

It is crucial to the sociological view of birth that it happens to, and within, a society, as well as to an individual who may, or may not, be the subject of medical control. Thus, the way in which birth is 'managed' has important implications for society as a whole; for its view of reproduction, for the position of women, for family relationships and for child socialization and the construction of adult personality. As a concrete example, whether or not newborn infants are routinely separated from their mothers may affect the long-term development of personality and family relationships. (It may be

methodologically extremely difficult to find out whether or not this is so; but the critical point is that birth and its management do have this potential.) A second implication flowing from the cultural status of birth is that, from the point of view of the individual woman, her career as a pregnant and parturient patient is not isolated from her other social roles. A woman giving birth may also be the mother of other children, a worker in the home and outside, a wife or daughter responsible for elderly parents, and so on. Beyond all these roles, women are also individuals.

Following the anthropological line of thought for one moment, let us consider what kind of transition rite motherhood in modern society really is. There are at least four key features of the transition to motherhood today. First, it is characteristic of motherhood in the developing world that there is a divorce between motherhood as an *institution* and motherhood as an *experience*. The 'institution' of motherhood is how society — including the medical professionals — defines motherhood. The experience of motherhood is how mothers themselves perceive it. This division has been articulated most clearly by the American writer Adrienne Rich. Motherhood as an institution cannot be touched or seen:

> When we think of motherhood, we are supposed to think of Renoir's blooming women with rosy children at their knees, Raphael's ecstatic madonnas, some Jewish mother lighting the candles in a scrubbed kitchen on Shabbos, her braided loaf lying beneath a freshly ironed napkin. We are not supposed to think of a woman lying in a Brooklyn hospital with ice packs on her aching breasts because she has been convinced she could not nurse her child; of a woman in Africa equally convinced by the producers of US commercial infant formula that her ample breastmilk is inadequate nourishment . . .'[130]

In other words, there is frequently a clash between the way that women are led to think about motherhood (before it happens) and the way it feels to them (when it does). In a study of the transition to motherhood carried out in the mid-1970s,[131] the majority of women interviewed experienced a contradiction between the idealized view of motherhood as a naturally happy state and the lived realities of being a mother. Second, it can be argued that, today, becoming a mother is physically safer than it has ever been, but that this gain in physical safety is more than balanced by an increase in psychosocial hazards. The most obvious manifestation of this is postpartum depression. Third, the major agents controlling and shaping motherhood today are the health professionals, particularly obstetricians. In itself, this is of no particular significance. But it does carry the risk that the needs of mothers as identified by health professionals may not be the needs identified

by mothers themselves. Fourth, motherhood is a life-crisis, a life-event —
threre are many different terms. The essential message is that, for the
individual woman, becoming a mother is an important transition — it is often
accomplished with some difficulty and the need for substantial personal
adjustment. As one mother once said, 'They told me I had a normal delivery,
but that's not what I would have called it'.[132]

Among the many changes that motherhood normally means are
patienthood, institutionalization and occupational career change. All these
carry implications for a mother's identity — that it needs to shift and reform
itself at the same time as preserving a nucleus of stability and consistency.
Again, a sociological perspective on birth highlights these features of the
normal rite of passage that otherwise might not be seen, and seen to be a
problem. Institutionalization, for example, was described by the sociologist
Erving Goffman in a famous essay, first published in 1957. Goffman said
about institutions that:

> First, all aspects of life are conducted in the same place and under the
> same single authority. Second, each phase of the member's daily
> activity is carried out in the immediate company of a large batch of
> others, all of whom are treated alike and required to do the same thing
> together. Third, all phases of [the day's] activities are tightly scheduled
> . . . the whole sequence of activities being imposed from above by a
> system of explicit formal rulings and a body of officials. Finally, the
> various enforced activities are brought together into a single rational
> plan purportedly designed to fulfill the official aims of the institution.[133]

This last point is extremely important, for it often seems to outsiders that an
institution such as a maternity hospital exists not to provide services for
mothers but to justify its own existence. One is led to the impression that
many people who run hospitals feel that they would do so much more
efficiently if there were no patients at all. This attitude is not, of course,
confined to the medical sphere. It exists among academics, for example
(where the progress of one's work is constantly hampered by the presence of
students), and is to be found also in department stores, which would get
along much better without shoppers, or among those responsible for railway
systems, whose trains suffer from the inconvenient and expensive
impediment of having to carry passengers from time to time.

Goffman also makes the point that a consequence of institutionalization is
that persons can be moved in blocks and are supervised by personnel whose
chief activity is not guidance or periodic inspection but, rather, simply
surveillance — in the interests of the policing of the institution itself. Some
personal consequences of these structures for the inmates of institutions are

that they lose their individual identity when they enter them – for instance, they cannot wear their own clothes. They lose their privacy, by becoming the public object of other people's attention; other people exchange information about them without consulting them. In Britain, hospital case-notes are marked 'confidential – the property of the hospital'. It is argued in favour of this system that patients would not understand, and/or might be worried by, what is written inside the notes. This, then, of course, becomes self-evidently true, as people write in the notes incomprehensible or worrying things.

Women's passage to motherhood, which is something of considerable importance both to women and to society, is rendered more difficult by its technical management – the fact that birth is medicalized, is bereft of its normality, almost by definition. The obstetrical definition of a normal birth is just that – the obstetrical definition. It is an expert's view of what constitutes normality, and, as such, may or may not (but is not very likely to) coincide with other people's. Normality and rationality are not the same thing. Indeed, following Lomas' interpretation, modern obstetric practice is in some fundamental way *irrational*, that is anti-reason and by implication internally illogical or contradictory. One particular aspect of motherhood – breastfeeding – provides a good illustration of this.

THE MILK OF KINDNESS?

Breastfeeding is regarded as good practice today. Women are encouraged to breastfeed and to continue breastfeeding for at least four to six months.[134] The health-promoting consequences of breastfeeding have been tracked as far as adulthood; adults who were breastfed as babies are less prone to coronary heart disease.[135] The long-term beneficial effects on the health of breastfeeding mothers are beginning to emerge, as the epidemiologists sort out the relation between parturition and risks of reproductive cancer, for example, on the one hand, and the possible impact of parturition plus sustained lactation on the other. But in the short term, and for babies, there is really no dispute about the fact that what babies ought to have is human milk. Breastfeeding is, in other words, a normal concomitant of birth. Birth does not end with the delivery of the baby, but rather with the delivery of a healthy young person into the adult world (a feat which is altogether much more difficult to accomplish than merely being allowed to give birth to them).

We have here, then, a clear example of a health practice which all the experts agree ought to be promoted. However, when we examine what is actually happening, we see that, in industrialized countries, the most important factor behind the decline in the incidence of breastfeeding which

started in the mid-nineteenth century was the promotion of artificial milk by the medical profession, at first only for sick babies and babies who could not be breastfed, but then subsequently for all infants. As Rima Apple puts it in her social history of infant feeding,

> Based on increasingly sophisticated analyses of human and cow's milk, the creation of 'scientific' infant formulas provided a rationale for growing medical intervention in childcare. Once their research had disclosed the variable nature of breastmilk, some physicians promoted artificial feeding with a food compounded of known ingredients in preference to the uncertainty of maternal nursing. For medical practitioners, artificial feeding came to represent an important and lucrative aspect of medical practice.[136]

The result was an epidemic switch to bottlefeeding, as many mothers came to believe doctors when they represented this as a better, more 'scientific' alternative to natural feeding. From the doctors' point of view, bottled milk had the advantage that its quantity could be measured. A concern with quantification – with quantity rather than quality – is built into the medical-scientific paradigm, with the result that what can be seen to be measured is also seen to be better. Hence Beazley's dismissal, quoted earlier, of maternal diagnoses of labour in preference to mechanical ones – the evidence of the needle that writes the pattern of uterine contractions on the graph paper. Hence the delight displayed at evidence of fetal vitality on an ultrasound scanner versus scepticism regarding women's reports – and so on. In relation to baby feeding, the concern with quantification *did* extend to breastfeeding, of course, and many health professionals worldwide persisted – still persist – in the iniquitous habit of 'test-weighing' breastfed babies before and after feeds, with a profound disregard for the fact that production of milk occurs in a body connected to a psyche – breastfeeding is the best exemplar of a psychosomatic process there is.

In the USA and the UK, the result of this was that, by the 1950s, most babies were bottlefed. Mothers' loss of confidence in natural feeding combined with changed notions of women's sexuality to produce genuine difficulties for those who wanted to breastfeed. Once bottlefeeding had become widespread, the female breast became an embarrassing private object. So private, in fact, that when historian Edward Shorter wrote his *A History of Women's Bodies*, he did not mention breasts at all. Female breasts lack a history – they lost it along with their status as organs of nutrition. More recently, the change in medical opinion about breastfeeding has been accompanied by a move back to the breast. In Britain, for example, while fifty per cent of mothers breastfed initially in 1975, sixty-seven per cent did so in

1980. The biggest increase is in mothers of second or subsequent babies, forty-two per cent of whom breastfed initially in 1975, while sixty per cent did so in 1980. Breastfeeding also lasts longer now, with two-thirds of mothers continuing beyond six weeks, as compared with half only five years ago. Despite these changes, only one in fourteen mothers in the UK breastfeeds as long as the officially recommended four months. The same social pattern still obtains as was found in earlier surveys: breastfeeding rates are higher among highly-educated middle-class mothers aged twenty-five or over and living in London or the South-East. For unknown reasons, Scottish mothers are significantly less likely to breastfeed than English or Welsh mothers.

We can document the social factors associated with breastfeeding as a concomitant of birth's status as a precursor of normal childcare, but we can also look more closely at the medical factors involved. There is a great deal of evidence showing that successful breastfeeding is jeopardized by the same medical structures that argue for its promotion. The two national surveys of infant feeding in Britain carried out in 1975 and 1980 indicate some of the mechanisms responsible. The first is the amount of time between delivery and the first feed. The likelihood that mothers will stop breastfeeding within two weeks of birth increases with the amount of time elapsing between birth and the first feed. Twice as many women stop breastfeeding when the interval to the first feed is twenty-four hours or more, as compared with less than one hour.[13] Fortunately, professional practice changes, and the three per cent of babies who went straight to the breast in 1975 had become sixteen per cent in 1980. This is particularly clear evidence of how professional behaviour can directly affect the process of becoming a mother. Other medical factors identified as especially important in the two feeding surveys were Caesarean delivery, a general anaesthetic, and the baby's admission to special care – all of which prejudiced the chances of successful breastfeeding independently of other factors. In the second survey, when the events of labour and delivery were looked at together, three factors had a strong and independent association with early termination of breastfeeding: the baby's birthweight, having a general anaesthetic and not putting the baby to the breast within four hours of birth. This survey also showed that the longer stays in hospital (more than six days) were associated with giving up breastfeeding by the time the baby was two weeks old, as was feeding at set times other than demand feeding.[138]

Any reasonable interpretation of these statistics would argue that the promotion of breastfeeding requires the prevention of medical intervention. Yet, while some things are improving (there was more demand feeding in hospital in 1980 than in 1975, for example), other things, for example the use

of Caesarean section, are becoming demonstrably worse. Some of this confused medical double-think is due to the division between obstetrics on the one hand and paediatrics on the other. This has always served to separate the interests of the mother and baby, whose destinies are inextricably linked together – and, of course, breastfeeding is *the* prime example of this. However, we can also note that, in relation to breastfeeding, obstetricians appear to want to have their cake and eat it too. The female breast has recently acquired a new status as a means of inducing labour. In a randomized controlled trial of nipple-stimulation, this was found to be an effective method of ripening the cervix and probably one that is safer and cheaper than medical methods such as 'sweeping the membranes' or the use of prostaglandins.[139] (Another natural method for inducing labour, which does not cost anything but is not yet popular with doctors, is sexual intercourse.)

Health professionals are important advisors to new mothers as to feeding, but so are non-professionals. Nearly half the women in the 1980 survey named midwives, nurses and doctors as giving advice about feeding, and a similar proportion said that they had also received advice from friends or relatives. The study of first-time motherhood in London, quoted earlier, found that sixty-three per cent of women were advised about feeding by their own mothers.[140] To be given advice is one thing; but one profound cultural change occurring over the last half-century in many countries is the loss of a collective knowledge about breastfeeding within the female community. Seeing mothers breastfeeding is no longer a normal part of childhood for most children. Part of this collective cultural loss concerns support for the breastfeeding mother: in her book *The Tender Gift*, the anthropologist Dana Raphael contends that mothers need mothering (the support of other women) for successful breastfeeding to take place.[141] However, health professionals often seem quite unhappy about such lay interventions in motherhood, possibly because the advice conveyed is contrary to the professional model and probably because 'the subversive power of sisterhood' is out of their control.

It is possible to demonstrate the role which such an intervention can play. In a study of social support in pregnancy carried out between 1985 and 1989, mothers who were offered social support were more likely to put their babies to the breast earlier than those who had not been given social support. It is worth noting that the purpose of the social support intervention was not to promote breastfeeding, but to promote health in a general sense. We did hypothesize that one result of enhanced support might be increased maternal self-confidence, and this finding, among others, would seem to bear this out.[142]

FRAMES OF REFERENCE

Breastfeeding is a specific example of a contradiction between two views: that birth is a normal process and that birth is a medical event. Some years ago, the sociologist Hilary Graham and I pooled data from two research projects concerning parenthood to explore the extent to which these different and conflicting perspectives marked the different positions of women and obstetricians.[143] This is what we found: that the emphasis on normality exists in mothers' accounts of childbirth with other features of this event, including its status as a normal and continuous part of a woman's life.

Criteria of the success of reproduction from the mother's point of view are not restricted to the prevention of perinatal mortality and physical morbidity, but are evaluated more holistically. Within this perspective, mothers view themselves as possessing an authentic and valid knowledge about reproduction. Conversely, obstetricians view birth primarily as a medical event and, as such, as isolated from the rest of life. Childbirth is about parenthood, not about personhood. Criteria of success hinge upon the production of low mortality statistics, and success is seen as dependent on the subjection of mothers to specialist medical knowledge. We called these differences conflicts between two opposing 'frames of reference', each of which is internally consistent, accepted within the relevant peer group. Indeed, its acceptance has so much of a taken-for-granted aspect that it may not be reflected upon or articulated directly.

It is often said that the point of greatest disagreement between mothers and obstetricians lies in the notion, espoused by mothers and not by doctors, that pregnancy and birth are not inherently illnesses but episodes of health. This is to oversimplify; many women's experiences of pregnancy and birth have characteristics in common with illness – for example, unpleasant physical symptoms and suffering – but the two sets of experiences differ primarily in *context*. Accordingly, when considering the issue of perspectives on normality, it is crucial to note that much of the discussion that goes on omits the fact that the world possesses a second group of professionals on birth whose training and rationale makes them, in important ways, the guardians of the normal – midwives. Their role in all this gives them an essential gatekeeping function. The future of childbirth – whether or not it is allowed to regain the status which it once had as a normal part of life – will depend largely on what happens to, and within, midwifery. If midwifery continues as an independent occupation oriented around the idea that childbirth is not about medicine at all, then the phrase 'birth as a normal process' will have some meaning. If, on the other hand, the present erosion and devaluation of midwifery skills and autonomy continues, then the

normality of birth will belong to a golden age of the past — or a science-fiction future.

The disjunction between medical and maternal frames of reference is linked to other differences of opinion about the *risks* and *responsibilities* of childbirth. These have been given a good deal of attention by sociologists over the past few years. As a subspeciality of sociology in general, medical sociology began to emerge in the 1950s as a response to the inability of mechanical-biological models of health and illness to explain *chronic* illness conditions. By this time, in industrialized countries, acute conditions were becoming much less important in the total pattern of morbidity. It was necessary to develop *multicausal* models of illness in which social factors could be identified as playing a major part.

Sociologists' interest in birth developed within the new multicausal model. This meant, and continues to mean, that sociologists draw attention to the impact on pregnancy outcome of factors such as poverty, bad housing, poor diet, stressful life-events, lack of social support and so on. The starting point for this exercise is very often the well-known picture of social-class differences in adverse pregnancy outcomes. These differences are found in all countries that collect occupational data on parents, and the gap between the life-chances of infants in socially disadvantaged as compared with advantaged families shows no sign of narrowing. As has been repeatedly said, however, to identify a social-class difference is not to explain anything; on the contrary, it is to point to a problem that requires an explanation.

One important corollary of the focus on social-class differences is the use made within the medical frame of reference of social class as a 'risk' factor. Central to the obstetric definition of birth as a medical event is the concern to predict risk, to identify in advance those factors which will mean that something is likely to go wrong. As a matter of fact, the general failure of this exercise has led to the reductio ad absurdum of the risk approach, which is that every woman and fetus is at risk until proved otherwise. This is like the nineteenth-century medical positivist view (at the time largely a consequence of doctors' ignorance about reproduction) that no woman could definitely be said to be pregnant until she had given birth to a baby.[144] Social class acquires status as a risk factor *because* working-class women have more medical and health problems than middle-class women. In the well-known prenatal risk-scoring system of Hobel and colleagues in the USA, low social class belongs in the 'miscellaneous' group of factors that should alert obstetricians to the likelihood of disaster.[145] In view of the evidence

about the statistical association between low social class and adverse pregnancy outcome, it may be argued in some quarters that this is a reasonable attitude to take. Consider, however, for a moment the implications of this for obstetric practice, and for women categorized as working-class. Not only do women perceived and classed in this way have to contend with the real effect of bad housing conditions, unemployment, insufficient income and so forth, but they also have to deal with the negative view imposed on them as a result of the medical labelling process.

The health risks of adverse social conditions are different from the other categories of risk in two senses, namely that individuals have rather little control over the possibility of correcting them, and that the medical frame of reference locates such factors squarely outside the scope of the personal health services. The fact that poverty is the biggest known risk to the health of mothers and babies is not something that most obstetricians wish to take on board. The problem of poverty belongs to the social workers or the sociologists or the politicians. Yet, at the same time, the room for obstetrical manoeuvre does include the attempt to correct some of the personal consequences of poverty – for example, the habit of smoking in pregnancy, which research has shown to be associated predominantly with the burden of caring work in difficult social circumstances rather than with women's ignorance of its adverse reproductive effects.[146] What is a risk is, from another point or view, also a matter of *responsibility*. This comes out very clearly in the literature on women's smoking, which demonstrates that, while smoking may be considered a risk to the fetus, it is very often a mechanism by means of which the mother acts out her responsibility to that child, to her other children, and to everyone for whom she cares, as smoking helps her to cope and to claim some authentic activity and personal space in an otherwise crowded and impossible life.

A sociological perspective on birth can put a broader context round these issues of risk and responsibility than it is possible to find in a medical textbook. For example, and globally speaking, one of the biggest risk factors for the healthy survival of infants is the orientation on the part of many of the world's governments to death – in the form of arms expenditure – rather than to life. Alternatively, we can put the risk of childbirth into the context of other kinds of risk that people voluntarily or involuntarily take: the risk of a woman in an industrialized country dying in childbirth is about the same as the risk of death posed by two years' factory work or by riding 200 miles as a motorcycle passenger, for example.[147] This kind of statistical picture can be interpreted on a number of levels. But it is evident from research on women's experiences of childbirth that many women feel that what medical management above all prevents them from doing is taking responsibility for

their own behaviour and decisions during the process of childbearing. The wish to be seen as morally responsible is in part a claim to be seen as properly adult, and is certainly viewed as preferable to the kind of moral culpability foisted on women by obstetricians who deem women irresponsible and selfish (or childish) in some of the decisions that we choose to make.

In the Hobel risk-prediction scheme, having given birth to a previous low-birthweight baby is deemed an obstetric risk, and indeed it is so seen and treated in many places, including the four hospitals in which the social support project mentioned above was carried out. All the women in this study had a history of low-birthweight babies, and all were subjected to intensified clinical surveillance as a result. We asked them how they saw low birthweight. Two-thirds of them did not see it as a problem in itself. Many made comments indicating that they found the medical view of a history of low birthweight being a risk factor in the current pregnancy distinctly unhelpful. This was what one woman said, referring to the research as a whole:

> I hope this information will lead to some kind of service being offered to mothers of prospective small babies. Why people have small babies in the first place is obviously the object of this survey, and I hope this question is answered. However, I do think the attitudes of medical and other persons to a second pregnancy do not help in the prevention of another small baby. Being told to rest, not to garden, iron, hoover, carry shopping etc., having extra scans booked when three months pregnant and generally being made to feel a failure as a pregnant woman must, I am sure, go a long way to producing further small babies . . . Perhaps a survey of larger-than-average babies would produce some interesting results.

She may well be right. But it is not normal to consult those who use the maternity services about the kind of research that they want to see done. The other side of the coin of unproductive medical advice is the tendency which many women note for health professionals not to take mothers' own worries seriously. Here is another woman on this very point:

> You didn't ask about the doctors; most of them treated you like a nobody, didn't want to take the time to explain anything to you. I was in hospital six times . . . and each time I saw different doctors and when I did see the same doctor twice he said, what are you doing here again, and he didn't mean it as a joke . . . they just don't know how you feel inside, sick with worry . . . I had a small, premature baby, then my second pregnancy ended in miscarriage, so it's no wonder that I was

worried when I was carrying this one. But it makes you feel worse when the doctors don't understand or don't want to understand the fear that you feel for your unborn baby.

These are some of the ways in which doctors' understandings about birth differ from the understandings of those for whom they care. In the process of becoming a matter for experts, the danger is that the real expert – the mother – loses her own right to knowledge and control.

11

The Changing Social Context
of Maternity Care

Childbirth has always been the subject of science fiction. From novels such as Aldous Huxley's *Brave New World* (1932) to Marge Piercy's *Woman on the Edge of Time* (1979), and countless others, the challenge has been to understand both the extent to which reproduction and the associated unequal roles of the sexes can be changed, and the ways in which these help to determine the different positions of men and women in the wider society. For the Director of Hatcheries and Conditioning in Huxley's *Brave New World*, it was simply a matter of obtaining the raw reproductive material and controlling not only gestation but also childrearing. Women received six months' salary in return for yielding one ovary, which in laboratory conditions was capable of growing thousands of identical individuals in a short space of time. 'Parent' and especially 'mother' were dirty words. In Marge Piercy's novel, describing another kind of future society, reproduction takes place in a brooder where genetic material is stored and mixed and where babies are grown in tanks, fed with sounds of the human heart and human voices. This is presented as a choice that a particular society has made.[148] More usually in science fiction, the novelist's speculative imagination obstinately refuses to face up to the archaic constraints of the old mode of reproduction. The American writer Marilyn Hacker recalls being repeatedly distressed as a teenage science-fiction reader with

a 3052 AD where all women mentioned were secretaries or housewives off somewhere invisible with the children; the one woman on the spaceship crew who develops a craving for pickles at the pre blast-off banquet – Guess Why? – and is left behind in a vine-covered cottage to Fulfil Her Real Function . . .'[149]

In thinking about the future, we must distinguish between those of our present social arrangements that we can expect, realistically, to change and those that we cannot expect to change. In making predictions about how, as a society, we will provide for childbirth in the future, we need to take on board a number of different considerations. These include cultural values about childbirth, children, women, men and families; the social positions of mothers and fathers; the social positions of midwives and doctors; the social organization of maternity care; the role of health professionals and of the community in securing its own health; and the division of welfare between public and private sectors. This chapter focuses on three themes within this broad agenda. The first of these is the *demographic context* within which maternity care is being, and will be, provided in the 1990s. Second, there are *changes in family life*. The third topic is the ways in which those who *use* the maternity services are likely to interact with those who *provide* them: how will we build on the challenges and the struggles of the 1980s?

THE DEMOGRAPHIC CONTEXT

Projecting from the 1980s to the 1990s, the following generalizations emerge from a number of different recent reports. First, childbirth is becoming less popular. Between 1970 and 1987 in the UK, the number of children per woman dropped from 2.44 to 1.82. In most other EC countries, the decrease was greater. Related to this, a woman's age at first childbirth is rising: from 23.9 in 1970 to 26.4 in 1987 for births within marriage, and from 24.5 in 1980 to 25.0 in 1987 for all births. There are proportionately more births among older women. The proportion of women who never have children is increasing; while ninety per cent of those born in 1945 are mothers, this is expected to fall to eighty-three per cent among women born in 1955. Again, similar trends are observable elsewhere in Europe. The birth rate is expected to peak in the early 1990s, when the large generation born in the 1960s are having children, and thereafter to decline. If these trends continue, births in the UK will exceed deaths until 2030, when the position will be reversed and there will be a net decline in the population (assuming, of course, no increase in immigration).[150]

Quite how this deferment of childbearing is being achieved is something of a mystery, given the decreased provision of contraceptive services. However, perhaps Kenneth Clarke was right when he suggested that there is little connection between the level of unwanted pregnancies and family planning services.[151] As a context for maternity care, the cuts in these services, and particularly the offloading of responsibility from family planning clinics to GPs, are serving to reduce women's choices. It is estimated that fewer than half of all GPs are trained to fit the cap or IUD,[152] which, given

the trend for oral contraception to become less popular,[153] may pose something of a problem. Pregnancy terminations have been increasing since 1983. Between 1988 and 1989, there was a fourteen per cent rise. At the same time, regional differences in the availability of termination of pregnancy continue; in south Birmingham in 1988, only one per cent of terminations carried out on women living in the district were within the NHS, whereas ninety-nine per cent of women in north Devon were able to obtain an NHS termination.[154] The increase in terminations is proportionately greater for younger women, among whom there has been a fourfold increase from the late 1960s to the late 1980s.[155] Indeed, the increased exposure of young women to the risks of pregnancy and childbirth is one of the most marked social trends of the 1980s. In the mid-1960s, one in fifty girls and one in seventeen boys said that they had had sexual intercourse before the age of sixteen. In 1988, these figures had risen to a striking one in two for girls and one in three for boys.[156] Although Victoria Gillick's attempts to prevent doctors from giving confidential contraceptive advice to under-sixteens were unsuccessful, we do not know the extent to which the sexually-experienced young are able to obtain the contraceptive information and help that they need, and we can only speculate on the long-term impact of earlier and earlier sexual experience on conception, pregnancy and childbirth.

The second major change likely to continue into the 1990s is that the attractions of marriage as a context for childbirth appear to have worn thin. One in four of all births are now to unmarried women. This represents an increase of nearly 250 per cent in a decade,[157] and is a new cultural pattern: before 1960, the proportion of births to unmarried women had remained stable at about four to five per cent for fifty years, with the exception of the two World Wars (which both produced a temporary increase in the proportion of women having babies without the benefits – or otherwise – of marriage). In some areas today, for example inner London, *more* than one in four births now take place outside marriage, and the rate is substantially higher in some ethnic groups, particularly Afro-Caribbean women, where births outside marriage may soon exceed those within, making so-called legitimate babies the deviation rather than the norm. Indeed, this is already the case in Sweden. Within the EC, the UK has the fourth-highest rate of births outside marriage. Our rate is also higher than that of the USA.[158]

However, it is not quite right to say that marriage is no longer popular; in fact, the UK also has the highest marriage rate in Europe. During the 1970s and 1980s, the rate of marriage among men and women at ages thirty and over remained more or less unchanged. It is among the young that the change has occurred, with only one-fifth the rate of marriages among the

under-twenties at the end of the 1980s compared to twenty years earlier.[159] As we all know, however, people's continued willingness to try marriage, at least in certain age groups, is meeting with decreasing chances of success. As well as having the highest marriage rate, the UK also has the second-highest divorce rate in Europe (Denmark is first).

OTHER CHANGES IN FAMILY LIFE

The second theme follows from the first, and is concerned with the extent to which *family life has changed.* It is, of course, one thing to cite the statistics of birth and marriage, and quite another to interpret their meaning. On the surface, at least, the declining popularity of marriage does not mean the disappearance of fathers. Along with the increase in births outside marriage has gone an increasing tendency for these to be registered by both parents. Whereas only four per cent of live births outside marriage were registered by both parents in 1971, one in five were so registered in 1989.[160] Many mothers who are not married to their children's fathers are living with them. Nonetheless, the result of these demographic and other changes has meant a decline in the traditional family – defined as a married couple living with their dependent children – as the context within which children are born and reared. Most people in the UK no longer live in such families. Over the last thirty years, there has been a large increase both in single-person households and in lone-parent families. The latter have more than doubled over this period. One in seven of all families with dependent children is now a lone-parent family,[161] and one in five children under sixteen does not live with both his or her natural parents.[162] But in the midst of this change, there is also stability: ninety per cent of all lone parents are women, a figure which has changed little over thirty years.[163] At the other end of the age range, long-term demographic changes resulting in an increase in the elderly as a group within the population also have an impact on family life, by increasing the amount of caring that has to be done within the community. The 1980 Women and Employment survey found that one in eight adult women provided regular caring services for another adult, usually a parent or parent-in-law.[164] With the government policy of community care, which serves as a euphemism for women's unpaid caring services, this burden of dependency is likely to increase.

The mother of the 1990s is therefore more likely than her own mother to have children later, and without being married, or, if married, to experience a change in her family circumstances precipitating her into lone motherhood. She is more likely to have other relatives to care for, as well as her own children. She is also considerably more likely to have paid employment of her own. Once again, the UK comes second to Denmark in terms of having

the highest economic activity rate for women. In more than half of all families with dependent children, both parents are employed.[165] A majority of mothers of dependent children are now employed, a figure which includes forty per cent of women with under-fives, rising to seventy-five per cent of those whose youngest child is aged between eleven and fifteen.[166] Structural changes in the distribution of jobs between different employment sectors mean that employment among women, including among mothers, is likely to rise further in the 1990s, becoming an important safety net to prevent families from falling into poverty with the rise in male unemployment and the increase in lone motherhood. Some three-quarters of potentially poor households are moved out of poverty by women's earnings.[167]

If this makes mothers sound as though they have too much to do, that is exactly the picture conveyed by division-of-labour and time-budget surveys. In all households, women have less leisure time than men; for example, women in full-time employment enjoy thirty-three hours' leisure per week compared with forty-four hours for similarly-employed men.[168] Other work has shown that the presence of a man in the household, irrespective of whether there are children or not, is what makes a difference to women's disposable time.[169] Time-budget surveys show that eighty-seven per cent of the care provided for children under five is given by their mothers, and only thirteen per cent by their fathers.[170] The British Social Attitudes survey data on the division of labour between men and women in the home shows almost no change over the 1980s in the gender-distribution of household tasks. For example, five per cent of men made the evening meal in 1983 compared with six per cent in 1987, while one per cent of men did the washing and the ironing in 1983 and two per cent in 1987. A consistent finding of many studies is that men are more likely to say that they do more in the house than women say they do.[171] When women are employed full-time, the men with whom they live do more in the way of household work than when women have part-time jobs or no employment at all, though which comes first here is difficult to disentangle – are helpful men making it possible for women to 'work', or is a 'working' woman a spur to male helpfulness?

Whatever men do, or do not do, they are present in maternity care now in a way that they were not thirty years ago, and there would seem to be no reason for this presence not to continue. From a more or less absolute ban at delivery in the late 1960s, we have now reached the point at which it is deviant for there not to be a man in the delivery room. In the 1955 edition of *Baby and Child Care*, Benjamin Spock described the modal paternal experience of childbirth at the time in the following, both optimistic and pessimistic terms: 'He helps to get his wife safely to hospital, where there are

dozens of people to take care of her. Then he's really alone . . . It's no wonder that a man may take this occasion to drink in company at a bar'.[172] Research carried out by Anne Woollett and colleagues shows that paternal attendance at birth was rare before 1970 but became the norm during that decade.[173] The study by Jo Garcia and colleagues of mothers' experiences in the Dublin electronic monitoring trial[174] found an increase of more than sixty per cent over four years in one hospital. But while it is clear that men are expected to be in the delivery room, it remains unclear as to what they are supposed to do there.[175] Some years ago, Joel Richman and colleagues concluded from a survey of 100 British fathers that

> In some ways the father's presence at birth can be likened to a small boy permitted to enter the sanctum of the school staffroom. He has to learn his way around the hospital. He can be dismissed at will when the doctor makes an examination. His rights to be present are limited and vague . . . At birth he is not certain what to do, where to stand or where to put his hands.[176]

In the study by Woollett and colleagues, men's inferior status at birth was emphasized in the clothes they were asked to wear – gowns, masks, hats and shoe covers. During a shortage of gowns, the men were even asked to don pink, flowery nightgowns, thus further emphasizing their lowly status (by making them look like women).[177] Once the baby is born, there is more for fathers to do. Not surprisingly, they do similar things to mothers at this point, such as hold the baby, touch it and admire it. Research shows that, when left alone with newborn babies, fathers spend more time looking at babies than holding them, though they are more likely to hold boys than girls.[178] In Woollett and colleagues' study, fathers stayed three-and-a-half minutes longer in the delivery room when boys were born, and talked much more to sons than daughters. Typical remarks were: 'Hello little fellow, you're here now', or 'That's it, let the world know you're here mate'.[179] By comparison, mothers did not distinguish between sons and daughters, except in the presence of fathers, when they were more likely to make comments about their daughters.

Compared to the delivery room, far fewer men – around eight per cent in some surveys – venture into the antenatal clinic.[180] Though some of the early enthusiasm for fathers' involvement in maternity care claimed that attending fathers were more likely to be involved with their infants subsequently, it now appears that an effect on male domestic participation washes out over time.[181] This was also the finding of a randomized controlled trial of social support in pregnancy, where the intervention of a home-visiting midwife succeeded in making men more likely to help the

mothers of their children in the period immediately after delivery, but this effect had disappeared by the time the children were one year old.[182]

Motherhood, and the ways in which mothers and babies are cared for or not, is not only a matter of fact — of establishing what people do and how they do it. At the heart of many of our past, present and future dilemmas in this area is the conflict between expectations and ideals on the one hand, and reality on the other. This is a problem on a number of levels, including for women undergoing the transition to motherhood, who may find the contrast between the way that they thought motherhood was going to be and the way that it is quite literally depressing,[183] and for children and young people exposed to school-based education-for-parenthood programmes, who are presented with a view of childbirth which bypasses the mother as main actor and is insensitive to emotional aspects of the experience.[184] But, in these respects, individual exposure merely mirrors cultural experience. The recent report of the Institute for Public Policy Research on *The Family Way*[185] highlights this fundamental tendency for there to be a gap between what people think ought to be happening in families and what is increasingly happening on the level of individual experience. More people hold to the notion of a proper family as one where the mother does not 'work' than are willing (or able) to practise it. More people advocate the participation of fathers in family life and household work than live in egalitarian households. For example, in the British Social Attitudes survey, caring for sick children equally was practised by thirty per cent of married couples, but viewed prescriptively as an ideal by fifty-one per cent.[186] The perception of family life as a set of ideals may in part be responsible for the high rate of remarriage leading to that abhorrently-phrased phenomenon, 'reconstituted families'. Following the general pattern observed earlier, men are more likely to remarry than women, more likely to do so sooner rather than later, and more likely to cohabit in the interim than women.[187] Reconstituted families are at high risk of dissolution, particularly where both husband and wife have children from previous unions. The same tendency for people to believe in the importance of heterosexual family life, while at the same time finding it difficult, may lie behind the fashion for admitting fathers to delivery rooms. It is the ritual and the beliefs that are important; the facts of the matter are less so.

One fact of the matter is money. Increasingly in the 1980s and the 1990s, the maternity services have had, and will have, to contend with the fact that Britain has an increasingly poor population, and that the poorest groups in the population are women and children. Around one in four of all British children now live in or on the margins of poverty. Poverty is a fact of life for two out of ten two-parent families and seven out of ten lone-parent families

(here, poverty is defined as not more than 140 per cent of the old supplementary-benefit or present income-support level).[188] An often-quoted fact is that, by the year 2000 in countries such as the UK and the USA, the poverty population is expected to consist entirely of women and children living on their own. Historical work has shown that, throughout the twentieth century, women and children have been more likely to live in poverty than men; it is just that recently the 'poverty division of labour' has been better documented.[189]

The reasons for this are complex. Important factors include the relative material disadvantage imposed on *people* through having children, the failure of *marriage* to protect women and children financially, and the culturally-imposed *inability of women as lone parents* to provide for their children at the same level as is possible for men. For example, when one looks at the financial fates and likely futures of families with children compared to those without, the figures show a pattern of increasing inequality. Households with children are coming to occupy a proportionately larger share of the low-income band.[190] Between 1979 and 1985, the proportion of couples with children in the bottom band of disposable income rose from three to eighteen per cent. Under the influence particularly of Thatcherite policies, the distribution of income and ownership of wealth became increasingly unequal in the 1980s.[191] Increased male unemployment contributes, although in a quarter of poor families the family 'head' is in full-time work.[192] There has been a corresponding increase in homelessness – between 1978 and 1989, there was a 240 per cent increase in the number of homeless families in Britain.[193]

Money is only one of a number of resources which contribute to health and well-being. Others, including space, time and food, also show a pattern of distribution which disadvantages women and children.[194] The title of Margaret Forster's recent novel *Have the Men Had Enough?*[195] describes a cultural system of prioritizing male needs which many of us might like to think of as belonging to the past but which is, unhappily, still with us, and is likely to form part of the context within which maternity care is provided in the 1990s.[196] Some years ago, the Maternity Alliance showed how the income of many families is unable to support an adequate diet for pregnant women,[197] and this is likely to become increasingly the case in the future. Although pregnant women and young children need to be prioritized in the policy agenda, this is often not what happens, though the intention may of course not be to discriminate. For example, research on transport use shows the crucially declining availability of, but need for, low-cost public transport among women and children in low-income families. In one study, a mother whose young child had swallowed bleach had to locate an unvandalized

telephone, organize a babysitter for her other children and make a complicated bus journey before getting the child to hospital.[198]

Behind both the misfortunes of families and the specific straits of female-headed lone-parent families is the social position of women as mothers. Despite the efforts of feminism in the 1970s and 1980s, women's status in the public world remains secondary and their role in the domestic world primary. As we have seen, within families, women still do the major share of caring work − not only of children, but also of men and of other family members. Within the paid workforce, they are far more likely to be in part-time, poorly-paid, low-status work than men. Eighty per cent of employed women are semi-skilled part-time workers.[199] Without social-policy changes permitting a different domestic division of labour to emerge, women's unequal burden of caring work will remain and intensify during the 1990s. As with the links between women's paid work and men's 'help' in the home, what happens in the public and private sectors is complementary and mutually reinforcing. If women do unpaid caring work, they cannot perform the same non-domestic roles as men; if women are allocated the lowest-status, worst-paid jobs, the rationale for doing the unpaid caring work is even greater. Using data from the 1980 Women and Employment survey, Heather Joshi has shown that a typical British mother who gives birth to and brings up two children will forego earnings of £122,000 over her lifetime. The lost earnings are consequent on a period of absence from the labour force, but part-time work and low-paid work make a heavy contribution.[200] Since the lost-earnings formula is sensitive to the interval between births − more earnings are foregone when the interval is larger − this fact may help to explain the tendency for intervals between births to have decreased recently among UK mothers.[201]

Women's work as childbearers and childrearers is performed mostly unpaid and in private, within the 'sanctity' of the home. A striking feature of British family life is the low level of provision for out-of-home child care. Both in absolute and relative terms, this is low, and the trend is towards less, not more. Fewer than one per cent of British under-fives have access to local-authority day nursery places, and fewer than one per cent of primary-school children have access to out-of-school care facilities.[202] Although employer-provided creches have received some media attention recently, a survey found only 198 out of 1,100,000 women were in a position to use these facilities.[203] In the European league, the UK does badly, providing publicly-funded child care for only two per cent of children under three, compared with forty-four per cent in Denmark, twenty-five per cent in France, five per cent in Italy and four per cent in Portugal.[204] Since British children are as likely as or more likely than their other European counterparts

to have no parent at home full-time to care for them, negotiating and resourcing child care is a difficult business carried out on an individual basis and consisting of piecemeal packages of relatives, friends, neighbours and paid childminders for the majority of working parents who cannot afford the middle-class convenience of a nanny.[205]

THE FUTURE OF THE CONSUMER MOVEMENT

The third theme has to do with the relationship between women and families as users of the maternity services on the one hand and the providers of these services on the other. What kind of relationship is this likely to be in the 1990s? How will it differ, if at all, from the relationship which we all know and love from the 1980s?

In the 1980s, pregnancy care as a branch of medicine had recently become the focus of 'much debate and controversy in both medical and lay circles'.[206] Contentious issues had been raised in relation to objectives of care, the role of the consumer and the contributions of the different professional groups. Other issues on the agenda were: the need to evaluate the effectiveness of antenatal care; consumer views; community-based initiatives; psychological aspects of childbirth and parent–child relationships; the advantages and disadvantages of home and hospital delivery; the roles of obstetrician, midwife and GP in modern obstetric care; and the desirability of preparation-for-parenthood programmes.[207]

The period from the early 1970s to the late 1980s stands out as *the* era of the consumer movement in maternity care. There is no doubt that by 1980 the professionals providing maternity care had had to assimilate a sustained attack on their expertise. Beginning as a protest against high induction rates, this had quickly generalized itself to become a complaint about the dominance of the medical model of childbirth, in which pregnancy is a pathology requiring institutionalization and care by high-technology means, and women are merely vessels for fetal transport – the best kind of incubator there is.[208] During these years, a range of new maternity-care pressure groups were set up, including the Maternity Alliance, the Stillbirth and Neonatal Death Society, the Foundation for the Study of Infant Deaths, the Pre-eclamptic Toxaemia Society, and many others. Important new developments took place in the two older organizations, AIMS and the NCT. The voluntary organizations now receive some £30,000,000 per annum core government funding,[209] and have achieved some notable successes in focusing the attention of the public, professionals and policy-makers on specific questions in maternity care. The potentially angry consumer has become an accepted fact, and few would dispute the rights of women to speak out about the kind of maternity care that they want to have. During a period when expenditure on health and social

services is being curtailed, the role of pressure groups in helping the professionals to defend the resourcing of services is critically important, as Lyn Durward and Ruth Evans[210] have pointed out. But the important question is of course whether this is all merely lip-service. What impact has the consumer movement had, and what is it likely to have, in the 1990s? Here, it would seem that the responsiveness of health professionals to the consumer demand for a more 'social' and participatory model of childbirth is at odds with several other important historical trends.

The first of these is the tendency within obstetrics as the dominant profession dealing with childbirth to assert the value of its own expert, interventionist perspective. Looking at the development of obstetrics over the whole period from the 1920s, Pamela Sumney and Marsha Hurst[211] point out how the development of an interventionist ideology in the 1920s and 1930s was linked with the need of obstetricians to differentiate themselves from general doctoring, and to establish links with the surgical speciality of gynaecology.

When the ideology of natural childbirth began to appear in the late 1940s, the challenge which this at first posed to obstetrical expertise was met with a two-pronged strategy: first, prepared women made better patients – a Presidential Address published in the American Journal of Obstetrics in 1955 even suggested that natural childbirth might succeed in replacing some of the confidence that women had lost in their doctors.[212] Second, the profession began to take a decided interest in women's psyches, extending its professional domain by capturing a version of the psychosocial within it, and putting forward various new versions of old arguments, including the idea that women who 'failed' at reproduction had a deep-seated desire to be men, and that dissatisfaction with maternity care was a manifestation of an underlying rejection of womanhood, which in turn was one of many malignant products of women's higher education. When the new consumer movement arrived in the 1970s, a different set of responses were in evidence. Control and management came to be emphasized less than monitoring and surveillance. More significantly, however, women began to lose their central role as obstetrical patients, and the professional gaze shifted to the fetus. It is increasingly being argued in medico-legal circles both in the USA and in Europe that pregnant women cannot be considered to be the guardians of their unborn children's best interests. In the USA, women are being sued for behaviour during pregnancy believed to damage the unborn, and for refusing to consent to obstetrical procedures deemed by obstetricians to be required in the interests of the unborn's health. The development of the fetal rights movement threatens any partnership of childbearing women and health professionals that has been achieved, by proposing that women

are not important in securing a good outcome of pregnancy. As the sociologist Barbara Katz Rothman has argued, fetal rights go hand-in-hand with a growing tendency for 'commodification' in maternity care. Genetic counselling and the screening and testing of fetuses in antenatal care serve the function of 'quality control' on the assembly line of the products of conception. If babies and children are products, mothers are producers – the unskilled workers on a reproductive assembly line:

> Think of the antismoking, antidrinking 'behave yourself' campaigns aimed increasingly at pregnant women. What are the causes of prematurity, fetal defects, damaged newborns – flawed products? Bad mothers, of course – inept workers. One New York City ad shows two newborn footprints, one from a full-term and one from a premature infant. The ads read, 'Guess which baby's mother smoked while pregnant?' Another asks 'Guess which baby's mother drank while pregnant?' And yet another: 'Guess which baby's mother didn't get prenatal care?' I look in vain for the ad that says, 'Guess which baby's mother tried to get by on welfare?' 'Guess which baby's mother had to live on the streets'; or 'Guess which baby's mother was beaten by her husband?'[213]

It is not because there is no evidence available about the health-damaging effects of poverty, domestic voilence and other social factors that the image of motherhood is constructed in this way. It is not because no-one understands the powerful logic of pregnant women's smoking as embedded in stressful lives that the idea is held up of mothers deliberately wrecking their babies by forcing them to inhale cigarette smoke.[214] It is, rather, because the strength of this evidence, its political power, has simply never gained the upper hand over the weight of accepted notions of motherhood as propounded by health and other professionals.

The commodification process is very clearly seen in the treatment of infertility, where modern techniques allow for the removal and insertion of body parts, and for the mixing of different bodies, in a way which would have been viewed as pure science fiction fifty or even twenty years ago. Though the development and application of these newer reproductive technologies proceeds outside the main field of maternity care, it is important to consider the needs of the involuntarily childless as well as those who do not have to tangle with the awful dilemmas of IVF and its like. It seems unlikely that the 1990s will see any increase in work on the primary prevention of infertility, that much-noted missing agenda item.

Furthermore, the increasing use of IVF and related technologies inserts the technological imperative back into the heart of maternity care. Other

incentives are relevant here, including the rise in private obstetric care with its associated higher intervention rate. Hospital In-patient Enquiry data for 1985 showed that ten per cent of women delivering under the NHS, seventeen per cent delivering in amenity beds and twenty-three per cent of those using pay beds had Caesarean sections.[215] Legal influences on clinical practice are undoubtedly highly significant as forces pulling the profession away from any sensitivity that developed during the 1970s and 1980s to the desire of many women to avoid intervention. The trebling of claims since late 1989 for compensation following birth injuries hailed by a leading firm of health-authority lawyers[216] draws attention to the importance of introducing a no-fault compensation scheme.

One of the criticisms made by consumers in the 1970s was of the kind of communication that characterizes maternity-care encounters. It was said, and there was evidence to support this,[217] that the typical encounter between pregnant women and obstetricians and/or midwives prevented many women from voicing their questions and anxieties. The spectre of the Guardian-reading middle-class woman as the sole possessor of information-seeking qualities was laid to rest by Ann Cartwright's survey of induction in 1979, which showed the only class difference to reside in the *articulation* of questions: working-class women had more unasked, and therefore unanswered, questions than their middle-class peers.[218] The extent to which maternity-care encounters retain their traditional hierarchical format is not known – though the same themes have been repeatedly thrown up in surveys over the years. One of the developments that has *not* happened as a result of the consumer critique is regular monitoring of women's satisfaction with the maternity services, despite the fact that, as Ann Jacoby and Ann Cartwright argue, 'there is a case for using repeat studies on a regular national basis to monitor the effectiveness of action, and to identify other changes, particularly at a time of considerable and increasing pressure on the maternity services'.[219] The British Social Attitudes survey does, however, include a question about general satisfaction with the NHS, and their 1988 report showed a substantial *decrease* in satisfaction since 1983: among women aged between eighteen and thirty-four, there was a seventeen per cent rise in dissatisfaction, with forty per cent in 1987 saying that they were very or quite dissatisfied with the NHS.[220]

Systematic research on user satisfaction is, therefore, one aspect of maternity care that requires attention in the 1990s. Another is medical education and the perspectives that doctors bring to the care which they provide for childbearing women. Although it may be widely believed that some of the rampant sexism of earlier decades has now gone missing, I am not sure that the evidence quite supports this. One recent American study of

advertisements in medical journals showed that readers were still being exposed to negative and outdated images of women.[221] Taking a stratified random sample of medical journals published in the first six months of 1986 yielding a total of 209 advertisements, findings showed that two-thirds of the women in them appeared as health-care users, whereas two-thirds of the men were in the role of providers of health care. The women in the advertisements were significantly more likely to have only one part of their body portrayed, to be naked, and (or should it be or) to be wearing a wedding ring. When men and women were portrayed in the same advertisements, the contrasts were particularly striking: in one, all the men were workers or professionals, one woman was in a robe with pink curlers in her hair, one was obese and eating, and one was holding a cat. Women were more likely to be portrayed as inactive, dependent, emotional and depressed. In one typical advertisement showing an outdoor scene, the woman was sitting on a log while the man was chopping wood. Advertisements for prenatal products implied that the woman alone was interested in or responsible for pregnancy and had no other role than that of homemaker.

Both in the USA and the UK, a major unmet challenge before the maternity services is to provide a type of care which does not reinforce gender, class and race inequalities. To do this will require more than the education of health professionals out of the repetition of outmoded stereotypes. Ann Phoenix and others have pointed out how some basic maternity-care practices are racially discriminatory in their effects; for example, all newborn babies in the UK are routinely screened for phenylketonuria, which has an incidence of about one in 10,000 births but is considerably more common in white than black populations, whereas newborn babies are not screened for condition such as sickle-cell disease which affect mostly black populations; an estimated one in 200 babies of Caribbean origin and one in 100 of those of West African origin are born with sickle-cell disease.[222]

CONCLUSION

In summary, then, pregnancy care in the 1990s will need to contend with a social context in which childbearing women and their families are themselves having to struggle with considerable social and economic odds. More pregnant women and more children will in future be economically dependent on themselves and on the state. The consequences of the health and social policies of the last ten years amount to a dismantling of the welfare state, which was set up in part to protect the health of this vulnerable group. Unless it is restored, however caring antenatally is the work of midwives, GPs and obstetricians, they will increasingly have to function without the safety net of other support services.

Second, those who provide maternity care will need to bear in mind the decreasing likelihood of the pregnant women whom they care for living in traditional families. The notion that behind every pregnant woman there is a supportive husband lurking ready to supply emotional companionship, domestic help and financial resources will increasingly be a piece of cultural mythology. The old classification 'marital status' is a poorer and poorer guide to women's living circumstances. Whether a woman is legally married or not does not inform her health-care providers either about her household arrangements or about the social and financial support available to her. In an analysis which we are currently doing of marital status and social support in the *Social Support and Pregnancy Outcome* study, we have found that, while only about two per cent of women had no partner at all, some of those who were married were not living with their husbands (in one case the husband was not the baby's father), and some of the most helpful and supportive men were not living with their partners.[223] Within the context of a multicultural society, it is especially important that health-care providers do not make any implicit or explicit judgments about conventional family arrangements. Similarly, it is important to be aware that there is no evidence that non-traditional family arrangements are health-damaging contexts for children. The poorer health outcomes observed in lone-parent and young-mother households, for example, are a consequence of poverty, and not of some adverse effect that follows from membership of such families.

Third, while the consumer movement will not go away, neither will other important influences on the shape of maternity care. We live in a world which values technology and which has relinquished control over many aspects of life to professionals. The pressure on obstetricians to maintain an interventionist pose, and to continue complex, perhaps unevaluated monitoring and surveillance systems, is likely to be intense. In view of this, the role of midwives and GPs in defending normality in pregnancy will be crucial. Midwives, in particular, may have to guard against some of the incentives to professionalization that seem to be gripping other health-care providers, including nurses. We need to think very carefully about our model of what a professional is, and to reconsider, as a society, whether assigning knowledge about, and control over, important aspects of our lives to other people is good for us or for them. In this process of rethinking what kind of services we want, the systematic evaluation of the effectiveness, appropriateness and safety of different treatments and procedures within maternity care will be all-important. The increased acceptability of evaluation is, along with the consumer movement, the greatest heritage of the 1970s. In the 1990s, we will need to build on the fruits of the attitude which says that merely to *believe* that something works is not sufficient; we

must set up studies to test the hypothesis that the new is better than the old. So many procedures have been shown to be worthless or dangerous when subjected to the scrutiny of the controlled trial that it is to be hoped that we may at last be learning a little from history.

Finally, I could end where I began – with science fiction. Only this time it would not be science fiction, it would be some of the developments in the arena of new reproductive technology which are creating a storm of protest from radical groups in Europe and North America at the present time. We no longer need to read *Brave New World*; we live in it. I think that the potential for learning from these developments is enormous. And the main lesson to be learnt for the antenatal services is what the consumer movement has been telling us all along, that pregnancy is above all a social relationship. It is this relationship, rather than its fragmentation into parts owned by different experts or fought over by the courts, or jeopardized by poverty and material deprivation, which remains the main challenge for the development of appropriate care in the 1990s: how to respect the integrity and autonomy of each woman and baby in their own, unique social context, while at the same time using the best endeavours and most appropriate resources of the health-care system to provide safe, sensitive and effective care.

Part III

Technology

12

The China Syndrome

Marie Stopes, the great pioneer of birth control in Britain, had a second, less well-known career as a writer. In 1926, she wrote a play called *Vectia* which was about a virgin wife's desire to have a baby by her husband. The play was banned just before its first performance by the Lord Chamberlain, who said: 'You have done it beautifully, there is not a word or a thing to which I can take exception, but I cannot allow the *theme*.'[1] The theme was, of course, taken from Marie Stopes' own life. Fifteen years previously, she had married a young botanist, Reginald Gates, and in the months following the wedding had experienced a growing realization that something was not quite right with the marriage. It took a visit to the British Museum for her to find out what this was. It was the British Museum that taught her the facts of life. The marriage had not been consummated and was annulled five years later.

No wonder, one might say, that Marie Stopes was inspired throughout her life by the desire to invest women with a basic level of information about, and control over, the functions and capacities of their own bodies. Yet, in this respect, Marie Stopes was not a pioneer; she was merely a more prominent and public pioneer than most. The real pioneers of fertility control have been the many women throughout history and in different cultures who have not needed a trip to the British Museum to teach them a very important fact about a woman's life – that without control over reproduction it may not be much of a life at all. In this chapter, I am going to ask some rather elementary questions about the concept of fertility control, beginning with the question of where the concept comes from, moving on to why it is important to women and to men, and ending with some speculations about the social implications of modern techniques of fertility control.

HISTORICAL CONTINUITIES IN FERTILITY CONTROL

Most self-respecting fertility controllers these days are aware that they are engaged in an activity as old as recorded human history, and at the same time as new as the medical profession. By this I mean that there is well-documented historical evidence about the social importance of controlling fertility in different societies. There are also anthropological data from contemporary preliterature cultures, showing that the impetus to devise ways of controlling fertility predates modern 'scientific' medicine.[2]

Within both the history of fertility control and its present-day medical practice lie two diametrically-opposed motives: promoting and preventing birth. Thus, the early fifteenth-century *Medieval Woman's Guide to Health*[3] contains both sorts of prescriptions. In order to conceive, a medicine containing fifteen different herbs mixed with six gallons of water and one gallon of wine is recommended, or alternatively a woman must swallow the dried testicles of a boar. Interestingly, a third suggestion involves a plaster of raw eggs, cloves, saffron and oil of roses on which *either* the woman or the man (or perhaps both?) was supposed to lie. The manuscript recognizes that infertility may at times be incurable, and advises a rather unpleasant test in which the urine of the infertile couple is mixed with wheat bran. After nine days, a terrible smell plus the presence of worms is considered absolutely diagnostic of incurable infertility.

It is easy to dismiss such remedies as magical nonsense, but in this context let me just mention the instructive example of crocodile and elephant dung. Egyptian papyri, discovered in 1889 and dating from about 1850 BC, contain a prescription for the contraceptive use of crocodile dung mixed with honey and sodium carbonate as a vaginal pessary.[4] Since greasy substances such as honey form the basis of some modern contraceptive suppositories and may inhibit the motility of sperm, the Egyptians may well have been on to something. But what about the crocodile dung? Enthusiastic biochemists in the 1920s set out to test this material for its pH value, but unfortunately could only get hold of Cuban crocodiles, whose dung showed a pH of 7.9, which did not suggest contraceptive efficacy. The mystery of the pH value of Egyptian crocodile dung remains, but what happened to the dung contraceptive was that over the centuries elephant dung came to be substituted, and there is no doubt that the pH value of elephant faeces would have had some spermicidal effect (the Indian elephant being preferable to the African elephant here).

When we look at such prophylactics, we do not, of course, know who first invented them, but we do know which sex they were used by, and we can guess the answer to two further key questions, namely who controlled the

availability of the remedy in question, and who was likely to have been most highly motivated to use it. Most methods of fertility control described in the historical and anthropological literature were used by women, and almost all the necessary technical resources (for example, elephant dung) were readily available. As to motivation for deployment of fertility control, I would say that there are good reasons why women as a social group are *always* more likely than men to be highly-motivated fertility controllers. That is, women are more likely than men to be interested in both the promotion and prevention of pregnancy. This is a most significant historical continuity, which I shall return to below.

If we compare the fertility-control scene today with that obtaining in fifteenth-century England, or in Egypt in 1850 BC, we can also say that, in all probability, a second common theme is the greater number of female over male fertility-control methods. Men would have practised *coitus interruptus* and used certain potions; women not only swallowed potions, used ointments and put all sorts of substances in their vaginas, but also practised abortion and relied on prolonged breastfeeding and/or sexual abstinence to protect themselves from unwanted pregnancy. Today, oral contraception is swallowed by women; the sheath, withdrawal and male sterilization are the only 'male' methods. Among contraceptive-using married populations in Britain and the USA, some sixty per cent or more use female methods.[5]

The biggest single difference between what one might call the 'traditional' and the 'modern' fertility-control scenes is, therefore, not one of who wants to use, or does use, fertility control. It is that the technical and knowledge resources for practising fertility control now belong to the medical profession. Hence the delivery of this lecture at a symposium held in an institution called the Royal College of Obstetricians and Gynaecologists – I am what you could call the odd woman out. Modern 'scientific' medicine has made fertility control a medical subject, whereas previously it belonged to the people. Fertility control is, in this sense, exactly like many other areas of modern life such as birth, child care and unhappiness – now know respectively by their medical titles as obstetrics, paediatrics and depression.

WHY IS FERTILITY CONTROL IMPORTANT TO WOMEN?

I am not sure how controversial it is to say that fertility control is more important to women than to men; I am also not sure how true it is. Obviously, some aspects of this question are self-evident. As Hawkins and Elder's *Human Fertility Control* puts it, 'if a woman has sexual intercourse, then she must accept a finite risk to her life – whether that risk be encountered by childbearing or by the prevention or termination of pregnancy'.[6] It is not necessary to be a militant feminist to note that when a

man has sexual intercourse with a woman, he does not risk his life in the same way, and that a different formulation of this risk problematic might be 'sex with men is dangerous to women's health'. By far the most important manifestation of this danger has been maternal mortality – female deaths due to, or associated with, pregnancy – but there has also been, and still is, an enormous amount of morbidity associated with childbearing. A recent study of 900 women having babies in Berkshire revealed, for example, that three months after childbirth twenty per cent of women were troubled with varying degrees of incontinence.[7]

Taking a broad view of the risks for women of sexual activity with men also means looking at the risks associated with pregnancy prevention. Hence the concept of 'reproductive' mortality promoted by Valerie Beral, a term that includes deaths due to spontaneous or induced abortion, complications of pregnancy, delivery and the puerperium and adverse effects of female contraception and sterilization. According to Valerie Beral's calculations, for British women aged twenty-five to forty-four, mortality from pregnancy alone has declined by more than eight-five per cent since 1950. Among women aged thirty-five to forty-four, eighty-five per cent of reproductive deaths were due to the pill, and these outweighed the fall in pregnancy mortality. Overall, for these older women, reproductive mortality had actually increased.[8]

Some time ago, a feminist parody of the possible hazards of modern contraception highlighted the ways in which these are handled by both a medical profession and a lay public accustomed to the idea that women probably do have to suffer in order to prevent pregnancy. Because it makes several important points well, I shall quote this parody nearly in full:

> The newest development in male contraception was unveiled recently at the American Women's Surgical Symposium held at the Ann Arbor Medical Centre. Dr Sophie Merkin . . . announced the findings of a study conducted on 763 . . . male undergraduates.
>
> The IPD (intrapenile device) resembles a tiny rolled umbrella which is inserted thought the head of the penis and pushed into the scrotum with a plunger-like device . . .
>
> Experiments on 1,000 white whales from the continental shelf proved the IPD to be 100 per cent effective in preventing the production of sperm, and eminently satisfactory to the female whale since it does not interfere with her rutting pleasure.
>
> Dr Merkin declared [the IPD] . . . to be statistically safe for the human male. She reported that of the 763 undergraduates tested with the device only 2 died of scrotal infection, only 20 developed swelling of

the testicles, and 13 were too depressed to have an erection. She stated that common complaints ranged from cramping and bleeding to acute abdominal pains. She emphasized that these symptoms were merely indications that the man's body had not yet adjusted to the device . . .

One complication caused by the IPD and briefly mentioned by Dr Merkin was the incidence of massive scrotal infection necessitating the surgical removal of the testicles. 'But this is rare', said Dr Merkin, 'too rare to be statistically important.' She and other distinguished members of the Women's College of Surgeons agreed that the benefits far outweighed the risk to any individual man.[9]

This uncomfortable rewriting of the fertility-control scene of course brings out the paradox that while women are the main users of modern contraception techniques, men are quite interested in getting them to use them. This is one of the senses in which fertility control is in men's interests as much as it is in women's. It is also a demonstration of the fact that we cannot hope to understand what fertility control is all about unless we see it in a context of social and sexual relations.

Control of fertility has been a plank in the political platform of every feminist movement. Control over one's own life and destiny, the very essence of feminism, is not possible without that first 'freedom' – freedom from unplanned and unwanted pregnancy. For this reason, the feminist struggle is nowhere near won in those countries where either the Church or the state forbids contraception, and where abortion is illegal. If there is one single lesson to be learnt from the history of fertility control, it is that whether abortion is legal or illegal, women will have abortions – it is just that they will die more often when abortion is against the law.

Defending the rights of women and advocating safe and effective fertility control have historically gone hand-in-hand, but the situation is more complex than that. In the first place, many non-feminists have argued the need for humane methods of fertility control. Second, from the sex-equality viewpoint, it is not enough to advocate safe and effective fertility control: one must ask who controls the fertility control. Third, the feminist perspective on fertility control has been, until very recently, extremely one-sided. Far more attention has been paid to preventing pregnancy than to promoting it. Female biology has been defined as a burden to be offloaded by the effective prevention of pregnancy. No particularly positive value has been attached to the achievement of motherhood. It was the American writer Adrienne Rich who, some years ago in a provocative book about motherhood, made a crucial distinction between the *experience* of motherhood, on the one hand, and the *institution* of motherhood, on the other. She says:

The institution of motherhood is not identical with bearing and caring for children, any more than the institution of heterosexuality is identical with intimacy and sexual love. Both create the prescriptions and the conditions in which choices are made or blocked: they are not reality but they have shaped the circumstances of our lives.[10]

What Rich means by this is that social forces beyond the control of the individual partly determine the shape of parenthood in any culture. Are children wanted? How many children are wanted? Are women needed in the labour force? What do cultural attitudes say about the role of women – what is the status of mothers and what is the status of non-mothers? Answers to these questions outline the social context within which motherhood is lived, but the actual relationship of mothers to their children – the day-to-day experience of joy, anger, labour, peace and love – may be very different. This clash between experience and institution, between the reality of motherhood on the one hand and social expectations of women-as-mothers on the other, has been, I think, one of those conflicts responsible for the very birth of feminism itself.

FERTILITY CONTROL TODAY

In comparing fertility control among the ancient Egyptians with modern fertility control, I identified the key difference as one of medicalization. Today's experts on fertility control are not its users but those who develop, market, prescribe, and thus control, fertility control. When we add the medicalization of fertility control to the medicalization of birth and child care, we have a situation in which reproduction as a human activity is increasingly divorced from sexual and social relations. Medical and technical considerations have come to dominate the management and shaping of parenthood. One example of this is the near-100 per cent hospitalization rate for childbirth, a policy which has evolved in many countries on a completely unscientific basis, since it has never been proved that the majority of women and their babies benefit from institutionalized birth.[11] More than this, the success of different ways of managing birth has been judged totally in terms of *physical* parameters – what happens to bodies rather than what happens to minds, emotions and interpersonal relationships.

There are many other examples of how the medicalization of reproduction ignores its character as a social process, from the husband who becomes impotent whenever his infertile wife is induced to ovulate, to the new terminology for describing female unhappiness as premenstrual tension and postpartum depression, a terminology which allows us to enquire more closely into the mechanics of female body-functioning and not into the social dynamics of women's situation. Consider, too, the idea of the 'perfect'

contraceptive as pursued by fertility controllers and, following them, the lay public. The perfect contraceptive is one that has no practical or temporal connection to the sexual act. It is just 'there', suspending the woman's body in a 'no-risk-of-pregnancy' state, so that whenever an act of intercourse occurs neither she nor her partner is forced to consider the necessity for contraception, or the biological and social consequences of their union. The 'perfect' contraceptive is one that encourages irresponsibility precisely because sexual intercourse is permitted to become a purely physical activity. This is the sense, of course, in which the pill has liberated women. It has encouraged them to place sexuality in one compartment of their lives and reproduction in another. Whether this was what women wanted and whether it is a good thing are ethical questions that have not been answered – I do not think there is much evidence suggesting that most women are happily able to separate childbearing and sexuality in this way. I would suggest that the separation is easier for men, who do not experience both in the same body. Certainly, the idea of the liberated woman as the 'woman-who-is-perfectly-protected-against-pregnancy' has been a new stereotype for women in the post-pill era to rail against – *sexual* liberation is not the same thing as liberation, and what is so sexually liberating anyway about a continuous medication that tends to suppress one's libido? Personally, I have always felt that women have been a great deal more liberated by the invention of tampons than by the pill – if, that is, one can somehow avoid toxic shock and frightening books such as *Everything You Must Know about Tampons*.[12]

I could produce many more examples of this divorce of reproduction from social relations, but will content myself with only one: so-called preconceptual care (an odd term: surely it should be 'preconceptional'?). What are the implications of extending medical care backwards to the period before pregnancy has even started? Stemming from a basically sound and commonsense idea – that parental health before conception is as important as parental health after conception – the new vogue for preconceptual care nevertheless conjures up a disturbing vision. In this vision, we see an epidemic of preconceptual clinics arising at which the purveyors of preconceptual care advocate a variety of dietary and vitamin packages on the basis of what is at the moment a very uncertain knowledge about which elements of diet are really needed for healthy reproduction.[13] In the end, perhaps, these enthusiastic purveyors of the new preconceptual expertise will find themselves asking 'but why don't women attend for preconceptual care?' in much the same way as the protagonists of antenatal care have repeated the question about women's non-attendance for antenatal care.[14]

As a matter of fact, we may also note that the same question has been

asked by birth controllers who have confronted over the years the results of population surveys showing that a significant proportion of women (and therefore of course men as well) indulge in the dangerous activity of sexual intercourse without using contraception. Why are women (and men) so silly? The two main answers to this question have been inadequate knowledge and availability of contraception, and inadequate personality. Neither of these theories has ever satisfactorily explained the fact that some couples clearly know about contraception, or do not suffer from confusions and unresolved conflicts over whether or not to have a baby, but still do not use an effective contraceptive method. In 1975, a Californian sociologist called Kristin Luker wrote a very important book called *Taking Chances*[15] which I think has not been taken nearly seriously enough by the medical profession. In this book, Luker argues, first, that it takes two to make a baby, a point that, mysteriously, sometimes seems most apt to be forgotten by those best acquainted with the facts of life. Second, she proposes that if you talk to women (and men) about why they do not use contraception when they do not want a baby, you are liable to find that they are actually able to give a rational account of their behaviour. Within this rational account, the most significant component is the citation of the personal, social, biological and economic costs of using contraception. It may be costly in personal terms to acknowledge that one is in a sexual relationship. Obtaining contraception may cost time and money. Using contraception may mean putting up with side-effects in the short term and unwanted consequences such as disturbed fertility in the long term. The balancing of costs and benefits can only be done by the individual, but the point is that it usually is done. Not using contraception may thus be a means of exercising control over one's fertility, though it challenges a basic precept behind the medicalization of fertility control — that in the struggle to avoid pregnancy, some form of contraception is always better than none.

I have not yet talked about the most extreme manifestation of the divorce of reproduction from social relations, namely artificial reproduction. This is a futuristic aspect of fertility control, which so far impinges on the lives of very few users or providers of fertility control; nevertheless, it raises in a particularly blatant manner the issue of whose responsibility fertility control is, or should be.

ARTIFICIAL REPRODUCTION: WHOSE BABY?

The new techniques of in vitro fertilization (IVF) and embryo transfer (ET) have achieved for the beginning of pregnancy what neonatal intensive care has done for its end — they have made the participation of the mother's body redundant. About half the total span of human pregnancy can in theory be

accomplished outside the body. In theory too, pregnancy can be the burden and the joy of both sexes, since an embryo could be transferred into a male abdomen rather than into a female uterus, leading the fantasy of the 1970 contraception advertisement which portrays a pregnant man to become a reality, albeit a highly uncomfortable one. If women can occasionally have successful abdominal pregnancies, why not men?

The idea of male gestation is perhaps the most advanced flight of fantasy engendered by recent advances towards artificial reproduction. Yet it illustrates how profoundly this infant scenario of new reproductive techniques is able to challenge a tradition of sex and gender roles which is itself as long as human history. People have speculated endlessly on just how far and in what ways the division of reproductive labour – female as gestator, male as inseminator – has influenced the social roles and statuses of men and women. Nobody has really come up with an answer, except to say that different cultures link reproduction and social gender roles differently, that the biological imperative of sex differences can be played up or down, that it is all a matter of what human beings decide is most important. If it is important that women be people first and women second, then all sorts of social arrangements are possible to facilitate reproduction without oppression. With the vista of artificial reproduction on the horizon, it appears that we may not need to answer these questions after all. The solution has come off the pages of science fiction into the world around us. Well, has it? It was the former US astronaut James Lovell who said: 'we will fly women into space and use them the same way we use them on earth – for the same purpose'.[16] Before taking a closer look at the present-day scientific reality of artificial reproduction, let us learn another instructive lesson (the lesson of the crocodile dung reversed, as it were) from the genre of science fiction.

Science-fiction writers are commonly supposed to invent fictional forms of science, to create worlds containing all sorts of exotic possibilities based on some future scientific mode. Yet, what most science-fiction writers actually do is subscribe to the conservative partisan (medicalized?) view that all social revolutions are a scientific product. Within that framework, the social relations of present-day society are astonishingly persistent. As science-fiction writer Pamela Sargent has put it:

> There are a vast number of science fiction stories which show the impact of labour-saving devices, computers, space travel, increased communications, and new scientific ideas on men. About all such things seem to accomplish for women, however, is to give them more leisure time in which to worry about their children, lounge about their

residences in futuristic fashions, oversee robotic or computerized 'servants' . . . and worry about retaining the affections of their husbands. . . . On other planets . . . they often quickly become involved primarily in childbearing.[17]

There *are* works of science fiction or futurology – Huxley's *Brave New World* is the most famous example – which *do* question the assumption that reproduction is a woman's job. Some, and Huxley's is not in this category, use the possibility of artificial reproduction completely to restructure gender roles. In Thomas M. Disch's *334*,[18] early twenty-first century New York is used as a setting for various permutations on laboratory-aided parenthood. A lesbian called Shrimp is caught up in a fantasy of childbearing by artificial insemination, and a man called Boz has a child brought to term in an artificial womb, after which he has a breast implant to enable him to breastfeed. There are a number of science-fiction novels in which reproduction is not relegated to the laboratory and to the hospital, but becomes a human rather than sex-specific activity. Men and women take it in turns to have children, or there are no men and women – everyone is bisexual. Alternatively, there are no men, and the science-fiction element is used to replace the male contribution in childbearing by technology.

My favourite among all these fictional diversions is a novel called *Woman on the Edge of Time* by the American writer Marge Piercy. The heroine (even science fiction has heroines) is a decayed, middle-aged and welfare-dependent Mexican American called Connie, who is an inmate in a public mental hospital. She participates in an experiment involving electronic implants in the brain, and an unintended consequence of the experiment is that she finds herself intermittently in a society where sex roles are unknown. It is a very untechnological society in which everyone lives ecologically and in harmony with nature, with one exception – childbearing is done mechanically in a 'brooder' which stores genetic material and replicates the conditions of the human uterus. The inhabitants of this world explain to Connie why they have allowed the intrusion of this technology:

> It is part of women's long revolution . . . Finally there was that one thing we had to give up too, the only power we ever had . . . The original production: the power to give birth. [Be]cause as long as we were biologically enchained, we'd never be equal. And males never would be humanized to be loving and tender. So we all became mothers.[19]

To summarize the lesson of science fiction, it could be said, then, that the limits and possibilities of artificial reproduction are not set by the technology

itself. Scientific discovery and social change do not exist in a one-to-one relationship. The kind of society in which we live determines the kind of scientific progress that is made – the areas where research effort and money are concentrated, the areas where they are not, the questions within these areas that are either pursued or ignored. What this means is that, as Virginia Woolf[20] put it, science is not sexless; she is a man. I am not suggesting any sort of simple male conspiracy theory here, for that does not adequately fit the facts. For example, the lack of research on male contraceptives is sometimes pointed to as evident misogyny. Yet it may be that it is genuinely technically easier to disrupt the mechanisms responsible for ovulation and implantation in the female than to interfere with those involved with sperm production in the male.[21] In any case, the arguments about the ethical superiority of shared contraceptive responsibility must compete with the argument about fertility control being essentially a woman's issue, and thus being better in the hands, bloodstreams or at least in the reproductive apparatuses of women.

One good illustration of the two-way relationship between scientific development and social relations is the issue of sex selection. Like fertility control itself, the desire to be able to decide the sex of children is not new – what is new is the technical capacity to do so. Of course, we already have that, with prenatal sex-chromosome analysis and selective termination of pregnancies containing the 'wrong'-sexed fetus.

But have we even begun to disentangle the ethical issues involved in disposing of fetuses merely because of their sex? According to studies of parents' sex preferences, there is a sustained bias towards males and against females. This is more marked among men than women, but women sometimes follow their husbands' preferences rather than their own.[22] If parents were able to decide fetal sex now, the sex ratio would show a marked change in favour of males. This is already happening in China. Sex predetermination functions also as birth control, since 'trying for a boy' or 'trying for a girl' become unnecessary motivations for increased family size. If the 'cereal packet' norm of a boy first and a girl second become reality, there would also be the 'birth order' effect to consider. Position in the family is known to affect personality and life-chances, with first-borns being generally more anxious, intelligent and achievement-oriented.[23] A consistent concentration of males among the first-born would therefore add to the gender division a further structural inequality in life-chances.

The implications of changes in the sex ratio are thus enormous. Yet the social consequences of this potential transformation are much less discussed than the technical status of the field. Most of all, scientists apparently do not feel it to be part of their brief to consider *why* fetal biological sex should be

regarded as so important that its manipulation is worth the expenditure of considerable amounts of time and money. At the same time, of course, most doctors probably do not feel prepared to terminate a 'wrong'-sexed pregnancy or even *diagnose* the sex of a pregnancy simply because the parents want it. One American case quoted in a recent discussion of the sex-predetermination issue concerned a pregnant woman and her husband who presented themselves to a paediatrician with a family history of haemophilia. Following amniocentesis, the paediatrician was glad to be able to tell the parents that the fetus was a girl and they need not worry about a sex-linked disorder, to which the parents replied that they were going off to get an abortion because they really wanted a boy and had merely made up the story about haemophilia in order to get the amniocentesis done.[24]

The new technologies for controlling reproduction take us – all of us – to the point at which it is impossible any longer to avoid confronting ethical issues. This dilemma is most clearly marked in the notion of 'the artificial family' created by the techniques of artificial insemination, in vitro fertilization and embryo transfer. Using these techniques, a whole scientific soap opera of parental roles can be written: an infertile woman implanted with another woman's in vitro fertilized egg – and fertilized with, perhaps, anonymously donated sperm; so-called surrogate motherhood – 'rent-a-womb' – in which, for payment, a woman bears a child by artificial insemination of the payer's sperm, giving up that child at birth; the insemination of women with Nobel prize sperm, or rather the sperm of Nobel prizewinners (not at all the same thing), according to the persisting science-fiction fantasy that the roots of scientific achievement lie firmly in the underworld of the genes.

Within this realm of ever-expanding possibilities, two stand out. The first is the possibility that the family is no longer necessary. The second is the possibility that men are no longer necessary. I am, of course, overstating the current situation a little. But the ease with which sperm may be collected and frozen for long periods of time, and the relative simplicity of the technique of artificial insemination, do mean that women can in theory bear children without ever relating to men. For the time being, until the era of the artificial placenta, real female wombs are still needed. The theoretical redundancy of men is itself a challenge to the family, but there are other challenges to the family in here too, some of which are apparent in the recent report of the Royal College of Obstetricians and Gynaecologists Ethics Committee on *in vitro* fertilization and embryo replacement or transfer.[25]

The report begins by considering the circumstances under which IVF and ER (as the Committee calls it) should be used. The first consideration of the medical profession in this field is whether technical interference in

conception risks an abnormal fetus – if it does, the doctors concerned may be the subject of legal action. The second consideration is the use of the techniques of IVF and ER within 'marriage', defined generously by the committee as comprising 'a heterosexual couple cohabiting on a stable basis'. Should doctors accept for treatment all 'married' people who request it? The answer is no, for it is the 'province' of the doctor to take on for treatment only those couples who are suitable on physical, genetic, psychiatric and social grounds. The third consideration is whether IVF and ER should be used outside 'marriage', and about this the committee has 'grave reservations'. Its argument here is that

> IVF and ER differ from other forms of treatment for infertility and put extra strain not only on patients but also on doctors. The latter are not acting only as 'enablers'; with IVF and ER they are taking part in the formation of the embryo itself. That role brings a special sense of responsibility for the welfare of the child thus conceived. The committee believes that most practitioners will intuitively feel that IVF and ER should be performed in the most 'natural' of family environments.

I have always wondered why donors preferred for artificial insemination are English, middle-class medical students[26] and here, perhaps, is part of the answer. Medical students are said to be preferred because an acceptable level of intelligence, a stable personality and character as a 'good all-rounder' is thereby assured,[27] but I am not sure either that studies on medical students are quite as reassuring as one would like them to be on these matters, or that being a good all-rounder is a qualification for fatherhood which is at all important to mothers.

The point that I am making in a roundabout way here is that the medical profession seems to have negotiated itself into an extremely difficult position of enormous power with respect to the new techniques of artificial reproduction. Doctors are making moral and social decisions about suitability for parenthood for which their training does not equip them. They are playing God as never before – God the Father; for, as the RCOG report so succinctly puts it, doctors are now actually participating in the formation of embryos. In the face of this new role, and in view of the ability of the new techniques to liberate men and women from traditional sexual relationships, it seems a little disingenuous to fall back on that 'intuitive' notion of the 'natural' family.

CONCLUSION

In his book *The Technological Society*, Jacques Ellul called ours 'a civilization committed to the quest for continually improved means to carelessly

examined ends'.[28] Perhaps this would also do as a description of the process of scientific discovery, and certainly it applies to the history of scientific development within the fertility-control field, including its most recent product of artificially-engineered conception.

Having acquired the technology, we now have to examine the reasons why we wanted it in the first place. Obviously, these new techniques are welcomed by infertile couples. But there is an issue about the possible uncontrolled growth of a technology that benefits only a minority. As I have indicated, there are good reasons why women throughout history have needed to control the mixed blessing of motherhood. That I am talking about this very subject owes something to the fact that I have spent a mere five-and-a-half years of my life either pregnant or lactating; the capacity which women have to experience themselves as persons apart from the function of reproduction is limited, first and foremost, by the choice that they are able to exercise over whether, when and how they will become mothers. In this sense, fertility control is not a feminist issue – though it is that as well. It is primarily a *woman's* issue.

In considering the implications of this, we need to take into account not only access to the means of controlling fertility, but also who owns the knowledge and the technical resources and who makes the decisions about the promotion and prevention of fertility in individual cases. Artificial insemination from a donor is a good example of a technique for which doctors per se are not actually needed, but which it is nevertheless argued should be under medical control. Radical feminist groups have been using AID without medical help successfully for years.[29]

In short, there are strong grounds for arguing that, because fertility control is a woman's issue, doctors should be prepared to share their expertise, and particularly their decision-making power, more equally with their patients. Like shared income-earning within the family (either natural or artificial), it seems to me that this shared responsibility could only in the long run be a relief to those who so manfully now shoulder it alone. The spectre of a future in which reproduction is entirely an artificial exercise is either horrific or wonderful. Which it is will depend on our willingness from this moment onwards to oversee the evolution of a brave new world which is truly brave in the human and humane sense of increasing freedom and engendering good human relationships, rather than trapping us in a technology that, as a society, we did not choose and do not wholly want.

13

Technologies of Procreation
Hazards for Women and the Social Order?

The topic of reproductive technology generates some of the fiercest and most passionate debates of our time. This is because it evokes many of our deepest human concerns: the desire for immortality — for lives that extend beyond our own graves into the cradles (laboratory dishes) of the next generation; the evolutionary promise of science as the great deliverer of humanity from all ills and suffering; and last, but not least, the social and biological division of populations into male and female, so often culturally hardened into exploitation and oppression. Fertility, science and gender are the themes which fuel the fire of the reproductive technology debate. They occupy us all, and we are consequently occupied by them: they inhabit our minds, emotions and imaginations with great practical and symbolic force. They make us ask questions, but, more than that, they demand answers.

The questions about reproductive technology asked in this chapter single out the way in which women's experiences in relation to motherhood are defined, fragmented and rendered internally contradictory by the system within which technological methods of controlling reproduction have achieved dominance as the 'real' science fiction of the closing years of the twentieth century. The discussion proceeds on two levels. The first is the micro-level: accepting that these technologies exist as part of the medical system in most countries today, what can we say descriptively about their nature and function? The second level of analysis is the macro-level, and its focus is this conceptual triad — fertility, gender and science. The question here is not whether women benefit from the new technologies, but what their *meaning* is in the context of a social order that oppresses women and of an industrial-capitalist system that alienates workers from the products of

their labour. What role is technology really playing in the social control of women as workers in the reproductive labour process? This chapter focuses on in vitro fertilization and related procedures as provided under the heading of 'treatment' for infertility. However, IVF work is intimately connected with the broader issue of genetic manipulation of embryos, which therefore also demands comment. And since all these particulars are enclosed within a whole – forming the 'deconstruction' of motherhood – issues such as surrogacy will need to be mentioned at certain points as well.

WHAT IS REPRODUCTIVE TECHNOLOGY?

The American sociologist Barbara Katz Rothman[30] observes that the term 'reproductive technology' is a misnomer. Human beings are not the result of a 'production' process, as no one of us reproduces ourselves unaided; in the famous phrase, it takes two to make a baby. (Perhaps we should say 'at least two', for in the IVF clinics many more are involved.) Thus, we should not speak of *reproductive* technologies, but of *procreative* technologies instead. Procreative technologies include the full range of biomedical/technical interferences during the process of procreation, whether aimed at producing a child or at preventing or terminating pregnancy. It is important to remember here what technology 'is'. Although commonsense usage may associate it primarily with physical artefacts such as needles, scanners, lasers and so forth, it needs to be defined more broadly than that. According to the US Office of Technology Assessment, medical technology is 'The set of technologies, drugs, equipment, and procedures used by health-care professionals in delivering medical care to individuals *and the systems within which such are delivered*'.[31] Thus, it is impossible to understand the implications of the new procreative technologies for women (or anyone else) without considering the nexus of *social relations* in which technology is embedded. Any technology is developed and utilized by one group of people for use on, or by, another group. It is not democratically selected, nor democratically distributed. Thus technology is never neutral – a thing to be considered in and for itself. Every technology in its mode of development and use will reproduce the power relations of the culture.

Procreative technologies fall into four groups: those concerned with the prevention of conception and/or implantation; those applied to the promotion of conception; those involved in the monitoring and management of pregnancy; and technologies applied to childbirth itself. As a matter of historical fact, none of these is really new, for anthropologists have shown us how even pre-scientific societies have developed quite sophisticated methods of controlling procreation, including treatments for infertility.[32]

Nonetheless, of the four groups I have listed, it is technologies for promoting conception that are commonly regarded as 'new'. These include IVF – in vitro fertilization – GIFT – gamete intrafallopian transfer – embryo replacement/transfer, and genetic diagnosis and preselection of embryos. IVF as the critical method here is a technical way of saying that sperm and egg first meet in a glass dish rather than in the respectable privacy of a woman's body. (One has only to consider the unseemly housekeeping ring of 'glass dish fertilization' to understand why the experts chose to call it IVF.) It was first suggested in 1937, achieved in mice in 1958 and then in humans in 1977. Not all the component procedures were new, of course; though the surgical retrieval of eggs and the method of making eggs ripen in the Petri dish had to be developed, the collection of sperm relies on an ancient, pretechnological method. Somewhat unsavoury ideologies of women are suggested by the fact that IVF clinics must provide masturbatory facilities, together with a supply of pornographic literature. The notion that sperm for AID is best provided by medical students[33] is a form of professional imperialism. As a report from the Hastings Centre has argued, the choice of medical students and/or doctors as suppliers of genetic material can only be regarded as a sociobiological stragegy to ensure the maximum spread of what doctors believe to be 'superior' genes.[34]

The claim to fame of IVF may be chronicled through the medium of the scientific publications devoted to it: ten per annum in 1977, more than 300 by 1985.[35] Some 5,000 IVF babies were born in the decade 1978–88, and a register held by one of the two specialist journals – *The Journal of In Vitro Fertilization and Embryo Transfer* – included 178 registered IVF clinics in 1988. In addition, there are many unregistered ones. Every major city in the world where western medicine is practised now has an IVF programme. There have also been six world congresses.

Two obvious questions about IVF and the treatments associated with it are: do they work, and who are they for?

JUDGING SUCCESS

As Ardine de Wit and David Banta have shown in their valuable study of the diffusion of IVF in the Netherlands and England,[36] accurate statistics for success rates are not easily available. A postal survey of IVF clinics in the two countries met with response rates of fifty per cent (UK) and seventy per cent (Netherlands). In other words, half of all clinics in the UK and a third in the Netherlands were not willing to provide information for a scientific study of IVF activities. Most careful scrutinies of the statistics on the success of IVF clinics that are available come up with a success rate of about ten per cent.[37] This rate is calculated on the basis of live births per IVF stimulation cycle: that

is, for every 100 women exposed to one episode of IVF stimulation, ninety will not take home a baby. Furthermore, it is reasonable to suppose that some of those who 'succeed' in the programme would have 'succeeded' anyway. The best comparison group here is infertile couples on the waiting list for IVF, some five per cent of whom conceive while waiting.[38] Thus, it is probably true to say that IVF is responsible for something in the order of a five per cent pregnancy rate. To put it the other way around, ninety-five per cent of women will not be helped by IVF. Additionally, of the five per cent who are helped, a healthy surviving child may not be gained. The risk of multiple birth is well known: women having IVF are twenty-seven times more likely than the general population to experience a multiple birth.[39] In 1987 in the UK, one in four IVF and GIFT pregnancies was multiple, and these procedures accounted for half of all the higher-order multiple pregnancies in the UK that year.[40] The preterm birth rate for IVF pregnancies is four times that of the general population, and the rate of low birthweight five times the general rate.[41]

Pregnancy complications are considerably more common. For example, the mother of the world's first 'test-tube baby' developed pre-eclampsia and toxaemia, and the baby was delivered by Caesarean section.[42] Four times more IVF babies than others die around the time of birth. There are no long-term data on health and survival among IVF babies, but, because both minor and major permanent neurological, visual and hearing disability occurs more often among babies born too early and/or too small, a clustering of these problems in the IVF population is to be expected. As an editorial in the *British Medical Journal* put it, 'Contrary to the happy image in the media of multiple births, the reality is often starkly different'.[43] This editorial went on to describe a recent US case of quintuplets delivered at twenty-seven weeks in which one baby died after two days, one had necrotizing enterocolitis and was blind, one had post-haemorrhagic hydrocephalus, one had chronic lung disease and the fifth had neonatal seizures. The cost of neonatal care was $300,000. Since low birthweight and disability are significantly less common among babies of couples who conceive while waiting for IVF, they must be due at least in part to the procedures themselves rather than to characteristics (for example, higher age or an excess of medical complications) of the women enrolled for IVF.[44]

Assessments of efficacy can be carried out in many ways. The ancient Greek physician Galen expressed the view that an effective remedy was one that enabled people to recover quickly, except for those whom it could not help, who would all die. The women whom IVF does not help do not die, but it is important and necessary to consider other effects on women, aside from pregnancy.

Hormonal induction of ovulation for IVF is not strictly necessary but is usually practised, largely because it affords physicians more control over the timing of their work.[45] The major immediate risk of ovulation-stimulation with fertility drugs is going too far – hyperstimulation. Symptoms of this are menstrual irregularities which continue for a prolonged time, premature menopause, ovarian hypertrophy and ovarian cancer. A recent World Health Organisation paper observed that

> These sequelae to the use of fertility drugs are under-reported because there is little follow-up of women having IVF, but it is reasonable to speculate that such treatment will be associated with an increased risk of endometrial, cervical, ovarian and breast cancer for two to three decades.[46]

Moreover, the procedure of harvesting eggs involves the additional ordinary risks of infection, anaesthesia and surgical intervention. Some deaths of women have been reported. Because of the way in which pregnancies subsequent to IVF are 'managed', further damage to women often ensues: in one series, nearly half of such pregnancies ended in Caesarean section, with accompanying risk to the woman's health. This computation of risk must also include the financial, psychological and social hazards of the IVF programmes. Most couples have to pay financially. There are few studies of the psychosocial implications. One, of women's experiences following multiple birth, echoes the 'stark reality' of the *BMJ* editorial in highlighting the acute and chronic stress occasioned by this fruition of the wish to have a child in the form of two, three, four, five or more babies demanding round-the-clock care simultaneously in a culture where childrearing remains firmly identified as women's work.[47] The media do not so often report the darker side of the new technologies. There are more than a few known cases of murder and suicide in families experiencing multiple birth.[48]

These are some of the known but hidden realities against which the joy of successful technology-achieved motherhood must be set. The costs and the benefits must be weighed against each other; only thus will individuals and societies be in a position to decide whether the new technologies are appropriate and desirable or not. However, we are far from a position in which such a cost-benefit assessment can be carried out. The first reason is lack of knowledge. Why is there almost no research on the experiences and viewpoints of the women undergoing IVF, for example? Why is there no long-term follow-up of the consequences for woman, child and family? Pushing the logic of this further back, we can ask: why have the practitioners and protagonists of IVF not been required to submit their claims to success to accepted canons of scientific evaluation? All new interventions in human life

need to be subjected to systematic evaluation before they enter routine practice. The most appropriate way to do this is in the form of a randomized controlled trial. When properly applied, use of this method permits valid comparisons of outcomes in two otherwise similar groups, one of whom received the intervention while the other did not. Only in this way can confident statements be made about the success, safety and acceptability of this or that procedure. Studies of this kind must include elucidation of the experiences of those on whom the particular treatment is used, and must be constructed so as to allow follow-up of populations over time, thus permitting accurate estimates to be made of damage and benefit attributable to the procedure. But despite the fact that RCTs are widely accepted within medicine as the only valid way to establish safety and success, no trial of any of the new procreative technologies has been done or is in progress. Many of those who are worried about the implications for women of the new technologies are also opposed to what they see as unwarranted experimentation in the form of a trial. While there may be a case for arguing that financial and social investment in the new technologies should be halted for other reasons, the opposition to evaluation is in itself misplaced.[49] If there is no controlled experimental evaluation, uncontrolled experimentation in the form of everyday medical practice will continue and probably escalate. This has been shown to be the pattern for many technologies.[50]

The rapid progress of diffusion of exciting high-technology innovations is well illustrated in the Amsterdam Institute for Medical Technology Assessment's report on IVF. 'Uncontrolled proliferation'[51] is the byword. Two features of technology development are marked in the case of IVF, according to the Dutch report: one is the general failure to consider the need for evaluation studies, which includes a dismissive attitude to evidence of negative effects. The other is the failure to consider *ethical* questions. There are multiple instances of both these features of technology in the field of reproductive care more generally – for example, the rise in hospital birth, the proliferation of antenatal care, ultrasound scanning, the use of diethystilboestrol to 'prevent miscarriage', induction of labour, the ever-expanding list of 'indications' for Caesarean section, the use of electronic fetal heart-rate monitoring, and oxygen treatment for preterm babies are only a few of the unevaluated and actually or potentially dangerous procedures foisted on uninformed women.[52] In every case, it is the new, high-technology alternative to the conventional treatment that is preferred by health professionals, irrespective of both the scientific rationale and the ethical considerations. Take, as one brief example, the use of EFHR monitoring in labour: enthusiastically promoted from promising report to standard procedure in many places, a controlled trial which was eventually carried out

showed that this procedure had no advantage over intermittent monitoring in preventing unnecessary intervention and infant disability.[53] Conversely, controlled trials[54] of the efficacy and acceptability of social support in labour, which show that providing support and comfort for the labouring mother avoids costly and harmful interventions, have had little or no impact on maternity-care policy. Scientific evidence and clinical practice inhabit different worlds. Another telling and relevant example is the use of DES as a treatment for miscarriage; although known for many years to be ineffective and dangerous, it is currently being used to 'decrease fetal wastage' in at least one IVF programme.[55]

WHO BENEFITS?

Twelve years ago, non-corporeal fertilization rested safely in the realms of science fiction. What accounts for its shifting from fiction to fact, and who really, is it *for*?

The common explanation is that IVF and the other procreative technologies are designed to help women who want babies to get what they want. In the words of one British Member of Parliament, 'The researchers are not monsters, but scientists. They are medical scientists working in response to a great humane need. We should be proud of them.'[56] Again, however, and on a purely factual level, there is no evidence to support this belief. No studies of the motives of the key figures behind the development of the new technology have been carried out that would satisfactorily answer this question. On the other hand, there is a fair amount of evidence suggesting that the motive of helping the infertile is not the only, or the dominant, one.

First of all, and as many have noted, if there is a concern to help the infertile, there is very little interest worldwide in the *prevention* of infertility in the first place. This may be something to do with the fact that medical technologies have themselves been instrumental in causing it. The two new contraceptive technologies of the twentieth century – the pill and the IUD – are both associated with problems in conceiving. Furthermore, many of the infections which cause pelvic damage would be prevented from doing so by screening and early treatment, but these facilities are not routinely provided. There is very little research into the causes of infertility.[57] Research into infertility is not a money-earner, nor is it an attention-getter for doctors wishing to advance their own professional status. The head of one of Israel's eighteen IVF clinics, when asked to justify this number of clinics in a country of 4,400,000 people, answered in one word: 'prestige'.[58] Worldwide, IVF is regarded as a highly profitable area for financial investment. Much IVF work is privately funded, and the interests of the pharmaceutical industry figure prominently in it.[59]

Second, whereas IVF was at first offered to women whose own medical conditions prevented pregnancy, it is significant that it is now being used in the treatment of *male* infertility. Since infertility in men means few and/or few normal sperm, the challenge is to make the best of what you have, even if this means subjecting a perfectly healthy and fertile woman's body to the effects of hormonal stimulation and egg-retrieval in order to do so. The logical extreme here is fertilization with a single sperm – 'successful' experiments have apparently already been reported with microsurgical injection into the cytoplasm of the egg. A further extension of the notion of new procreative technology as a treatment for male problems is their reported use as a way of curing cases of infertility due to death. The removal of live sperm from dead men truly promises immortality.[60] In the UK, 'spare' embryos are used in research on male fertility; the head of one research team said that this work 'is of enormous importance, because forty per cent of infertile people are male and these men are desperate'.[61]

Third, IVF is *not* for everyone who wants it, and it is not even for everyone who can pay for it. For example, so far as is known, no IVF programme in the world accepts lesbians and few accept single women. Access to IVF is controlled by an outdated ideology which sees the heterosexual nuclear family as the only proper recipe for parenthood. In the words of the British Warnock Committee Report,

> many believe that the interests of the child dictate that it should be born into a home where there is a loving, stable, heterosexual relationship and that, therefore, the *deliberate* creation of a child for a woman who is not a partner in such a relationship is *morally* wrong. . . . we believe that as a general rule it is better for children to be born into a two-parent family, with both father and mother . . .[62]

Moral gatekeeping of this kind has historically been an effective way of ensuring uneven access to health resources. Here, the ideal of the heterosexual two-parent family is held up as a screen behind which women as the actual mothers of children are made to loiter, shadowy figures in disguise. Note, too, that pungent phrase in 'the interests of the child'. There is, as a matter of fact, no evidence that the interests of the child are compromised by living in a non-nuclear family unit.[63] The essential difficulties experienced by children in single-parent families are problems of poverty, not of father-deprivation.[64] The defence of restrictive practices in the interest of the child mirrors those regarding women as the containers of fetuses whose best interests they are supposedly unable to protect. The point is that the assertion and codification in legal and social policy of this notion of 'the child's best interests' frequently bears little relation to the

viewpoint of the child. For instance, in cases of child sexual abuse perpetrated by fathers, the fact that the child's best interests would normally be served by the removal of the father from the opportunity to continue the abuse, is frequently overlaid by an ideological appeal to the notion of the ideal of the unbroken nuclear family, which results in his being restored to the abusing relationship.[65] It is no accident that Dr Robert Edwards, one of the two 'fathers' of IVF, told a world congress on IVF that the main duty of doctors and scientists involved in this technique is to the children – and that the interests of IVF children are best served by researching spare embryos in an attempt to detect and prevent the causes of abnormality.[66]

If fertility should be a couple matter, it follows logically that infertility, too, should be so treated. Accordingly, infertility is not what happens to a *woman*, it is a condition of *couples*. Thus, the practice in UK IVF clinics is to use one consent form per couple, which speaks of 'we' all the way through. On one such form, the couple is asked to consent to the following, among other procedures: 'preparation for egg retrieval by the administration of hormones and other drugs; egg retrieval by means of laparoscopy or ultrasound, and selection by the medical and scientific staff of the most suitable pre-embryos for such replacement'.[67] The form does not note that it is the woman, and not the man, who is to be 'prepared' for egg-retrieval. The form also asks for the consent of the *couple* to all such drugs, anaesthetics and operative measures applied to the *woman* as are found necessary. There is no parallel in any other area of health care where *two* adults are required to give their consent to procedures that only *one* will undergo. This process is reminiscent of nineteenth-century ideologies of women in which, on marriage, their personhood was subsumed in that of a man – and, more recently, of the long-lived practice of requiring the husband's consent for the insertion of IUDs and for hysterectomies, on the premise that men own women's bodies.

In other words, the major beneficiaries of the new procreative technologies are not women as a group. Individual women may feel that they benefit, but that is different. This failure to benefit women as a group derives from the fact that the interests of women are not represented anywhere in the system that delivers the promised benefit; women have no control over what is done, how or where, and, as we have seen, the main stratagem accomplishing women's invisibility in the decision-making process is the archaically simple device of stating that they do not exist. By annexing women's identities and bodies to the heterosexual unit, it becomes possible for those providing these techniques to ignore the subjective and material reality of women's existence and experiences. The fact that this invisibility coexists with women's bodies being the stage on which the dramas of the new technologies are daily enacted produces the contradiction

responsible for the implacable opposition of some feminist groups to these technologies. Seeing the doctors and scientists truly as chauvinist monsters (to return to the British MP's phrase), groups such as FINRRAGE (Feminist International Network of Resistance to Reproductive and Genetic Engineering) turn doctors' sanitary claims of 'helping the infertile' into rather more savage metaphors of egg-farming and prenatal femicide,[68] and speak of an ideological system within which women are viewed and treated as interchangeable reproductive objects. Much of their argument makes sense; but there is one major problem with it. As Hilary Rose has said, talking of the world's first test-tube baby and her mother, Lesley Brown, 'It is one thing to argue against a specific technological development which is against the interest of women . . . it is quite another to say to Lesley Brown (or any other infertile woman) that it was wrong for her to have Louise'.[69] If we say that the industry of the new procreative technologies should be halted, what do we say to women who want to become mothers, and who believe that investment in this industry is their only means of doing so? In order to answer this question, it is necessary to proceed to a second level of analysis and ask: what is the significance of these technologies for women's position as mothers, and what meaning does the reshaping of motherhood have in terms of social values and practices in the closing years of the twentieth century?

MECHANICAL BODIES IN A MAN'S WORLD

The essential point, the point from which we begin and to which we must always return, is summed up in a statement of Nancy Chodorow's: 'Only women mother'.[70] But motherhood, as a female capacity and experience, is also a social institution. Fitted into different cultures in different ways, it is also constrained by them. Very often, though by no means always, motherhood seems to become precisely what it ought not to be – the core, the rationale, the manifestation, the cause even, of women's oppression. There are times, of course, when this situation is challenged. What happens when the exploitation of women as mothers and in other ways is subject to attack is that the old order reasserts itself, though in a different guise; the symbolic and political effect of the new procreative technologies is to reiterate women's secondary status: they are a means of bringing women under control, of reasserting those values which tie women to the judgments of men and to servicing the welfare of others, not themselves.

In her book *Recreating Motherhood*,[71] Barbara Katz Rothman argues that the new procreative technologies belong to a wider, sinister move in the direction of the commodification of human life. People, and bits of people, are objects to which price tags are attached in a commercial market-place.

Babies and children are products, and mothers merely producers – the unskilled workers on a reproductive assembly line. They are producing not only babies but also fetal material which has commercial value as a component in particular medical therapies – for example, the use of fetal cells in Parkinson's disease or of umbilical veins in bypass operations.[72] These situations involve ownership as well as ethical issues and are paralleled in other areas of medicine – for instance, in the recent legal claim in the USA by a cancer patient that cells from his spleen were developed into a $3 billion business venture from which he as well as the doctors involved should benefit financially.[73]

In her analysis of the fate of motherhood today, Rothman sees three overlapping and interacting ideologies as important: those of patriarchy, technology and capitalism. Through the ideology of patriarchy, what women experience as mothers becomes what mothers and babies mean to *men*. The value system of capitalism, defining the family as an economic unit, and children not as workers but as items in a process of production, treats women somewhere in between objects and unskilled workers. And the ideology of technology is a mechanical world-view, a vantage point that incorporates bodies into the language of engineering, so that doctors and scientists are mechanics manipulating mechnical body structures in the interests of efficient functioning. The individuality of the person is bypassed. In the case of the new procreative technologies, this is amply illustrated in the medical language used to describe these. In one major state-of-the-art review on research in IVF and ET in the *British Medical Journal*, for example, individual women are represented in seven uses of the word 'patient' or 'patients' in a piece of 3,500 words, and in three uses of the word 'woman' or 'women' in the following contexts: 'women with disease', 'the infertile woman' and 'women with absent or nonfunctional ovaries'.[74]

The history of medical technology charts the rise of the modern physician as technological 'man' with his barrage of instruments – the stethoscope, the microscope, the thermometer, the electrocardiograph – a new form of doctor who does not need to talk to people about their bodies (or their minds), as he is in the business of gathering objective data by means of machines in order to repair *the* basic machine – the body.[75] The work of the embryo researchers, the IVF men, the technocrats of fetal medicine, proceeds, as does all science and technology, and all our modern institutions and understandings, with a view of human beings, nature and the social order as composed of interchangeable atomized parts that can be repaired or replaced from the outside. Hence the attraction of getting conception out of the body and into the laboratory where what might only have been *felt* by mothers can be *seen* by scientists. The privileging of the visual as the primary means

to knowledge in the western scientific tradition has the function of debasing direct sensory experiences: not for nothing is the French word for the lens of a camera 'l'objectif'.[76] And what the scientist can see as separate from himself can also be the subject of his manipulations: the pre-embryo in the Petri dish, and fetus imaged on ultrasound and lifted from and replaced in the mother's body for surgical repair. Hence, too, the driving image of the conceptus as a machine composed of alterable genetic parts. The bodies of women as mothers are subject to the same historical process. The chief impetus for 'advances' such as pregnancy X-rays and obstetric ultrasound was the obstetrician's need to claim a greater knowledge of the pregnancy than the mother herself.[77] Though this process of distancing was/is imbued with a particular stereotyping of women as unreliable sources of information about their bodies, it rests more fundamentally on doctors' needs to establish themselves as *the* experts in charge of all health-care matters.

The motive of claiming professional expertise combined with a profoundly *uncritical* attitude to technological work is the reality behind the media image of doctors involved in the new procreative technologies as scientists carrying forward the indomitable march of progress. The project of science, as writers such as Keller, Rose, Hartsock and Harding[78] have shown, is not to discover truth, but to present *as* truth certain partial representations of some people's experiences. It is not that scientists cannot be trusted, but rather that science is too important to be left to men.

So too, is motherhood. All the evidence is that doctors and scientists do not understand what motherhood 'is' in the sense that the only way they have of comprehending it is in terms of two patriarchal concepts – those of fatherhood and of citizenship. The citizen is an individual, separate in a bodily and civil sense from others; fathers are those who must know who their inheritors, their children, are, who must establish biological and therefore social rights of ownership and lineage. But are mothers like this? How is their relationship to children and to their own experiences to be comprehended?

IN WHOSE BEST INTERESTS?

The declarations of the IVF doctors, that women are biologically motivated to reproduce and if thwarted will become 'disturbed',[79] are both a statement of the dominant ideology – women need motherhood – and part of the professional claim to an area of work (not just *some* women who want children but *all* women). The desire for children – that 'desperation' which confronts the IVF doctors – is not biological but socially-driven. The relationship between biological capacity and social desire is, however, so linked that it does not make sense to separate out 'biology' and 'society' as

distinct from one another. We must recognize that each is there, but the mixture will vary between individuals, and across and within cultures. The statement 'I want a baby' is part cultural imperative, part learned response, and part something which is more difficult to handle – a response to living in a body which promises to be able to do this for you. It is this 'living-in-the-body' aspect of motherhood which is so poorly represented in the dominant frame of reference. Some of the most ludicrous and damaging conclusions drawn as a result are evident in debates about fetal rights – both those that have long gone on under the heading of anti-abortion campaigns, and those that have more recently emerged in the domain of maternity care in the USA, where, in the 'best' interests of the fetus, women are being legally coerced into receiving obstetrical interventions that they do not want. A national survey in 1987 showed that in eleven states, court orders had been obtained for Caesarean sections, in two for hospital detentions and in one for intrauterine transfusions. In eighty-six per cent of the cases, the women involved were black, Asian or Hispanic, forty-four per cent were unmarried and twenty-four per cent did not speak English as their primary language.[80] Court orders are also being used to enforce prenatal care attendance on women, and to forbid certain behaviours in pregnancy. One man has successfully sued his wife on behalf of their child because she needed to take a medically-prescribed antibiotic while pregnant which stained her child's teeth.[81] Though we in the UK have not gone as far as this, we are moving in the same direction. For example, the major pressure group Action on Smoking and Health has proposed that pregnant women who smoke should be prosecuted for criminal neglect.[82]

Are women and the babies whom they carry in their bodies really at odds with one another? Consider here, too, the language of 'surrogate' motherhood. The woman who carries a child for someone else, whether conceived of her own genetic material or not, can only be called 'surrogate' if there is something unreal about the experience of pregnancy, or pregnancy is not part of motherhood at all. (The Dutch word here – 'draagmoederschap', or 'carry mother' – is better, but unfortunately is not likely to come into common usage.) The denial of the bodily experiences of motherhood brings to mind Mary Beth Whitehead's account in the famous 'Baby M' case of the forced removal of the breastfeeding Sara by police under a court order from the child's genetic father.[83] The breastfeeding relationship and experience of mother and child counted for nothing by comparison with the man's claim that some of his genetic material had been planted there.

Such events and namings are only explicable if one understands the need for a newly unrelenting and restrictive language of motherhood which *follows*

from and is required to *legitimate* the new procreative technologies themselves. In this new language, two contradictory ideological shifts must be accomplished simultaneously: on the one hand, women's biologically-rooted tie to children must be denied, because it is being interfered with; but, on the other hand, women themselves must be yoked more strongly to some particular version of motherhood in case they themselves get out of hand. An alternative statement of the meanings of motherhood to women resists this commodification of the fetus and its alienation from the mother, and women's consequent alienation from themselves. This statement brings to the fore the biology of motherhood as social relationship: the fact that children are known by their mothers and know them before birth means that the two are bound in a social relationship in which what one does affects the other – that older description of pregnancy as 'with child' rather than 'expecting' one. In this description, the relationship of mother and child cannot be reduced to atomistic individualism; it is about a kind of connection which goes beyond the mechanical language of modern politics and medicine, and is lifelong in a sense beyond the commodification of life. The people who care for children throughout their long and often difficult lives are not obstetricians, not IVF specialists, not judges, not police and not fathers. They are women. Only women mother. Or, as Rothman has succinctly put it, 'Men may own their sperm but children are not sperm grown up'.[84]

PERFECT BABIES IN A PERFECT WORLD

For a long time, the most insidious promise held up to women by doctors is the image of the perfect baby that will result if women do as they are told. Within these limits, women are free to seek the perfect pregnancy experience or the perfect birth, but it is doctors who decide how the perfect baby is to be obtained, and what procedures their mothers must comply with to achieve this goal. (The fact that doctors, being far from superhuman, cannot promise a perfect baby is conveniently left out of the picture.) Let us now go back to the 'informed consent' form used in IVF clinics. One of the things which these forms ask couples to agree to is that 'decisions as to the *suitability* of eggs or pre-embryos for replacement will be at the *absolute and sole discretion* of the medical and scientific staff'.[85] The new procreative technologies are, as many have pointed out, eugenics in a new guise. Experimental work with human fertilization makes possible research on how to get the perfect embryo – the embryo that will turn into a human being with no observable physical or other defects. The list of defects to be avoided goes rapidly from major to minor. Down's Syndrome, Tay-Sachs disease or thalassaemia are less debatable than club-foot or hare-lip (already reasons for terminating pregnancy in some centres). Identifying the genetic causes and

manifestations of these diseases and selectively aborting affected fetuses is, however, no longer the first choice. The first choice, made possible by the techniques of IVF, is to diagnose after conception but before implantation, and eventually to introduce new genetic material in a form designed to replace the faulty gene in all the body cells.

Unfortunately, for medical scientists to decide that this selection of 'perfect' individuals should be a goal of their work involves all of us in a commitment to eugenic policies. What would it mean to live in a world where none of us could admit to physical and other imperfections? Would black people be regarded as less perfect than white people? Would short-sighted people be outlawed? Who is to decide what imperfection is? What is the point of life anyway?

These are important questions, and they are not being asked by those who are pushing the new techniques on us. Moreover, selective eugenics are already being practised. Girl fetuses are being selectively killed in favour of boys — except where the notorious inferiority of the male sex[86] as the expressor of genetically-inherited diseases means that girls are preferred. The mother of the world's first test-tube baby signed a written statement agreeing to abort the child if the obstetrician thought that it might be abnormal.[87] Screening of pregnancies by amniocentesis or chorionic villus sampling is thus dependent in many places on women agreeing to abortion before having the test. In some IVF clinics, it is a condition of being accepted into treatment that the couple also agree to yield spare pre-embryos for research. One form for a large private facility in London has a section headed 'Agreement for the Use of Pre-embryos for Research' on its standard 'informed consent' form.[88]

WOMEN, THE SOCIAL ORDER AND THE DEATH OF NATURE

To sum up then, in discussing the new procreative technologies, we must be agile in moving between different levels of discourse. We must concern ourselves with the practical details of what is being done here and now, at the same time as putting these events into perspective, and asking a series of political and ethical questions, including about what the future is for motherhood and for women if these developments continue to proliferate unhampered by legislative and other social brakes. In asking such questions, we must also seriously attend to the position of the infertile. In particular, we need to respect the double bind that they are in — of deeply wanting motherhood, the 'natural' relationship of a woman 'with child', but at the cost of engaging in a technology that is known to be dehumanizing and 'against nature'.

Because the three central issues in the debate about the new procreative

technologies are the control of technology, the power of medicine and the position of women, all of these must be addressed in any programme of amelioration. Some strategies are obvious. Medical technologies need to be subject to formal technology-assessment procedures in all countries. The guidelines for such assessment should be those that flow from the concept of 'appropriate technology' as advanced by WHO and others. To be appropriate, any technology must be effective and culturally acceptable – it must 'fit into the hands, minds and lives of its users without disrupting a social fabric that may already be fragile; it must be affordable, sustainable and politically responsible'.[89] Procedures for technology-assessment must be set up in such a way as to override medical professionals' invidious claims to clinical freedom, which have disguised some of the worst forms of hormonal, surgical and institutional abuse of women. The type of arrangement set up in the UK following the Warnock Report – a Voluntary Licensing Authority sponsored by the Medical Research Council and the Royal College of Obstetricians and Gynaecologists – is not adequate, as history teaches us that, when monitoring of medical practice is carried out by doctors, only those who want to be monitored will submit themselves to the critical scrutiny of their peers. These are not the ones to worry about. Furthermore, any mandatory licensing or technological-assessment authority needs to be an organization with significant 'lay' representation, including women. I believe that there also needs to be central state monitoring of ethical issues in medical treatment and research. Ethics cannot just be 'made up on the way', as they have been with the development of IVF and embryo research: like science, ethics are certainly too important not to be everyone's business. Given these provisos, and if IVF is to continue, then the benefits of the technology should be evaluated in a controlled trial which includes as a major outcome measure the experiences of infertile women, and does not lose these in the heterosexual fiction of his interests including hers. It goes without saying that if IVF is found to be effective, it should be democratically available, and not only to those who can pay, or to those who fit some value-laden caricature of the 'normal' family.

But this is to attend to the problem of adjusting the social relations of procreative technology at the micro-level. A more general conclusion is that what is not in the best interests of women is also not in the best interests of the social order. The social order – the world system of western industrialized-capitalist societies and, increasingly, the Third World, on which the 'benefits' of biotechnology are unethically imposed – is in a technological fix. We are spending large sums of money and intellectual and social energy on technologies that benefit a few, when most of the world's parents and children lack the basic prerequisites of health – safe drinking-

water, hospitable shelter, education and primary health care. On a global level, every IVF programme is a human choice *not* to do other things – not to educate women so that they can understand what kind of future awaits them and their children, not to give money to the poor so that they can have food, not to care for the sick, the elderly and the disabled so that the phrase 'community care' becomes more than women's extra burden; and, on the level of obstetric and gynaecological care, IVF and embryo research are alternatives to expending time and money on ways of improving women's health care, so that the problem of infertility is treated at its source, and medical care for childbearing women becomes what it has never been – sensitive, appropriate and safe.

Technologies for procreation are themselves the creation of a society which has foregone an earlier image of the earth as 'alive' and considered to be a 'beneficent, receptive, nurturing female' in Caroline Merchant's[90] words, and chosen instead a representation of itself in which the machine is the dominant metaphor. In asserting the best interests of women and of the social order, we need to return to this older view of the world itself as a living thing, composed of interrelated, interdependent, indivisible parts. Instead of seeing motherhood as a machine, and mothers as insignificant, we need to take the metaphor of motherhood as unfragmented connection and experience, and apply it to our understanding of the world itself. In order to do this, and to bring about the necessary changes in the social relations of procreative technology at the micro-level, we need above all to do one thing: we need to empower women to take these issues in their hands for their own and the world's future. Empowerment means many things at the same time. It means taking women seriously by providing them with an education that values their humanity rather than their own superficial, socially-ascribed femininity. It means respecting rather than penalizing them as mothers. It means giving them information about their situation rather than stories about what other people might like their situation to be. For, in the beginning and in the end, it seems to me that this is what the proponents of procreative technology do: they tell women stories about motherhood. Like the fairy-stories read to us as children, we listen and are lulled into a false sense of security by the neat morals which they contain. But fables wear thin. By constantly reiterating and inflating the 'desperation' of some women to become mothers, uncritical advocates of procreative technologies trade on the cultural denigration of women as less than human, and contribute to a situation in which it is difficult for women to accept that there *are* ways of expressing motherhood other than 'having' – in that redolent capitalist phrase – a child of one's own. Neither infertility nor women are the central problem in this analysis. The problem is the definition of motherhood in a

social order opposed in fundamental ways to the mothering project.[91] Because motherhood is an archaic social relation in a commercialistic and commodified world, so the argument goes, it must be brought into line — and women with it. Resistance to the shaping of motherhood by the new technologies is also critical, therefore, to the defence of women as autonomous, unfragmented human beings. Finally, it is crucial to the safeguarding of the human world as a caring place to be inherited by all our children, however conceived and born.

14

A History Lesson
Ultrasound in Obstetrics

In one of his novels, the Irish writer James Joyce said that 'History is a nightmare from which I am trying to awake'.[92] Thomas Carlyle said that 'The history of the world is but the biography of great men'.[93] Edward Gibbon complained that history is 'little more than the register of the crimes, follies and misfortunes of mankind'.[94] The industrialist Henry Ford, being a practical soul, simply described history as 'bunk',[95] while the German philosopher Hegel is said sensibly to have reflected that 'what experience and history teach is this – that people and governments never have learnt anything from history, or acted on principles deduced from it'.[96]

These quotations do not adequately reflect the value of historical work, although I am more in sympathy with Hegel's than Henry Ford's view of what history is able to teach us. I do not think history is bunk. But it is apparent that people frequently fail to benefit from its lessons because, in their excitement for what is happening now, they lose sight of the need for a scientific approach to the evaluation of human experience. In what follows, I am going to tackle two questions about the use of ultrasound in obstetrics: first, and specifically, why and how did obstetric ultrasound develop? Second, and more generally, what does the development of obstetric ultrasound tell us about the nature of technical developments within medicine (and the nature of technical developments in society more broadly)? What lessons can we learn, despite Hegel, from this?

My own view of history is that there is no single 'right' way to 'do' it. While one may, and must, attempt to be fair to all perspectives, in the end certain choices have to be made about the important questions and about the most appropriate way to approach these. My background as a social scientist

leads me to focus on questions to do with the social relations of medicine. Histories written from within the profession are concerned rather more narrowly with medical 'achievements'.[97] This is a difference of emphasis with, of course, quite a number of implications. Reverting to Carlyle's remark about history being the same thing as biography, I take the view that the development of such medical techniques as ultrasound cannot be explained without understanding the pioneer work of key individuals. Yet, at the same time, this individual endeavour must be set in a context; that is, we need to know how this work fits in with other developments, including those in the social field.

OBSTETRIC ULTRASOUND: BEGINNINGS

The basic technique of ultrasound does not have its roots in obstetrics or in medicine, but in warfare.[98] During the First World War, detection by sound waves of underwater objects developed as a useful way of identifying underwater submarines. After the war, the technique of ultrasonic echo sounding was applied to mapping the ocean floor for the shipping and navigation industry and for locating deep-sea herring shoals. The pioneer medical work on soft-tissue ultrasonography was carried out in the USA in the late 1940s and early 1950s, and the translation into obstetrics occurred in the mid-1950s, with much of the original work being done by Professor Ian Donald and his colleagues in Glasgow.

The original clinical task spurring Donald and his team to apply ultrasound to the female abdomen was not the surveillance of pregnancy but the diagnosis of abdominal tumours, particularly the diagnostic separation into benign and malignant tumours. Glasgow was a city with heavy engineering commitments, where ultrasound was already used in the metal industry. Donald was familiar with this work, and it occurred to him to try on human tumours the industrial ultrasound equipment used for detecting flaws in metals. The technique worked, and, from the summer of 1955, women patients presenting with obscure abdominal complaints were liable to find the doctor putting transformer oil on their tummies as an acoustic coupling medium for an industrial metal-flaw detector. Since, with one of these detectors, nothing showed up within eight centimetres of penetration, women had water tanks with flexible latex bottoms balanced on their stomachs. The many resulting wet beds led Donald to think of contraceptive condoms as a solution to the problem. However, being rather reticent himself, he sent a professor colleague from Cape Town into a surgical rubber goods store in a disreputable area of Glasgow, to buy some. The professor was asked if he wanted teat-ended or plain, and proceeded to astonish the sales assistant by saying that he would go back to his friend and ask.

Every technical development has its lighter side, but if the new role of the metal-flaw detector seemed bizarre, one has only to reflect on that well-known obstetrical saying that 'the commonest abdominal tumour in women is pregnancy' and also, perhaps, on the fact that the fetus hidden in its amniotic fluid behind the surface of the maternal abdomen is not unlike the submarine skulking in obscurity on the ocean floor.

By 1965, the technique of fetal biparietal diameter measurement had been worked out, pregnancy had shown up on ultrasound as early as seven weeks, and early, blighted ova were being recognized, although other obstetric challenges such as the localization of the placenta had not yet been successfully taken up. Other teams of research workers in the USA were taking further this initial experimental work. By 1966, the ultrasound case-load in the Glasgow centre was described as nearly 'unmanageable', with twenty-eight per cent of all that hospital's obstetric patients receiving ultrasound.

Not long after this, ultrasound began to appear in other obstetric departments. Since we do not in this (or any other) country monitor the use of new medical techniques by means of routine data-collection systems, it is hard to find out just when and how use of a new techology escalates. Indeed, this is one of the central problems in constructing the history of ultrasound and other medical techniques. We do not know how many pregnant women and fetuses have been exposed to ultrasound. It is remarkable how unwilling obstetricians are to give information about their use of ultrasound − one postal survey of fellows of the American College of Obstetricians and Gynecologists in 1981 yielded only a 28.2 per cent response rate, meaning that nearly seventy-five per cent of obstetricians would not say how frequently they used it.[99]

Against this lack of evidence, we also know that professional contacts and informal social networks promote doctors' adoption of new techniques, so it is not surprising to learn that the first large obstetric ultrasound centre in England was started by a junior member of Donald's Scottish team, Stuart Campbell. Within a year of Campbell's arrival at Queen Charlotte's Maternity Hospital in London in 1968, ultrasound had become a routine method for estimating fetal growth and maturity. Four years later, nearly half of Queen Charlotte's patients received ultrasound in pregnancy, and by 1978 ultrasound coverage of the pregnant population attending that hospital was virtually complete.

We cannot understand the history of one technique (ultrasound) applied to one medically-defined condition (pregnancy) except by considering it in the context of all such techniques, and in the context of the medical definition of the condition itself. Ultrasound is one technique for acquiring knowledge

about what is happening inside the womb. Another such technique is the X-ray, and the use in obstetrics of both X-rays and ultrasound are stages in a long history of clinicians' attempts to secure a better knowledge of what is happening inside the womb than mothers themselves have. Although it has been suggested that the reason for this is obstetricians' ungratified childhood curiosity about where babies come from, the urge to possess superior knowledge is more appropriately explained as an important part of the process of professionalization. Thus, a new technique such as ultrasound rapidly generates a new subspeciality within obstetrics, including diplomas, certification and specialist journals. One other consequence of professionalization is a strong impetus to expand the use of new techniques. By the late 1970s, ultrasound had become a common method of fetal surveillance in many countries, and it now appears to be used intensively, especially in those countries with insurance-based health-care systems. Indeed, commercial motives and interests are an essential area to be considered when we are trying to understand the spread of a new technique – although an area about which it is extremely hard to obtain reliable information.

SOME HISTORICAL LESSONS

I have deliberately described, in some detail, how ultrasound developed in Britain, because I think that this is necessary to abstract the more general lessons. These I would list as follows:

1. Technical innovation in medicine is usually a serendipitous rather than a rational process. Thus, for example, the obstetric applications of ultrasound developed somewhat incidentally, and the main initial target area for ultrasound was not obstetrics at all.

2. Scientific evaluation of a new technique is not a necessary precondition for the introduction into routine practice of that technique. Or, in other words, ultrasound entered routine use in obstetrics before its effectiveness and possible hazards had been scientifically evaluated. The first controlled trial of obstetric ultrasound was not reported until 1980,[100] which was fourteen years after the obstetric ultrasound case-load at the first British centre was described as unmanageable.

3. The time between the initial experimental use of a new technique, such as ultrasound, and its introduction into routine practice may be very short.

4. Because techniques such as ultrasound form part of the professional resources of clinicians, the experiences, opinions and consent of childbearing women (and their partners) are rarely considered as either necessary or valid data in decisions about on whom the technique should be used, or for what kind of indication.

5. Those who advocate a new technique are liable to suffer from a strange condition called certainty.

EVALUATION

Ultrasound is not the only obstetric technique which has been subjected rather late in its history to the scrutiny of a controlled trial. In fact, it is the rule rather than the exception that clinical practice absorbs new techniques on the basis of inadequate evidence as to their effectiveness and safety. The 'seven stages in the career of a medical innovation'[101] run as follows: (1) 'promising reports' begin to appear in the literature; (2) the innovation is adopted by professional organizations; (3) the lay public begins to demand the technique; and (4) there ensues the era of routine use or 'standard procedure'. Only next does history expand to include controlled experimental evaluation (5). Finally, we have the last two stages, at which there is professional disbelief in, and denunciation of, the results of scientific evaluation, especially when these challenge the wisdom of routine use (6). This stage merges with one of general discredition (7), in which a technique hailed earlier in its history as universally applicable comes to be seen as useful only in some cases.

With obstetric ultrasound, I suggest that we are now somewhere between stages (5) and (6). We are beginning to look seriously at routine use of ultrasound, but perhaps not all of us are equally willing to translate the findings of clinical trials into clinical practice.

One of the lessons of history is, of course, that history repeats itself. The development of obstetric ultrasound thus mirrors the application to human pregnancy of diagnostic X-rays: both, within a few years of their 'discovery', were being used to diagnose pregnancy and to measure the growth and normality of the fetus. In 1935, it was said 'that antenatal work without the routine use of X-rays is no more justifiable than would be the treatment of fractures'.[102] In 1978, 'It can be stated without qualification that modern obstetrics and gynaecology cannot be practised without the use of diagnostic ultrasound'.[103] And two years later, it was said that 'ultrasound is now no longer a diagnostic test applied to a few pregnancies regarded on clinical grounds as being at risk. It can now be used to screen all pregnancies and should be regarded as an integral part of antenatal care.'[104] On neither of these dates did evidence qualify the speakers to make these assertions. As the sociologist J. B. McKinlay has said,

> It is reasonable then to argue that the success of an innovation has little to do with its intrinsic worth (whether it is measurably effective, as determined by controlled experimentation) but is dependent upon the

power of the interests that sponsor and maintain it, despite the absence or inadequacy of empirical support.[105]

On this question of evaluation and ethics, we do not only learn from the history of ultrasound and other similar techniques how rarely and how late the randomized controlled trial has been used for scientific evaluation. Another important question is the uncontrolled use of the technique in experimental research. This is what was said in 1926 about X-rays: 'The use of the X-rays or radium clinically should have been preceded by exhaustive studies, but as a matter of fact the practical application followed promptly upon their discovery and much of the experimental work has been done on human beings'.[106] The same is true of obstetric ultrasound. Among a variety of aspects of the fetal lifestyle, ultrasound has over the last fifteen years been used to 'discover' fetal breathing movements and fetal hiccups, monitor fetal eye movements and fetal activity in general, and find out how often fetuses empty their bladders and stomachs. Now this is doubtless fascinating work, but what is its ethical justification? Are the women involved in these experiments (none of whom are receiving it because they 'need' it) informed about the unknown long-term effects of ultrasound? What is learnt from all this experimental activity that is likely to be of overall benefit to the welfare of the childbearing population? Selecting one of these studies at random — one focused on fetal movements in pregnancy — I came across the following statements:

> As experience in monitoring fetal movements accumulated, it became obvious that the fetus does not always move in one and the same manner.
>
> Fetal motor behaviour is a complex of spontaneous movements and a motionless period between them.
>
> Strong movements correlate with a high motor rate, while slow movements tend to occur at a lower rate.[107]

This hardly adds up to outstandingly original wisdom justifying the use of a potent technology. Any mother can tell you that fetuses do not always move in the same way, and that sometimes a healthy fetus does not move at all; in fact, it sleeps — like the rest of us.

CERTAINTY

When I referred earlier to that stage in the history of a procedure at which people 'fervently believe' that it is unethical to withhold that procedure, I chose my words carefully. Any historian of techniques for seeing into the womb, or otherwise monitoring the behaviour of people's bodies, cannot fail

to be impressed by the *certainty* which is expressed on certain key issues, particularly the *safety* of the technique in question. In 1937, for example, a standard textbook on antenatal care commented that 'It has been frequently asked whether there is any danger to the life of the child by the passage of X-rays through it; it can be said at once that there is none if the examination is carried out by a competent radiologist or radiographer'.[108] But the same textbook declared in a later edition (1960): 'It is now known that the unrestricted use of X-rays may be harmful to mother and child'.[109] The 'knowledge' referred to was of course the report by Alice Stewart and her colleagues in 1956 on fetal X-rays and childhood cancer.[110] It is worth noting that the 1955 edition of the said textbook still carried a section on 'X-rays in Diagnosis of Pregnancy'.

Questions of safety, both in the short and the long term, have also been raised with respect to ultrasound. While the early practitioners of obstetric ultrasound seem to have been reasonably cautious about claiming 'no known harmful effects', what appears to happen is the following: as the technique begins to be used, and as it begins to be used more and more, and as no harmful effects emerge (which generally they do not because no mechanism for finding such effects has been set up), people become more and more certain in their claim that the technique is a safe one. Hence the words of one textbook on *Ultrasound in Gynecology and Obstetrics* in 1978: 'One of the great virtues of diagnostic ultrasound has been its apparent safety. At present energy levels, diagnostic ultrasound appears to be without any injurious effect . . . all the available evidence suggests that it *is* a very safe modality'[111] (my italics). Note the leap from 'appears to be' to 'is'.

CONCLUSION

So, to summarize the history lesson:

First of all, in observing the historical parallels between the development of X-rays and ultrasound as components of obstetric practice, I certainly do not intend to suggest that the techniques are likely to be equal in their effects. It is rather that both have been taken up and explored for the potential access to the interior life of the womb that they afford obstetricians. What I am saying is that the power of, and behind, the motive helps to explain the extent of their use. I do not think that it is mere coincidence that the use of X-rays in obstetrics declined rapidly in the late 1950s — which was also the time at which the pioneering work on obstetric ultrasound was done.

Second, while I have drawn out of all this the historical lesson that there is not nearly enough scientific evaluation of techniques that enter clinical practice, I have not commented on the lessons of the evaluation that has been done. One issue is that of *whether* any evaluation of a procedure

entering clinical practice has taken place. A second concerns what such evaluation, once it is done, actually demonstrates. Yet another is whether anyone pays attention to research findings, that is, what kind of relationship exists between evaluative research, on the one hand, and what clinicians decide to do, on the other.

Finally, technology brings about a profound shift in the knowledge base of medicine. Before the present era of medical knowledge, the 'subjective' knowledge of patients about their condition constituted information without which physicians could not practise. The danger of technologies such as ultrasound is that they substitute so-called 'objective' data for the earlier patient-generated kind. But the problem is that this is to substitute one partial view of 'illness' for another. Innovations such as ultrasound have a tendency to transform the social relationships of those who use them. For example, the obstetrician who can view an ultrasound scan, or a chart describing ultrasonically-surveyed fetal growth, has that much less time to spend conversing with the owner of the surveyed fetus – the mother. The machine tells the doctor what the doctor wants to know. For example, too, it has been claimed that ultrasound in pregnancy now enables obstetricians to 'introduce' mothers to their fetuses and facilitate a new phenomenon called prenatal bonding. In exactly the same way, the medical innovation of hospital delivery enabled paediatricians to discover the phenomenon of postnatal bonding. I would suggest that all this is rediscovering-the-wheel activity of a most primitive kind. Mothers and newborn babies bonded before hospitalized delivery disturbed the natural process. Mothers and fetuses were in a relationship with one another before they met on the ultrasound screen. The implication for social relations of medical innovations are nowhere more important than in the case of pregnancy, which is in itself not an illness condition and is, furthermore, a condition in which social and emotional factors play a profoundly important part, requiring that repertoire of traditional clinical skills that simply cannot be replaced by machines.

I will end with an observation made by obstetric ultrasound's original great enthusiast, Ian Donald. In 1980, Donald said:

> Perhaps the time has now come to stand and stare and to take stock of where we are going and where we are most likely to settle, bearing in mind that sonar, like radiology and biochemistry, must never lose their subservience to the medical art and the paramount importance of the patient who is the clinician's chief concern. Viewed with this sense of proportion sonar comes as a commodity only . . . out of control it can be an obsession . . . sonar is not a new medical religion . . . nor an end in itself.[112]

And, coming back to the definitions of history – with which I started – the following remark of Samuel Taylor Coleridge is unfortunately true: 'If men [sic] could learn from history, what lessons it might teach us! But passion and party blind our eyes, and the light which experience gives us is a lantern on the stern, which shines only on the waves behind us.'[113]

15

tamoxifen — In Whose Best Interests?

The proposed trial of the hormone drug tamoxifen in healthy women as a means of preventing breast cancer raises many different issues. These include the ethics of medical research; the kind of information given by health professionals to their clients; the use of medical as distinct from public-health strategies to prevent disease; and last, but by no means least, the medical regulation and control of women's bodies.

Breast cancer is a serious disease. One in twelve women in the UK will develop it in their lifetime. It is the commonest cause of death among women aged thirty-five to sixty-four, accounting for some 12,000 deaths every year. Both the incidence and the mortality rate of breast cancer have been increasing over the past twenty years.[114] These are good reasons for carrying out research into different ways of treating and preventing breast cancer. Like many such medical questions, it is more appropriate to search for answers to the question of whether drugs can prevent breast cancer by means of the controlled experimentation of a trial than through the uncontrolled experimental conditions of routine medical practice. If doctors give the treatment of their choice to patients of their choice, then no-one will ever know what works and what does not work, and, equally importantly, there will be no systematic long-term monitoring of adverse effects. The subjection of tamoxifen to the rigorous evaluation of a randomized controlled trial is thus, in principle, to be welcomed.

There are good trials and bad trials, however. It is important that the information given to women recruited to trials is clear and complete. So far as the trial of tamoxifen is concerned, the information given to women should cover what is known about this drug, including the fact that its

long-term effects are unknown. The design of trials also needs to have built-in procedures for allowing participants to evaluate their health symptoms and experience of inclusion in the trial. Not being listened to by doctors is the commonest complaint in the field of women's health.[115] Quality-of-life measures are as important as quantity-of-life ones. The specific question here is not only whether tamoxifen prevents breast cancer, but also what the quality of life is like for women taking tamoxifen.

Britain badly needs a proper system for monitoring the ethics of medical research, and for ensuring that research is designed in such a way that these kinds of questions can be answered. The present arrangement, whereby research protocols are reviewed by hospital or district health-authority ethics committees with varying memberships and procedures, is extremely unsatisfactory: a recent review of twenty-three such committees found that less than half wanted to know how outline consent would be obtained, and only a few asked detailed questions, for example what procedures would be used for people whose first language is not English.[116]

In the feasibility study for the tamoxifen trial, about half the women who were asked, because of their family history of breast cancer, to take part declined to do so, and one in five who did say yes dropped out later on. Although tamoxifen is generally reckoned to be a relatively safe and effective drug, the context in which it has been assessed is that of treatment for breast cancer, where its side-effects compare favourably with the devastating impact of chemotherapy.[117] Nonetheless, tamoxifen does have side-effects in some women. Jean Robinson, lay member of the General Medical Council and long-time women's health activist, reports a steady trickle of complaints over the years about the side-effects of tamoxifen,[118] a long litany of which is listed in the pharmaceutical handbooks. If women in the tamoxifen trial are clearly informed about the possibility of such symptoms as hot flushes, headaches, depression, dizziness and pruritus, then they may be better informed than those who are being prescribed it outside a trial. A survey by the breast-cancer group ASPECT of women with breast cancer taking either tamoxifen or another drug showed that seventy-five per cent said they had been given *no* information about side-effects.[119]

As important as carrying out trials of new drugs is the improvement of routine practice to meet women's needs for information, counselling and *care*, as well as treatment. However, beyond these specific issues of research and practice, there are wider issues concerning the cultural definition of women's bodies as legitimate terrain for medical manipulation. It is not simply that a hormone, tamoxifen, is proposed as a means of preventing breast cancer, but that tamoxifen is seen in partnership with artificial oestrogen and progesterones as a package that will 'adjust' women's bodies

to the 'natural' event of the menopause and to the 'natural' risks of being female. The anthropologist Margaret Mead remarked many years ago[120] that childbirth is nowhere 'natural' – everywhere it is defined differently by different societies. So it is with the menopause. There are many cultures, for example, where it is viewed positively and not as an oestrogen-deficiency disease.[121] Furthermore, any proposal for long-term medication of healthy bodies must be carefully scrutinized: who is proposing medication for whom and for what purpose? The history of women's health contains many unprincipled examples of interference by doctors according to an ideology of 'women's best interests', from the proscription of higher education in nineteenth-century Britain and the USA as against the interests of women's reproductive function,[122] to the more recent administration of Depo-Provera as a 'convenient' contraceptive.[123] Why is long-term medication not proposed for men, whose mortality rates throughout life exceed those of women, and whose bodies are also containers of hormones which fluctuate and decline with age?

Finally, there is the question of primary prevention. Breast-cancer rates in some countries – for instance Japan – are low, and it seems probable that diet is important. It is known that an early full-term pregnancy reduces the risk. Breastfeeding may protect, though little of the research has looked at the protective effect of prolonged breastfeeding on demand, which is likely to have a different impact from the more usual practice of regulated breastfeeding stopped after the early weeks.[124] Where, then, is the research on diet and breast cancer, and why are health professionals not doing anything to make early motherhood and lengthy breastfeeding on demand more possible and congenial experiences for those women who might prefer a more 'natural' way of reducing their breast-cancer chances?

Part IV

Methodology

16

Ways of Knowing
Feminism and the Challenge to Knowledge

In 1974, the great writer, political thinker and feminist, Simone de Beauvoir, played for a while the role of her best-known title, *The Second Sex*, and interviewed her lifelong companion, Jean-Paul Sartre, about his life and hers. There is a passage in the resulting book, *Adieux*, about the moon. Sartre described his feeling as a child about the moon – that 'one knew from experience . . . it was always there . . . I saw it at night and it was important to me in some way; I couldn't tell exactly how'. Later on, when informed that the moon was a satellite of the earth, Sartre, characteristically, took this personally and believed the moon to be *his* satellite: 'It seemed to me', he tells de Beauvoir, 'that I had thoughts that came because I was looked at by the moon.' De Beauvoir asks Sartre next why he speaks in the past. He replies: 'Because the moon means less to me since people go there. The moon was all that I've said up until the time they started going to it . . . it changed the moon into a scientific object, and it lost the mythical character it had until then.'[1]

In *Adieux*, there are also many passages about Sartre's complicated relations with women. De Beauvoir asks him what it was that he found attractive about other women. (One supposes she includes herself in the term 'women', as she did in the term 'other', although she does not say.) Sartre answers that 'it was above all an atmosphere of feeling, of sentiment. Not of sexuality properly so-called, but of feeling, with a sexual background.' He talks about his role in these other liaisons as 'the more active and reasonable one' and the woman's as being on the emotional plane. 'That did not mean', he explains,

that women were not as capable of exercising reason as men – it simply meant that most of the time a woman had emotional and sometimes sexual values; and it was that aggregate which I drew towards myself, because I felt that having a connection with a woman like that was to some extent taking possession of her affectivity. Trying to make her feel it for me, feel it deeply, meant possessing that affectivity – it was a quality that I was giving myself. . . . Sometimes in my notes, sometimes in my books, I have stated – and I think it still – that sensibility and intelligence are not separated, that sensibility produces intelligence, or rather that it is also intelligence, and that in the end the rational man, taken up with theoretical problems, is an abstraction . . . [The women] were perfectly capable of doing the same things as men, but a certain tendency, arising to begin with from their upbringing . . . put affectivity first. And since for the most part they did not rise very high . . . they retained their sensitivity unimpaired. This sensibility included an understanding of others.[2]

WOMEN LOOKING AT THE MAN IN THE MOON

These conversations between Sartre and de Beauvoir yield two main themes. The first theme is the articulation of Sartre's use of women to give himself that understanding of social relations which he cannot obtain in any other way. Removing this insight from the context of Sartre's troubled sexuality, the question becomes one about the kind of understanding of the social world which women possess by virtue of their status as an oppressed minority group. Sensitivity to others may be a cultural strength, but it can be a weakness for women themselves. Virginia Woolf called it the 'Angel in the House' syndrome. She admonished those women who wanted to be writers to kill the Angel before the Angel killed them.[3] Women's sensitivity to others has broad implications, for example for the study of moral choice. Carol Gilligan[4] has shown not only that women typically make different moral choices from men, but also that the basis on which they do so is considerably more complex.

The second theme is the face of the moon, a comfort in the darkness, a satellite of all kinds, but a mythical object until Neil Armstrong started trudging around in his moon boots making evolutionary claims on behalf of mankind. This act of colonization converted the moon from the status of unreal heavenly body to the class of scientific object. Our scientific knowledge of the moon has deprived us of another kind. In slotting the moon into all the other things that we 'know' about – in the same way as the viruses that make us ill, the behaviour of the seasons, the child's comprehension of space and time, the construction of buildings supposed to

withstand earthquakes, and so forth – we have devalued its enormous aesthetic and symbolic significance. We have fitted it into a pre-existing framework of understanding not on its own terms but on ours. Our knowledge is consequently limited. And because it is limited, it is also limiting. So, I shall argue, has been the case with women's studies. Women's studies are Sartre's moon: a mode of understanding which offered more before it was captured by 'man' (even embracing women) – before it was implanted in men's studies.

WOMEN'S STUDIES: STUDYING WOMEN?

Since the late 1960s in the USA, in Britain and in many other countries, there has been an attempt to reform academic knowledge, practice and education (and the three terms are importantly not synonymous) so that these are less exclusively concerned with male representations of the world.[5] The consequence of this is that in many places there are women's studies courses or components of courses in universities, polytechnics and schools. In setting up women's studies courses, women have wanted to draw attention to the ways in which women are either a hidden constituency in conventional mainstream or 'malestream' knowledge, or subject to various kinds of stereotypical misrepresentations.

It is hard to remember today what the world was like before women's studies. When I went to university almost thirty years ago, there were no women's studies courses. I remember studying economic and political theory, moral philosophy and sociology, with a sense of inchoate puzzlement about the representations of humankind embedded in these subjects. In economics, for example, there was rational man, a bit like Piltdown Man, or some other archaeological relic. Rational Man's behaviour was guided by unbelievably simple notions of economic cost and benefit, and not by any consideration of social relations at all. Next to him in the economic theory textbooks was The Housewife, who spent her entire life in shops choosing what to buy and being responsible for the shape of supply and demand curves. She was portrayed as rather a silly kind of creature, whose inability to grasp the interplay between individual market behaviour and national economic policy could be depended on. She had, moreover, apparently no consciousness at all of the basis of her own decision-making. Not surprisingly, none of this worked very well as an explanation of what happened in real life, and after a term or two of economic theory we moved on to economic organization, which proved the inability of the theory to explain anything. But no-one went on to argue that the theory should be rewritten, or questioned who The Housewife was anyway, and whether anyone would really behave like this. The sexist bogs of philosophy were

equally oppressive. But the Platonic ideal of philosophy as an activity that must rise above the ordinary mundanities of life at least gave me the answer to the question about what The Housewife was doing in economic theory. She was out there consuming commodities so that he could sit and think and devise theories about the world that would not work.

During the 1970s, all this changed. By the end of the decade, it had become legitimate to mention women's experiences and opinions in an academic context. One review of Work on Women within social science in Britain in 1979 put it thus: 'Over a relatively short period of time, and after decades of indifference and neglect, the study of women has developed from a minority interest into a major area of activity and debate'.[6] Many people would agree with this statement as almost the commonsense view of the development of a feminist consciousness within academia. It is obviously true that there are many activities going on in the institutions of higher education which are concerned with studying women, in one way or another. It is perhaps less obvious how much of the rest of what goes on in such institutions is the study of men. But it is necessary to unpack a little of what we might call the 'Darwinian' view of women's studies — that the study of women gets better and better all the time. First, there are significant social science (broadly defined) works 'about women' that predate the 1960s women's movement — most notably, of course, Simone de Beauvoir's *The Second Sex*,[7] but also Viola Klein's *The Feminist Character*,[8] and the book she wrote with the Swedish sociologist Alva Myrdal in 1954, *Women's Two Roles*[9]; community studies such as Madeleine Kerr's *People of Ship Street*[10]; works by women anthropologists, again most notably Margaret Mead's *Sex and Temperament in Three Primitive Societies*[11] and her later *Male and Female*,[12] but also ethnographies such as Phyllis Kaberry's *Women of the Grassfields*,[13] and works of theory such as Barbara Wootton's *Social Science and Social Policy*,[14] which, by carrying out a careful appraisal of John Bowlby's work on maternal deprivation, began the task of clarifying the basis of cultural assumptions about gender roles.

None of these, however, has the same cultural resonance as the books that started the infusion of feminism into academic knowledge in the early 1970s — Betty Friedan's *The Feminine Mystique*,[15] Germaine Greer's *The Female Eunuch*,[16] Kate Millett's *Sexual Politics*,[17] Juliet Mitchell's *Women's Estate*,[18] and her earlier *New Left Review* piece *Women: The Longest Revolution*,[19] and Shulamith Firestone's *The Dialectic of Sex*.[20] Though each of these was in its own way a political statement, they were all written by women academics who brought different theoretical and disciplinary perspectives to bear on 'the problem of women'. Mitchell, for instance, who was teaching English at Reading University at the time, began with Marx's prioritization of the

relations of production and with Althusser's concept of the 'over-determination' of social position through interlocking economic and political structures. Kate Millett's version of women's mistreatment as the subjects of knowledge took a literary route through the works of Norman Mailer, D. H. Lawrence et al. and brought the instruments of literary criticism to bear on the reconstruction of the known world from women's point of view.

To answer the question of why these works were accepted and read as legitimate commentary when earlier ones were not, we have to turn to an analysis of the relationship between feminism as a political movement and women's social position, and indeed to an analysis of what feminism itself 'is'. Important here is the difference between the intellectual and cultural history of feminist ideas, on the one hand, and the practice of an organized women's movement, on the other. For example, Mary Wollstonecraft's *Vindication of the Rights of Women*, published in 1792, may appear to have been followed by a period of feminism's absence from political and social life, but, if one traces the cultural transmission and representations of Wollstonecraft's ideas, they can be seen to be taken up within utopian socialism of the period.[21] It is a mistake to conclude that, in the absence of organized feminism, feminism 'itself' does not exist. Feminism as political practice is an ever-present possibility because it rests on, and grows out of, a coherent system of ideas which has its own autonomous cultural existence. These ideas and their longevity stem from the material and political system of women's oppression, which is historically contingent rather than biologically determined.

The question about the origin of feminist movements then becomes not 'why feminism?' but 'why feminism now?' In our own recent past, the radical student politics and the black movement of the 1960s provided the political impetus for the dissatisfaction of some women with the postwar retrenchment of women's position to mobilize itself into a recognizable women's movement. In the same way, too, the repressive return to family values and nostalgia for the culture of sexual difference of the late 1980s appear to bury the political movement of feminism as a thing of the past. The works of authors such as George Gilder,[22] Christopher Lasch[23] and Brigitte and Peter Berger,[24] trading on later pronouncements of cultural feminists such as Greer and Friedan, manoeuvre the nuclear family into position as the only right repository for a strongly-modelled female consciousness. In their book on this topic, Janice Doane and Devon Hodges[25] remind us of Kate Millet's able sketching in *Sexual Politics* of the counterrevolutionary ideologies produced as a response to first-wave feminism. History is repeating itself.

What *is* knowledge? Like feminism, knowledge can be many things. But

the model of knowledge that dominates the academic and scientific world is narrow and specific. The constituents of knowledge are objectively-determined facts. What we know are collections of things derived from studying the world not as our oyster but as a laboratory: observing, documenting, describing as detached observers, we build up portfolios of objectively-determined and replicable findings. The object of collecting these facts is to test predetermined theories about the relation between events and processes, or to generate theories which can in turn be taken back to the laboratory and checked out for their capacity to map and predict what 'really' exists and happens.

This model dominates both the natural and the social (the 'unnatural') sciences. Indeed, a large part of sociology's own quest for professional status has been spent wandering around the maze of habits and practices that call themselves natural science 'proper'. Central to the clash between feminism or feminisms and knowledge is the perspective of the knower, and the purpose of knowing. In the conventional model, the knower is separable from what is known, and the purpose of knowledge is knowledge. From the feminist perspective, the person who knows, what they know and what is to be known are joined in a nicely heretical confusion. Moreover, there is no point in knowledge for its own sake. Knowledge must serve social ends. It must improve the human predicament either directly or indirectly, either concretely or diffusely. There follow some examples from recent feminist work which illustrate this confrontation between feminism and the construction of knowledge as a body of objectively-known facts.

The Search for Things Real, Deep and Hard

The first example is taken from a study of social support and pregnancy. The design of this study adopted the experimental scientific model. We set out to test the impact of friendship on health by offering one group of pregnant women the social support of a research midwife and comparing the impact of this with a group of pregnant women who were not offered this help. We used a table of random numbers to decide which women would be offered the help and who would not. At the end of the experiment, we counted and added up facts such as the birthweight of the baby and how many times the woman and the baby went into hospital − as well as, of course, other dimensions of the experience of those who took part in the research. The story of this research and of how and why in terms of my own personal biography I switched methodological modes is long and complicated and is being told in other places.[26] As part of this story, it is important to note that the quantitative/qualitative divide is basic to the methodology of all the sciences. As Louise Kidder has said,

the division between qualitative and quantitative research is entrenched in several disciplines. In psychology it appears as a tension between experimental and clinical methods. In sociology it appears in the separation of fieldwork and statistical work. In the logic of scientific enquiry it appears as a difference between hypothetico-deduction and analytic induction. The difference between qualitative and quantitative researchers appears also in caricatures – the former are considered 'soft' and the latter 'hard', and the former called 'navel gazers' and the latter 'number crunchers'.[27]

Or, as the American sociologist Zelditch put it many years ago,

> Quantitative data are often thought of as 'hard' and qualitative as 'real and deep' – thus, if you prefer 'hard' data you are for quantification and if you prefer 'real', 'deep' data, you are for qualitative participant observation. What to do if you prefer data that are real, deep *and* hard is not immediately apparent.[28]

Sociologists who have grappled with the description and measurement of concepts such as intimacy or well-being or happiness will appreciate the attraction of simple number-crunching for a change. Some of the critical outcomes in our study were numerically defined, for example the birthweight of the baby. We did not at the outset regard the operationalization of these concepts as problematic. Yet they were. For example, some babies had seven different birthweights, depending on the source of the information (the midwife's notes or the doctor's notes; the mothers' answers to a survey question, etc.). In only twenty cases out of 507 did the mothers and the hospital records agree about how much the babies weighed. In many cases, the disagreement was a few ounces only, but in some it was a pound or more. There were many other categories of information for which we found it impossible to determine what was the 'right' answer. Perhaps the most blatant example was the babies' sex. In thirteen out of the 507 cases, the mother said that the baby was one sex and the hospital records said that it was the other sex.

We may laugh at such puzzles, but laughter always has a point to it. The point here is that we are forced to recognize that sex and birthweight are just as much a matter of perception as anything else. There is no such thing as the truth. The truth is not simple – any such cliché will do.

A Feeling for the Organism

The second example comes from the scientific field, and is relatively well known. In Evelyn Keller's elegant biography of geneticist Barbara

McClintock,[29] we learn a good deal about how scientific discovery proceeds in practice as distinct from theory; the book's title, *A Feeling for the Organism*, is suggestive. Keller shows how McClintock's discoveries concerning the cytogenetics of maize were derived from a method of 'understanding' plants in their individuality and their environment that has no place in traditional canons of the scientific method which stress the necessary objective data-gathering and pre-formed hypothesis-testing of the 'true' scientist:

> As if without distinguishing between the two, [McClintock] knew by seeing and saw by knowing. Especially illustrative is the story she tells of how she came to see the Neurospora chromosomes. Unwilling to accept her failure to see these minute objects under the microscope – to pick them out as individuals with continuity – she retreated to sit and meditate, beneath the eucalyptus trees. There she 'worked on herself'. When she felt she was ready, she returned to the microscope and the chromosomes were now to be seen, not only by her, but, thereafter by others as well.[30]

It is important to note that McClintock's method was based on the same assumptions held by other scientists, which are that nature is lawful and that the scientist's task is to probe for these laws and then frame them in objective, logical language. But reason and experiment are not enough on their own. What is needed instead is a capacity for union with that which is to be known – a mode of understanding in which the knower and the to-be-known have equal status and in which the knower's different senses are not pressed into the dampening dichotomies of mind *or* heart and passion, reason *or* feeling.

McClintock's work was poorly recognized at the time. One reason was because her perspective and way of working could not be heard within the prevailing model of molecular biology in which genetic programmes were thought to be inscribed as static linear messages in sequences of DNA. The somewhat contrary view, that they should be thought of as dynamic structures whose transposition was encoded in instructions derived in part from the environment, was unacceptable.

DEADLY WORDS

Next, we have a study of witchcraft. In 1969, ethnographer Jeanne Favret-Saada[31] went to live in a village in the Bocage region of western France. She went equipped with the usual academic and fieldwork training and ready to wait for some time, taking extensive notes, until she found an informant or informants who trusted her enough to tell her about witchcraft, which was well known to be an endemic phenomenon in that part of France.

She encountered some difficulties, however. First of all, there was the immediate conflict that confronted her between what the academics said about the beliefs of peasants practising witchcraft and the way in which the peasants presented themselves to her. The academic literature on the subject says that peasants believe in witchcraft because they are credulous, backward and do not understand causality. Peasants attribute to witchcraft happenings which educated people know have other causes. Peasants have beliefs, other (superior) people have scientific theories. Thus, as Favret-Saada became immersed in the life of the people whom she was studying, she came to ask two questions of her own: 'Does the "scholar" or the "man of our own age" need to comfort himself with the myth of a credulous and backward peasant?', and 'Do you really have to do thirty months of fieldwork to be in a position to say that country people are just as well able to cope with causal relations as anyone else?'[32]

The second problem which Favret-Saada confronted had to do with a main tenet of the anthropological method: the notion that an 'anthropology' of anything is based on information conveyed by natives in the field and presented in the form – of course – of words. Thus, to find out about witchcraft practices, you get someone to tell you about them. Informer and informant must talk to each other, and must see language as a means of conveying information. But this was the problem. So far as witchcraft was concerned, it was the same thing as language: witchcraft *was* the spoken word. The spoken word, language, had the status of power rather than knowledge or information. There was no concept of wanting, or being able, to know something for its own sake. So it was impossible for the ethnographer to find out about witchcraft by collecting facts about it through the medium of language. If she tried to talk to would-be informants about witchcraft, Favret-Saada became involved in it. There was no way to learn about witchcraft except by becoming involved.

FROM RATS TO MEN

The fourth example concerns a piece of research which Helen Longino carried out with Ruth Doell[33] on the influence of sex hormones on behaviour and cognitive performance. The aim of the research was critically to review studies of the relationship between sex hormones at various stages of human development and later behaviour. Longino and Doell found numerous instances of sexist assumptions in the way that data were described – as anyone who has even a passing acquaintance with the literature on the psychology of sex differences will know, 'scientists' in this field reveal their values in such strategies as using the male as the norm and commenting on how females measure up to this, in emphasizing the pursuit of differences

rather than similarities and even in such apparently innocent devices as using a solid black line on a graph to represent male performance, and a hesitant, broken one to represent female performance.[34] Sometimes the sexism can be even more rampant, though hidden. For example, most psychological experiments using rats only use male rats, although they do not say so. The female rat, like the female human being for much of her life, has a reproductive cycle that is thought to complicate things far too much. It is a small step from here to the argument used, with academic and scientific respectability, of women for a long time that because of their reproductive function it was far too complicated to let them do anything outside the home, including voting, acquiring an education and playing a role in the paid labour force (though this latter disqualification was only held to apply to middle-class women).

But what was most interesting about Longino and Doell's work was that they did not find that such grossly sexist assumptions mediated inferences from data to theory in any notably prejudicial way. What did mediate such inferences was the model of linearity – the assumption that there are direct one-way causal relationships between variables such as prenatal sex hormones and postnatal cognitive development. The model of unidirectional programming which scientists believed they had observed in animals was imposed on the human data without any consideration for the fact that humans are more than animals. Thus, Longino and Doell argue for the replacement of the linear model with one that 'includes psychological, environmental, historical and psychological elements'. 'Such a model', they argue, 'allows not only for the interaction of physiological and environmental factors but also for the interaction of these with a continuously self-modifying, self-representational (and self-organizing) central processing system.'[35]

The point of this example is threefold. One, sexism takes many forms and must be challenged on many levels. The fact that in Longino and Doell's research the assumption of linear causality proved more limiting than more blatant instances of masculine bias is important. Two, the story of feminist understanding is not simple. Three, and related to this, it takes someone, a woman – or rather two of them – sensitive to a range of meanings and explanations, to recognize a theory that is not so.

BACK TO THE KITCHEN

The fifth example is a book called *Democracy in the Kitchen* by Valerie Walkerdine and Helen Lucey.[36] Its subtitle is 'regulating Mothers and Socializing Daughters'. The book is based on a reanalysis of data from a study of how young children learn at home and at school. The conclusion of

the original research, which was done with an all-female sample of four-year-olds, was that young children learn a good deal more at home than they do at school, as mothers are more sensitive to children's needs than teachers; however, some mothers are more sensitive than others. The original report of the research, which was published as *Young Children Learning* by Barbara Tizard and Martin Hughes,[37] is a powerful argument, inadvertently — or perhaps not inadvertently — for mothering being a good deal more than the romantic patriarchal view says that it is. Tizard and Hughes show just how much information is conveyed by mothers to children in the course of everyday conversations, for example, while mother and child are eating lunch or putting the shopping away. This, perhaps, is the obverse of the witchcraft case: whereas Favret-Saada found herself up against the barrier that words were not ways of passing on information, Tizard and Hughes show that the ordinary banter of the mother–daughter relationship, normally considered merely domestic or expressive in the gendered functionalist paradigm of the family, is educative in a way that few educational institutions have learnt to be. The problem however, uncovered by Walkerdine and Lucey in their reanalysis of this material, was with the addendum to all this — but some mothers are more sensitive than others. From working-class backgrounds themselves, Walkerdine and Lucey re-examined the original transcripts of mother–daughter conversations and found that those deemed to be least successful in terms of young children learning were those taped in working-class homes. They ask, then, 'what is a sensitive mother?' The answer that they give to this question expounds on both class and gender oppression — not separately but together. For a sensitive mother is one who, while peeling potatoes, educates her child about how and where potatoes grow, who explains about urban sewage systems while cleaning the lavatory, and who lectures about microbes when pegging the washing on the line (if indeed she still engages in this outmoded activity). Domestic labour is a pedagogy of its own: the foundation within the patriarchal paradigm of children's cognitive development. In addition, though, the sensitive mother is one who regulates her child's development without appearing to. Regulation must be underground; there should be no overt power struggles. As Walkerdine and Lucey put it,

> Successful parenting rests on creating an illusion of autonomy so convincing that the child actually believes itself to be free. We believe that this fiction, the illusion of autonomy, is central to the travesty of the word 'freedom' embodied in a political system that has to have everyone imagining they are the better to regulate them. In locating the problem of democracy in the home it is the mother who has come

to the rescue and the working-class mother who has to be watched above all others.[38]

These examples illustrate the fact that there are different ways to tell a story and, in the process, the story itself becomes different. In this sense, feminism may be compared to the fairy godmother in *Cinderella*. In writer Sara Maitland's words,

> Cinderella is sitting at home rather pissed off, wanting to go to the ball and not having a thing to wear, when the fairy godmother whizzes in and puts it all right. One of the important things about the fairy godmother is that she transforms all the old stuff around Cinderella into new and useful equipment: the rags, the pumpkin, the rats and so forth. This little girl's fairy godmother turned out to be called Feminism. As well as cheering the little girl up no end, Feminism also transformed all the old things around her. Above all she transformed the old stories. Suddenly the little girl could see that the stories were just vehicles; they had been told over and over again for different purposes and could be told one more time at least; they could be told through brand new shining feminist eyes. What excitement![39]

The methods used to build knowledge constitute part of that knowledge — methodological, theoretical and empirical issues are not easily separable. Quantitative and qualitative methods are not as easily distinguished as malestream knowledge says they are. Quantitative data are mediated by the perception and position of the observer just as much as, though less obviously than, accounts of experience or feeling. Language is not only a method for obtaining knowledge, it may also be knowledge itself. The assumption of a one-to-one relationship between cause and effect might be the way that some of us would like to see the world, but it is not necessarily any help in understanding it. The orthodox story of how scientists work is a story — much scientific work is not careful plodding hypothesis, experiment and observation, but steered by passion and intuition and shaped by random social events. Most important of all, the stance of the knower — the academic theorist or researcher — influences what is known. Mainstream knowledge pretends that personal values are left behind in intellectual work; feminist knowledge knows that they are not, and that an awareness and articulation of what these are and how they may be represented in knowledge as a product is essential, not to prevent the shaping of knowledge by personal perspective, but to understand, to know, when and how this happens. Of the examples given, the clearest illustration of this

point is in relation both to gender and to class, namely Walkerdine and Lucey's example of how mother–daughter conversations are interpreted by non-feminist middle-class researchers as illustrative of individual mothering practices, whereas a working-class feminist perspective questions the description of these practices by locating it in particular material and political circumstances.

As feminist intellectual work has developed and has challenged the simplistic models of mainstream knowledge, in part by pointing out its biases, in part by carrying out a kind of housework of the knowledge-building process, so it has become obvious that the contribution of the feminist approach is not to create a less sound, stable, integrated system of knowledge than existed before, but rather to produce a more integrated, sounder, indeed more 'scientific' one. The view that feminist knowledge is inherently 'better' than mainstream knowledge according to the canons of mainstream knowledge is developed by feminist writers such as Hartsock,[40] Rose [41] and Harding.[42] The argument proceeds thus: if social experiences are unevenly and hierarchically structured for different social groups, then the vision of each will represent an inversion of the other. More specifically, the vision of the dominant group will be more partial and thus more perverse than the vision of the subordinate group. The reason for this is because the subordinate group needs to understand not only itself but also its place in the world. Women need to understand not only themselves but also men. It is by studying themselves and men that they learn to survive, to make their way in the system and even, occasionally, to beat it. Men can do all this without much understanding of any kind. Understanding is a bonus, not a necessity. Moreover, men do not have to understand their own point of view. All of this carries the most important, indeed quite world- or knowledge-shattering corollary – that feminist-constituted knowledge will be more scientific than knowledge which is not so constituted, as it originates in and is tested against a more complete and less distorting kind of social experience. This argument has been most thoroughly developed in relation to the natural sciences. Writers such as Keller[43] and Harding[44] have argued that the logic of science is not simply influenced by the masculine world but is in essence the logic of patriarchal domination itself. Within social science, Hilary Graham[45] has provided a neat illustration of this in her critique of the development of the survey method. Graham observes that one important impetus for the development of sociology as a 'science' was that the social changes of capitalism disturbed traditional values and practices so that men (and it was men) no longer understood the world around them. This created the need for a method of finding out, and the most attractive method was one patterned on the model of the natural sciences. Urbanization and the congregation of

people in large cities, where they had the status of units rather than individuals, promoted the notion that human beings could indeed be studied as units, as objects. Graham goes on to observe that, as the survey method is modelled on the form of labour relations prescribed for capitalist production, it may well be incompatible with the social relations which determine women's lives. She argues that there are specific areas of tension. First, the fact that surveys deal with social units imposes the idea of a unit on the realities of the way in which people live. This is one of the difficulties in the notion of social class as based on the occupation of one person – the 'head' of the household. Also problematic is the fact that we know that, within a unit such as a household, labour, rights, responsibilities and resources are often divided very unequally. Another problem is the assumption of measurement – that what you are researching can be counted, can be quantified. One can only quantify in the terms made available by the culture, and these are impoverished. This is a central problem with the analysis of women's household work, which lacks the monetary value of other work because it is done in the private domain and is attached to the emotional and psychic relations of women under patriarchy.

The same problem is evident when we talk about the lack of any sociology of feelings and emotions. Emotions, like women, who are closely associated with them, are devalued by the male world – one needs only to think about how the term 'sentimental' has come to have an entirely derogatory meaning. So, while activities can be measured and counted, emotions are much more difficult for researchers to handle – not intrinsically, but because mainstream knowledge considers them unimportant and has consequently developed no methodology for studying them.[46]

A third problem with the survey method is the idea that social phenomena have an existence separate from the social relations in which they are embedded. Does depression, for example, exist separately from the experience of depression? Modern feminist scholarship would say that it does not. Most influential here is the work of the American sociologist Dorothy Smith, which has highlighted the purpose of knowledge for women as producing not a knowledge *of* them, but knowledge *for* them. Smith's central observation is that the starting point for all knowledge is personal, everyday experience. In her words, 'there is no entry to the abstracted conceptual mode of working without passing through and making use of the concretely and immediately experienced'.[47]

This is true whatever sex or gender you are. But for women living in a male-dominated and anti-women society, the mediation and determination of knowledge by everyday experience results in the probability that women will experience what Smith calls a 'line of fault' in their social geography:

they will, at some point or other, and in one way or another, stumble on a point of rupture between the experience of being a woman and the forms in which experience is socially expressed. Stumbling on the fault line is the starting point for women's studies.

With the wisdom of hindsight (which knows no gender), it is clear that all of this is what I was struggling to recognize when I was studying philosophy as a student in the 1960s. I did not feel the need – it did not make sense to me – to argue that the goal of intellectual work is to rise above everyday life as if this were seen as tedious, trivial and boring and not at all, incidentally, the realm of women. But at the time I could not articulate this. In Dorothy Smith's terms, culture is not born spontaneously out of people's everyday experiences but is manufactured by the 'ruiling classes'. The forms of thought available to us are put together from a place that women do not occupy.

THE GENDERING OF EVERYDAY LIFE

In order to study gender, it is necessary to analyse sociological data by gender on an individual basis. For a long time, sociological work was dominated by the tradition of taking the family or the household as the unit of analysis. The result was a screen which effectively prevented gender from coming into view as an axis of inequality. Thus, the tradition of social-class analysis based on male occupation created a whole genus of work which was restricted to class as a male concept.[48] The present tense would do as well here. Numerous books about social class and/or social mobility are about male social class and male social mobility – they tell us nothing about women at all. A recent example is a book with a fascinating and challenging title, *Height, Health and History: Nutritional Status in the UK 1750–1980*. On page four of the preface, the following statement can be found: 'We have been able to say virtually nothing about the heights of women. Our sources are primarily military and do not contain any records of women.'[49] It is important to consider how people would react if the book, though pretending still to be about *Height, Health and History*, contained no data about *men*. Dorothy Smith's examples[50] are Philippe Aries' *Centuries of Childhood*,[51] which is properly *Centuries of the Childhood of Men*, and Christopher Jencks' influential *Inequality*,[52] which is a study of the educational system and its implications for equality among *men*.

'Man' means 'woman', and 'household' and 'family' means 'individual' – except that of course this is not the case. One particular and important error flowing from the idea that the unit of analysis is not the individual but the household concerns income. For a long time, it was assumed that household income and other material resources were shared equally by all its members.

But work on household resources[53] has shown that this is far from being the case. A particular paradox is that, though the earning power of men may be recognized by both men and women to be the arbiter of family living standards, women, particularly in low-income households, also recognize that theirs is the responsibility for family well-being. This translates into the understandable finding that women in poor single-parent families may feel better off than women in poor dual earner households because they have more control over the management of money.[54]

As Margaret Stacey[55] has pointed out, the two principal sociological theories about the social division of labour both feature Adam – one in the Garden of Eden and one not. Theories of the division of labour by sex refer to Adam's seduction by Eve into increasing his vitamin C intake, while theoretical understandings of the division of economic labour begin with Adam Smith in *The Wealth of Nations*. In these two key accounts, public and private labour are irreconcilably divided, with the result that theoretical explanations of human labour are also divided. There is no single theoretical perspective which can be applied to labour in the home – work 'on' people, and labour outside it – work *for* people.

One consequence of this is that any, however partial, sociology of household work takes up Eve's role in and outside the Garden of Eden, while men and the wealth or poverty of nations stagger on, more or less unchanged. Another consequence is that the removal of the masculine bias in – the introduction of women's studies to – sociology is itself a project weakened by the lack of a suffcient theoretical base.

A crucial arena of labour that has been reconceptualized in the last fifteen years is that concerned with caring work. Caring about someone is not necessarily the same as caring for them; yet the two tend to be confused within the sociological analysis of labour because of the dominance of the paradigm of motherhood as the prototype of women's caring work. Sensitivity to others' needs and the undertaking of practical labour necessary to fulfil these needs are built into the psychological socialization of women in western society, in such a way that women are often caught in the trap of 'doing good' and 'feeling bad'.[56] One implication of this is that the duality of caring as both labour and love can be taken to define the experience of being a woman in a male-dominated and capitalist social order. Caring work has implications for women's mental, emotional and physical health; it has implications for health policy in the widest possible sense and, increasingly in the 1990s, it has implications for the policies of both central and local government directed towards the care of dependent members of the community.

CONCLUSION

There have been changes in knowledge discourses over the last twenty years as women, conscious of their treatment as an oppressed group, have identified the ways in which the constitution of knowledge is itself an instrument of oppression. However, these changes do not add up to a revolution. Women have mapped their exclusion from male knowledge, but have not transformed it. On the other hand, it could be said that women could not have been *expected* to transform male knowledge. We might also ask whether male knowledge is worth transforming. We might say that the mapping of women's knowledge is extraordinarily important in its own right.

Sylvia Walby[57] has described four stages in the development of academic knowledge under the political impact of feminism. The first stage consists of the initially total neglect of women's social position, which includes their treatment in a brief aside or footnotes. The first stage lasted until the early 1970s. In the second stage, the flaws and fallacies of this reduction of women through biology and footnotes (often both together) is revealed for the hedonistic practice that it is. In the resulting criticism, assumptions about women and gender re-emerge as research questions. This happened from the mid-1970s through the 1980s, and is of course an extremely important point in itself. For the research questions of women's studies were not initially derived from the political practice of feminism; they came, rather, from the traditional practice of academia. His assumptions became her questions. To understand the full meaning of this, consider the sentence the other way round: her assumptions became his questions.

The third of Walby's stages is the additive one, and it proceeded in parallel with the emergence of research questions concerning women. Women are added in, or on, as a special case in order to compensate for their previous omission. This practice results in the multiple conjunctions of titles such as 'women and politics', 'women and stratification', 'women and employment', and so forth. Again, to murmur these phrases with 'men' substituting for 'women' is to appreciate the force of circumstances against us.

The fourth stage is the full theoretical integration of the analysis of gender into the central questions of the discipline. There are many reasons why this has not happened. In the first place, women's studies, wherever introduced, have been situated within the organizational and ideological structures of the very mode of understanding — that of patriarchal knowledge — which they set out to challenge. Universities are patriarchal hierarchies. As Adrienne Rich[58] has argued, the notion of the university rests on assumptions of social inequality and competitiveness, and on false ideas of objectivity.

A second reason why the feminist critique of knowledge in the shape of women's studies has not transformed the nature of academic knowledge is because the position of women retains some of its old pre-women's-movement contours. A third reason lies with the nature of malestream knowledge and its social construction, which is such that women's ways of knowing cannot be incorporated into it. These ways of knowing challenge not simply what is known, but the entire methodology and epistemiology of knowledge.

The most we can hope for is the continuation of women's ways of knowing and their institutional representations in women's studies courses. However, this is not only the most we can hope for, but also the best. A project carried out by Mary Belenky and colleagues[59] on how women see knowledge describes, on the basis of interviews with 135 women, a mode of knowing which links characteristics normally separated – for example, people's sense of self-worth, moral values, intellectual development, vision, everyday experience. The authors suggest that designing an education for women must begin by asking, not what most women learn, but what women know. That is the core of women's studies, both of the texts and of the process. This is the potential transformation of knowledge itself at the heart of the enterprise of women's studies.

Finally, there is the issue of how knowledge, however defined, is disseminated. It is another paradox that many of us consider, often apparently against all the evidence, the universities as places where this can be achieved. Somehow we continue obstinately to believe in the potential of the university for enriching life – that of both individuals and the community. The process whereby knowledge produced in the university reaches the public domain deserves a good deal of study and attention as the critical factor in the social uses to which knowledge is, and can be, put. When I was at a low point in believing in the value of my own work, someone drew to my attention the fact that the following limerick had won a competition in the *New Statesman and Society*:

> A jaded young housewife from Wapping
> Said her life was all cleaning and shopping.
> Her husband said jokily
> Try reading Ann Oakley
> So she did and left home without stopping.[60]

It could be argued that to produce work that comes out of, and hence resonates with, people's lived experiences is the very essence of the feminist challenge to knowledge.

17

Interviewing Women
A Contradiction in Terms?

Interviewing is rather like marriage: everybody knows what it is, an awful lot of people do it, and yet behind each closed front door there is a world of secrets. Despite the fact that much of modern sociology could justifiably be considered 'the science of the interview',[61] very few sociologists who employ interview data actually bother to describe in detail the process of interviewing itself. The conventions of research reporting require them to offer such information as how many interviews were done and how many were not done; the length of time the interviews lasted; whether the questions were asked following some standardized format or not; and how the information was recorded. Some issues on which research reports do not usually comment are: social/personal characteristics of those doing the interviewing; interviewees' feelings about being interviewed and about the interview; interviewers' feelings about interviewees; and quality of interviewer–interviewee interaction; hospitality offered by interviewees to interviewers; attempts by interviewees to use interviewers as sources of information; and the extension of interviewer–interviewee encounters into more broadly-based social relationships.

I shall argue in this chapter that social science researchers' awareness of those aspects of interviewing which are 'legitimate' and 'illegitimate' from the viewpoint of inclusion in research reports reflect their embeddedness in a particular research protocol. This protocol assumes a predominantly masculine model of sociology and society. The relative undervaluation of women's models has led to an unreal theoretical characterization of the interview as a means of gathering sociological data which cannot and does not work in practice. This lack of fit between the theory and practice of

interviewing is especially likely to come to the fore when a feminist interviewer is interviewing women (who may or may not be feminists).

Let us consider first what the methodology textbooks say about interviewing. First, and most obviously, an interview is a way of finding out about people. 'If you want an answer, ask a question . . . The asking of questions is the main source of social scientific information about everyday behaviour.[62] According to Johan Galtung:

> The survey method . . . has been indispensable in gaining information about the human condition and new insights in social theory.
>
> The reasons for the success of the survey method seem to be two: (1) *theoretically relevant* data are obtained, (2) they are amenable to *statistical treatment*, which means (a) the use of the powerful tools of correlation analysis and multi-variate analysis to test substantive relationships, and (b) the tools of statistical tests of hypotheses about generalizability from samples to universes.[63]

Interviewing, which is one means of conducting a survey, is essentially a conversation, 'merely one of the many ways in which two people talk to one another',[64] but it is also, significantly, an *instrument* of data-collection: 'the interviewer is really a tool or an instrument'.[65] As Benney and Hughes express it,

> Regarded as an information-gathering tool, the interview is designed to mimimise the local concrete, immediate circumstances of the particular encounter — including the respective personalities of the participants — and to emphasise only those aspects that can be kept general enough and demonstrable enough to be counted. As an encounter between these two particular people the typical interview has no meaning; it is conceived in a framework of other, comparable meetings between other couples, each recorded in such fashion that elements of communication in common can be easily isolated from more idiosyncratic qualities.[66]

Thus an interview is 'not simply a conversation. It is, rather, a pseudo-conversation. In order to be successful, it must have all the warmth and personality exchange of a conversation with the clarity and guidelines of scientific searching.'[67] This requirement means that the interview must be seen as 'a specialised pattern of verbal interaction — initiated for a specific purpose, and focussed on some specific content areas, with consequent elimination of extraneous material'.[68]

The motif of successful interviewing is 'be friendly but not too friendly'. For the contradiction at the heart of the textbook paradigm is that interviewing necessitates the manipulation of interviewees as objects of study/sources of data, but this can only be achieved via a certain amount of humane treatment. If the interviewee does not believe that he/she is being kindly and sympathetically treated by the interviewer, then he/she will not consent to be studied and will not come up with the desired information. A balance must then be struck between the warmth required to generate 'rapport' and the detachment necessary to see the interviewee as an object under surveillance; walking this tightrope means, not surprisingly, that 'interviewing is not easy',[69] although mostly the textbooks do support the idea that it *is* possible to be a perfect interviewer and both to obtain reliable and valid data and to make interviewees believe that they are not simple statistics-to-be. It is just a matter of following the rules.

A major preoccupation in spelling out the rules is to counsel potential interviewers about where necessary friendliness ends and unwarranted involvement begins. Goode and Hatt's statement on this topic says:

> Consequently, the interviewer cannot merely lose himself [sic] in being friendly. He must introduce himself as though beginning a conversation but from the beginning the additional element of respect, of professional competence, should be maintained. Even the beginning student will make this attempt, else he will find himself merely 'maintaining rapport', while failing to penetrate the cliches or contradictions of the respondent. Further he will find that his own confidence is lessened, if his only goal is to maintain friendliness. He is a professional researcher in this situation and he must demand and obtain respect for the task he is trying to perform.[70]

Claire Selltiz and her colleagues give a more explicit recipe. They say:

> The interviewer's manner should be friendly, courteous, conversational and unbiased. He [sic] should be neither too grim nor too effusive; neither too talkative nor too timid. The idea should be to put the respondent at ease, so that he[71] will talk freely and fully . . . [Hence] A brief remark about the weather, the family pets, flowers or children will often serve to break the ice. Above all, an informal, conversational interview is dependent upon a thorough mastery by the interviewer of the actual questions in his schedule. He should be familiar enough with them to ask them conversationally, rather than read them stiffly; and he should know what questions are coming next, so there will be no awkward pauses while he studies the questionnaire.[72]

C. A. Moser, in an earlier text, advises of the dangers of 'overrapport':

> Some interviewers are no doubt better than others at establishing what the psychologists call 'rapport' and some may even be too good at it — the National Opinion Research Centre Studies found slightly less satisfactory results from the . . . sociable interviewers who are 'fascinated by people' . . . there is something to be said for the interviewer who, while friendly and interested, does not get too emotionally involved with the respondent and his problems. Interviewing on most surveys is a fairly straightforward job, not one calling for exceptional industry, charm or tact. What one asks is that the interviewer's personality should be neither over-aggressive nor over-sociable. Pleasantness and a business-like nature is the ideal combination.[73]

'Rapport', a commonly-used but ill-defined term, does not mean in this context what the dictionary says it does ('a sympathetic relationship'[74]), but the acceptance by the interviewee of the interviewer's research goals, and the interviewee's active search to help the interviewer in providing the relevant information. The person who is interviewed has a passive role in adapting to the definition of the situation offered by the person doing the interviewing. The person doing the interviewing must actively and continually construct the 'respondent' (a telling name) as passive. Another way to phrase this is to say that both interviewer and interviewee must be 'socialized' into the correct interviewing behaviour:

> it is essential not only to train scientists to construct carefully worded questions and draw representative samples but also to educate the public to respond to questions on matters of interest to scientists and to do so in a manner advantageous for scientific analysis. To the extent that such is achieved, a common bond is established between interviewer and interviewee. [However] It is not enough for the scientist to understand the world of meaning of his informants; if he is to secure valid data via the structured interview, respondents must be socialised into answering questions in proper fashion.[75]

One piece of behaviour that properly-socialized respondents do not engage in is asking questions back. Although the textbooks do not present any evidence about the extent to which interviewers do find in practice that this happens, they warn of its dangers and in the process suggest some possible strategies of avoidance: 'Never provide the interviewee with any formal indication of the interviewer's beliefs and values. If the informant poses a question . . . parry it.'[76] 'When asked what you mean and think, tell

them you are here to learn, not to pass any judgement, that the situation is very complex.'[77] 'If he [the interviewer] should be asked for his views, he should laugh off the request with the remark that his job at the moment is to get opinions, not to have them'[78] – and so on. Goode and Hatt offer the most detailed advice on this issue:

> What is the interviewer to do, however, if the respondent really wants information? Suppose the interviewee does answer the question but then asks for the opinions of the interviewer. Should be give his honest opinion, or an opinion which he thinks the interviewee wants? In most cases, the rule remains that he is there to obtain information and to focus on the respondent, not himself. Usually, a few simple phrases will shift the emphasis back to the respondent. Some which have been fairly successful are 'I guess I haven't thought enough about it to give a good answer right now', 'Well, right now, your opinions are more important than mine', and 'If you really want to know what I think I'll be honest and tell you in a moment, after we've finished the interview'. Sometimes the diversion can be accomplished by a head-shaking gesture which suggests 'That's a hard one!' while continuing with the interview. In short, the interviewer must avoid the temptation to express his own views, even if given the opportunity.[79]

Of course, the reason why the interviewer must pretend not to have opinions (or to be possessed of information that the interviewee wants) is because behaving otherwise might 'bias' the interview. 'Bias' occurs when there are systematic differences between interviewers in the way in which interviews are conducted, with resulting differences in the data produced. Such bias clearly invalidates the scientific claims of the research, since the question of which information might be coloured by interviewees' responses to interviewers' attitudinal stances and which is independent of this 'contamination' cannot be settled in any decisive way.

The paradigm of the social research interview described in the methodology textbooks does, then, emphasize

1. its status as a mechanical instrument of data-collection;
2. its function as a specialized form of conversation in which one person asks the questions and another gives the answers;
3. its characterization of interviewees as essentially passive individuals, and
4. its reduction of interviewers to a question-asking and rapport-promoting role.

Actually, two separate typifications of the interviewer are prominent in the literature, though the disjunction between the two is never commented on.

In one, the interviewer is 'a combined phonograph and recording system';[80] the job of the interview 'is fundamentally that of a reporter not an evangelist, a curiosity-seeker, or a debater'.[81] It is important to note that, while the interviewer must treat the interviewee as an object or data-producing machine which, when handled correctly, will function properly, the interviewer herself/himself has the same status from the point of view of the person/people, institution or corporation conducting the research. Both interviewer and interviewee are thus depersonalized participants in the research process.

The second typification of interviewers in the methodology literature is that of the interviewer as psychoanalyst. The interviewer's relationship to the interviewee is hierarchical, and it is the body of expertise possessed by the interviewer that allows the interview to be successfully conducted. Most crucial in this exercise is the interviewer's use of non-directive comments and probes to encourage a free association of ideas which reveals whatever truth the research has been set up to uncover. Indeed, the term 'non-directive interview' is derived directly from the language of psychotherapy and carries the logic of interviewer impersonality to its extreme:

> Perhaps the most typical remarks made by the interviewer in a non-directive interview are: 'You feel that . . .' or 'Tell me more' or 'Why?' or 'Isn't that interesting?' or simply 'Uh huh'. The non-directive interviewer's function is primarily to serve as a catalyst to a comprehensive expression of the subject's feelings and beliefs and of the frame of reference within which his feelings and beliefs take on personal significance. To achieve this result, the interviewer must create a completely permissive atmosphere, in which the subject is free to express himself without fear of disapproval, admonition or dispute and without advice from the interviewer.[82]

Sjoberg and Nett spell out the premises of the free association method:

> the actor's [interviewee's] mental condition [is] . . . confused and difficult to grasp. Frequently the actor himself does not know what he believes; he may be so 'immature' that he cannot perceive or cope with his own subconscious thought patterns . . . the interviewer must be prepared to follow the interviewee through a jungle of meandering thought ways if he is to arrive at the person's true self.[83]

It seems clear that both psychoanalytic and mechanical typifications of the interviewer and, indeed, the entire paradigmatic representation of 'proper' interviews in the methodology textbooks, owe a great deal more to a masculine social and sociological vantage point than to a feminine one. For

example, the paradigm of the 'proper' interview appeals to such values as objectivity, detachment, hierarchy and 'science' as an important cultural activity which takes priority over people's more individualized concerns. Thus, the errors of poor interviewing comprise subjectivity, involvement, the 'fiction' of equality and an undue concern with the ways in which people are not statistically comparable. This polarity of 'proper' and 'improper' interviewing is an almost classical representation of the widespread gender-stereotyping which has been shown, in countless studies, to occur in modern industrial civilizations. Women are characterized as sensitive, intuitive, incapable of objectivity and emotional detachment and immersed in the business of making and sustaining personal relationships. Men are thought superior through their own capacity for rationality and scientific objectivity, and are thus seen to be possessed of an instrumental orientation in their relationships with others. Women are the exploited, the abused; they are unable to exploit others through the 'natural' weakness of altruism – a quality which is also their strength as wives, mothers and housewives. Conversely, men find it easy to exploit, although it is most important that any exploitation be justified in the name of some broad political or economic ideology ('the end justifies the means').

Feminine and masculine psychology in patriarchal societies is the psychology of subordinate and dominant social groups. The tie between women's irrationality and heightened sensibility, on the one hand, and their materially disadvantaged position, on the other, is, for example, also be to found in the case of ethnic minorities. The psychological characteristics of subordinates

> form a certain familiar cluster: submissiveness, passivity, docility, dependence, lack of initiative, inability to act, to decide, to think and the like. In general, this cluster includes qualities more characteristic of children than adults – immaturity, weakness and helplessness. If subordinates adopt these characteristics, they are considered well adjusted.[84]

It is no accident that the methodology textbooks refer to the interviewer as male. Although not all interviewees are referred to as female, there are a number of references to 'housewives' as the kind of people whom interviewers are most likely to meet in the course of their work.[85] Some of what Jean Baker Miller has to say about the relationship between dominant and subordinate groups would appear to be relevant to this paradigmatic interviewer–interviewee relationship:

> A dominant group, inevitably, has the greatest influence in determining a culture's overall outlook – its philosophy, morality, social theory and

even its science. The dominant group, thus, legitimizes the unequal relationship and incorporates it into society's guiding concepts . . .

Inevitably the dominant group is the model for 'normal human relationships'. It then becomes 'normal' to treat others destructively and to derogate them, to obscure the truth of what you are doing by creating false explanations and to oppose actions toward equality. In short, if one's identification is with the dominant group, it is 'normal' to continue in this pattern . . .

If follows from this that dominant groups generally do not like to be told about or even quietly reminded of the existence of inequality. 'Normally' they can avoid awareness because their explanation of the relationship becomes so well integrated *in other terms*; they can even believe that both they and the subordinate group share the same interest and, to some extent, a common experience . . .

Clearly, inequality has created a state of conflict. Yet dominant groups will tend to suppress conflict. They will see any questioning of the 'normal' situation as threatening; activities by subordinates in this direction will be perceived with alarm. Dominants are usually convinced that the way things are is right and good, not only for them but especially for the subordinates. All morality confirms this view and all social structure sustains it.[86]

To paraphrase the relevance of this to the interviewer–interviewee relationship, we could say that: interviewers define the role of interviewees as subordinates; extracting information is more to be valued than yielding it; the convention of interviewer–interviewee hierarchy is a rationalization of inequality; what is good for interviewers is not necessarily good for interviewees.

Another way to approach this question of the masculinity of the 'proper' interview is to observe that a sociology of feelings and emotion does not exist. Sociology mirrors society in not looking at social interaction from the viewpoint of women. While everyone has feelings,

Our society defines being cognitive, intellectual or rational dimensions of experience as superior to being emotional or sentimental. (Significantly, the terms 'emotional' and 'sentimental' have come to connote excessive or degenerate forms of feeling.) Through the prism of our technological and rationalistic culture, we are led to perceive and feel emotions as some irrelevancy or impediment to getting things done.

Hence their role in interviewing. But, 'Another reason for sociologists' neglect of emotions may be the discipline's attempt to be recognized as a

"real science" and the consequent need to focus on the most objective and measurable features of social life. This coincides with the values of the traditional "male culture".[87]

Becoming involved with the people whom you interview is doubly bad: it jeopardizes the hard-won status of sociology as a science and it is indicative of a form of personal degeneracy.

WOMEN INTERVIEWING WOMEN, OR OBJECTIFYING YOUR SISTER

Before I became an interviewer, I had read what the textbooks said interviewing ought to be. However, I found it very difficult to realize the prescription in practice, in a number of ways which I describe below. It was these practical difficulties which led me to take a new look at the textbook paradigm. In the rest of this chapter, the case which I want to make is that, when a feminist interviews women,

1. use of prescribed interviewing practice is morally indefensible;
2. general and irreconcilable contradictions at the heart of the textbook paradigm are exposed; and
3. it becomes clear that, in most cases, the goal of finding out about people through interviewing is best achieved when the relationship of interviewer and interviewee is non-hierarchical and when the interviewer is prepared to invest his or her own personal identity in the relationship.

Before arguing the general case, I will briefly mention some relevant aspects of my own interviewing experience. I have interviewed several hundred women over a period of some ten years, but it was the most recent research project, one concerned with the transition to motherhood, that particularly highlighted problems in the conventional interviewing recipe. Salient features of this research were that it involved repeated interviewing of a sample of women during a critical phase in their lives (in fact, fifty-five women were interviewed four times each: twice in pregnancy and twice afterwards, and the average total period of interviewing was 9.4 hours). It included, for some, my attendance at the most critical point in this phase: the birth of the baby. The research was preceded by nine months of participant observation chiefly in the hospital setting of interactions between mothers or mothers-to-be and medical people. Although I had a research assistant to help me, I myself did the bulk of the interviewing – 178 interviews over a period of some twelve months. The project was my idea, and the analysis and writing-up of the data were entirely my responsibility.

My difficulties in interviewing women were of two main kinds. First, they asked me a great many questions. Second, repeated interviewing over this kind of period, and involving the intensely personal experiences of

Table 17.1: Questions that interviewees asked (total 878), Transition to Motherhood Project (percentage).

Information requests	76
Personal questions	15
Questions about the research	6
Advice questions	4

pregnancy, birth and motherhood, established a rationale of personal involvement which I found it problematic and ultimately unhelpful to avoid.

ASKING QUESTIONS BACK

Analyzing the tape-recorded interviews which I had conducted, I listed 878 questions that interviewees had asked me at some point in the interviewing process. Three-quarters of these (see Table 17.1) were requests for information (e.g. 'Who will deliver my baby?'; 'How do you cook an egg for a baby?'). Fifteen per cent were questions about me, my experiences or attitudes in the area of reproduction ('Have you got any children?'; 'Did you breastfeed?'); six per cent were questions about the research ('Are you going to write a book?'; 'Who pays you for doing this?'), and four per cent were more directly requests for advice on a particular matter ('How long should you wait for sex after childbirth?'; 'Do you think my baby's got too many clothes on?'). Table 17.2 goes into more detail about the topics on which interviewees wanted information. The largest category of questions concerned medical procedures – for example, how induction of labour is done, and whether all women attending a particular hospital are given episiotomies. The second-largest category related to infant care or development – for example, 'How do you clean a baby's nails?'; 'When do babies sleep through the night?' Third, there were questions about organizational procedures in the institutional settings where antenatal or delivery care was done; typical questions were concerned with who exactly would be doing antenatal care and what the rules were for husbands' attendance at delivery. Last, there were questions about the physiology of reproduction – for example, 'Why do some women need Caesareans?' and (from one very frightened mother-to-be) 'Is it right that the baby doesn't come out of the same hole you pass water out of?'

It would be the understatement of all time to say that I found it very difficult to avoid answering these questions as honestly and fully as I could. I was faced, typically, with a woman who was quite anxious about the fate of herself and her baby, who found it either impossible or extremely difficult to ask questions and receive satisfactory answers from the medical staff with whom she came into contact, and who saw me as someone who could not

Table 17.2: Interviewees' requests for information (total 664), Transition to Motherhood Project (percentage).

Medical procedures	31
Organizational procedures	19
Physiology of reproduction	15
Baby care/development/feeding	21
Other	15

only reassure but also inform. I felt that I was asking a great deal from these women in the way of time, cooperation and hospitality at a stage in their lives when they had every reason to exclude strangers altogether in order to concentrate on the momentous character of the experiences being lived through. Indeed, I *was* asking a great deal – not only 9.4 hours of interviewing time but also confidences on highly personal matters such as sex and money and 'real' (i.e. possibly negative or ambivalent) feelings about babies, husbands, etc. I was, in addition, asking some of the women to allow me to witness them in the highly personal act of giving birth. Although the pregnancy interviews did not have to compete with the demands of motherhood for time, ninety per cent of the women were employed when first interviewed and seventy-six per cent of the first interviews had to take place in the evenings. Although I had timed the first postnatal interview (at about five weeks postpartum) to occur after the disturbances of very early motherhood, for many women it was nevertheless a stressful and busy time. And all this in the interest of 'science' or for some book that might possibly materialize out of the research – a book which many of the women interviewed would not read and none would profit from directly (though they hoped that they would not lose too much).

THE TRANSITION TO FRIENDSHIP?

In a paper on 'Collaborative Interviewing and Interactive Research', Laslett and Rapoport[88] discuss the advantages and disadvantages of repeated interviewing. They say that the gain in terms of collecting more information in greater depth than would otherwise be possible is partly made by 'being responsive to, rather than seeking to avoid, respondent reactions to the interview situation and experience'. This sort of research is deemed by them 'interactive'. The principle of a hierarchical relationship between interviewer and interviewee is not adhered to and 'an attempt is made to generate a collaborative approach to the research which engages both the interviewer and respondent in a joint enterprise'. Such an approach explicitly does not seek to minimize the personal involvement of the interviewer, but, as Rapoport and Rapoport put it, relies 'very much on the formulation of a

relationship between interviewer and interviewee as an important element in achieving the quality of the information . . . required'.[89]

As Laslett and Rapoport note, repeated interviewing is not much discussed in the methodological literature: the paradigm is of an interview as a 'one-off' affair. Common sense would suggest that an ethic of detachment on the interviewer's part is much easier to maintain where there is only one meeting with the interviewee (and the idea of a 'one off' affair rather than a longer-term relationship is undoubtedly closer to the traditional masculine world-view which I discussed earlier).

In terms of my experience in the childbirth project, I found that interviewees very often took the initiative in defining the interviewer–interviewee relationship as something which existed beyond the limits of question-asking and answering. For example, they did not only offer the minimum hospitality of accommodating me in their homes for the duration of the interview: at ninety-two per cent of the interviews I was offered tea, coffee or some other drink; fourteen per cent of the women also offered me a meal on at least one occasion. As Table 17.1 suggests, there was also a certain amount of interest in my own situation. What sort of person was I, and how did I come to be interested in this subject?

In some cases, these kind of 'respondent' reactions were evident at the first interview. More often, they were generated after the second interview, and an important factor here was probably the timing of the interviews. There was an average of twenty weeks between the first and second interviews, an average of eleven weeks between the second and third interviews and an average of fifteen weeks between the third and fourth interviews. Between the first two interviews, most of the women were very busy. Most were still employed and had the extra work of preparing equipment/clothes/a room for the baby – which sometimes meant moving house. Between the second and third interviews, most were not out at work and, sensitized by the questions that I had asked in the first two interviews to my interest in their birth experiences, probably began to associate me in a more direct way with their experiences of the transition to motherhood. At the second interview, I gave them all a stamped addressed postcard on which I asked them to write the date of their baby's birth so I would know when to contact them again for the first postnatal interview. I noticed that this was usually placed in a prominent position (for example, on the mantelpiece) to remind the woman or her partner to complete it, and it probably served in this way as a reminder of my intrusion into their lives. One illustration of this awareness comes from the third interview with Mary Rosen, a twenty-five-year-old exhibition organizer: 'I thought of you after he was born, I thought she'll *never* believe it – a six-hour labour, a 9 lb 6 oz baby and *no* forceps – and all without an

epidural, although I had said to you that I wanted one'. Sixty-two per cent of the women expressed a sustained and quite detailed interest in the research; they wanted to know its goals, any proposed methods for disseminating its findings, how I had come to think of it in the first place, the attitudes to it of doctors whom I had met or collaborated with, and so forth. Some of the women took the initiative in contacting me to arrange the second or a subsequent interview, although I had made it clear that I would get in touch with them. Several range up to report particularly important pieces of information about their antenatal care – in one case a distressing encounter with a doctor who told a woman keen on natural childbirth that this was 'for animals; in this hospital we give epidurals'; in another case to tell me of an ultrasound result that changed the expected date of delivery. Several also got in touch to correct or add to things that they had said during an interview – for instance, one contacted me several weeks after the fourth interview to explain that she had had an emergency appendicectomy five days after my visit, and that her physical symptoms at the time could have affected some of her responses to the questions that I had asked.

Arguably, these signs of interviewees' involvement indicated their acceptance of the goals of the research project rather than any desire to feel themselves participating in a personal relationship with me. Yet, the research was presented to them as *my* research in which I had a personal interest, so it is not likely that a hard-and-fast dividing line between the two was drawn. One index of their and my reactions to our joint participation in the repeated interviewing situation is that, some four years after the final interview, I am still in touch with more than a third of the women whom I interviewed. Four have become close friends, several others I visit occasionally, and the rest write or telephone when they have something salient to report, such as the birth of another child.

A FEMINIST INTERVIEWS WOMEN

Such responses as I have described on the part of the interviewees to participation in research, particularly that involving repeated interviewing, are not unknown, although they are almost certainly underreported. It could be suggested that the reasons why they were so pronounced in the research project discussed here is because of the attitudes of the interviewer – that is, the women were reacting to my own evident wish for a relatively intimate and non-hierarchical relationship. While I was careful not to take direct initiatives in this direction, I certainly set out to convey to the people whose cooperation I was seeking the fact that I did not intend to exploit either them or the information which they gave me. For instance, if the interview clashed with the demands of housework and motherhood, I offered to, and often did,

help with the work that had to be done. When asking the women's permission to record the interview, I said that no-one but I would ever listen to the tapes; in mentioning the possibility of publications arising out of the research, I told them that their names and personal details would be changed and that I would, if they wished, send them details of any such publications, and so forth. The attitude that I conveyed could have had some influence in encouraging the women to regard me as a friend rather than purely as a data-gatherer.

The pilot interviews, together with my previous experience of interviewing women, led me to decide that when I was asked questions I would answer them. The practice which I followed was to answer all personal questions and questions about the research as fully as was required. For example, when two women asked if I had read their hospital case-notes, I said that I had, and when one of them went on to ask what reason was given in these notes for her forceps delivery, I told her what the notes said. On the emotive issue of whether I experienced childbirth as painful (a common topic of conversation), I told them that I did find it so, but that in my view it was worth it to get a baby at the end. Advice questions I also answered fully, but made it clear when I was using my own experiences of motherhood as the basis for advice. I also referred women requesting advice to the antenatal and childbearing advice literature or to health visitors, GPs, etc. when appropriate – though the women usually made it clear that it was my opinion in particular that they were soliciting. When asked for information, I gave it if I could or, again, referred the questioner to an appropriate medical or non-medical authority. Again, the way in which I responded to interviewees' questions probably encouraged them to regard me as more than an instrument of data-collection.

Dissecting my practice of interviewing further, there were three principal reasons why I decided not to follow the textbook code of ethics with regard to interviewing women. First, I did not regard it as reasonable to adopt a purely exploitative attitude to interviewees as sources of data. My involvement in the women's movement in the early 1970s and the rebirth of feminism in an academic context had led me, along with many others, to reassess society and sociology as masculine paradigms, and to want to bring about change in the traditional cultural and academic treatment of women. 'Sisterhood', a somewhat nebulous and problematic, but nevertheless important, concept, certainly demanded that women re-evaluate the basis of their relationships with one another.

The dilemma of a feminist interviewer interviewing women could be summarized by considering the practical application of some of the strategies recommended in the textbooks for meeting interviewees'

questions. For example, these advise that such questions as 'Which hole does the baby come out of?', 'Does an epidural ever paralyze women?' and 'Why is it dangerous to leave a small baby alone in the house?' should be met with such responses from the interviewer as 'I guess I haven't thought enough about it to give a good answer right now', or 'a head-shaking gesture which suggests "That's a hard one!" '[90] Also recommended is laughing off the request with the remark that 'my job at the moment is to get opinions, not to have them'.[91]

A second reason for departing from conventional interviewing ethics was that I regarded sociological research as an essential way of giving the subjective situation of women greater visibility, not only in sociology, but also, more importantly, in society, than it has traditionally had. Interviewing women was, then, a strategy for documenting women's own accounts of their lives. What *was* important was not taken-for-granted sociological assumptions about the role of the interviewer, but a new awareness of the interviewer as an instrument for promoting a sociology *for* women, that is, as a tool for making possible the articulated and recorded commentary of women on the very personal business of being female in a patriarchal capitalist society. Note that the formulation of the interviewer role has changed dramatically from being a data-collecting instrument for researchers to being a data-collecting instrument for those whose lives are being researched. Such a reformulation is enhanced where the interviewer is also the researcher. It is not coincidental that in the methodological literature the paradigm of the research process is essentially disjunctive, that is, researcher and interviewer functions are typically performed by different individuals.

A third reason why I undertook the childbirth research with a degree of scepticism about how far traditional precepts of interviewing could, or should, be applied in practice was because I had found, in my previous interviewing experiences, that an attitude of refusing to answer questions or to offer any kind of personal feedback was not helpful in terms of the traditional goal of promoting 'rapport'. A different role, which could be termed 'no intimacy without reciprocity', seemed especially important in longitudinal in-depth interviewing. Without feeling that the interviewing process offered some personal satisfaction to them, interviewees would not be prepared to continue after the first interview. This involves being sensitive not only to those questions that are asked (by either party) but also to those that are not asked. The interviewee's definition of the interview is important.

The success of this method cannot, of course, be judged from the evidence that I have given so far. On the question of the rapport established in the Transition to Motherhood research, I offer the following cameo:

AO: Did you have any questions you wanted to ask but didn't when you last went to the hospital?

MC: Er, I don't know how to put this really. After sexual intercourse I had some bleeding, three times, only a few drops and I didn't tell the hospital because I didn't know how to put it to them. It worried me first off, as soon as I saw it I cried. I don't know if I'd be able to tell them. You see, I've also got a sore down there and a discharge and you know I wash there lots of times a day. You think I should tell the hospital; I could never speak to my own doctor about it. You see I feel like this but I can talk to you about it and I can talk to my sister about it.

More generally, the quality and depth of the information given to me by the women whom I interviewed can be assessed in *Becoming a Mother*,[92] the book arising out of the research which is based almost exclusively on interviewee accounts.

So far as interviewees' reactions to being interviewed are concerned, I asked them at the end of the last interview the question, 'Do you feel that being involved in this research – my coming to see you – has affected your experience of becoming a mother in any way?' Table 17.3 shows the answers. Nearly three-quarters of the women said that being interviewed had affected them, and the three most common forms that this influence took were in leading them to reflect on their experiences more than they would otherwise have done; in reducing the level of their anxiety and/or in reassuring them of their normality; and in giving a valuable outlet for the verbalization of feelings. None of those who thought that being interviewed had affected them regarded this effect as negative. There were many references to the 'therapeutic' effect of talking: 'getting it out of your system'. (It was generally felt that husbands, mothers, friends, etc. did not provide a sufficiently sympathetic or interested audience for a detailed recounting of the experiences and difficulties of becoming a mother.) It is perhaps important to note here that one of the main conclusions of the research was that there is a considerable discrepancy between the expectations and the reality of the different aspects of motherhood – pregnancy, childbirth, the emotional relationship of mother and child, the work of childrearing. A dominant metaphor used by interviewees to describe their reactions to this hiatus was 'shock'. In this sense, a process of emotional recovery is endemic in the normal transition to motherhood and there is a general need for some kind of 'therapeutic listener' that is not met within the usual circle of family and friends.

Table 17.3: 'Has the research affected your experience of becoming a mother?' (percentage).

No	27
Yes:	73
Thought about it more	30
Found it reassuring	25
A relief to talk	25
Changed attitudes/behaviour	7

(Percentages do not add up to 100 per cent because some women gave more than one answer.)

On the issue of cooperation, only two out of eighty-two women contacted initially about the research actually refused to take part in it, making a refusal rate of two per cent, which is extremely low. Once the interviewing was under way, only one woman voluntarily dropped out (because of marital problems); an attrition from sixty-six at the first interview to fifty-five at the fourth interview was otherwise accounted for by miscarriage, moves, etc. All the women who were asked if they would mind my attending the birth said that they didn't mind, and all got in touch either directly or indirectly through their husbands when they started labour. The postcards left after the second interview, for interviewees to return after the birth, were all completed and returned.

IS A 'PROPER' INTERVIEW EVER POSSIBLE?

Hidden among the admonitions on how to be a perfect interviewer in the social research methods manuals is the covert recognition that the goal of perfection is actually unattainable: the contradiction between the need for 'rapport' and the requirement of between-interview comparability cannot be solved. For example, Dexter, following Paul,[93] observes that the pretence of neutrality on the interviewer's part is counterproductive: participation demands alignment. Selltiz et al. say that 'Much of what we call interviewer bias can more correctly be described as interviewer *differences*, which are inherent in the fact that interviewers are human beings and not machines and that they do not work identically'.[94] Richardson and his colleagues, in their popular textbook on interviewing, note that:

> Although gaining and maintaining satisfactory participation is never the primary objective of the interviewer, it is so intimately related to the quality and quantity of the information sought that the interviewer must always maintain a dual concern: for the quality of his respondent's participation and for the quality of the information being sought. Often . . . these qualities are independent of each other and occasionally they may be mutually exclusive.[95]

It is not hard to find echoes of this point of view in the few accounts of the actual process of interviewing that do exist. For example, Zweig, in this study of *Labour, Life and Poverty,*

> dropped the idea of a questionnaire or formal verbal questions . . . instead I had casual talks with working-class men on an absolutely equal footing . . .
>
> I made many friends and some of them paid me a visit afterwards or expressed a wish to keep in touch with me. Some of them confided their troubles to me and I often heard the remark: 'Strangely enough, I have never talked about that to anybody else'. They regarded my interest in their way of life as a sign of sympathy and understanding rarely shown to them even in the inner circle of their family. I never posed as somebody superior to them or as a judge of their actions but as one of them.[96]

Zweig defended his method on the grounds that telling people they were objects of study met with 'an icy reception' and that finding out about other people's lives is much more readily done on a basis of friendship than in a formal interview.

More typically and recently, Marie Corbin, the interviewer for the Pahls' study of *Managers and Their Wives,* commented in an Appendix to the book of that name:

> Obviously the exact type of relationship that is formed between an interviewer and the people being interviewed is something that the interviewer cannot control entirely, even though the nature of this relationship and how the interviewees classify the interviewer will affect the kinds of information given . . . simply because I am a woman and a wife I shared interests with the other wives and this helped to make the relationship a relaxed one.

Corbin goes on:

> In these particular interviews I was conscious of the need to establish some kind of confidence with the couples if the sorts of information required were to be forthcoming . . . In theory it should be possible to establish confidence simply by courtesy towards and interest in the interviewees. In practice it can be difficult to spend eight hours in a person's home, share their meals and listen to their problems and at the same time remain polite, detached and largely uncommunicative. I found the balance between prejudicing the answers to questions which covered almost every aspect of the couples' lives, establishing a

relationship that would allow the interviews to be successful and holding a civilized conversation over dinner to be a very precarious one.[97]

Discussing research on copper-mining on Bougainville Island in Papua New Guinea, Alexander Mamak describes his growing consciousness of the political context in which research is done:

> as I became increasingly aware of the unequal relationship existing between management and the union, I found myself becoming more and more emotionally involved in the proceedings. I do not believe this reaction is unusual since, in the words of the wellknown black sociologist Nathan Hare, 'If one is truly cognizant of adverse circumstances, he would be expected, through the process of reason, to experience some emotional response'.[98]

And, a third illustration of this point, Dorothy Hobson's account of her research on housewives' experiences of social isolation contains the following remarks:

> The method of interviewing in a one-to-one situation requires some comment. What I find most difficult is to resist commenting in a way which may direct the answers which the women give to my questions. However, when the taped interview ends we usually talk and then the women ask me questions about my life and family. These questions often reflect areas where they have experienced ambivalent feelings in their own replies. For example, one woman who said during the interview that she did not like being married, asked me how long I had been married and if I liked it. When I told her how long I had been married she said, 'Well I suppose you get used to it in time, I suppose I will'. In fact the informal talk after the interview often continues what the women have said during the interview.
>
> It is impossible to tell exactly how the women perceive me but I do not think they see me as too far removed from themselves. This may partly be because I have to arrange the interviews when my own son is at school and leave in time to collect him.[99]

As Bell and Newby note, 'accounts of doing sociological research are at least as valuable, both to students of sociology and its practitioners, as the exhortations to be found in the much more common textbooks on methodology'.[100] All research is political, 'from the micropolitics of interpersonal relationships, through the politics of research units, institutions and universities, to those of government departments and finally to the state'

– which is one reason why social research is not 'like it is presented and prescribed in those texts. It is infinitely more complex, messy, various and much more interesting'.[101] The 'cookbooks' of research methods largely ignore the political context of research, although some make asides about its 'ethical dilemmas': 'Since we are all human we are all involved in what we are studying when we try to study any aspect of social relations';[102] 'frequently researchers, in the course of their interviewing, establish rapport not as scientists but as human beings; yet they proceed to use this humanistically gained knowledge for scientific ends, usually without the informants' knowledge'.[103]

These ethical dilemmas are generic to all research involving interviewing, for reasons that I have already discussed. But they are greatest where there is least social distance between the interviewer and interviewee. Where both share the same gender-socialization and critical life-experiences, social distance can be minimal. Where both interviewer and interviewee share membership of the same minority group, the basis for equality may impress itself even more urgently on the interviewer's consciousness. Mamak's comments apply equally to a feminist interviewing women:

> I found that my academic training in the methodological views of Western social science and its emphasis on 'scientific objectivity' conflicted with the experiences of my colonial past. The traditional way in which social science research is conducted proved inadequate for an understanding of the reality, needs and desires of the people I was researching.[104]

Some of the reasons why a 'proper' interview is a masculine fiction are illustrated by observations from another field in which individuals try to find out about other individuals – anthropology. Evans-Pritchard reported this conversation during his early research with the Nuers of East Africa:

I: Who are you?
Cuol: A man.
I: What is your name?
Cuol: Do you want to know my *name?*
I: Yes.
Cuol: You want to know *my* name?
I: Yes, you have come to visit me in my tent and I would like to know who you are.
Cuol: All right, I am Cuol. What is your name?

I: My name is Pritchard.

Cuol: What is your father's name?

I: My father's name is also Pritchard.

Cuol: No, that cannot be true, you cannot have the same name as your father.

I: It is the name of my lineage. What is the name of your lineage?

Cuol: Do you want to know the name of my lineage?

I: Yes.

Cuol: What will you do with it if I tell you? Will you take it to your country?

I: I don't want to do anything with it. I just want to know it since I am living at your camp.

Cuol: Oh well, we are Lou.

I: I did not ask you the name of your tribe. I know that. I am asking you the name of your lineage.

Cuol: Why do you want to know the name of my lineage?

I: I don't want to know it.

Cuol: Then why do you ask me for it? Give me some tobacco.

I defy the most patient ethnologist to make headway against this kind of opposition [concluded Evans-Pritchard].[105]

Interviewees are people with considerable potential for sabotaging the attempt to research them. Where, as in the case of anthropology or repeated interviewing in sociology, the research cannot proceed without a relationship of mutual trust being established between interviewer and interviewee, the prospects are particularly dismal. This inevitably changes the interviewer/anthropologist's attitude to the people whom he/she is studying. A poignant example is the incident related in Elenore Smith Bowen's *Return to Laughter*, when the anthropologist witnesses one of her most trusted informants dying in childbirth:

> I stood over Amara. She tried to smile at me. She was very ill. I was convinced these women could not help her. She would die. She was my friend but my epitaph for her would be impersonal observations scribbled in my notebook, her memory preserved in an anthropologist's file: 'Death (in childbirth)/Cause: witchcraft/Case of Amara'. A lecture from the past reproached me: 'The anthropologist cannot, like the chemist or biologist, arrange controlled experiments. Like the astronomer, his mere presence produces changes in the data he is trying to observe. He himself is a disturbing influence which he must endeavour to keep to the minimum. His claim to science must therefore

rest on a meticulous accuracy of observations and on a cool, objective approach to his data.'

A cool, objective approach to Amara's death?

One can, perhaps, be cool when dealing with questionnaires or when interviewing strangers. But what is one to do when one can collect one's data only by forming personal friendships? It is hard enough to think of a friend as a case history. Was I to stand aloof, observing the course of events?[106]

Professional hesitation meant that Bowen might never see the ceremonies connected with death in childbirth. But, on the other hand, she would see her friend die. Bowen's difficult decision to plead with Amara's kin and the midwives in charge of her case to allow her access to western medicine did not pay off and Amara did eventually die.

An anthropologist has to 'get inside the culture'; participant observation means 'that . . . the observer participates in the daily life of the people under study, either openly in the role of researcher or covertly in some disguised role'.[107] A feminist interviewing women is by definition both 'inside' the culture and participating in that which she is observing. However, in these respects, the behaviour of a feminist interviewer/researcher is not extraordinary. Although

Descriptions of the research process in the social sciences often suggest that the motivation for carrying out substantive work lies in theoretical concerns . . . the research process appears a very orderly and coherent process indeed . . . The personal tends to be carefully removed from public statements; these are full of rational argument [and] careful discussion of academic points. [It can equally easily be seen that] all research is 'grounded', because no researcher can separate herself from personhood and thus from deriving second order constructs from experience.[108]

A feminist methodology of social science requires that this rationale of research be described and discussed, not only in feminist research, but also in social science research in general. It requires, further, that the mythology of 'hygienic' research with its accompanying mystification of the researcher and the researched as objective instruments of data-production be replaced by the recognition that personal involvement is more than dangerous bias – it is the condition under which people come to know each other and to admit others into their lives.

18

Some Problems of the Scientific Research Method and Feminist Research Practice

This chapter focuses on the nature and uses of the methodology of the randomized controlled trial (RCT) in the light of recent critiques of science, including the feminist concern with the social structure of science as representing an inherently sexist, racist, classist and culturally coercive practice and form of knowledge. Using the example of one specific RCT aimed at promoting women's health, the chapter outlines some of the dilemmas thus raised for the pursuit of 'good' research practice. The particular viewpoint is that of a feminist sociologist who has been responsible for designing and carrying out a randomized trial in the field of prenatal health care.[109] While the focus is on the use of the methodology of random allocation in health research, it is important to note that it has also been used in other areas of experimental research within the social sciences, for instance in psychology in the evaluation of educational interventions,[110] and in the assessment of professional social-work services.[111] Although the study discussed here and some of the other data drawn on are British, the issues highlighted are of general relevance to all communities where importance is attached to the goal of researching and promoting women's health in the broadest sense.

FROM GUINEA PIGS TO THE CAMEL'S NOSE: ORIGINS AND PROBLEMS OF THE RCT AS A TOOL FOR RESEARCHING WOMEN'S HEALTH

The randomized controlled trial as a research method applicable to human subjects is generally said to have been invented in 1946. In that year, a new drug, streptomycin, was thought to cure tuberculosis in guinea pigs, and

initial use on human beings suggested therapeutic effectiveness. Because supplies of the new drug were scarce, the Medical Research Council in Britain decided to administer it in the form of a controlled trial, giving it on the basis of selection according to a table of random numbers to some people with tuberculosis and not to others.[112]

Behind this apocryphal story of the origins of the randomized controlled trial lies an intermittent history of previous attempts to carry out unbiased comparisons of the effectiveness of different medical treatments. The RCT is essentially an experimental test ('trial') of a particular treatment/approach (or set of treatments/approaches) comparing two or more groups of subjects who are allocated to these groups at random, i.e. according to the play of chance. Conclusions about the effectiveness of treatments based on an RCT rest upon two issues – an assessment of *significance* and a judgment about *causation.* Tests of statistical significance are used to determine whether any observed difference between trial groups is due to sampling variability or is evidence of a 'real' difference. If a difference is significant in this sense, then, as Schwartz and colleagues put it in their classical text *Clinical Trials,*

> a judgement of causation allows us to attribute it to the difference between [the] two treatments. This is only possible if the two groups are strictly comparable in all respects apart from the treatments given. Providing two such comparable groups is another statistical problem the correct solution of which is obtained by randomization.[113]

It is important to note that the prerequisite for any RCT is *uncertainty* about the effects of a particular treatment. If something is known to work (and to be acceptable and without harmful effects), then there is no reason to put it to the test in the form of a trial. It is, however, this very issue of certainty/uncertainty that constitutes one of the central problems of the contemporary debate about RCTs. People can be certain that something (e.g. streptomycin, social workers) *is* effective but have no 'real' basis for their certainty; conversely, unless they are able to admit uncertainty, 'real' knowledge can never be gained.

The RCT has been increasingly promoted over the last twenty years as *the* major evaluative tool within medicine. Over the same period, a new critical perspective has emerged towards what counts as 'knowledge' and the methods and techniques appropriate to its accumulation. Sources of this critique include the radical science movement,[114] the emergence of 'ethnomethodology' within sociology,[115] and the broad consensus located within the women's movement about the 'masculinist' orientation of much scientific activity.[116] The result of these various critiques has been a heightened awareness of the contribution made by different kinds of

research strategies to extending human knowledge in the domain both of the 'natural' and the 'social' sciences.

Over the last twenty years, feminists have increasingly criticized the ways in which the construction of what counts as 'knowledge' omits women's perspectives and experiences and is embedded with masculinist values.[117] The orbit of feminist concern has included science.[118] At the same time as the feminist critique has developed, medical science has expanded its control of life in general and of women's lives in particular. This process has highlighted the need to evaluate all interventions claimed to promote health, and has given prominence to the role of the RCT. But, although feminist researchers have taken to task in recent years many methodologies in both the natural and 'unnatural' sciences, there has been virtually no discussion to date of this particular, increasingly advocated approach.

The notion of 'feminist' research as discussed here is taken to mean research that relates to an understanding of women's position as that of an oppressed social group, and which adopts a critical perspective towards intellectual traditions rendering women either invisible and/or subject to a priori categorizations of one kind of another. The research process itself is subject to the same stipulations: that it should not employ methods oppressive either to researchers or to the researched, and that it should be oriented towards the production of knowledge in such a form and in such a way as can be used by women themselves.[119] These strictures are also a formula for 'good' research practice as applied to human subjects in general. However, the practice of feminist research is often located by its advocates on one side of the divide between 'qualitative' and 'quantitative' research methods. Qualitative methods involving in-depth interviewing are seen to be more suited to the exploration of individual experiences – the representation of subjectivity within academic discourse – and to facilitate (in practice if not in theory) a non-hierarchical organization of the research process.[120] Conversely, quantitative methods (large-scale surveys, the use of prespecified scoring methods, e.g. in personality tests) are cited as instituting the hegemony of the researcher over the researched, and as reducing personal experience to the anonymity of mere numbers. The feminist/ masculinist and qualitative/quantitative divisions are paralleled conceptually by a third, that between the physical and the social sciences. As Hedges has commented, 'Those of us in the social and behavioural sciences know intuitively that there is something "softer" and less cumulative about our research results than those of the physical sciences'.[121]

In terms of this debate about good research practice, the starting point of this chapter is Davies and Esseveld's observation that the problem about the feminist rejection of quantitative methods as necessarily alienating is that it

bars discussion both of the ways in which these methods are used, and of those in which they could be used to generate knowledge relevant to the exercise of improving women's situation.[122] Although feminist research practice requires a critical stance towards existing methodology (the abolition of 'methodolatry', to use Daly's[123] term), at the same time it has to be recognized that the universe of askable research questions is constrained by the methods allowed. To ban any quantitative (social) science therefore results in a restriction to certain kinds of questions only; this restriction may very well be counter to the same epistemological goal that a code of feminist research practice is designed to promote.

According to an Arabic saying deployed by Harris,[124] the problem about letting a camel's nose into your tent is that you are likely then to have to let the whole camel in. The essential question for feminist research posed by the RCT is whether there are benefits of this methodology which can and should be harnessed, without simultaneously dragging into the tent the entire unwieldy superstructure of mixed benefits and hazards (the rest of the camel). Existing published work and the experience drawn on in this chapter suggest that RCTs pose three particular problems for feminist researchers. First, and most obviously, there is the principle of *random allocation*, which uses chance – 'the absence of design' (OED) to determine the treatment received by participants in the research. The extent to which individuals are able to choose the form of their participation in the research is thereby limited. Linked with this is the much-debated issue of *informed consent*. What is the meaning of consent, and how much of what kind of information is required by whom? The third problem concerns the epistemology, ownership and distribution of *certainty*. As already noted, the rationale for undertaking an RCT is uncertainty about the effectiveness/acceptability of a particular procedure. But the professionals may be certain and the lay public not; or the lay public may be convinced about the benefits of a procedure which meets with professional scepticism. It would appear that this issue in particular has provoked a good deal of unclear thinking among those concerned with the promotion of women's health.

Before examining each of these problems in turn, I shall briefly outline the study which highlighted these specific areas of conflict between the practice of *feminist* research one the one hand, and the model of *randomized controlled evaluation*, on the other.

WHO CARES FOR WOMEN? AN RCT OF SOCIAL SUPPORT

The history of the medical care and surveillance of childbearing women is not one of tested and proven effectiveness.[125] Studies of how women experience the maternity services have for long revealed an iceberg of

dissatisfaction, with lack of information, poor communication, long waiting times and absence of continuity of care coming top of the list.[126] The complaints that women make about their care resonate with an expanding literature on the importance of social support to the promotion of health.[127] It appears (not surprisingly) that friends are as good as or better than the famous apple in keeping the doctor away.[128] (This may be one instance of modern scientific knowledge catching up with women's experiential understanding of the world.[129])

For these reasons, a study of social support in pregnancy was undertaken in 1985. The broad aim of the project was to establish whether social support provided as a research intervention has the capacity to make things better for women and their babies. Most previous work on this topic is problematic, because of the repetitive methodological problem that, although better health is generally associated with more support, it is impossible to rule out the explanation that healthier, more supported mothers are different in other ways from less supported, less healthy mothers and babies.[130] Although the better-done observational studies make multiple adjustments for confounding variables, still one can only adjust for those variables known to confound; there may be others, equally confounding, of which the researcher is ignorant. For this reason, our study was planned as an *intervention* study, in which the intervention of providing additional social support would be offered to some women and not to others, and various indices of their experiences, including their health and that of their babies, would be compared at the end of the study. Over a fifteen-month period, a total of 509 women agreed to take part in the study. Random allocation was used to determine who received the intervention, and social support was given by four research midwives who visited women at home during pregnancy, offered a listening ear for individual problems, provided various forms of practical and emotional help when required, and were available twenty-four hours a day to be contacted in case of need. The Department of Health and Social Security (as was), who funded the study, were keen for us to have midwives, rather than any other professional or lay group, giving social support because of the study's possible policy implications. The Department expressed the view that, were the study to be successful in demonstrating the clinical effectiveness of social support, the intervention used should be one that related to existing maternity-care provision. In order to increase our chances of detecting an effect of social support, we specified that the women needed to have given birth to a small baby in the past and thus constitute a 'high-risk' group. The theory behind this was that women with problematic medical histories would be more likely than those without to benefit from extra support.

Additionally, use of this criterion would lead to a largely working-class sample (as two-thirds of low-birthweight babies but only half of all babies in Britain are born in working-class households), and this concentration of social disadvantage might also result in higher benefit. The 'effectiveness' of this social support intervention in terms of a range of outcomes, including women's satisfaction and infant birthweight, was evaluated after delivery, using obstetric case-note information from the four hospitals where the study was done, and by sending all the women a long and detailed postal questionnaire.

Methods used in this study fit more closely within the medical model of controlled evaluation of therapeutic strategies, rather than with the social-science model of qualitative research, in which in-depth interviewing is used to build up interpretative accounts of social processes. However, the study began life as a desire to test the idea that in-depth social-science interviewing can in itself have a supportive effect for those interviewed.[131] The midwives giving social support also carried out semi-structured interviews with the women in their intervention group; these interviews were partially tape-recorded in order to enable some qualitative analysis of women's experiences.

CHANCE OR CAUSATION? THE ROLE OF RANDOM NUMBERS

The first of the three problems referred to earlier in combining a feminist research consciousness with the technique of an RCT concerns the process of random allocation itself. We had some interesting and some disturbing difficulties with this. Before discussing these, it is worth considering the history of randomization as a research technique. According to Silverman, 'The central question in the study of living things is how to decide whether an observed event is to be attributed to the meaningless play of chance, on the one hand, or to causation . . . on the other'.[132] Until the 1920s, scientists were not able to overcome the problem that very long series of observations were needed in order to estimate the frequency of occurrence of chance variations. R. A. Fisher, a statistician working at an Agricultural Research Station in Harpenden, then devised new techniques for reducing the number of observations needed, by dividing the ground into *randomly* ordered blocks to be treated in different ways.

As a research technique, randomization is said to offer three principal advantages. First, each study unit (plot of earth, person, institution, etc.) has an equal chance of being or not being in the experimental group. Estimates of chance variability are consequently much easier to come by. Second, assignment on the basis of a table of random numbers eradicates the potential for *bias*: researchers are unable to influence their results by

choosing to load their experimental group with 'favourable' factors – 'good' seeds, middle-class women, well-resourced institutions. Third, the method allows the researchers evenly to distribute both those factors *known* to be associated with different outcomes and those which may be, but are *unknown*. An instructive example of the latter is discussed by Chalmers[133] in a paper addressing the competing claims of scientific inquiry and authoritarianism in perinatal care. In a trial of a cholesterol-lowering drug versus placebo in the prevention of repeat myocardial infarction in men,[134] no overall benefit for the active drug was found. However, twenty per cent of those prescribed the drug had not actually taken it, and mortality in this group was significantly higher, which might lead to the conclusion that the drug really did work. Researchers then went on to look at the group given placebo pills: twenty per cent of these had also not taken their pills, and *their* mortality was also significantly higher than those who had. In fact, the group that fared best of the four (drug-prescribed compliers/non-compliers/ placebo-prescribed compliers/non-compliers) were men who took the placebo as prescribed. The *behavioural* factor of 'non-compliance' had an unanticipated importance greater than that of *physical* risk factors, and use of random allocation distributed the propensity to disobey doctors' orders equally between treatment groups, thus permitting valid conclusions to be drawn about the 'real' value of the 'active' drug.

These advantages have led to a characterization of RCTs within medicine and health-care research more generally as 'the most scientifically valid method' of evaluating different procedures or types of care.[135] According to proponents of the method, the advantage of random allocation is predominantly *scientific*. It improves the *design* of a study, in part by ensuring that the basic premise – of truly random sampling – underlying the use of statistical tests of significance is correct, in part by clearing the field of unknown 'biases', including those of both researchers and the researched. This removal of the human, subjective element is in line with what Reinharz[136] and others have described as the 'conventional' or 'patriarchal' research model: research design is laid down in advance, research objectives are concerned with testing hypotheses, units of study are predefined, the researcher's attitudes to research subjects is detached, data are manipulated using statistical analyses, replicability of the study findings is stressed, and research reports are cast in the form of presenting results only in relation to preset hypotheses and for approval in an academic community where neither researcher nor researched are allowed identities or personal values. It is, however, worth noting that one of the attributed weaknesses of RCTs – their concern with quantity rather than quality, of life measures – is not a weakness of the method itself, but of its application.[137]

Having acquired research funds, we then needed to discuss the use of the method with those whom we were asking to use it, namely the four research midwives. In our discussions with them, we emphasized the dual facts that, first, it was by no means clear that social support was of global benefit to pregnant women (too much social support might be too much of a good thing: at least it was a research question as to which subgroups of women might benefit); and that, second, we wanted to be able to say something definite about the usefulness of giving social support to pregnant women at the end of the study; use of this method was more likely than any other to enable us to do this. Randomization was done by the midwives telephoning us in London with the names of women who had agreed to take part. The study 'secretary' had sheets of allocations derived from a table of random numbers, and she wrote down each woman in order, then informing the midwife of the result of the allocation.

As the study progressed, we had many discussions about how everyone felt about this procedure. The midwives were sometimes unhappy about both the process and the results of the randomization. They considered it a problem that random allocation was being used to determine which women received additional social support, as this meant that the women themselves could not choose their fates; it also meant that, in agreeing to participate in the study, they were agreeing to a fifty per cent chance of either receiving additional social support or not doing so. Also, the midwives worried because sometimes women whom they thought were in need of social support were allocated to the control grup (standard care), or those whom they considered to have enough of it already were allocated to receive it. One midwife wrote compellingly in a questionnaire which we gave them halfway through the study, about the conflict between random allocation and the principles of her midwifery training:

> It's very strange in that, if this was practice and not research, you would evaluate each woman and decide if she needed the extra care for various reasons. . . . It's hard if you recruit someone who obviously has major problems and is desperate for extra help, and then she becomes control. I can feel guilty at showing her that extra care is available, and then not offering it to her – even more so if she eventually has a poor outcome to her pregnancy. Conversely, if she becomes intervention and has obvious major problems, I may wilt a little at finding the extra time and stamina to help her!
>
> It can be a shame if, at first interview, you feel that a woman has no problems, is well-informed and supported, and yet you know you will keep on visiting, when you could spend that time with someone who

would benefit more. But it's often not until you visit two or three times that problems become apparent.

There were other observations from the midwives about the initial invisibility of women's support needs. The following dialogue occurred during one of our regular research team meetings:

> *Midwife 1:* I think sometimes after the first interview, I wouldn't mind writing down which group I thought they needed to be in. I mean, you see them the first time, and their history's nothing, but when you talk to them, you know how awful it is.
>
> *Midwife 2:* And it may not be anything to do with their obstetric history.
>
> *Midwife 1:* Very often it isn't. I went to a lady the other day. On the first visit, everything seemed fine. We were talking away and I got to the section on major worries. She said well, yes, I suppose I have, and it turned out that her older son and her husband, who was not his father, had never got on, which could have had a bearing on the pregnancy in which she'd had a small baby. He'd been in trouble with the police, writing cheques, and so had her son; she brought out all these problems existing in her family since she'd remarried, and she said she can see such a difference in her life now. But I mean that sort of thing doesn't come out at first does it?

In other words, random numbers have the edge over human intuition because human beings are not always right in the judgments that they make. The professional ideology of midwifery, along with that of other health professionals, has been shown to lead to discriminatory stereotyping of women, based on such characteristics as working-class or ethnic minority status.[138]

The midwives in our study also tried various ploys to control the randomization process. These included: attempting to spot a pattern in the allocations, so that the order of intervention and control allocations could be predicted, and women entered in accordance with what the midwives thought would suit the women best; and good-humouredly trying to persuade the study secretary to tell them in which order to enter different women (they were quick to realize that the secretary would have the preset allocation order in front of her when they telephoned). As well as the factor of women's own needs for social support, the four midwives openly

confessed concern about the distances that they had to travel to carry out the home visits, and about other aspects of their work conditions, such as having to visit possibly dangerous, ill-lit housing estates late in the evening. They understandably hoped that their intervention group women would live close to home in places which were comfortable and safe to visit.

My own concerns as project 'director' on the issue of random allocation were, and remained, confused. In the first place, I was committed to the goal of evaluating the effectiveness of social support in a scientific manner acceptable to the scientific community and to policy-makers, which raises its own problems – for instance about the ethics and relevance to women's situation of targeting research at those in power. It is arguable that the usefulness of research in terms of effecting change is greatest when made accessible to the powerless, rather than the powerful. However, the escalating use of unevaluated technology in the maternity-care field is a compelling reason for focusing at least some attention directly on those responsible for formulating policy. Because of this goal of reaching policy-makers, I felt that it *was* important to carry out the study according to the rules. This, I think was achieved; indeed, our commitment to open discussion of these difficult issues may even have produced greater rigour and consistency in terms of the orthodox model than is normally obtained.

Professional discussions of RCTs are replete with 'anecdotes' concerning people's natural human attempts to control the randomization process. In a trial described by Silverman, for instance, of the effect of artificial light on the occurrence of retrolental fibroplasia (oxygen-induced blindness) in babies,

> Assignment to 'light' or 'no-light' was made on the basis of blue and white marbles in a box. One day, I noted that our head nurse reached into the box for a marble and then replaced it because it wasn't the colour that corresponded to her belief about the best treatment for her babies. I became convinced that we had to shift to sealed envelopes, as used in the British streptomycin trial. When the first sealed envelope was drawn, the resident physician held it up to the light to see the assignment inside! I took the envelopes home and my wife[139] and I wrapped each assignment-sticker in black paper and resealed the envelopes.[140]

Such revelations draw attention to the discrepancy between the model of 'scientific' research on the one hand and its practice on the other. This discrepancy has been increasingly discussed in recent years, with reports drawing attention to such aspects as the subjective bias inherent in the peer-review process,[141] or the tendency for medical researchers to write up and publish research favouring new, as opposed to standard, therapies.[142]

CONSENTING ADULTS?

The issue of randomization is closely bound up with the question of the extent to which participants in a research project (either an RCT or any other) consent on the basis of full information to take part in it. The issue of informed consent is the second area of conflict between the principles of feminist research practice and the use of the RCT technique.

In most, if not all, research studies in the social sciences and the market research/opinion survey domain, the people from whom, or on whom, information is gathered are given the opportunity not to take part. This convention accounts for the citation of what, perhaps revealingly, are called 'refusal' and 'non-response' rates: high refusal or non-response rates are considered to call into question the validity (generalizability) of the research findings, whereas low refusal or non-response rates are generally hailed as an achievement for the researchers.

Consent to participate in research is not, however, the rule in medical research, where, according to Faulder,[143] a considerable proportion of the ten per cent of British patients whom she estimates to be included currently in RCTs of one kind or another are likely to be in varying states of ignorance about their status as research subjects. The practice of informing people about their inclusion in RCTs appears to have lagged behind their introduction by many years, and to remain uneven between countries. In the USA, written signed consent came into fashion in the 1960s, although more as protection for the doctor than for the patient, given the different organizational base of the US health-care sustem and its more obvious domination by the practice and threat of litigation. Until the late 1950s, there was almost no discussion, either in Europe or North America, of informed consent in medical or health research. The term itself seems to have been created in legal circles in 1957, and this legal base has been a continuing important pressure on doctors and medical researchers to consider the issue of what patients should know. In Britain, the current legal position is that, in seeking informed consent, doctors are not obliged fully to disclose all the risks of any procedure, particularly when disclosure is thought by the doctor likely to cause the patient undue anxiety and/or persuade her/him not to accept treatment medically deemed to be beneficial.[144] The essential conflict is between what Fader and Beauchamp[145] term the 'principle of consent' on the one hand and a 'methodology of deception' on the other.

There is the issue of *what* patients are told; but there is also the issue of *which* patients are told, *when*, and on whom data are collected. From this point of view, it has been customary to design RCTs in a number of ways. The differences between the designs centre on two issues: the relationship

between randomization and consent, and whether or not the trial analysis is done on an 'intention to treat' basis (so that data are collected on all randomly-allocated subjects) or only on those who *were* treated. Figure 18.1 shows three variations on the possible combinations of these practices. In design A, which has been in common use, informed consent is sought only after randomization from the experimental group. But data are collected on all randomized subjects, whether or not their consent to take part in the research was requested and obtained, so that the subgroup of subjects randomized to the experimental group who do not give their consent nonetheless involuntarily contribute data. In design B, consent is solicited before randomization; but, because data-collection and analysis proceed on the 'intention to treat' principle, once again data on all patients are collected, whether or not they regard themselves as participating in the research; data are also collected on those who did not consent to take part in the trial. This seems to be the most frequently-used RCT design at the moment in UK medical research. In design C, like design B, consent is sought before randomization. But, by contrast with design B, only those who agree have information collected on them; those who refuse either initially or subsequently are excluded from data-collection and analysis. In our study, we used design C.

The implications of the different designs for *what* people are told are also quite different (although clearly other factors also influence the extent of disclosure characterizing the consent process). In designs B and C, as opposed to design A for example, what people are asked to consent to is not either to receive a particular intervention or not to receive it. They are asked to agree to putting themselves in a position where they have a fifty-fifty chance of receiving a particular treatment or not receiving it. In our study, using design C, the midwives were asked to follow a text explaining this, prepared by us, when talking to the women eligible to enter the study. Women who agreed to take part were randomized and then informed of the result. Twenty-five women out of 534 asked said that they would rather not take part in the research. After randomization, two women changed their minds – one in the control and one in the intervention group.

Design C is not in common use in RCTs of medical care carried out in Britain. The reasons why we chose to use it can be deduced from the arguments advanced in favour of the other methods, particularly design A. A leading article in the journal *Science* in 1979, 'Informed Consent May Be Hazardous to Health', says, for example:

> Before human subjects are enrolled in experimental studies, a variety of
> preliminary rituals are now required. These include an explanation of

Figure 18.1: Different designs for randomized controlled trials.

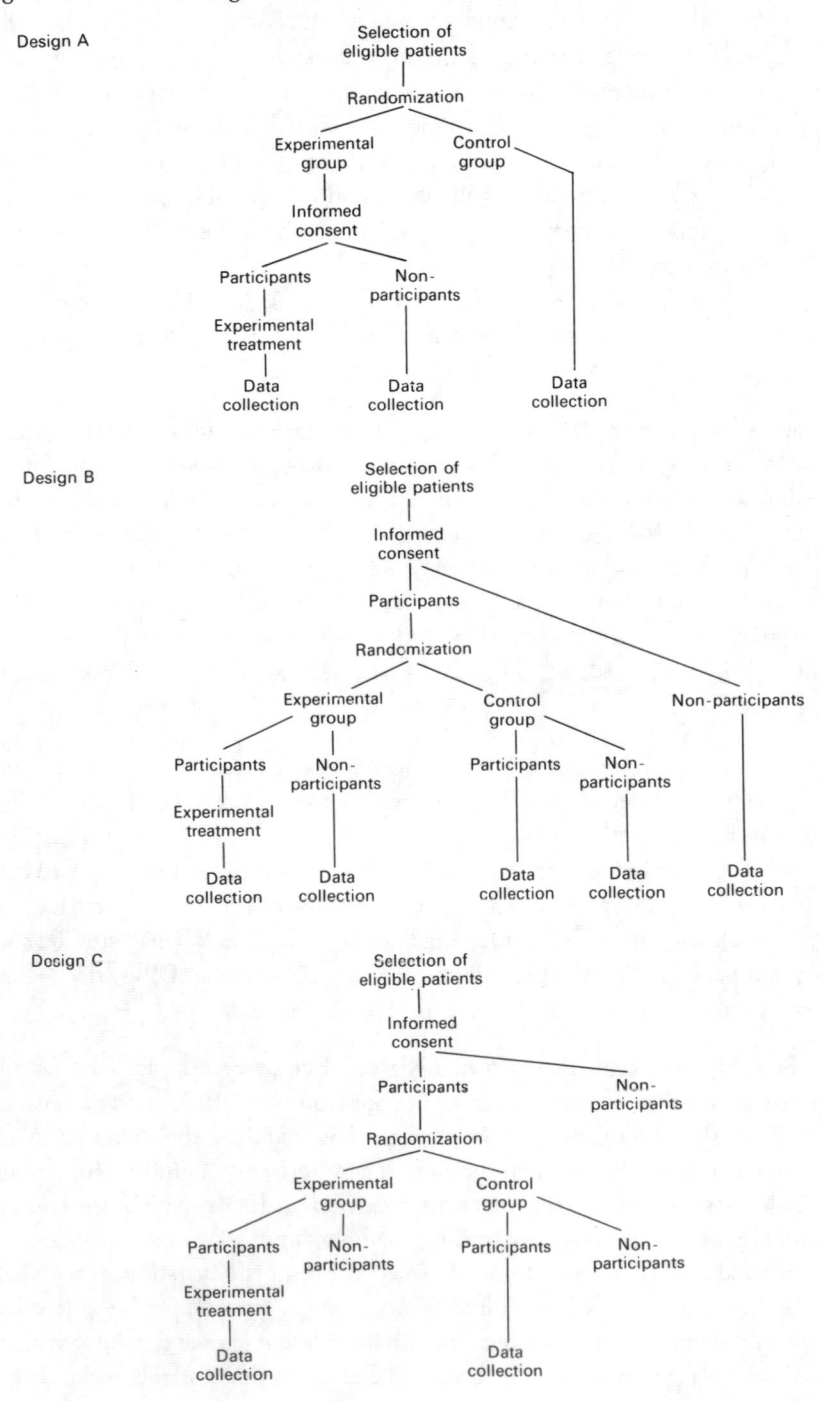

Source: Author's own compilation.

the nature of the experimental procedure and a specific elaboration of possible adverse reactions . . . These rituals are said to increase the subjects' understanding of the procedures . . .

A considerable body of psychological evidence indicates that humans are highly suggestible . . . This alone would lead one to suspect that adverse reactions might result from information given during an informed consent discussion . . . possible consequences of suggested symptoms range from minor annoyance to, in extreme cases, death.

If protection of the subject is the reason for obtaining informed consent, the possibility of iatrogenic harm to the subject as a direct result of the consent ritual must be considered.[146]

This is an extreme statement of a position quite commonly stated in the medical literature. The term 'ritual', used in a derogatory sense, immediately tells one how these investigators regard the task of informing people what is being done to them. In another version of this response, the danger that the stress of receiving information may affect health directly results in the conclusion not that *all* patients in a trial should be equally informed, irrespective of group allocation, but rather that *no* patient should be informed at all. Instead, this job is best left to 'ethical'[147] committees, because:

Only such committees have the experience, skill, information, and emotional detachment to judge the merits of a research protocol; the individual patient has none . . .

As a rule, patients will consent to randomization on the basis of skeleton information only, if they know that a committee of professional and other interested people has on their behalf studied and approved the scientific merits and ethical aspects of the trial. Most patients will not need, want, or ask for more.[148]

Such a viewpoint invites a number of obvious responses. First of all, reliance on the efficacy or ethical behaviour of ethics committees is dangerously ill-informed. In Britain, no law requires the submission of research proposals to such bodies. There are no statutory or other regulations governing the practices followed in them, which are widely variable, as are the rules controlling membership.[149]

Second, in the debate about informed consent, the question as to what patients want is rarely constituted as an empirical question, to be settled by appropriate inquiry. Dissatisfaction with the amount and kind of information that they are given is the most common complaint that patients make about

medical care in both the UK and the USA.[150] A number of studies show that even among people with fatal conditions, over eighty per cent would prefer to know the truth.[151] Studies by Mattson and colleagues[152] show that among participants in two large trials of drugs to prevent heart disease, increased knowledge was ranked in first or second place as benefits which they personally derived from taking part in research. A major finding of these studies was that altruistic motivation ('to help others') was almost as important as the incentive of gaining better care for themselves. Altruism has been an important finding in other fields, including maternity care[153] and the non-commercial blood-donation system that exists in Britain.[154] In our study, altruistic motives were referred to by a number of the women. Comments included:

> 'Happy to be of help in getting information to others, and hope to help to improve the system.'

> 'Very glad to do anything which might help women to cope better with pregnancy.'

> 'Took part in research to help other people.'

> 'Quite willing to help with future knowledge for all mothers. Hope it will be helpful.'

> 'I feel it is very good that things are being researched about childbirth.'

In an interesting account of a 'failed' RCT concerning methods of delivering very low-birthweight babies in Australia, Lumley and colleagues[155] describe how women's reluctance to subject their obstetric care to the play of chance on a basis of informed consent was anticipated by professionals as a problem before the trial started; however, the reason why it proved impossible to carry out in practice turned out instead to be the unwillingness of professionals to subject their own behaviour to systematic evaluation. But it is nonetheless true that research on people's attitudes to information and consent in both health care generally, and health research specifically, is astonishingly limited. One obstacle is that doctors think that patients want to know somewhat less than they do actually want to know.[156] Very little research, for example, has been devoted to the question of how best to give information. One survey of surgical consent forms used in the USA found that readability presupposed a university education and that four out of five were written at the level of a scientific journal.[157] Growing concern about the informed consent issue has now bred the ultimate in RCTs: an RCT of informed consent procedures itself.[158] This compared 'total disclosure' with written consent to an 'individual approach' with verbal consent in patients with cancer who were candidates for RCTs. 'Total disclosure' resulted in more

knowledgeable and informed patients who were also less willing to take part in RCTs and were judged to have more anxiety than the less informed group; since anxiety is assumed to be a negative outcome, it is commonly taken to count against the use of 'total disclosure' procedures.

In a chapter advocating the use of RCTs in perinatal research, Bracken introduces two further favoured medical reasons against informing patients when he says that:

> Patients are blinded in clinical trials for two major reasons. First, if blind, they are unlikely to withdraw from an RCT after being randomized into what they believe to be the less effective treatment. Such selective withdrawal would be extremely serious for the success of a trial. Second, blinding the patient avoids placebo effects.[159]

Not telling people that they are part of a research project thus unsurprisingly results in the advantage (for the researcher) that they cannot refuse to cooperate. But what are 'placebo effects', and what are they doing in this argument?

People's belief in the efficacy of what is being done to them has measurable effects on their health.[160] Medical professionals hold interestingly divided views on this point. On the one hand, much of the historical efficacy of medical care must have rested on this basis,[161] since, until the twentieth century, relatively few medical procedures could be shown to have any other mechanism of therapeutic effect. The 'placebo' (literally 'I please') response also shores up the notion, close to the heart of many professionals, that the relationship which they have with their patients may in itself be healing. These considerations reveal the tension of the physicalist model of health, since it is evident that mind and body interact, and that medicine's very claim to effectiveness depends on this, at the same time as disputing it. From a research point of view, however, the placebo effect is nothing more than inconvenient nonsense. A well-designed trial must assess it, in order to be assured of credibility.

The giving of information is also said to sound the death-knell for the double-blind RCT itself. Brownell and Stunkard's paper, 'The Double-blind in Danger: untoward consequences of informed consent', reports a trial of fenfluramine in 'obese women' in which information given in advance about possible side-effects of medication enabled four out of five patients to guess correctly that they were taking the medication. In turn, this correct estimate was associated with greater weight-loss. According to Brownell and Stunkard, 'The implications of these findings are grave: the double-blind methodology . . . can be breached and may be endangered by the demands of institutional review boards for increasingly detailed informed consent'.[162]

What is highlighted are the consequences for the scientific method of allowing people to know what is happening to them, rather than the therapeutic effect of empowering them with this knowledge.

We encountered various difficulties in our study with the method and content of the informed consent procedure which we used. Much the most important of these was the extent to which our informing women who were subsequently allocated to the control group what the study was about may have resulted in their feeling deprived (see the midwife's comment above, p. 250). One example is this experience described by one of the midwives:

> Dawn Benn[163] (Control). She was absolutely desperate to be intervention and she was so upset when I phoned her because of her social circumstances that when she asked me if I knew the address of any mother and toddler groups, NCT groups, anything, because she's just moved into the area, I gave her a couple of phone numbers before I'd even got her allocated. She was heartbroken.

In other instances, control-group women got in touch with the midwives for help even though they knew they had been assigned to the no-support group. We asked the midwives to respond minimally in such situations, conscious that responding fully would be to jeopardize the aims of the study. It is interesting to note that control-group women were only able to request this help because the midwives felt that it was unethical for them not to give all the women in the study a contact address and telephone number. They did so, although this was not part of the study design, and partly in response to our discussions about the informed consent issue.

Evidence of a 'deprivation' response was also gleaned from a few of the women who took part, in the questionnaires which they filled in after delivery: for example,

> 'Pleased to help. I would have welcomed home visits from a midwife.'

> 'I was very pleased to help, but would have enjoyed the visits . . .'

> 'Happy . . . (to take part in the research) if it can help anyone in the future. Would have preferred to be in group visited.'

For other control-group women, the desire to feel included took such a form that they felt they had been. One of the sections of the questionnaire asked women to tick a list of possibly helpful people, including the research midwife ('if she visited'), and thirteen control-group women ticked this, though they had not in fact been visited at all. Other appreciative remarks included:

> 'I wanted to take part and kept a note of how I was feeling at the time of my son's birth.'

> 'Pleased to have even a small interest taken in my feelings and opinions only inasmuch as feeling I would have some "right to reply" had I been treated very badly.'

> 'I didn't mind, especially if it helps to understand or prevent premature birth. By filling in this form it helped me to understand any problems I have because I had to write them down.'

One woman in the control group even went so far as to say that she felt special as a result of taking part in the research; it was 'like belonging to an elite group'.

Because we gave information to all the women whom the midwives identified as eligible for the study, the women in the control group *were* part of a research project in which they had *chosen* to participate. In this sense, it is probably true to say that rigorous testing of the hypothesis that social support can improve pregnancy outcome is at odds with the principle of informed consent. A further complication is that the standard scientific model of RCTs presupposes that there is no 'contamination' of the control group by the experimental group; the purpose of the control group is, after all, to act as a 'control' for the experiment. (In French, the term for 'control group' is 'le groupe témoin', literally 'witness' group, which carries an interestingly different connotation.) Again, the actual practice, as opposed to theory, of research reveals the chimerical nature of this model. It is assumed, for instance, that people do not talk to one another. In our study, had we not told the control-group women about the study, we would have needed to rely on the intervention-group women remaining silent about their receipt of social support – at home, with friends and neighbours, in antenatal clinics. But women are not silent. Although this human tendency to communicate may be overcome by randomizing groups (areas, institutions) rather than individuals, the tension between the scientific requirements of research and the humane treatment of individuals remains, and is expressed in the very strategy of designing an experiment so as to restrict people's freedom to discuss with one another the commonality of the process in which they are engaged. A potent example of the scientific disruptiveness of this was described in an RCT of health-screening for the elderly in Finland which failed to test the effectiveness of this form of health surveillance, as a local media campaign raised the rate of follow-up examinations in the control group to a figure that was ten per cent higher than the rate in the experimental group.[164]

A second problem which we encountered with our informed consent procedure was in deciding how to present the aims of the study to the women whom we asked to take part in it. The standard procedure for an RCT involves the researcher setting out to test something affectionately known as 'the null

hypothesis'. Adoption of the scientific method requires that one should begin from the standpoint that there is no difference between the treatment and the lack of treatment, or between the treatments that are being compared. But, since we had designed our study to test the hypothesis that social support might affect the baby's weight, as well as to investigate other factors such as the type of delivery that mothers had, and how they felt about their experiences, the dilemma was whether we should say so; or, if we said 'we want to see if social support can make babies grow better' (for example), were we somehow biasing the study from the start? Might we turn the study into a self-fulfilling prophecy, the results of which would never be believed except as such? This formulation of the question is interesting, for it leads to the next question, which is: if the hypothesis is that a *social* process may be therapeutic in a *clinical/physical* sense, what sensible arguments are there for concealing the purpose of the exercise from those taking part in it? The reason why researchers are wary about the placebo response is, after all, because of the possible beneficial impact on someone of feeling that they are being cared for: it is the very presence and effect of the social process that is counted as disturbing. But, for us, the social process was of central concern. It was for this very reason that we decided to enlist the midwives' confidence in the aims of the study from the start: not to have done so would, we felt, have been not only unethical but also intuitively counter to its aims. For the same reason, we were also open with the women in the study about what we were trying to do. In saying that we wanted to see if social support could achieve the stated aims, we were conscious of the tension with the principle that women allocated to the control group should not feel deprived. Thus, we also stated what we also believed, that we did not *know* whether social support could improve the health of all women and their children in this sense.

THE IMPORTANCE OF BEING (UN)CERTAIN

The last of the issues raised at the beginning of this chapter as especially problematic in this type of research is the question of uncertainty.

Much of the literature on informed consent refers to an uncomfortable prerequisite for the seeking of consent, which is that of researcher or practitioner uncertainty (our not knowing whether social support works). Certainty can be a consequence of very different political and ideological positions. Medical certainty, for example, lies behind one of the most commonly-used informed consent/randomization procedures (design A above). According to Zelen, whose advocacy of this design has been influential, the main advantage of withholding information from the control group is that clinicians do not need to admit to these patients 'that they do not know which treatment is best'. Zelen explains that

many investigators and patients are reluctant to participate in randomized clinical trials . . . One of the principal reasons why clinical investigators decline to participate in randomized studies is that they believe that the 'patient–physician relation' is compromised.[165]

For this reason, use of the RCT is sometimes said to be 'unethical'; the question of ethics enters the medical debate at the point at which the traditional paternalism of the doctor–patient relationship is threatened. From a vantage point outside medicine, however, such professional understandings are precisely the reason why RCTs have an ethical advantage over routine medical practice. They subject to external assessment the medical claim to therapeutic effectiveness (which rests partly on the ambiguous notion of trust). As Freidson has observed, technological/scientific autonomy is *the* premise on which the professionalization of medicine rests; medicine is 'free to develop its special area of knowledge and to determine what are 'scientifically acceptable' practices'.[166] The aphorism 'doctor knows best' is both a manifestation of this control and its translation into the politics of the doctor–patient relationship. As Freidson also observes, the *claim* to sole ownership of scientific wisdom says nothing about the *actual* scientific status of the knowledge thus claimed.

However, certainty is not the prerogative of medical professionals. It is also possessed by lay people and by women. The women's health movement has been guilty of a fair amount of misguided certainty over the years, as for example in the recently fashionable demand that cervical screening programmes be made more readily available to all women. As Robinson[167] has noted, 'Neither the ethics, the efficacy, nor the adverse effects of screening have been adequately discussed by women's organizations'. In the childbirth field, many attempts systematically to evaluate different modes of care have been shipwrecked on the rock of women's certainty about the effectiveness of apparently natural and innocuous methods such as childbirth education, vitamin supplements or raspberry leaf tea. (While such methods may have this effect, there is, as yet, no scientific evidence, and even some to the contrary.[168] Perhaps best-publicized of recent examples in Britain has been the response of maternity-service user groups to the Medical Research Council's RCT on vitamin supplementation in pregnancy. The trial was designed to test the hypothesis that such supplements, taken around the time of conception, can reduce the chances of a baby having a neural tube malformation. User groups such as the National Childbirth Trust and the Association for Improvements in the Maternity Services contended that the need for a good diet in pregnancy was well established, making the trial unethical.[169] The point is that, whatever form it takes, and whoever professes

it, certainty blocks progress towards greater understanding of the role of chance versus causation in the patterning, and human experience of events and processes, including those responsible for health or its absence.

Genuine scepticism about something is probably rare. It appears that researchers must merely possess sufficient *un*certainty about something in order to want to find out about it. The issue of certainty was complicated in our study. None of us was prepared to say that we did not know whether social support was a good thing (in the same way as we would have been prepared to say, for example, that we did not know whether it is helpful for women prone to premature labour to be admitted to hospital during pregnancy). But while it may seem almost axiomatic that social support, like love, is something that we all want, what is at issue is the range and type of event/process that social support is capable of affecting, and the mechanism by which it does so.[170] Assumptions about the inevitably therapeutic effects of social support may prove unfounded when subject to systematic evaluation. This was the case, for example, in the Cambridge-Somerville Youth Study, an early attempt initiated in 1935 to evaluate the long-term effectiveness of social-work help in preventing delinquency and other 'undesirable' outcomes.[171]

CONCLUSION

The RCT is a method of *experimental* research, and the term 'experiment' has been linked with what Chalmers[172] has called the 'Auschwitz' view of scientific inquiry, according to which all experimental research is inherently suspect. The view of experimental research as inherently unethical is central to the feminist critique,[173] but also comes from other quarters.[174] Much of it misses the absolutely crucial point that the condemnation of experimentation under the heading of 'research' allows a great deal of experimentation to pass unnoticed under the heading of standard practice. The frequency with which doctors impose on patients experiments of an uncontrolled nature has been one of the strongest objections to professionalized medicine made by the women's health movement over the last twenty years in Europe and North America.[175] The fact that very large numbers of women have been treated with medical and surgical procedures of unknown or suspect effectiveness and potentially or actually harmful consequences has been taken to signal both women's status as a minority group and medicine's essentially unscientific standing. For this reason, women have been, and continue to be, important beneficiaries of the advocacy of randomized controlled evaluation within medicine. One significant example concerns the treatment of breast cancer, a disease which affects one in twelve women in the UK at some point in their lives. Analysis of

the results of trials of breast-cancer treatments has been responsible for the production of persuasive evidence that 'conservative' treatments are superior to 'radical' treatments both in prolonging life and in assuring a better quality of life. Overviews of RCTs concerned with systematic treatment (chemotherapy or endocrine therapy) of the disease show important differences between the effectiveness of such treatments in older and younger women. They also provide evidence that short courses of treatment are as effective as longer courses – an important consideration, given their sometimes unpleasant side-effects.[176] It is, however, crucial to note that the benefits that accrue to women as a result of their willingness to participate in such studies cannot be held out as a carrot to those who do except by trading on altruism. It is the *future* health of *other* women that stands to benefit by the willingness of *some* to be experimented on *now*.

What our experience with an RCT of social support in pregnancy has shown is the need to subject every precept of the traditional scientific method to scrutiny. Is it necessary? Do its benefits outweigh its hazards? It is as important to ask these questions of a trial of something as apparently harmless as social support as it is of trials of other more obviously ambiguous therapies. The argument against 'methodolatry' is then transformed into the case for an *appropriate* methodology which, like its namesake, appropriate technology, requires that individuals involved in it be treated with sensitivity and respect, and *that there be no division between this ethical requirement and other requirements of the method.* This is not, of course, to say that the procedure of randomized controlled evaluation is the *only* means to reliable knowledge, is *sufficient* in itself, or is *always* the right approach; for the pursuit of truth in human affairs is, as we all know, ultimately an illusion, and reliable knowledge definitely not a good in itself. The point is that what Rowbotham[177] has called 'the attraction of spring cleaning' should be seen as a means to an end, not an end in itself. The frenetic housewife is unable to enjoy the product of her labours. In Evelyn Keller's words,

> The intellectual danger resides in viewing science as pure social product; science then dissolves into ideology and objectivity loses all intrinsic meaning. In the resulting cultural relativism, any emancipatory function of modern science is negated, and the arbitration of truth recedes into the political domain.[178]

Notes

INTRODUCTION

1 A. Oakley *Taking it Like a Woman* London, Jonathan Cape, 1984.
2 Oscar Wilde, quoted in B. Anderman (ed.) *The Book Lover's Birthday Book* New York, Metropolitan Museum of Art and the New York Public Library, 1984.
3 I. Dinesen *On Modern Marriage and Other Observations* New York, St Martin's Press, 1986, p. 33.
4 E. Cederborg 'Introduction: Karen Blixen – her life and writings'. In Dinesen, op. cit., p. 23.
5 C. Heilbrun *Writing a Woman's Life* London, The Women's Press, 1989.
6 A. Cross *Death in a Tenured Position* New York, E. P. Dutton, 1981. Published in the UK as *A Death in the Faculty* Virago, London, 1988.
7 Heilbrun, op. cit., pp. 130–1.

PART 1

1 For a summary of the evidence, see A. Oakley *Subject Women* Oxford, Martin Robertson, 1981, chapter 3.
2 S. Houd and A. Oakley 'Alternative Perinatal Services in the European Region and North America: a pilot survey', unpublished paper, WHO, Copenhagen, 1983.
3 J. MacGuire 'Nursing: none is held in higher esteem' in R. Silverstone and A. Ward (eds) *Careers of Professional Women* London, Croom Helm, 1980.
4 Department of Health and Social Security, Statistics and Research Division, Hospital Medical Staff, England and Wales, National Tables, 30 September 1977 (February 1978).
5 M. A. Elston 'Medicine: half our future doctors?' in R. Silverstone and A. Ward (eds) *Careers of Professional Women* London, Croom Helm, 1980.
6 C. P. Gilman 'The Yellow Wallpaper' *The New England Magazine* January 1982. Reprinted in *The Charlotte Perkins Gilman Reader: The Yellow Wallpaper and Other Fiction* London, The Women's Press, 1981.
7 T. Olsen *Silences* London, Virago, 1980.
8 C. P. Gilman 'Why I wrote "The Yellow Wallpaper"' *The Forerunner* October 1913. Reprinted in *The Charlotte Perkins Gilman Reader: The Yellow Wallpaper and Other Fiction* London, The Women's Press, 1981.
9 E. Boulding *Women in the Twentieth Century World* New York, Sage Publications, 1977.
10 B. Chiplin and P. J. Sloane *Tackling Discrimination at the Workplace* Cambridge, Cambridge University Press, 1982.
11 L. Hamill *Wives as Sole and Joint Breadwinners* Government Economic Service Working Papers no 13, London, HMSO, 1978.

12 H. Land 'The family wage' *Feminist Review* **6**, 1980, pp. 55–77.

13 V. Beral 'Reproductive morality' *British Medical Journal* 15 September 1979, pp. 632–4.

14 A. Cochrane *Effectiveness and Efficiency* The Nuffield Provincial Hospitals Trust, 1971, p. 64.

15 M. Shepherd, B. Cooper, A. C. Brown and G. W. Kalton *Psychiatric Illness in General Practice* London, Oxford University Press, 1966.

16 G. V. Stimson 'GPs, "trouble" and types of patient' in M. Stacey (ed.) *The Sociology of the National Health Service* Sociological Review Monograph **22**, University of Keele, Staffordshire, 1976.

17 For a discussion of this dilemma in relation to premenstrual tension, see S. Laws 'The sexual politics of premenstrual tension' *Women's Studies International Forum* **6**, 1983, pp. 19–31.

18 V. Woolf 'Professions for women', reprinted in V. Woolf *Women and Writing* London, The Women's Press, 1979.

19 A. Rich 'Women and honor: some notes on lying' in *On Lies, Secrets, Silence* London, Virago, 1980.

20 A point made by J. Hirsch and cited in S. B. Ruzek *The Women's Health Movement* New York, Praeger, 1979, p. 58.

21 J. Robinson 'Cervical cancer: a feminist critique' *Times Health Supplement* 1981, 5, p. 16.

22 I. Illich *Medical Nemesis* London, Calder and Boyars, 1975.

23 T. McKeown *The Role of Medicine* Oxford, Basil Blackwell, 1979.

24 M. P. M. Richards 'Innovation in medical practice: obstetricians and the induction of labour in Britain' *Social Science and Medicine* **9**, 1975, p. 598.

25 Figure cited by the Dutch obstetrician G. J. Kloosterman.

26 I have discussed this fully in 'Normal motherhood: an exercise in self-control?' in B. Hutter and G. Williams (eds) *Controlling Women: The Normal and the Deviant* London, Croom Helm, 1981.

27 British Medical Association, Family Doctor Publication 'From pregnancy to birth' *You and Your Baby, Part 1* 1977, p. 22.

28 R. Cooperstock and H. L. Lennard 'Some social meanings of tranquiliser use' *Sociology of Health and Illness* 1979, **1**, 3, pp. 331–47.

29 I. Broverman, D. Broverman, F. Clarkson, P. Rosenkrantz and S. Vogel 'Sex-role stereotypes and clinical judgements of mental health' *Journal of Consulting and Clinical Psychology* 1970, **34**, pp. 1–7.

30 See the discussion in A. Oakley and G. Chanberlain 'Medical and social factors in postpartum depression' *Journal of Obstetrics and Gynaecology* **1**, 1981, pp. 182–7.

31 For a fuller discussion of these themes and references to the literature, see A. Oakley *Women Confined: Towards a Sociology of Childbirth* Oxford, Martin Robertson, 1980, chapter 2, 'Psychological Constructs'.

32 S. Wolkind 'Prenatal emotional stress – effects on the fetus' in S. Wolkind and E. Kajicek (eds) *Pregnancy: A Psychological and Social Study* London, Academic Press, 1981.

33 For example, W. S. Kroger and S. T. DeLee 'The psychosomatic treatment of hyperemesis gravidarum by hypnosis' *American Journal of Obstetrics and Gynecology* 1946, p. 51.

34 For example A. Nilsson 'Perinatal emotional adjustment' in N. Morris (ed.) *Psychosomatic Medicine in Obstetrics and Gynaecology* 3rd International Congress, London 1971, Basel, Karger, 1972.

35 A. Milinski 'Different behaviour of women in labour as a symptom of different psychic patterns' in H. Hirsch (ed.) *The Family* 4th International Congress of Psychosomatic Obstetrics and Gynaecology, Basel, Karger, 1975.

36 M. Heiman 'Psychiatric complications: a psychoanalytic view of pregnancy' in J. J. Rovinsky and A. F. Guttmacher (eds) *Medical, Surgical and Gynecological Complications of Pregnancy* Baltimore, Williams and Wilkins, 1965.

37 Ibid.
38 L. Chertok *Motherhood and Personality* London, Tavistock, 1969.
39 D. Breen *The Birth of the First Child* London, Tavistock, 1975, p. 193.
40 M. B. Parlee 'Psychology' *Signs: Journal of Women in Culture and Society* 1975, **1**, Autumn, pp. 119–35.
41 T. Parsons and R. F. Bales *Family: Socialisation and Interaction Process* London, Routledge and Kegan Paul, 1956.
42 S. Macintyre 'The management of childbirth: a review of sociological research issues' *Social Science and Medicine* **11**, 1977, pp. 477–84.
43 R. Dahrendorf *The Listener* **92**, 1974, p. 624.
44 A. Oakley *The Captured Womb: A History of Medical Care for Pregnant Women* Oxford, Basil Blackwell, 1984.
45 A. Oakley 'Social consequences of obstetric technology: the importance of measuring "soft" outcomes' *Birth* **10**, 2, 1983, pp. 99–108.
46 T. Szasz *The Theology of Medicine* Baton Rouge, Louisiana State University Press, 1977.
47 E. Freidson *Profession of Medicine: A Study in the Sociology of Applied Knowledge* New York, Dodd, Mead and Co., 1972.
48 P. S. Byrne and B. E. L. Long *Doctors Talking to Patients* London, HMSO, 1976.
49 E. J. Cassell *The Healer's Art: A New Approach to the Doctor–Patient Relationship* Philadelphia, J. B. Lippincott, 1976, p. 18.
50 H. Brody *Placebos and the Philosophy of Medicine* Chicago, Chicago University Press, 1980.
51 Richards, op. cit.
52 A. Cartwright *The Dignity of Labour?* London, Tavistock, 1979.
53 L. Hudson and B. Jacot 'Education and eminence in British medicine' *British Medical Journal* **2**, 1971, pp. 162–3.
54 A. K. Ladas, B. Whipple and J. D. Perry *The G Spot and Other Recent Discoveries about Human Sexuality* London, Corgi Books, 1983.
55 E. D. M. Riley ' "What do women want?" – The question of choice in the conduct of labour' in T. Chard and M. Richards (eds) *Benefits and Hazards of the New Obstetrics* London, Spastics International Medicine Publications, 1977.
56 A. Cartwright *Human Relations and Hospital Care* London, Routledge and Kegan Paul, 1964.
57 W. Wilson 'Correlates of avowed happiness' *Psychological Bulletin* **67**, 4, 1967.
58 P. R. Kaim-Caudle and G. N. Marsh 'Patient satisfaction survey in General Practice' *British Medical Journal* **1**, 1975, pp. 262–4.
59 R. S. Ledward 'Communication in hospital' *British Medical Journal* **2**, 1978, p. 505 (letter).
60 A. Oakley *Becoming a Mother* Oxford, Martin Robertson, 1979; H. Graham and L. McKee *The First Months of Motherhood*, London, Health Education Council, 1980.
61 Cartwright, 1964, op. cit.
62 D. Locker and D. Dunt 'Theoretical and methodological issues in sociological studies of consumer satisfaction with medical care' *Social Science and Medicine* **12**, 1978, pp. 283–92.
63 A. Cartwright *Health Surveys in Practice and in Potential: A Critical Review of Their Scope and Methods* London, King's Fund, 1983.
64 Oakley, 1980, op. cit.
65 J. Y. Green, M. Weinberger and J. J. Mamlin 'Patient attitudes towards health care: expectations of primary care in a clinic setting' *Social Science and Medicine* **14**, 1980, pp. 133–8.
66 C. L. Shear, B. T. Gipe, J. K. Mattheis and M. Riery 'Provider continuity and quality of medical care' *Medical Care* **21**, 12, 1983, pp. 1204–10.
67 G. V. Stimson 'Obeying doctor's orders: a view from the other side' *Social Science and Medicine* **8**, 1974, pp. 97–104.

68 Macintyre, op. cit.

69 M. Millman *The Unkindest Cut: Life in the Backrooms of Medicine* New York, William Morrow, 1977; S. Danziger 'On doctor watching: field work in medical settings' *Urban Life* **7**, 4, 1979, pp. 513–32.

70 W. R. Arney *Power and the Profession of Obstetrics* Chicago, University of Chicago Press, 1982; D. Scully *Men Who Control Women's Health* Boston, Houghton Mifflin, 1980.

71 A. Cartwright 'Professionals as responders: variations in and effects of response rates to questionnaires 1961–77' *British Medical Journal* **2**, 1978, pp. 1419–21.

72 J. B. McKinlay 'Who is really ignorant – physician or patient?' *Journal of Health and Social Behaviour* **16**, 1, 1975, pp. 3–11.

73 R. M. Titmuss *Essays on the Welfare State* London, Allen and Unwin, 1958, pp. 200–2.

74 T. B. Brewin 'The cancer patient: communication and morale' *British Medical Journal* **2**, 1977, pp. 1623–7.

75 G. P. Maguire, E. G. Lee, D. J. Bevington, C. S. Kuchemann, R. J. Crabtree and C. E. Cornell 'Psychiatric problems in the first year after mastectomy' *British Medical Journal* **1**, 1978, pp. 963–5.

76 Illich, op. cit.

77 R. J. Haggerty 'Life stress, illness and social supports' *Developmental Medicine and Child Neurology* **22**, 1980, pp. 391–400.

78 S. Cobb 'Physiologic changes in men whose jobs were abolished' *Journal of Psychosomatic Research* **18**, 1974, pp. 245–58.

79 H. R. Bourne 'The placebo – a poorly understood and neglected therapeutic agent' *Rational Drug Therapy* November 1971, pp. 1–6.

80 A. Anderson and A. Turnbull 'Effect of oestrogens, progestogens and betamimetics in pregnancy' in M. Enkin and I. Chalmers (eds) *Effectiveness and Satisfaction in Antenatal Care* London, Spastics International Medical Publications, 1982.

81 H. H. Meyhoff, T. C. Gerstenberg and J. Nordling 'Placebo – the drug of choice in female motor urge incontinence' *British Journal of Urology* **55**, 1983, pp. 34–7.

82 N. Cousins *Anatomy of an Illness as Perceived by the Patient* New York, W. W. Norton, 1979.

83 Cited in B. Abel-Smith *A History of the Nursing Profession* London, Heinemann, 1960.

84 Ibid., p. 5.

85 See C. Davies (ed.) *Rewriting Nursing History* London, Croom Helm, 1980.

86 C. Woodham-Smith *Florence Nightingale 1820–1910* London, Constable, 1950.

87 C. Magges 'Nurse recruitment to four provincial hospitals 1881–1921' in Davies, op. cit.

88 R. Lewis and A. Maude *Professional People* London, Phoenix House, 1952.

89 1905 comment, cited in E. Gamarnikow 'Sexual division of labour: the case of nursing' in A. Kuhn and A. Wolpe (eds) *Feminism and Materialism* London, Routledge and Kegan Paul, 1978, p. 105.

90 Nightingale, 1881, ibid., p. 115.

91 Cited in Woodham-Smith, op. cit., p. 340.

92 See, for example, S. B. Ruzek, op. cit.

93 J. M. MacGuire *From Student to Nurse* Oxford Area Nurse Training Committee, 1966.

94 E. Hughes, H. Hughes and I. Deutscher *Twenty Thousand Nurses Tell Their Story* Philadelphia, J. B. Lippincott, 1958.

95 R. L. Coser *Life in the Ward* East Lansing, Michigan, Michigan State University Press, 1962.

96 E. R. Anderson, *The Role of the Nurse* Royal College of Nursing of the United Kingdom, 1973.

97 Hughes et al., op. cit.

98 M. Johnston 'Communication of patients' feelings in hospital' in A. E. Bennett (ed.) *Communication between Doctors and Patients* Oxford, Oxford University Press, 1976.

99 J. B. Miller *Toward a New Psychology of Women* Boston, Beacon Press, 1977.

100 J. G. Rosen and K. Jones 'The male nurse' *New Society* 9 March 1972, pp. 493–4.

101 Anderson, 1973, op. cit., pp. 90–1.

102 See, for example, A. M. Carr-Saunders and P. A. Wilson *The Professions* Oxford, Clarendon Press, 1933; Freidson, op. cit.

103 A. Etzioni (ed.) *The Semi-Professions and Their Organization: Teachers, Nurses and Social Workers* New York, The Free Press, 1969.

104 I. Illich 'Disabling professions' in I. Illich, I. K. Zola, J. McNight, J. Caplan and H. Shaiken *Disabling Professions* London, Marion Boyars, 1977, p. 15.

105 J. A. Ashley *Hospitals, Paternalism, and the Role of the Nurse* New York, Teachers College Press, 1976.

106 Cited in Woodham-Smith, op. cit., p. 341.

107 Miller, op. cit., p. 71.

108 Joint Committee of the Royal College of Obstetricians and Gynaecologists and the Population Investigation Committee *Maternity in Great Britain* London, Oxford University Press, 1948, p. vi.

109 Ibid., p. 47.

110 See Oakley, 1984, op. cit.

111 B. A. Beech 'The work of the Association for Improvements in the Maternity Services'. Unpublished paper presented at the fourth *Human Relations in Obstetric Practice* seminar, University of Glasgow, Scotland, 1981.

112 S. Arms *Immaculate Deception* New York, Bantam Books, 1975, p. xiii.

113 See Research Unit in Health and Behavioural Change *Changing the Public Health* Chichester, Sussex, John Wiley, 1989.

114 Oakley, 1979, op. cit.

115 J. Cornwell *Hard-earned Lives* London, Tavistock, 1984.

116 See e.g. I. Chalmers and M. Richards 'Intervention and causal inference in obstetric practice' in T. Chard and M. Richards (eds) *Benefits and Hazards of the New Obstetrics* London, Heinemann, 1977.

117 R. G. DeVries *Regulating Birth: Midwives, Medicine and the Law* Philadelphia, Temple University Press, 1985.

118 Oxford English Dictionary.

119 Social Services Committee Session 1979–80 *Perinatal and Neonatal Mortality* London, HMSO, p. 16.

120 M. Hall, S. Macintyre and M. Porter *Antenatal Care Assessed* Aberdeen, Aberdeen University Press, 1985.

121 L. I. Zander, M. Watson, R. W. Taylor and D. C. Morrell 'Integration of general practitioner and specialist antenatal care' *Journal of the Royal College of General Practitioners* August 1978, pp. 455–8.

122 B. Beech *Whose Baby Is It Anyway?* London, Camden Press and Health Rights, 1987, p. 84.

123 Ibid., pp. 84–5.

124 J. E. Tyson, J. A. Furzan, J. S. Reisch and S. G. Mize 'An evaluation of the quality of therapeutic studies in perinatal medicine' *Journal of Pediatrics* **102**, 1983, pp. 10–13.

125 Cartwright, 1979, op. cit.

126 A. Macfarlane 'Variations in numbers of births and perinatal mortality by day of the week in England and Wales' *British Medical Journal* **2**, 1978, pp. 1670–3.

127 Cartwright, 1979, op. cit.

128 I. Chalmers, J. E. Zlosnik, K. A. Johns and H. Campbell 'Obstetric practice and outcome of pregnancy in Cardiff residents 1965–73' *British Medical Journal* **1**, 1976, pp. 735–8.

129 See P. Romito 'Unhappiness after childbirth' in I. Chalmers, M. Enkin and M. J. N. C. Keirse (eds) *Effective Care in Pregnancy and Childbirth* Oxford, Oxford University Press, 1989.

130 W. Farrant 'Stress after amniocentesis for high serum alpha-fetoprotein concentrations' *British Medical Journal* 1980, 281, p. 452.

131 Select Committee, op. cit., p. 91.

132 Arney, 1982, op. cit.

133 Editorial 'Helping mothers to love their babies' *British Medical Journal* **2**, 1977, p. 595.

134 N. Jeffcoate 'Medicine versus nature' *Journal of the Royal College of Surgeons of Edinburgh* **21**, 1976, pp. 263–77.

135 D. Stewart *The Five Standards for Safe Childbearing* Marble Hill, Missouri, NAPSAC International, 1981.

136 M. P. M. Richards and N. R. C. Robertson 'Admission and discharge policies for special-care unit' in F. S. W. Brimblecombe, M. P. M. Richards and N. R. C. Robertson (eds) *Early Separation and Special Care Nurseries* London, Heinemann, 1978.

137 Cartwright, 1964, op. cit.

138 See pp. 34–5, this volume.

139 M. K. Nelson 'Working-class women, middle-class women, and models of childbirth' *Social Problems* 1983, 30 **3**, pp. 284–97.

140 M. H. Hall 'Crisis in the maternity Services' *British Medical Journal* 1988, 297, pp. 500–1.

141 J. Brannen and P. Moss *New Mothers at Work* London, Unwin Hyman, 1988.

142 W. Savage *A Savage Enquiry* London, Fontana Books, 1986.

143 H. J. Garrigues *A Textbook of the Art and Science of Midwifery* Philadelphia, J. B. Lippincott, 1902, pp. 211–16.

144 See e.g. R. W. Newton and L. P. Hunt 'Psychosocial stress in pregnancy and its relation to low birthweight' *British Medical Journal* 1984, 288, pp. 1191–4.

145 See e.g. M. H. Klaus, J. H. Kennell, S. Robertson and R. Sosa 'Effects of social support on maternal and infant morbidity' *British Medical Journal* 1986, 293, pp. 585–7.

146 G. Dick-Read *Childbirth Without Fear* London, Heinemann, 1942, p. 12.

147 S. Sontag *Illness as Metaphor* New York, Farrar, Strauss and Giroux, 1977.

148 N. Pfeffer 'The hidden pathology of the male reproductive system' in H. Homans (ed.) *The Sexual Politics of Reproduction* London, Gower, 1985.

149 N. Devitt 'The statistical case for elimination of the midwife: fact versus prejudice 1890–1936, Part II' *Women and Health* 1979, 4, **2**, pp. 169–86.

150 N. Devitt 'The statistical case for elimination of the midwife: fact versus prejudice 1890–1936, Part I' *Women and Health* 1979, 4, **1**, pp. 81–96.

151 M. C. Versluysen 'Midwives, medical men and "poor women labouring with child": lying-in hospitals in the eighteenth century' in H. Roberts (ed.) *Women, Health and Reproduction* London, Routledge and Kegan Paul, 1981.

152 J. B. DeLee 'Progress towards ideal obstetrics' *Transactions of the American Association for the Study and Prevention of Infant Mortality* **6**, 1915, pp. 114–38.

153 Devitt, op. cit.

154 J. B. Donnegan *Women and Men Midwives* Westport, Connecticut, Greenwood Press, 1978.

155 Cited in R. W. Wertz and D. C. Wertz *Lying-in: A History of Childbirth in America* New York, Free Press, 1977, p. 137.

156 J. W. Williams 'Medical education and the midwife problem in the United States' *Journal of the American Medical Association* **58**, 1912, pp. 1–7.

157 Versluysen, op. cit.

158 See A. Oakley 'Wisewoman and medicine man: changes in the management of childbirth' in J. Mitchell and A. Oakley (eds) *The Rights and Wrongs of Women* Harmondsworth, Penguin, 1976.

159 Cited in J. Towler and J. Bramall *Midwives in History and Society* London, Croom Helm, 1986, p. 56.

160 R. Taylor *Medicine out of Control* Melbourne, Sun Books, 1979, pp. 3–4.

161 See A. Oakley *Social Support and Motherhood: The Natural History of a Research Project* Oxford, Basil Blackwell, 1992, for a discussion.

162 M. C. Saunders, J. S. Dick, I. M. Brown, K. McPherson and I. Chalmers 'The effects of hospital admission for bed rest on the duration of twin pregnancy: a randomised trial' *Lancet* 12 October 1985, pp. 793–5.

163 I. Donald 'Sonar – its present status in medicine' in A. Kurjak (ed.) *Progress in Medical Ultrasound* vol. 1, Amsterdam, Excerpta Medica, 1980, p. 2.

164 World Health Organization *Health Services in Europe, Volume 1* Copenhagen, WHO Regional Office for Europe, 1981.

165 International Confederation of Midwives.

166 See pp. 243–64 above.

167 L. Runnerstrom 'The effectiveness of nurse-midwifery in a supervised hospital environment' *Bulletin of the American College of Nurse-Midwives* 14, 1969, pp. 40–52.

168 C. Slome, H. Westerbee, M. Daly, K. Christenssen, M. Meglen and H. Thiede 'Effectiveness of certified nurse-midwives. A prospective evaluation study' *American Journal of Obstetrics and Gynecology* 15 January 1976, pp. 177–82.

169 N. Spira, F. Audras, A. Chapel, E. Debuisson, C. Jacquelin, C. Kirchhoffer, C. Lebrun and C. Prudent 'Surveillance à domicile des grossesses pathologiques par les sages-femmes' *Journal Gynecologie, Obstetriques, Biologie et Reproduction* 10, 1981, pp. 543–8.

170 J. Lumley 'Review article. The prevention of preterm birth: unresolved problems and work in progress' *Australian Paediatric Journal* 24, 1988, pp. 101–11.

171 D. L. Olds, C. R. Henderson, R. Tatelbaum and R. Chamberlin 'Improving the delivery of prenatal care and outcomes of pregnancy: a randomized trial of nurse home visitation' *Pediatrics* 77, 1986, pp. 16–28.

172 J. Dance 'A social intervention by linkworkers to Pakistani women and pregnancy outcome'. Unpublished, 1987.

173 N. M. Nelson, M. W. Enkin, S. Saigail, K. J. Bennett, R. Milner and D. L. Sackett 'A randomized clinical trial of the Leboyer approach to childbirth' *New England Journal of Medicine* 20 March 1980, pp. 656–86.

174 M. M. Timm 'Prenatal education evaluation' *Nursing Research* 1979, 28, **6**, pp. 338–42.

175 E. Z. Zimmer, M. Y. Divon, A. Vilensky, Z. Sarna, B. A. Peretz and E. Paldi 'Maternal exposure to music and fetal activity' *European Journal of Obstetrics and Gynaecological and Reproductive Biology* 13, 1982, pp. 209–13.

176 M. E. Reid, S. Gutteridge and G. M. McIlwaine 'A comparison of the delivery of antenatal care between a hospital and peripheral clinic' Report to Health Services Research Committee, Scottish Home and Health Department, 1983.

177 M. Klein, A. Papageorgiou, R. Westreich, L. Spector-Dunsky, V. Elkins, M. S. Kramer and M. M. Gelfand 'Care in the birth room versus a conventional setting: a controlled trial' *Canadian Medical Association Journal* 131, 1984, pp. 1461–6.

178 J. Carpenter, K. Aldrich and H. Boverman 'The effectiveness of patient interviews. A controlled study of emotional support during pregnancy' *Archives of General Psychiatry* 19, 1968, pp. 110–12.

179 C. Flint and P. Poulengeris 'The "Know Your Midwife" scheme' London, Report published by authors, 1987.

180 A. Lovell and D. Elbourne 'Holding the baby – and your notes' *Health Service Journal* 19 March 1987, p. 335.

181 A. E. Reading, S. Campbell, D. N. Cox and C. M. Sledmere 'Health beliefs and health care behaviour in pregnancy' *Psychological Medicine* 1982, pp. 379–83.

182 R. E. Gordon and K. K. Gordon 'Social factors in prevention of postpartum emotional problems' *Obstetrics and Gynecology* 15, 1960, pp. 433–8.

183 M. F. Gutelius, A. D. Kirsch, S. MacDonald, M. R. Brooks and T. M. McErlean 'Controlled study of child health supervision: behavioural results' *Pediatrics* 60, 1977, pp. 294–304.

184 See Oakley, 1992, op. cit.

185 C. Sakala 'Content of care by independent midwives: assistance with pain in labour and birth'. Unpublished paper.

186 J. F. Walker 'Midwife or obstetric nurse? Some perceptions of midwives and obstetricians of the role of midwife' *Journal of Advanced Nursing* 1, 1976, pp. 129–38.

187 S. Robinson, J. Golden and S. Bradley 'The midwife: a developing or diminishing role?' Research and the Midwife Conference, 1980.

188 J. Green, V. Coupland and J. Kitzinger 'Great Expectations: a prospective study of women's expectations and experiences of childbirth' Child Care and Development Group, University of Cambridge, unpublished report, 1988, p. 14.

PART 2

1 M. Mead *Blackberry Winter* New York, Pocket Books, 1975, p. 225.

2 Quoted in A. Davin 'Imperialism and motherhood' *History Workshop Journal* Spring 1978, p. 17.

3 E. Key *The Century of the Child* New York, G. P. Putman, 1909, pp. 100–1.

4 Cited in B. Ehrenreich and D. English *For Her Own Good* London, Pluto Press, 1979, p. 171.

5 C. P. Gilman 'The Home: its work and influence' 1903, in R. Salper (ed.) *Female Liberation* New York, Knopf, 1972, p. 113.

6 A. Oakley *Women Confined: Towards a Sociology of Childbirth* Oxford, Martin Robertson, 1980.

7 G. W. Brown and T. Harris *Social Origins of Depression* London, Tavistock, 1978.

8 D. C. Skegg, R. Doll and J. Perry 'Use of medicines in general practice' *British Medical Journal* 18 June 1977, pp. 1501–3.

9 H. Graham and L. McKee 'The first months of motherhood', unpublished report, London, Health Education Council, 1980.

10 J. B. Miller *Toward a New Psychology of Women* Boston, Beacon Press, 1976.

11 N. Chodorow *The Reproduction of Mothering* Berkeley, California, University of California Press, 1978.

12 L. W. Hoffman and F. I. Nye (eds) *Working Mothers: An Evaluative Review of the Consequences for Wife, Husband and Child* San Francisco, Jossey-Bass, 1974.

13 A. Rossi 'Transition to parenthood' *Journal of Marriage and the Family* February 1968, pp. 26–39.

14 D. Levy *Maternal Overprotection* New York, Columbia University Press, 1943, pp. 3–4.

15 M. Mead *Blackberry Winter* p. 269.

16 J. F. Bernal and M. P. M. Richards 'Why some babies don't sleep' *New Society* 28 February 1974, p. 509.

17 For example, D. Breen *The Birth of a First Child* London, Tavistock, 1975.

18 S. de Beauvoir *The Second Sex* London, Four Square Books, 1960, p. 233.

19 Central Policy Review Staff *Services for Young Children with Working Mothers* London, HMSO, 1978.

20 A. Rich *On Lies, Secrets, Silence* London, Virago, 1980, pp. 263–4.

21 World Health Organization *Primary Health Care* Geneva, World Health Organization, 1978.

22 Quoted in C. Tomalin *Katherine Mansfield: A Secret Life* Harmondsworth, Penguin, 1988, p. 230.

23 F. Nightingale (1852) intro. M. Stark (1979) *Cassandra* New York, The Feminist Press.

24 See J. S. Haller and R. M. Haller *The Physician and Sexuality in Victorian America* New York, W. W. Norton, 1977.

25 Nightingale, op. cit., pp. 25, 30.

26 Ibid., p. 34.

27 Ibid., p. 38.

28 H. Graham *Women, Health and the Family* Brighton, Sussex, Harvester Press, 1984, pp. 150–3.

29 R. M. Titmuss 'The position of women' in *Essays on the Welfare State* London, Allen and Unwin, 1958.

30 See p. 141 above.

31 J. Brannen and P. Moss *Managing Mothers: Dual Earner Households after Maternity Leave* London, Unwin Htman, 1991.

32 J. Brannen and G. Wilson (eds) *Give and Take in Families: Studies in Resource Distribution* London, Allen and Unwin, 1987.

33 C. Glendinning and J. Millar (eds) *Women and Poverty in Britain* Brighton, Sussex, Wheatsheaf, 1987.

34 de Beauvoir, op. cit.

35 Graham and McKee, op. cit.; see also A. Oakley *Social Support and Motherhood: The Natural History of a Research Project* Oxford, Basil Blackwell, 1992.

36 A. Oakley and L. Rajan 'Obstetric technology and maternal emotional wellbeing: a further research note' *Journal of Reproductive and Infant Psychology* 8, 1990, pp. 45–55.

37 See A. Oakley 'Normal motherhood: an exercise in self-control?' in B. Hutter and G. Williams (eds) *Controlling Women: The Normal and the Deviant* London, Croom Helm, 1981.

38 G. Jones 'Cigarettes, health and gender: a study of smoking among parents in Britain', unpublished paper.

39 J. Balding *Young People in Britain* Exeter, University of Exeter, 1987.

40 S. G. Gabbe 'Reproductive hazards of the American life style' in G. Chamberlain (ed.) *Pregnant Women at Work* London, Macmillan, 1984.

41 H. Graham 'The limits of health promotion: some unfiltered tips from women who smoke', Paper presented at the Social Policy Association Annual Conference, Edinburgh, July 1988.

42 Institute of Medicine *Preventing Low Birthweight* Washington, National Academy Press, 1985.

43 G. Chamberlain, E. Phillipp, B. Howlett and K. Masters *British Births 1970* London, Heinemann, 1978.

44 W. J. Simpson 'A preliminary report of cigarette smoking and the incidence of prematurity' *American Journal of Obstetrics and Gynecology* 73, 1957, pp. 807–15.

45 Z. Stein and J. Kline 'Smoking, alcohol and reproduction' *American Journal of Public Health* 73, 1983, pp. 1154–6.

46 See R. Everson 'Individuals transplacentally exposed to maternal smoking may be at increased cancer risk in adult life' *Lancet* 19 July 1980, pp. 123–7; M. Sternfeldt, K. Berglund, J. Lindsten and J. Ludvigsson 'Maternal smoking during pregnancy and risk of childhood cancer' *Lancet* 14 June 1986, pp. 1350–2; R. J. Stevens, R. C. Becker, G. L. Krumpos, L. J. Lanz and C. J. Tolan 'Postnatal sequelae of parental smoking during and after pregnancy' *Journal of Reproductive and Infant Psychology* 6, 1988, pp. 61–81.

47 R. Davie, N. R. Butler and H. Goldstein *From Birth to Seven* London, Longman, 1972; N. R. Butler and H. Goldstein 'Smoking in pregnancy and subsequent child development' *British Medical Journal* 4, 1973, pp. 573–5.

48 K. R. Fogelman and O. Manor 'Smoking in pregnancy and development into early adulthood' *British Medical Journal* 1988, 297, pp. 1233–6.

49 Institute of Medicine, op. cit.

50 C. MacArthur, J. K. Newton and E. G. Knox 'Effect of anti-smoking health education on infant size at birth: a randomized controlled trial' *British Journal of Obstetrics and Gynaecology* 94, 1987, pp. 295–300; M. Sexton and J. R. Hebel 'A clinical trial of change in maternal smoking and its effect on birth weight' *Journal of the American Medical Association* 1984, 251, pp. 911–15; R. A. Windsor, G. Cutter, J. Morris, Y. Reese, B. Manzela, E. E. Bartlett, C. Samuelson and D. Spanos 'The effectiveness of smoking

cessation methods for smokers in public health maternity clinics: a randomized trial' *American Journal of Public Health* **75**, 1985, pp. 1389–92; see, for a review, J. Lumley and J. Astbury 'Advice for pregnancy' in I. Chalmers, M. Enkin and M. J. N. C. Keirse (eds) *Effective Care in Pregnancy and Childbirth* Oxford, Oxford University Press, 1989.

51 K. E. Bauman, E. S. Bryan, C. W. Dent and G. G. Koch 'The influence of observing carbon monoxide level on cigarette smoking by public prenatal patients' *American Journal of Public Health* 1983, 73 (9), pp. 1089–91.

52 J. W. Donovan 'Randomized controlled trial of anti-smoking advice in pregnancy' *British Journal of Preventive and Social Medicine* **31**, 1977, pp. 6–12.

53 H. Graham 'Smoking in pregnancy: the attitudes of expectant mothers' *Social Science and Medicine* **10**, 1976, pp. 399–405.

54 See A. Oakley 'Smoking in pregnancy: smokescreen or risk factor? Towards a materialist analysis' *Sociology of Health and Illness* 1989, 11, **4**, pp. 311–35.

55 A. Oakley *Social Support and Motherhood: The Natural History of a Research Project* Oxford, Basil Blackwell, 1992.

56 Jones, op. cit.

57 Brown and Harris, op. cit.; W. Grove 'Sex differences in mental illness among adult men and women' *Social Science and Medicine* **12B**, 1978, pp. 1887–98; R. Jenkins 'Sex differences in minor psychiatric morbidity' *Psychiatric Medicine* Monograph Supplement 7, 1985.

58 See Oakley, 1989, op. cit.

59 World Health Organization *IARC Monographs on the Evaluation of the Carcinogenic Risk of Chemicals in Humans: Tobacco Smoking* International Agency for Research in Cancer, vol. 38, 1985.

60 P. A. Gillies, F. Kristmundsdottir, B. Wilcox and J. C. G. Pearson 'The quantification of passive exposure to smoking amongst children' *Hygiene* **5**, 1986, pp. 861–7.

61 D. H. Rubin, P. A. Krasilnikoff, J. M. Leventhal, B. Weile and A. Berget 'Effect of passive smoking on birthweight' *Lancet* 23 August 1986, pp. 415–17.

62 *Hansard* 14 June 1988.

63 J. Popay and M. Bartley 'Conditions of labour and women's health' in C. Martin and D. McQueen (eds) *Readings for a New Public Health* Edinburgh, Edinburgh University Press, 1989.

64 World Health Organization 'Women, Health and Development. A report by the Director-general' Geneva, World Health Organization, 1985.

65 World Health Organization *Health Services in Europe* Copenhagen, World Health Organization Regional Office for Europe, 1981.

66 W. Farr *Vital Statistics* London, Edward Stanford, 1885, p. 132.

67 See the discussion in A. Oakley *The Captured Womb: A History of the Medical Care of Pregnant Women* Oxford, Basil Blackwell, 1984.

68 J. Campbell *The Protection of Motherhood* Reports on Public Health and Medical Subjects no 48, Ministry of Health, London, HMSO, 1927.

69 Departmental Committee on Maternal Mortality and Morbidity *Final Report* London, HMSO, 1932, p. 50.

70 M. Pfaundler 'Studien über Frühtod, Geschlechtsverhältnis und Selection' in M. Heilung (ed.) *Zur Intrauterinen. Absterbeordnung. 2 Kinderheilk.* **57**, 1936, 185–227.

71 Cranbrook Committee *Report of the Maternity Services Committee 1959*, London, HMSO, p. 67.

72 'Perinatal mortality' *Lancet* 16 December 1978, pp. 1319–20.

73 *New Society* 16 November 1978.

74 *Guardian* 13 February 1979.

75 Social Services Committee Second Report from the Social Services Committee *Perinatal and Neonatal Mortality* London, HMSO, 1980 (The Short Report), p. 6.

76 *United Nations Population Commission 15th Session. CICN 91231* Geneva, 1969, p. 82.

77 See M. G. Kerr 'The influence of information on perinatal practice' in I. Chalmers and G. McIllwaine (eds) *Perinatal Audit and Surveillance* Proceedings of the Ninth Study Group of the Royal College of Obstetricians and Gynaecologists, London, 1980.

78 I. Chalmers and A. Macfarlane 'Interpretation of perinatal statistics' in B. A. Wharton (ed.) *Topics in Perinatal Medicine* Bath, Pitman Medical, 1980.

79 Institute of Medicine, op. cit.

80 A. Macfarlane and M. Mugford *Birth Counts: Statistics of Pregnancy and Childbirth* vol. 1, London, HMSO, 1984.

81 H. J. Hoffman 'Perinatal mortality rates in relation to preterm birth and intrauterine growth retardation' in US Department of Health and Human Services *Proceedings of the International Collaborative Effort on Perinatal and Infant Mortality* vol. 1, Hyattsville, Maryland, 1985.

82 A. Macfarlane and I. Chalmers 'Problems in the interpretation of perinatal mortality statistics' in D. Hull (ed.) *Recent Advances in Paediatrics* Edinburgh, Churchill Livingstone, 1981.

83 Macfarlane and Mugford, op. cit., chapter 5.

84 World Health Organization *A WHO Report on Social and Biological Effects on Perinatal Mortality* vol. 1, Budapest, Hungary, WHO, 1978.

85 R. Illsley *Professional or Public Health?* London, Nuffield Provincial Hospitals Trust, 1980.

86 I. Chalmers 'Short, Black, Baird, Himsworth and social class differences in fetal and neonatal mortality rates' *British Medical Journal* 27 July 1985, pp. 231–2.

87 See, for a review, L. S. Bakketeig, H. J. Hoffman and A. Oakley 'Perinatal mortality' in M. Bracken (ed.) *Perinatal Epidemiology* New York, Oxford University Press, 1984.

88 P. Rantakallio 'Social background of mothers who smoke during pregnancy and influence of these factors on the offspring' *Social Science and Medicine* 13A, 1979, pp. 423–9.

89 N. Mamelle and B. Laumon 'Occupational fatigue and preterm birth' in G. Chamberlain (ed.) *Pregnant Women at Work* London, Macmillan, 1984.

90 J. W. B. Douglas 'Some factors associated with prematurity' *Journal of Obstetrics and Gynaecology of the British Empire* 57, 1950, pp. 143–70.

91 N. Hart 'Inequalities in health: the individual versus the environment' *Journal of the Royal Statistical Society* 1986, Part 3, pp. 228–46.

92 D. Baird 'Epidemiologic patterns over time' in D. M. Reed and F. J. Stanley (eds) *The Epidemiology of Prematurity* Baltimore, Maryland, Urban and Schwarzenberg, 1977.

93 D. Rush 'Effects of changes in protein and calorie intake during pregnancy on the growth of the human fetus' in M. Enkin and I. Chalmers (eds) *Effectiveness and Satisfaction in Antenatal Care* London, Spastics International Medical Publications, 1982.

94 D. Rush, Z. Stein, G. Christakis and M. Susser 'The prenatal project: the first 20 months of operation' in M. Winick (ed.) *Malnutrition and Human Development* New York, Wiley, 1974.

95 J. Winter 'The impact of the First World War on civilian health in Britain' *Economic History Review* 30, 1977, pp. 487–507.

96 R. M. Titmuss *Problems of Social Policy* London, HMSO, 1950.

97 Ibid., p. 530.

98 D. Dwork *War is Good for Babies and Other Young Children* London, Tavistock, 1987.

99 Oakley, 1984, op. cit.

100 The Short Report, op. cit., p. 21.

101 M. Enkin and I. Chalmers *Effectiveness and Satisfaction in Antenatal Care* Chapter 18 of Enkin and Chalmers (eds), op. cit.

102 A. Macfarlane and I. Chalmers, 1981, op. cit.; Bakketeig et al., op. cit.; I. Chalmers and M. Richards 'Intervention and causal inference in obstetric practice' in T. Chard and M. Richards (eds) *Benefits and Hazards of the New Obstetrics* London, Spastics International Medical Publications, 1977.

103 P. Bergsjo, E. Schmidt and D. Pusch 'Differences in the reported incidences of some obstetric interventions in Europe' in J. M. L. Phaff (ed.) *Perinatal Health Services* London, Croom Helm, 1986.

104 Leading article 'Caring for babies of very low birthweight' *British Medical Journal* 21 October 1978, pp. 1105–6.

105 A. Macfarlane 'Infant deaths after four weeks' (letter) *Lancet* 23 October 1982, pp. 929–30.

106 R. A. Jones, M. Cummins and P. A. Davis 'Infants of very low birthweight: a 15-year analysis' *Lancet* 23 June 1987, pp. 1332–5.

107 B. Hagberg, G. Hagberg and L. Olow 'The changing panorama of cerebral palsy in Sweden' *Acta Paediatrica Scandinavia* **73**, 1984, pp. 433–40.

108 E. Alberman 'Why are stillbirth and neonatal mortality rates continuing to fall?' *British Journal of Obstetrics and Gynaecology* **92**, 1985, pp. 559–64.

109 'Quality not quantity in babies' *British Medical Journal* 9 February 1980, p. 347.

110 W. Z. Billewicz 'Some implications of self-selection for pregnancy' *British Journal of Preventive and Social Medicine* **27**, 1973, pp. 49–52; N. M. Morris, J. R. Udry and C. L. Chase 'Shifting age-parity distribution of births and the decrease in infant mortality' *American Journal of Public Health* **65**, 1975, pp. 359–62.

111 M. E. Brennan and P. Lancashire 'Association of childhood mortality with housing stress and unemployment' *Journal of Epidemiology and Community Health* **32**, 1978, pp. 28–33.

112 C. J. Martin, S. D. Platt and S. M. Hunt 'Housing conditions and ill health' *British Medical Journal* 2 May 1987, pp. 1125–7.

113 Office of Health Economics *Perinatal Mortality in Britain – A Question of Class* Briefing no 10, 1979.

114 A. L. Cochrane '1931–71: A critical review with particular reference to the medical profession' in G. Teeling-Smith and N. E. J. Wells (eds) *Medicines for the Year 2000* New York, Basic Books, 1979.

115 *Lancet* 15 June 1985, pp. 1375–8.

116 I. Chalmers 'Perinatal epidemiology: strengths, limitations and possible hazards' in R. W. Beard and S. Campbell (eds) *Current Status of Fetal Monitoring and Ultrasound* London, Royal College of Obstetricians and Gynaecologists, 1978.

117 J. Russell 'Perinatal mortality: the current debate' *Sociology of Health and Illness* 1982, 4, 3, pp. 302–19.

118 H. Graham 'Prevention and health: every mother's business. A comment on child health policies in the 1970s' in C. Harris, M. Anderson, R. Chester, D. H. J. Morgan and D. Leonard (eds) *The Sociology of the Family* Sociological Review Monograph 28, 1979.

119 F. Capra *The Turning Point* New York, Bantam Books, 1983, p. 149.

120 A. Oakley, D. Elbourne and I. Chalmers 'The effects of social interventions in pregnancy' in G. Breart, N. Spira and E. Papiernik (eds) *Proceedings of a Workshop on Prevention of Preterm Birth – New Goals and New Practices in Prenatal Care* Paris, INSERM, 1986; D. Elbourne, A. Oakley and I. Chalmers 'Social and psychological support during pregnancy' in I. Chalmers, M. Enkin and M. J. N. C. Keirse (eds) *Effective Care in Pregnancy and Childbirth* Oxford, Oxford University Press, 1989.

121 World Health Organization 'Maternal mortality: helping women off the road to death' *WHO Chronicle* 1986, 40, **5**, pp. 175–83.

122 A. Macfarlane 'The downs and ups of infant mortality' *British Medical Journal* 23 January 1988, pp. 230–1.

123 W. Farr, op. cit.

124 A. van Gennep *The Rites of Passage* London, Routledge and Kegan Paul, 1960.

125 P. Lomas 'An interpretation of modern obstetric practice' in S. Kitzinger and J. A. Davis (eds) *The Place of Birth* Oxford University Press, 1978.

126 Ibid., pp. 176–7.

127 J. M. Beazley 'Controlled parturition' *British Journal of Hospital Medicine*, March 1977, pp. 237–44.

128 M. L. Romney 'Predelivery shaving: an unjustified assault?' *Journal of Obstetrics and Gynaecology* **1**, 1980, pp. 33–5.

129 Caroline Flint, personal communication.

130 A. Rich *Of Woman Born* London, Virago, 1977, pp. 274–5.

131 A. Oakley *Becoming a Mother* Oxford, Martin Robertson, 1979.

132 J. Lumley, personal communication.

133 E. Goffman *Asylums: Essays on the Social Situation of Patients and Other Inmates* New York, Anchor Books, 1961, p. 6.

134 Department of Health and Social Security *Present-day Practice in Infant Feeding* Third Report, London, HMSO, 1988.

135 E. Wynder 'Coronary heart disease prevention: should it begin in childhood?' Proceedings of a conference held by the Coronary Prevention Group, May 1988.

136 R. Apple *Mothers and Medicine: A Social History of Infant Feeding* Madison, Wisconsin, University of Wisconsin Press, 1987, p. 4.

137 J. Martin and J. Monk *Infant Feeding 1980* OPCS, Social Survey Division, London, HMSO, 1982.

138 Ibid.

139 J. P. Elliot and J. F. Flaherty 'The use of breast stimulation to ripen the cervix in term pregnancies' *American Journal of Obstetrics and Gynecology* 1 March 1983, pp. 553–6.

140 Oakley, 1979, op. cit.

141 D. Raphael *The Tender Gift: Breastfeeding* Englewood Cliffs, New Jersey, Prentice-hall, 1973.

142 See A. Oakley *Social Support and Motherhood: The Natural History of a Research Project* Oxford, Basil Blackwell, 1992.

143 H. Graham and A. Oakley 'Competing ideologies of reproduction: medical and maternal perspectives on pregnancy and birth' in H. Roberts (ed.) *Women, Health and Reproduction* London, Routledge and Kegan Paul, 1981.

144 See Oakley, 1984, op. cit.

145 C. J. Hobel 'Risk assessment in perinatal medicine' *Obstetrics and Gynecology* **21**, 1978, pp. 287–95.

146 See pp. 102–4 above; Oakley, 1989, op. cit.

147 R. H. Nicholson (ed.) *Medical Research with Children: Ethics, Law and Practice* Oxford, Oxford University Press, 1986.

148 M. Piercy *Woman on the Edge of Time* London, The Women's Press, 1979, p. 105.

149 M. Hacker *Introduction* to J. Russ *The Female Man* Boston, Gregg Press, 1977, pp. xi–xii.

150 Central Statistical Office *Social Trends 21* London, HMSO, 1991.

151 Quoted in A. Coote, H. Harman and P. Hewitt *The Family Way* Social Policy Paper no 1, London, Institute for Public Policy Research, 1990, p. 46.

152 Ibid., p. 47.

153 Central Statistical Office, op. cit., pp. 45–6.

154 Coote et al., op. cit., p. 47.

155 *Guardian* 'One in five pregnancies aborted as terminations reach record' 20 September 1990.

156 V. Estaugh and J. Wheatley *Family Planning and Family Well-being* Occasional Paper no 12, London, Family Policy Studies Centre, 1990, p. 42.

157 Central Statistical Office, op. cit., p. 43.

158 Ibid., p. 44.

159 Ibid., p. 39.

160 Ibid., p. 44.

161 Ibid., p. 38.

162 Coote et al., op. cit., p. 16.

163 Ibid.

164 J. Martin and C. Roberts *Women and Employment: A Lifetime Perspective* London, HMSO, 1984.

165 Coote et al., op. cit.

166 Central Statistical Office, op. cit., p. 69.

167 L. Morris *The Workings of the Household* Cambridge, Polity Press, 1990, p. 137.

168 Central Statistical Office, op. cit., p. 169.

169 H. Joshi 'The cash opportunity costs of childbearing: an approach to estimation using British data' London, Centre for Economic Policy Research, Discussion paper no 208, 1987.

170 K. Kiernan and M. Wicks *Family Change and Future Policy* London, Family Policy Study Centre, 1990, p. 30.

171 R. Jowell, S. Witherspoon and L. Brook (eds) *British Social Attitudes: The 5th Report* London, Gower, 1988.

172 Cited in A. Woollett, D. White and L. Lyon 'Observations of fathers at birth' in N. Beail and J. McGuire (eds) *Fathers: Psychological Perspectives* London, Junction Books, 1982, p. 72.

173 Ibid.

174 J. Garcia, M. Corry, D. MacDonald, D. Elbourne and A. Grant 'Mothers' views of continuous electronic fetal heart monitoring and intermittent auscultation in a randomized controlled trial' *Birth* **12**, 1985, pp. 79–85.

175 See R. S. Barbour 'Fathers: the emergence of a new consumer group' in J. Garcia, R. Kilpatrick and M. Richards (eds) *The Politics of Maternity Care* Oxford, Oxford University Press, 1990.

176 J. Richman, W. O. Goldthorp and C. Simmons 'Fathers in labour' *New Society* 16 October 1975.

177 Woollett et al., op. cit., p. 75.

178 M. Rodholm and K. Larsson 'Father–infant interaction at the first contact after delivery' *Early Human Development* **3**, 1979, pp. 21–7.

179 Woollett et al., op. cit., p. 82.

180 Barbour, op. cit.

181 N. Beail 'Role of the father during pregnancy and childbirth' in N. Beail and J. McGuire (eds) *Fathers: Psychological Perspectives* London, Junction Books, 1982, p. 11.

182 Oakley, 1992, op. cit.

183 Oakley, 1980, op. cit.

184 P. Prendergast and A. Prout 'Learning about birth: parenthood and sex education in English secondary schools' in J. Garcia, R. Kilpatrick and M. Richards (eds) *The Politics of Maternity Care* Oxford, Oxford University Press, 1990.

185 Coote et al., op. cit.

186 Jowell et al., op. cit.

187 Kiernan and Wicks, op. cit., p. 15.

188 Ibid.

189 J. Lewis and D. Piachaud 'Women and poverty in the twentieth century' in Glendinning and Millar, op. cit.

190 J. Roll 'Family fortunes: parents' incomes in the 1980s' London, Family Policy Studies Centre Occasional Paper no 7, 1988.

191 Central Statistical Office, op. cit.

192 Ibid.

193 Coote et al., op. cit., p. 23.

194 J. Pahl *Money and Marriage* London, Macmillan, 1989.

195 M. Forster *Have the Men Had Enough?* London, Chatto and Windus, 1989.

196 N. Charles and M. Kerr *Women, Food and Families* Manchester, Manchester University Press, 1988.

197 Maternity Alliance *Poverty – a Crisis for Babies* London, Maternity Alliance, 1985.
198 *Guardian* 'Women main victims of public transport cuts' 3 January 1991.
199 Martin and Roberts, op. cit.
200 Joshi, op. cit.
201 Central Statistical Office, op. cit.
202 Coote et al., op. cit.
203 *The Independent* 'Firms failing to provide childcare' 9 April 1990.
204 Coote et al., op. cit.
205 Brannen and Moss, op. cit.
206 L. Zander and G. Chamberlain (eds) *Pregnancy Care for the 1980s* London, Macmillan, 1984, p. xiii.
207 Ibid.
208 Oakley, 1984, op. cit.
209 L. Durward and R. Evans 'Pressure groups and maternity care' in J. Garcia, R. Kilpatrick and M. Richards (eds) *The Politics of Maternity Care* Oxford, Oxford University Press, 1990.
210 Ibid.
211 P. S. Summey and M. Hurst 'Ob/Gyn on the rise: the evolution of professional ideology in the twentieth century – Part I' *Women and Health* 11, **1**, pp. 133–45 and Part II: 11, **2**, pp. 103–22, 1986.
212 H. C. Mack 'Back to Sacajawea' Presidential Address *American Journal of Obstetrics and Gynecology* **69**, 1955, pp. 933–49.
213 B. K. Rothman *Recreating Motherhood: Ideology and Technology in Patriarchal Society* New York, W. W. Norton, 1989, p. 21.
214 Oakley, 1989, op. cit.
215 A. Macfarlane 'Holding back the tide of Caesareans' (letter) *British Medical Journal* 1988, 297, p. 852.
216 *Guardian* 'NHS faces crisis over birth claims' 18 October 1990.
217 See e.g. S. Fisher *In the Patient's Best Interests: Women and the Politics of Medical Decisions* New Jersey, Rutgers University Press, 1986; H. Roberts *Patient Patients: Women and their Doctors* London, Pandora Press, 1985.
218 A. Cartwright *The Dignity of Labour?* London, Tavistock, 1979.
219 A. Jacoby and A. Cartwright 'Finding out about the views and experiences of maternity-service users' in J. Garcia, R. Kilpatrick and M. Richards (eds) *The Politics of Maternity Care* Oxford, Oxford University Press, 1990, p. 251.
220 Jowell et al., op. cit., pp. 98–9.
221 J. W. Hawkins and C. S. A. Aber 'The content of advertisements in medical journals: distorting the image of women' *Women and Health* 14, **2**, 1988, pp. 43–59.
222 A. Phoenix 'Black women and the maternity services' in J. Garcia, R. Kilpatrick and M. Richards (eds) *The Politics of Maternity Care* Oxford, Oxford University Press, 1990.
223 J. Garcia, L. Rajan, A. Oakley and P. Robertson 'Marital status and social support for childbearing women (forthcoming).

PART 3

1 M. C. Stopes *A Banned Play and a Preface on the Censorship* London, 1926, p. 15.
2 M. Mead and N. Newton 'Cultural patterning of perinatal behaviour' in S. Richardson and A. F. Guttmacher (eds) *Childbearing – Its Social and Psychological Aspects* Baltimore, Williams and Wilkins, 1967.
3 B. Rowland *Medieval Woman's Guide to Health* London, Croom Helm, 1981.
4 N. E. Himes *Medical History of Contraception* New York, Gamut Press, 1963.
5 K. Dunnell *Family Formation* London, Office of Population Census and Surveys, 1979; National Center for Health Statistics *Contraceptive Utilization* US Department of Health Education and Welfare, 1978.

6 D. F. Hawkins and M. Elder *Human Fertility Control* London, Butterworth, 1979, p. 129.

7 J. Sleep, A. Grant, J. Garcia, D. Elbourne, J. Spencer and I. Chalmers 'The West Berkshire Perineal Management Trial' Paper presented at the 23rd British Congress of Obstetrics and Gynaecology, Birmingham, 23 July 1983.

8 V. Beral 'Reproductive Mortality' *British Medical Journal* II, 1979, pp. 632–4.

9 The East Bay Men's Center Newsletter, USA (undated).

10 A. Rich *Of Woman Born* London, Virago, 1977, p. 42.

11 M. P. M. Richards 'A place of safety? An examination of the risks of hospital delivery' in S. Kitzinger and J. A. Davis (eds) *The Place of Birth* Oxford, Oxford University Press, 1978.

12 N. Friedman *Everything You Must Know about Tampons* New York, Berkeley, 1981.

13 D. Rush 'Effects of changes in protein and calorie intake during pregnancy on the growth of the human fetus' in M. Enkin and I. Chalmers (eds) *Effectiveness and Satisfaction in Antenatal Care* London, Spastics International Medical Publications, 1982.

14 A. Oakley *The Captured Womb* Oxford, Basil Blackwell, 1984.

15 K. Luker *Taking Chances: Abortion and the Decision Not to Contracept* Berkeley, University of California Press, 1975.

16 J. Zimmerman 'Technology and the future of women: haven't we met somewhere before?' *Women's Studies International Quarterly* 4, 1981, pp. 335–67.

17 P. Sargent (ed.) *More Women of Wonder*, Harmondsworth, Penguin, 1979, p. 30.

18 T. Disch *334* New York, Avon Books, 1970.

19 M. Piercy *Woman on the Edge of Time* London, The Women's Press, 1979, p. 105.

20 V. Woolf *Three Guineas* Harmondsworth, Penguin, reprinted 1977.

21 W. J. Bremner and D. M. de Kretser 'Contraceptives for males' *Signs: Journal of Women in Culture and Society* 1, 1975, pp. 387–96.

22 R. Steinbacher 'Futuristic implications of sex preselection' in H. B. Holmes, B. B. Hoskins and M. Gross (eds) *The Custom-made Child?* Clifton, New Jersey, The Humana Press, 1981; N. E. Williamson 'Sex preferences, sex control and the effects on women' *Signs: Journal of Women in Culture and Society* 1, 1976, pp. 847–62.

23 L. Belmont and F. Marolla 'Birth order, family size and intelligence' *Science* **182**, 1973, pp. 1096–101.

24 M. R. Nentwig 'Technical aspects of sex preselection' in Holmes et al., op. cit.

25 Royal College of Obstetricians and Gynaecologists *Report of the RCOG Ethics Committee on In Vitro Fertilization and Embryo Replacement or Transfer* London, RCOG, 1983.

26 R. Snowden and G. D. Mitchell *The Artificial Family* London, Unwin, 1983.

27 E. Philipp *Childlessness* London, Arrow Books, 1975.

28 J. Ellul *The Technological Society* New York, Alfred Knopf, 1964, p. vi.

29 Feminist Self Insemination Group *Self Insemination* London, 1980.

30 B. K. Rothman *Recreating Motherhood: Ideology and Technology in a Patriarchal Society* New York, W. W. Norton, 1989.

31 Office of Technology Assessment *The Implications of Cost-effectiveness Analysis of Medical Technology* Washington, DC, Government Printing Office, 1980.

32 Mead and Newton, op. cit.

33 N. Pfeffer and A. Woollett *The Experience of Infertility* London, Virago, 1983, p. 68.

34 G. J. Annas *Hastings Center Report* 1979, p. 14.

35 A. de Wit and D. Banta *The Diffusion of In Vitro Fertilization in the Netherlands and England: An Exploratory Study* Maastricht, Netherlands, Institute for Medical Technology Assessment, 1990.

36 Ibid.

37 World Health Organization *Is In Vitro Fertilization Appropriate Technology?* European Regional Office, Copenhagen, 1989.

38 Ibid.

39 Australian In Vitro Fertilization Collaborative Group 'High incidence of preterm births

and early losses in pregnancy after in vitro fertilization' *British Medical Journal* 1985, 291, pp. 1160–4.

40 P. Braude and M. Johnson 'Embryo research: yes or no?' *British Medical Journal* 2 December 1989, pp. 1349–51.

41 Australian In Vitro Fertilization Collaborative Group, op. cit.

42 P. C. Steptoe and R. G. Edwards 'Birth after the reimplantation of a human embryo' (letter) *Lancet* 12 August 1978, p. 366.

43 B. Howie 'Selective reduction in multiple pregnancy' *British Medical Journal* 1988, 297, pp. 433–4.

44 World Health Organization, op. cit.

45 A. Trounson and A. Conti 'Research in human in vitro fertilization and embryo transfer' *British Medical Journal* 1982, 285 (24 July), pp. 244–8.

46 World Health Organization, op. cit.

47 B. Botting, A. Macfarlane and F. Price *Three, Four and More: A Study of Triplet and Higher-order Births* London, HMSO, 1990.

48 *Sunday Times* 'Super-births: how joy can turn to tears' 23 June 1985.

49 See pp. 243–64 above.

50 J. B. McKinlay 'From "Promising Report" to "Standard Procedure" – seven stages in the career of a medical intervention' *Millbank Memorial Quarterly* **59**, 1981, pp. 374–411.

51 A. de Wit and D. Banta, op. cit., p. 8.

52 I. Chalmers, M. Enkin and M. J. N. C. Keirse (eds) *Effective Care in Pregnancy and Childbirth* Oxford, Oxford University Press, 1989.

53 A. Grant, M.-T. Joy, N. O'Brien, E. Hennessy and D. Macdonald 'Cerebral palsy among children born during the Dublin randomized controlled trial of intrapartum monitoring' *Lancet* 25 November 1989, pp. 1233–6.

54 See e.g. M. Klaus, J. H. Kennell, S. Robertson and R. Sosa 'Effects of social support on maternal and infant morbidity' *British Medical Journal* 1986, 293, pp. 585–7.

55 P. Spallone *Beyond Conception* London, Macmillan, 1989, p. 96.

56 House of Commons Debates (Unborn Child Protection Bill), 1984–5, pp. 633–700.

57 N. Pfeffer 'Artificial insemination, in-vitro fertilization and the stigma of infertility' in M. Stanworth (ed.) *Reproductive Technologies* Cambridge, Polity Press, 1987.

58 World Health Organization, op. cit.

59 See Spallone, op. cit., p. 98.

60 Rothman, op. cit., p. 137.

61 *Guardian* 'NHS to open test-tube baby clinic in London' 27 October 1982.

62 Warnock Committee *Report of the Committee of Inquiry into Human Fertilization and Embryology* London, HMSO, 1987, p. 11.

63 M. P. M. Richards *Separation, Divorce and the Development of Children: A Review* Child Care and Development Group, University of Cambridge, 1982.

64 H. Graham and J. Popay (eds) 'Women and poverty: exploring the research and policy agenda' *Thomas Coram Research Unit Occasional Papers* Institute of Education, University of London, 1989.

65 B. Campbell *Unofficial Secrets* London, Virago, 1987.

66 *Guardian* 'Doctor wants more embryo research' 15 May 1984.

67 'Agreement for In Vitro Fertilization or Gamete Intra-Fallopian Transfer' Embryo and Gamete Research Group, Department of Obstetrics and Gynaecology, The Rosie Maternity Hospital, Cambridge, no date.

68 See R. Arditti, R. Duelli-Klein and S. Minden (eds) *Test-tube Women* London, Pandora Press, 1989.

69 H. Rose 'Victorian values in the test-tube' in M. Stanworth (ed.) *Reproductive Technologies* Cambridge, Polity Press, 1987, pp. 152–3.

70 N. Chodorow *The Reproduction of Mothering: Psychoanalysis and the Sociology of Gender* Berkeley, California, University of California Press, 1978.

71 Rothman, op. cit., pp. 19–21.

72 'Umbilical vein for bypass operations' *British Medical Journal* 23 July 1983, pp. 244–5.

73 *Guardian* 'Court to rule on property rights to body tissue' 8 May 1990. (California's Supreme Court ruled against the patient in this case: *Guardian* 11 July 1990.)

74 Trounson and Conti, op. cit.

75 S. J. Reiser *Medicine and the Reign of Technology* Cambridge, Cambridge University Press, 1978.

76 R. P. Petechsky 'Foetal images: the power of visual culture in the politics of reproduction' in M. Stanworth (ed.) *Reproductive Technologies* Cambridge, Polity Press, 1987.

77 Oakley, 1984, op. cit.

78 See e.g. S. Harding *The Science Question in Feminism* Milton Keynes, Open University Press, 1986.

79 See Stanworth, op. cit., p. 15.

80 See Spallone, op. cit., p. 44.

81 See Rothman, op. cit., p. 160.

82 See Rose, op. cit., p. 168.

83 P. Chester *Sacred Bond* London, Virago, 1990.

84 Rothman, op. cit., p. 242.

85 Embryo and Gamete Research Group, op. cit.

86 A. Montague *The Natural Superiority of Women* New York, Macmillan, 1968.

87 Rose, op. cit. p. 163.

88 'Agreement for In Vitro Fertilisation' The Hallam Medical Centre, London, no date.

89 Editorial 'Appropriate technology' *British Medical Journal* 28 April 1984, pp. 1251–2.

90 C. Merchant *The Death of Nature: Women, Ecology and the Scientific Revolution* San Francisco, Harper and Row, 1980.

91 See S. Ruddick *Maternal Thinking* London, The Women's Press, 1989.

92 J. Joyce *Ulysses*.

93 T. Carlyle *Heroes and Hero-worship*.

94 E. Gibbon *Decline and Fall of the Roman Empire*, chapter 2.

95 H. Ford, reported to have been said in the witness box when suing the *Chicago Tribune*, July 1919.

96 G. W. Hegel cited in G. B. Shaw *The Revolutionists' Handbook*.

97 For example H. R. Spencer *The History of British Midwifery from 1650 to 1800* London, John Bale Sons and Danielsson Ltd, 1927.

98 References for statements made in this chapter, unless otherwise indicated, are to be found in Oakley, 1984, op. cit.

99 C. W. Hohler and L. D. Platt, American College of Obstetrics and Gynecology Office Ultrasound Survey (personal communication) quoted in National Institutes of Health *Consensus Development Conference* 'The Use of Diagnostic Ultrasound Imaging in Pregnancy' 6–8 February 1984, Washington, DC, USA.

100 J. W. Wladimiroff and L. Laar 'Ultrasonic measurement of the fetal body size: a randomized controlled trial' *Acta Obstetrica et Gynaecologica Scandinavica* 59, 1980, pp. 177–9.

101 McKinlay, op. cit.

102 L. N. Reece 'The estimation of fetal maturity by a new method of X-ray cephalometry: its bearing on clinical midwifery' *Proceedings of the Royal Society of Medicine* 18 January 1938, p. 489.

103 S. N. Hassani *Ultrasound in Gynecology and Obstetrics* New York, Springer Verlag, 1978, p. vii.

104 S. Campbell and D. J. Little 'Clinical potential of real-time ultrasound' in M. J. Bennett and S. Campbell (eds) *Real-time Ultrasound in Obstetrics* Oxford, Basil Blackwell, 1980.

105 McKinlay, op. cit., p. 398.

106 W. A. N. Dorland and M. J. Huberry *The X-ray in Embryology and Obstetrics* London, Henry Kimpton, 1926, p. viii.

107 E. Reinold 'Fetal movements in early pregnancy' in A. Kurjak (ed.) *Progress in Medical Ultrasound* I, Amsterdam, Excerpta Medica, 1980, pp. 64–6.

108 R. W. A. Salmond 'The uses and value of radiology in obstetrics' in F. J. Browne (ed.) *Antenatal and Postnatal Care* 2nd ed., London, J. and A. Churchill, 1937, p. 497.

109 J. Chassar Moir 'The uses and value of radiology in obstetrics' in F. J. Browne and J. C. McClure-Browne (eds) *Antenatal and Postnatal Care* 9th ed., London, J. and A. Churchill, 1960, p. 389.

110 A. Stewart, J. Webb, D. Giles and D. Hewitt 'Malignant disease in childhood and diagnostic irradiation in utero' *Lancet* **2**, 1956, p. 447.

111 Hassani, op. cit.

112 I. Donald 'Sonar – its present status in medicine' in A. Kurjak (ed.) *Progress in Medical Ultrasound* I, Amsterdam, Excerpta Medica, 1980, p. 1.

113 S. T. Coleridge 18 December 1831, quoted in McKinlay, op. cit.

114 M. Roberts and S. Adam 'Breast cancer and benign breast disease' in A. McPherson (ed.) *Women's Problems in General Practice* Oxford, Oxford University Press, 1987.

115 See H. Roberts *The Patient Patients* London, Pandora Press, 1985.

116 M. Ginzler, J. Davies, K. McPherson and N. Black 'Ethics committees and health services research' *Journal of Public Health Medicine* **12**, 1990, pp. 190–6.

117 Consensus Development Conference 'Treatment of primary breast cancer' *British Medical Journal* 1986, 293, pp. 946–7.

118 J. Robinson, personal communication.

119 ASPECT *Breast Cancer Counselling and Drugs* Ramsgate, Kent, ASPECT, 1990.

120 See Mead and Newton, op. cit.

121 See G. Greer *The Change* London, Hamish Hamilton, 1991.

122 G. J. Barker-Benfield *The Horrors of the Half-known Life* New York, Harper and Row, 1976.

123 B. Seaman and G. Seaman *Women and the Crisis in Sex Hormones* New York, Bantam Books, 1978.

124 See M. Minchin *Breastfeeding Matters* Australia, Allen and Unwin and Alma Publications, 1985.

PART 4

1 S. de Beauvoir *Adieux: A Farewell to Sartre* New York, Pantheon, 1984, pp. 240–1.

2 Ibid., p. 298.

3 V. Woolf 'Women and fiction' in L. Woolf (ed.) *Collection Essays: Virginia Woolf* vol. II, London, Chatto and Windus, 1972.

4 C. Gilligan *In a Different Voice: Psychological Theory and Women's Development* Cambridge, Harvard University Press, 1982.

5 See A. Oakley 'Women's studies in British sociology: to end at our beginning?' *British Journal of Sociology* 1989, 40, **3**, pp. 442–70.

6 M. Evans and D. Morgan *Work on Women: A Guide to the Literature* London, Tavistock, 1979.

7 S. de Beauvoir *The Second Sex* London, Four Square Books, 1960.

8 V. Klein *The Feminine Character: History of an Ideology* London, Kegan Paul, Trench, Trubner and Co., 1949.

9 A. Myrdal and V. Klein *Women's Two Roles: Home and Work* London, Routledge and Kegan Paul, 1956.

10 M. Kerr *The People of Ship Street* London, Routledge and Kegan Paul, 1958.

11 M. Mead *Sex and Temperament in Three Primitive Societies* New York, William Morrow, 1935.

12 M. Mead *Male and Female* Harmondsworth, Penguin, 1962.

13 P. Kaberry *Women of the Grassfields* London, HMSO, 1952.

14 B. Wootton *Social Science and Social Pathology* London,, Allen and Unwin, 1959.

15 B. Friedan *The Feminine Mystique* London, Gollancz, 1963.

16 G. Greer *The Female Eunuch* London, MacGibbon and Kee, 1971.

17 K. Millett *Sexual Politics* London, Rupert Hart-Davis, 1971.

18 J. Mitchell *Woman's Estate* Harmondsworth, Penguin, 1971.

19 J. Mitchell 'Women: the longest revolution' *New Left Review* 40, 1966.

20 S. Firestone *The Dialectic of Sex* London, Paladin, 1972.

21 R. Delmar 'What is feminism?' in J. Mitchell and A. Oakley (eds) *What Is Feminism?* Oxford, Basil Blackwell, 1986.

22 G. Gilder *Sexual Suicide* New York, Quadrangle Books, 1973.

23 C. Lasch 'The politics of nostalgia' *Harper's Magazine* November 1984.

24 B. Berger and P. L. Berger *The War over the Family: Capturing the Middle Ground* Garden City, Anchor Press/Doubleday, 1984.

25 J. Doane and D. Hodges *Nostalgia and Sexual Difference* New York, Methuen, 1987.

26 See A. Oakley *Social Support and Motherhood: The Natural History of a Research Project* Oxford, Basil Blackwell, 1992.

27 L. H. Kidder 'Qualitative research and quasi-experimental frameworks' in M. B. Brewer and B. E. Collins *Scientific Enquiry and the Social Sciences* San Francisco, Jossey Bass, 1981, p. 227.

28 M. Zelditch 'Some methodological problems of field studies' *American Journal of Sociology* **67**, 1962, pp. 566–76.

29 E. F. Keller *A Feeling for the Organism: The Life and Work of Barbara McClintock* New York, W. H. Freeman, 1983.

30 Ibid., p. 148.

31 J. Favret-Saada *Deadly Words: Witchcraft in the Bocage* Cambridge, Cambridge University Press, 1980.

32 Ibid., p. 5.

33 H. E. Longino 'Can there be a feminist science?' in A. Garry and M. Pearsall (eds) *Women, Knowledge and Reality: Explorations in Feminist Philosophy* Boston, Unwin Hyman, 1989.

34 A. Oakley *Sex, Gender and Society* Revised edition, London, Gower, 1985.

35 Longino, op. cit., p. 210.

36 V. Walkerdine and H. Lucey *Democracy in the Kitchen* London, Virago, 1989.

37 B. Tizard and M. Hughes *Young Children Learning* London, Fontana, 1984.

38 Walkerdine and Lucey, op. cit., p. 29.

39 S. Maitland 'A feminist writer's progress' in M. Wandor (ed.) *On Gender and Writing* London, Pandora, 1983, p. 18.

40 N. Hartsock *Money, Sex and Power* Boston, Northeastern University Press, 1984.

41 H. Rose ' "Hand, brain and heart": a feminist epistemology for the natural sciences' *Signs: Journal of Women in Culture and Society* 1984, 9, **1**, pp. 73–90.

42 S. Harding *The Science Question in Feminism* Milton Keynes, Open University Press, 1986.

43 E. F. Keller 'Feminism and science' in A. Garry and M. Pearsall (eds) *Women, Knowledge and Reality: Explorations in Feminist Philosophy* Boston, Unwin Hyman, 1989.

44 Harding, op. cit.

45 H. Graham 'Do his answers fit her questions?' in E. Gamarnikow, D. Morgan, J. Purvis and D. Taylorson (eds) *The Public and the Private* London, Heinemann, 1983.

46 G. Bendelow *Gender Differences in Perceptions of Pain: Towards a Phenomenological Approach* Unpublished PhD thesis, University of London, 1992.

47 D. E. Smith 'A sociology for women' in J. A. Sherman and E. T. Beck (eds) *The Prism of Sex: Essays in the Sociology of Knowledge* Madison, Wisconsin, University of Wisconsin Press, 1979.

48 R. Crompton and M. Mann (eds) *Gender and Stratification* Cambridge, Polity Press, 1986.

49 R. Floud, K. Wachter and A. Gregory *Height, Health and History* Cambridge, Cambridge University Press, 1990.

50 D. E. Smith *The Everyday World as Problematic* Milton Keynes, Open University Press, 1988.

51 P. Aries *Centuries of Childhood* London, Jonathan Cape, 1962.

52 C. Jencks with M. Smith, H. Acland, M. J. Bane, D. Cohen, H. Gintis, B. Heyns and S. Michelson *Inequality: A Reassessment of the Effect of Family and Schooling in America* New York, Basic Books, 1972.

53 J. Brannen and G. Wilson (eds) *Give and Take in Families: Studies in Resource Distribution* London, Unwin Hyman, 1987.

54 H. Graham *Caring for the Family* London, Health Education Council, 1986.

55 M. Stacey 'The division of labour revisited, or overcoming the two Adams' in P. Abrams, R. Deem, J. Finch and P. Rock (eds) *Practice and Progress: British Sociology 1950–80* London, Allen and Unwin, 1981.

56 J. B. Miller *Toward a New Psychology of Women* Harmondsworth, Penguin, 1976.

57 S. Walby 'Gender politics and social theory' *Sociology* 1988, 22, **2**, pp. 215–32.

58 A. Rich 'Toward a woman-centred university' in A. Rich *On Lies, Secrets, Silence* London, Virago, 1980.

59 M. B. Belenky, B. M. Clinchy, N. R. Goldberger and J. M. Tarule *Women's Ways of Knowing* New York, Basic Books, 1986.

60 *New Statesman and Society* 30 June 1989.

61 M. Benney and E. C. Hughes 'Of sociology and the interview' in N. Denzin (ed.) *Sociological Methods: A Source Book* London, Butterworth, 1970, p. 190.

62 M. D. Shipman *The Limitations of Social Research* London, Longman, 1972, p. 76.

63 J. Galtung *Theory and Methods of Social Research* London, Allen and Unwin, 1967, p. 149.

64 Benney and Hughes, op. cit., p. 191.

65 W. J. Goode and P. K. Hatt 2Methods in Social Reseach New York, McGraw-Hill, 1952, p. 185.

66 Benney and Hughes, op. cit., pp. 196–7.

67 Goode and Hatt, op. cit, p. 191.

68 R. L. Kahn and L. F. Cannell *The Dynamics of Interviewing* New York, John Wiley, 1957, p. 16.

69 N. Denzin (ed.) *Sociological Methods: A Source Book* London, Butterworth, 1970, p. 186.

70 Goode and Hatt, op. cit., p. 191.

71 Most respondents appear to be female.

72 C. Selltiz, M. Jahoda, M. Deutsch and S. W. Cook *Research Methods in Social Relations* London, Methuen, 1965.

73 C. A. Moser *Survey Methods in Social Investigation* London, Heinemann, 1958, pp. 187–8, 195.

74 *Oxford English Dictionary*

75 G. Sjoberg and R. Nett *A Methodology for Social Research* New York, Harper and Row, 1968, p. 210.

76 Ibid., p. 212.

77 Galtung, op. cit., p. 161.

78 Selltiz et al., op. cit., p. 576.

79 Goode and Hatt *Methods in Social Research*, p. 198.

80 A. M. Rose 'A research note on experimentation in interviewing' *American Journal of Sociology* **51**, 1945, p. 143.

81 Selltiz et al., op. cit., p. 576.

82 Ibid., p. 268.

83 Sjoberg and Nett, op. cit., p. 211.

84 J. B. Miller *Toward a New Psychology of Women* Boston, Beacon Press, 1967, p. 7.

85 For example Goode and Hatt *Methods in Social Research*, p. 189.

86 Miller *Toward a New Psychology of Women*, pp. 6–8.

87 A. R. Hochschild 'The sociology of feeling and emotion: selected possibilities' in M. Millman and R. M. Kanter (eds) *Another Voice: Feminist Perspectives on Social Life and Social Science* New York, Anchor Books, 1975, p. 281.

88 B. Laslett and R. Rapoport 'Collaborative interviewing and interactive research' *Journal of Marriage and the Family* November 1975, p. 968.

89 R. Rapoport and R. Rapoport *Dual Career Families Re-examined* London, Martin Robertson, 1976, p. 31.

90 Goode and Hatt, op. cit., p. 189.

91 Selltiz et al., op. cit., p. 576.

92 A. Oakley *Becoming a Mother* Oxford, Martin Robertson, 1979.

93 L. A. Dexter 'Role relationships and conceptions of neutrality in interviewing' *American Journal of Sociology* 1956, 61, **4**, p. 156; B. Paul 'Interview techniques and field relationships' in A. L. Kroeber (ed.) *Anthropology Today* Chicago, Chicago Press, 1954.

94 Selltiz et al., op. cit., p. 583.

95 S. A. Richardson, B. S. Dohrenwerd and D. Klein *Interviewing: Its Forms and Functions* New York, Basic Books, 1965, p. 129.

96 F. Zweig *Labour, Life and Poverty* London, Gollancz, 1949.

97 M. Corbin 'Appendix 3' in J. M. and R. E. Pahl *Managers and Their Wives* London, Allen Lane, 1971, pp. 303–5.

98 A. F. Mamak 'Nationalism, race-class consciousness and social research on Bougainville Island, Papua New Guinea' in C. Bell and S. Encel (eds) *Inside the Whale* Oxford, Pergamon Press, 1978, p. 176.

99 D. Hobson 'Housewives: isolation as oppression' in Women's Studies Group, Centre for Contemporary Cultural Studies, *Women Take Issue* London, Hutchinson, 1975.

100 C. Bell and H. Newby *Doing Sociological Research* London, Allen and Unwin, 1977, pp. 9–10.

101 C. Bell and S. Encel, op. cit., p. 4.

102 M. Stacey *Methods of Social Research* Oxford, Pergamon Press, 1969, p. 2.

103 Sjoberg and Nett, op. cit., pp. 215–16.

104 Mamak, op. cit., p. 168.

105 E. E. Evans-Pritchard *The Nuer* London, Oxford University Press, 1940, pp. 12–13.

106 E. S. Bowen *Return to Laughter* London, Gollancz, 1956, p. 163.

107 H. S. Becker and B. Geer 'Participant observation and interviewing: a comparison' *Human Organization* 1957, **16**, p. 28.

108 L. Stanley and S. Wise 'Feminist research, feminist consciousness and experiences of sexism' *Women's Studies International Quarterly* **2**, 3, 1979, pp. 359–79.

109 See Oakley, 1992, op. cit.

110 See R. M. Rapoport (ed.) *Children, Youth and Families – the Action–Research Relationship* Cambridge, Cambridge University Press, 1985.

111 See J. Fischer 'Is casework effective? A review' *Social Work* January 1973, pp. 5–20; J. McCord 'Consideration of some effects of a counselling programme' in S. E. Martin, L. B. Sechrest and R. Redner (eds) *New Directions in the Rehabilitation of Criminal Offenders* Washington, National Academy Press, 1981.

112 W. A. Silverman *Retrolental Fibroplasia: A Modern Parable* New York, Grune and Stratton, 1980.

113 D. Schwarz, R. Flamant and J. Lellouch *Clinical Trials* London, Academic Press, 1980, p. 7.

114 See H. Rose and S. Rose 'Radical science and its enemies' in R. Miliband and J. Saville (eds) *Socialist Register* Atlantic Highlands, NJ Humanities Press, 1979.

115 See E. Goffman *Stigma: Notes on the Management of Spoiled Identity* Harmondsworth, Penguin, 1968.

116 S. Harding *The Science Question in Feminism* Milton Keynes, Open University Press, 1986.

117 See e.g. J. B. Elshtain *Public Man, Private Woman* Oxford, Martin Robertson, 1981; M. Millman and R. M. Kanter (eds) *Another Voice: Feminist Perspectives on Social Life and Social Science* New York, Anchor Books, 1975; Sherman and Beck, op. cit.

118 E. F. Keller 'Feminism and science' *Signs: Journal of Women in Culture and Society* 1982, 7, **3**, pp. 589–602; Rose, op. cit.

119 J. Acker, K. Barry and J. Esseveld 'Objectivity and truth: problems in doing feminist research' *Women's Studies International Forum* 1983, 6, **4**, pp. 423–35; H. Roberts (ed.) *Doing Feminist Research* London, Routledge and Kegan Paul, 1981.

120 See this volume pp. 221–42.

121 L. V. Hedges 'How hard is hard science? How soft is soft science?' *American Psychologist* May 1987, pp. 443–55.

122 K. Davies and J. Esseveld 'Reflections on research practices in feminist research' Paper presented at the fourth Nordiska Symposiet for Kvinnoforskning i Samhallsgeografi, Uppsala, Sweden, 22–24 May 1986, p. 9.

123 M. Daly *Beyond God the Father* Boston, Beacon Press, 1973.

124 H. Harris 'Prenatal diagnosis and selective abortion'. The Rock-Carling Fellowship, London, Nuffield Provincial Hospitals Trust, 1974.

125 See R. W. Wertz and D. C. Wertz *Lying-in: A History of Childbirth in America* Glencoe, The Free Press, 1977; I Chalmers, M. Enkin and M. J. N. C. Keirse (eds) *Effective Care in Pregnancy and Childbirth* Oxford, Oxford University Press, 1989.

126 J. Garcia 'Women's views of antenatal care' in M. Enkin and I. Chalmers (eds) *Effectiveness and Satisfaction in Antenatal Care* London, Spastics International Medical Publications, 1982.

127 S. Cohen and S. L. Syme *Social Support and Health* New York, Academic Press, 1987.

128 L. F. Berkman 'Assessing the physical health effects of social networks and support' *American Review of Public Health* **5**, 1984, pp. 413–32.

129 M. Chamberlain *Old Wives' Tales* London, Virago, 1981.

130 A. Oakley 'Social support in pregnancy: the "soft" way to increase birthweight?' *Social Science and Medicine* 1985, 21, **11**, pp. 1259–68; A. Oakley 'Is social support good for the health of mothers and babies?' *Journal of Reproductive and Infant Psychology* **6**, 1988, 3–21.

131 See this volume pp. 221–42; J. Finch ' "It's great to have someone to talk to": the ethics and policies of interviewing women' in C. Bell and H. Roberts (eds) *Social Researching: Politics, Problems, Practice* London, Routledge and Kegan Paul, 1984.

132 Silverman, op. cit.

133 I. Chalmers 'Scientific inquiry and authoritarianism in perinatal care and education' *Birth* 1983, 10, **3**, pp. 151–64.

134 Coronary Drug Project Research Group 'Influence of adherence to treatment and response of cholesterol on mortality in the coronary drug project' *New England Journal of Medicine* 1980, 303, pp. 1038–41.

135 M. Bracken 'Clinical trials and the acceptance of uncertainty' *British Medical Journal* 1987, 294, pp. 1111–12, p. 1111.

136 S. Reinharz 'Experimental analysis: a contribution to feminist research' in G. Bowles and R. Duelli-Klein (eds) *Theories of Women's Studies: II* Berkeley, California, University of Berkeley, Women's Studies Department, 1981.

137 See, for an exception, A. H. Laing, R. J. Berry, C. R. Newman and J. Peto 'Treatment of inoperable carcinoma of bronchus' *Lancet* 13 December 1975, pp. 1161–4.

138 H. Graham and A. Oakley 'Competing ideologies of reproduction: medical and maternal perspectives on pregnancy and birth' in H. Roberts (ed.) *Women, Health and Reproduction* London, Routledge and Kegan Paul, 1981; S. Macintyre 'To have or have not – promotion and prevention in gynaecological work' in M. Stacey (ed.) *The Sociology of the NHS* Sociological Review Monograph 22, Staffordshire, University of Keele, 1976.

139 The role of wives in medical research is interesting.

140 Silverman, op. cit., p. 140.

141 D. Peters and S. Ceci 'Peer-review practices of psychology journals: the fate of published articles submitted again' *The Behavioural and Brain Sciences* **5**, 1982, pp. 187–255.

142 K. Dickersin, S. Chan, T. C. Chalmers, H. S. Sachs and H. Smith 'Publication bias and clinical trials' *Controlled Clinical Trials* **8**, 1987, pp. 343–53.

143 C. Faulder *Whose Body Is It? The Troubling Issue of Informed Consent* London, Virago, 1985.

144 D. Brahms 'Informed consent does not demand full disclosure of risks' *Lancet* 2 July 1983, p. 58.

145 R. Fader and T. L. Beauchamp *A History and Theory of Informed Consent* New York, Oxford University Press, 1986.

146 E. F. Loftus and J. F. Fries 'Informed consent may be hazardous to health' *Science* **204**, 1979, p. 11.

147 The correct term is 'ethics' committees (they may, or may not, be ethical).

148 A. Papaioannou 'Informed consent after randomisation' (letter) *Lancet* 9 October 1982, p. 828.

149 British Medical Association 'Local ethical committees' *British Medical Journal* 1981, 282, p. 1010.

150 J. King 'Informed consent' *Bulletin of the Institute of Medical Ethics* December 1986, Supplement no 3.

151 See e.g. N. H. Cassem and R. S. Stewart 'Management and care of the dying patient' *International Journal of Psychiatry in Medicine* **6**, 1975, pp. 229–38; J. Aitken-Swan and E. C. Easson 'Reactions of cancer patients on being told their diagnoses' *British Medical Journal* **1**, 1959, pp. 779–83; J. Macintosh 'Patients' awareness and desire for information about diagnosed but undisclosed malignant disease' *Lancet* **7**, 1976, pp. 300–3.

152 M. E. Mattson, J. D. Curb, R. McArdle and the AMIS and BHAT Research Groups 'Participation in a clinical trial: the patient's point of view' *Controlled Clinical Trials* **6**, 1985, pp. 156–67.

153 D. Elbourne 'Subjects' views about participation in a randomised controlled trial' *Journal of Reproductive and Infant Psychology* **5**, 1987, pp. 3–8.

154 R. M. Titmuss *The Gift Relationship* London,, Allen and Unwin, 1970.

155 J. Lumley, A. Lester, P. Renon and C. Wood 'A failed RCT to determine the best method of delivery for very low birthweight infants' *Controlled Clinical Trials* **6**, 1985, pp. 120–7.

156 H. Waitzkin and J. Streckle 'Information control and the micropolitics of health care: summary of original research project' *Social Science and Medicine* **10**, 1976, pp. 263–76.

157 T. M. Grunder 'On the readability of surgical consent forms' *New England Journal of Medicine* 17 April 1980, pp. 900–2.

158 R. J. Simes, M. H. N. Tattersall, A. S. Coates, D. Radhaven, H. J. Solomon and H. Smart 'Randomized comparison of procedures for obtaining informed consent in clinical trials and treatment for cancer' *British Medical Journal* 1986, 293, pp. 1065–8.

159 M. D. Bracken 'Design and conduct of randomized clinical trials in perinatal research' in M. D. Bracken (ed.) *Perinatal Epidemiology* New York, Oxford University Press, 1984, p. 406.

160 H. Brody *Placebos and the Philosophy of Medicine* Chicago, University of Chicago Press, 1977.

161 E. J. Ballantine 'Objective measurements and the double-blind procedure' *American Journal of Opthalmology* **79**, 1975, pp. 763–7.

162 K. D. Brownell and A. J. Strunkard 'The double-blind in danger: untoward consequences of informed consent' *American Journal of Psychiatry* 1982, 139, **11**, pp. 1487–9.

163 A pseudonym.

164 S. Antilla and M. Isokoski 'Unexpected control-group behaviour in an intervention study' (letter) *Lancet* 5 January 1985, p. 43.

165 M. Zelen 'A new design for randomized clinical trials' *New England Journal of Medicine* 31 May 1979, pp. 1242–5, p. 1242.

166 E. F. Freidson *Professional Dominance: The Social Structure of Medical Care* Chicago, Aldine, 1970, p. 83.

167 J. Robinson 'Cervical cancer – doctors hide the truth?' in S. O'Sullivan (ed.) *Woman's Health: A Spare Rib Reader* London, Pandora Press, 1987.

168 See Chalmers, op. cit.

169 P. Micklethwait, C. C. Jenkins, G. L. Flanagan, R. Mansfield, B. Beech, A. Wynn and M. Wynn (letter) in *The Observer* 25 July 1982.

170 See N. Madge and M. Marmot 'Psychosocial factors and health' *The Quarterly Journal of Social Affairs* 1987, 3 (2), pp. 81–134.

171 See McCord, op. cit.; J. McCord 'The Cambridge-Somerville Youth Study: a sobering lesson on treatment, prevention and evaluation' in A. J. McSweeny, W. J. Freeman and R. Hawkins (eds) *Practical Program Evaluation in Youth* Springfield, Illinois, Charles C. Thomas, 1982.

172 See Chalmers, op. cit.

173 P. Spallone and D. L. Steinberg (eds) *Made to Order: The Myth of Reproductive and Genetic Progress* Oxford, Pergamon Press, 1987; L. Birke *Women, Feminism and Biology* Brighton, Sussex, Wheatsheaf Books, 1986.

174 W. A. Silverman *Human Experimentation: A Guided Step into the Unknown* Oxford, Oxford University Press, 1985.

175 S. B. Ruzek *The Women's Health Movement* New York, Praeger, 1979.

176 Consensus Development Conference 'Treatment of primary breast cancer' *British Medical Journal* 1986, 293, pp. 946–7.

177 S. Rowbotham 'What do women want? Women-centred values and the world as it is' *Feminist Review* **20**, 1985, pp. 49–69.

178 Keller, op. cit., p. 593.

Index

interviews, 221–42
  problems, 243–64
rites of passage, and birth, 125–30

satisfaction
  doctors, 33–4
  patients: with medical care, 34–6; with
    nurses, 46
  perinatal health care, 58
science
  childbirth, 71–2
  feminist knowledge, 215
  obstetrics, 58–60
  research methods, 243–64
science fiction
  childbirth, 139
  fertility control, 165–6
Second World War, and perinatal
    mortality, 117
  diet, 116
self-esteem and motherhood, 87, 89, 91–2
self-help, 16
self-identity and motherhood, 87, 88–9, 91
sensitivity and women, 204, 213
separation of mothers and babies, 62, 82,
    127–8
sex hormones, 211–12
sexism, 151–2
sexual abuse of children, 179
sexual intercourse, and age, 141
sexuality, studies of, 34
shaving of pubic hair, 127
sickle-cell disease, 152
single parents
  control of money, 218
  perinatal mortality, 114, 119
  social changes, 99, 141, 142
smoking in pregnancy, 100–4, 136, 150
  fetal rights, 183
  passive, 104
  perinatal mortality, 116
social causes of perinatal mortality, 108–9,
    120–1, 122
social class
  and communication, 151
  mother–daughter education, 213–14,
    215
  perinatal mortality, 114–15

and risk, 135–6
  and smoking, 100
  social support research, 248
social distance, and interviews, 240
social motherhood, 84–5
social order and procreative technology,
    186–7
social science studies, 36–7
social support
  breastfeeding, 133–4
  childbirth, 74–5
  effects, 75–6
  feminism and knowledge, 208–9
  research, 246–8, 250–2, 259–61, 263–4
sociology
  interviewing process, 221–42
  normality of birth, 124–38
  women and reproduction, 28–30
state
  child care provision, 147
  and motherhood, 92–3
stillbirths, 119
Stopes, Marie, 157
stress and pregnancy, 102–3
surrogate motherhood, 168, 183
survey method, 215–16
  interviews, 221–42
  problems, 243–64

tamoxifen, 198–200
terminations
  extent, 141
  fertility control, 161
  fetal defects, 184–5
  fetal rights, 183
traditional health care, 5

ultrasound, 189–97
uncertainty and research, 244, 246, 261–3
universities, 219
unmarried parents, *see* single parents
unwanted pregnancies, 140–1

witchcaft, 210–11
women's studies, 205–10, 219–20
work, *see* employment

X-rays, fetal, 192, 193–4, 195

Essays on
W O M E N ,
M E D I C I N E
& H E A L T H

In this collection of essays, Ann Oakley, one of the most influential social scientists of the last twenty years, brings together the best of her work on the sociology of women's health. She focuses on four main themes ~ divisions of labour, motherhood, technology and methodology ~ and in her own inimitable style, combines serious academic discourse from a feminist sociological perspective with a practical understanding of what it is to be a women facing the often impersonal world of twentieth-century medicine. Updating and expanding substantially on her earlier work, *Telling the Truth About Jerusalem*, this new collection bridges the medical/social divide in an accessible and personable way.

ANN OAKLEY is Professor of Sociology and Social Policy at the University of London's Institute of Education, and Director of the Social Science Research Unit there. She has written extensively on gender roles and medical sociology, and is author of eighteen books ~ both academic and fiction~including *The Captured Womb* (Blackwell, 1984), *The Sociology of Housework* (Blackwell, 1985) and *The Men's Room* (Virago, 1988).

Jacket illustration: *Cornucopia*, 1960, by Alan Davie. Reproduced by kind permission of the artist. Photography: Glasgow Museums.

EDINBURGH UNIVERSITY PRESS   22 George Square, Edinburgh
ISBN 0 7486 0450 2

A N N   O A K L E Y

ISBN 0-7486-0450-2

9 780748 604500 >